2016 | World Development Indicators

D1402025

WORLD BANK GROUP

Preface

In September 2015, leaders of 193 countries agreed on a set of 17 Sustainable Development Goals to guide global action over the next 15 years. Set out in the 2030 Agenda for Sustainable Development, the Sustainable Development Goals take over where the Millennium Development Goals before them left off—and in many cases aim to finish the job. Eradicating poverty, an objective shared by the World Bank Group, is a key element of this unfinished business. It remains the world's greatest challenge.

World Development Indicators will report on progress toward the Sustainable Development Goals, as it did with the Millennium Development Goals. The Sustainable Development Goals cover a broader range of issues, and this edition expands coverage in the *World view* section. For each of the 17 goals, key indicators have been selected to identify important trends and challenges and elicit discussion on measurement issues. An accompanying set of dashboards, showing trends by country, region, and income level, are available at http://data.worldbank.org/sdgs.

Implementing the Sustainable Development Goals and measuring and monitoring progress toward them will require much more data than are currently available, with more accuracy, better timeliness, greater disaggregation, and higher frequency. The institutions fundamental to this effort should be supported through strong and renewed global partnerships. A new Global Partnership for Sustainable Development Data was launched alongside Agenda 2030 in September 2015 (see http://data4sdgs.org). A key aim is to bring different groups together to ignite a data revolution for development.

Where possible, this edition of *World Development Indicators* includes new indicators to reflect the 169 targets of the Sustainable Development Goals, but the structure of the book remains the same as in previous editions: *World view, People, Environment, Economy, States and markets,* and *Global links.* Each section includes a brief introduction, a global map of a key indicator, a table, a section about the data, and an index of other indicators accessible online. *World view* retains the two tables showing progress toward the World Bank Group's goals of eradicating poverty and promoting shared prosperity.

Motivated by the universal agenda of the Sustainable Development Goals, this edition of *World Development Indicators* also introduces a change in the way that global and regional aggregates are presented in tables and figures. Unless otherwise noted, there is no longer a distinction between developing countries (defined in previous editions as low- and middle-income countries) and developed countries (defined in previous editions as high-income countries). Regional groupings are based on geographical coverage rather than a subset of countries that were previously referred to as developing. Two implications of this change are that a new aggregate for North America has been included in tables, and aggregates for Europe and Central Asia include countries of the European Union. Aggregates restricted to low- and middle-income countries are still available in the World Development Indicators database at http://databank.worldbank.org/wdi.

World Development Indicators is the result of a collaborative partnership of international agencies, statistical offices of more than 200 economies, and many more. I want to acknowledge their efforts and thank them for their tireless work, which is at the heart of development and the fight to eradicate poverty and promote shared prosperity.

Haishan Fu
Director
Development Economics Data Group

Acknowledgments

This book was prepared by a team led by Bala Bhaskar Naidu Kalimili under the management of Neil Fantom and comprising Parul Agarwal, Azita Amjadi, Peter Bourke, Maja Bresslauer, Tamirat Yacob Chulta, Liu Cui, Biokou Mathieu Djayeola, Mahyar Eshragh-Tabary, Juan Feng, Saulo Teodoro Ferreira, Timothy Herzog, Masako Hiraga, Haruna Kashiwase, Buyant Erdene Khaltarkhuu, Tariq Khokhar, Elysee Kiti, Hiroko Maeda, Cynthia Nyanchama Nyakeri, Ana Florina Pirlea, Malvina Pollock, William Prince, Elizabeth Purdie, Leila Rafei, Evis Rucaj, Umar Serajuddin, Sun Hwa Song, Rubena Sukaj, Emi Suzuki, Jomo Tariku, Dereje Wolde, and Junhe Yang, working closely with other teams in the Development Economics Vice Presidency's Development Data Group.

World Development Indicators electronic products were prepared by a team led by Soong Sup Lee and comprising Prasanth Alluri, Ying Chi, Rajesh Danda, Jean-Pierre Djomalieu, Ramgopal Erabelly, Shelley Fu, Omar Hadi, Gytis Kanchas, Siddhesh Kaushik, Karthik Krishnamoorthy, Ugendran Machakkalai, Nacer Megherbi, Parastoo Oloumi, Atsushi Shimo, and Malarvizhi Veerappan.

All work was carried out under the direction of Haishan Fu. Valuable advice was provided by Carter Brandon, Poonam Gupta, David Rosenblatt, and Jos Verbeek.

The choice of indicators and writeups on Sustainable Development Goals content was shaped through close consultation with and substantial contributions from staff in the World Bank's various Global Practices, Cross-Cutting Solution Areas, and other units: Agriculture; Business and the Law; Climate Change; Education; Energy and Extractives; Enterprise Surveys; Environment and Natural Resources; Finance and Markets; Fragility, Conflict, and Violence; Gender; Global Facility for Disaster Reduction and Recovery; Governance; Health, Nutrition, and Population; Jobs; Macroeconomics and Fiscal Management; Poverty; Public-Private Partnerships; Social Protection and Labor; Social, Urban, Rural, and Resilience; Trade and Competitiveness; Transport and Information and Communication Technologies; and Water; in addition to staff of the International Finance Corporation and the Multilateral Investment Guarantee Agency. The team also received substantial help, guidance, and data from external partners. For individual acknowledgments of contributions to the book's content, see *Credits*. For a listing of key partners, see *Partners*.

Communications Development Incorporated provided overall design direction, editing, and layout, led by Bruce Ross-Larson and Christopher Trott. Elaine Wilson created the cover and graphics and typeset the book. Peter Grundy, of Peter Grundy Art & Design, and Diane Broadley, of Broadley Design, designed the report. Jewel McFadden, Nora Ridolfi, and Janice Tuten from the World Bank's Publishing and Knowledge Division oversaw printing and dissemination of the book.

Table of contents

Partners

Defining, gathering, and disseminating international statistics is a collective effort of many people and organizations. The indicators presented in *World Development Indicators* are the fruit of decades of work at many levels, from the field workers who administer censuses and household surveys to the committees and working parties of the national and international statistical agencies that develop the nomenclature, classifications, and standards fundamental to an international statistical system. Nongovernmental organizations and the private sector have also made important contributions, both in gathering primary data and in organizing and publishing their results. And academic researchers have played a crucial role in developing statistical methods and carrying on a continuing dialogue about the quality and interpretation of statistical indicators. All these contributors have a strong belief that available, accurate data will improve the quality of public and private decision making.

The organizations listed here have made *World Development Indicators* possible by sharing their data and their expertise with us. More important, their collaboration contributes to the World Bank's efforts, and to those of many others, to improve the quality of life of the world's people. We acknowledge our debt and gratitude to all who have helped to build a base of comprehensive, quantitative information about the world and its people.

For easy reference, web addresses are included for each listed organization. The addresses shown were active on March 1, 2016.

International and government agencies

Carbon Dioxide Information Analysis Center

http://cdiac.ornl.gov

Centre for Research on the Epidemiology of Disasters

www.emdat.be

Deutsche Gesellschaft für Internationale Zusammenarbeit

giz

www.giz.de

The DHS Program

www.dhsprogram.com

Emission Database for Global Atmospheric Research

http://edgar.jrc.ec.europa.eu/

Eurostat

 eurostat

http://ec.europa.eu/eurostat

Food and Agriculture Organization

www.fao.org

Institute for Health Metrics and Evaluation

 IHME

www.healthdata.org

Internal Displacement Monitoring Centre

iDMC

www.internal-displacement.org

International Civil Aviation Organization

www.icao.int

Partners

International
Diabetes Federation

www.idf.org

International
Energy Agency

www.iea.org

International
Labour Organization

www.ilo.org

International
Monetary Fund

www.imf.org

International Telecommunication
Union

www.itu.int

Joint United Nations
Programme on HIV/AIDS

www.unaids.org

National Science
Foundation

www.nsf.gov

The Office of U.S. Foreign
Disaster Assistance

www.usaid.gov

Organisation for Economic
Co-operation and Development

www.oecd.org

Stockholm International
Peace Research Institute

www.sipri.org

Understanding Children's Work

www.ucw-project.org

United Nations

www.un.org

United Nations Centre for Human Settlements, Global Urban Observatory

www.unhabitat.org

United Nations Children's Fund

www.unicef.org

United Nations Conference on Trade and Development

www.unctad.org

United Nations Department of Economic and Social Affairs, Population Division

www.un.org/esa/population

United Nations Department of Peacekeeping Operations

www.un.org/en/peacekeeping

United Nations Educational, Scientific and Cultural Organization, Institute for Statistics

www.uis.unesco.org

United Nations Environment Programme

www.unep.org

United Nations High Commissioner for Refugees

www.unhcr.org

Partners

United Nations Industrial
Development Organization

www.unido.org

United Nations
International Strategy
for Disaster Reduction

www.unisdr.org

United Nations Office on
Drugs and Crime

www.unodc.org

United Nations
Population Fund

www.unfpa.org

United Nations Statistics Division

http://unstats.un.org/unsd/

Upsalla Conflict
Data Program

www.pcr.uu.se/research/UCDP

World Bank

http://data.worldbank.org

World Health Organization

www.who.int

World Intellectual
Property Organization

www.wipo.int

World Tourism
Organization

www.unwto.org

World Trade
Organization

www.wto.org

Private and nongovernmental organizations

Center for International Earth Science Information Network

www.ciesin.org

DHL

www.dhl.com

International Institute for Strategic Studies

www.iiss.org

Lloyd's List

www.lloydslist.com/ll
/sector/containers/

Netcraft

http://news.netcraft.com

PwC

www.pwc.com

Standard & Poor's

www.standardandpoors.com

World Conservation Monitoring Centre

www.unep-wcmc.org

World Economic Forum

www.weforum.org

World Federation of Exchanges

www.world-exchanges.org

World Resources Institute

www.wri.org

User guide to tables

World Development Indicators is the World Bank's premier compilation of cross-country comparable data on development. The database contains more than 1,300 time series indicators for 214 economies and more than 30 country groups, with data for many indicators going back more than 50 years.

The 2016 edition of World Development Indicators offers a condensed presentation of the principal indicators, arranged in their traditional sections, along with regional and topical highlights and maps.

 World view   People   Environment

Economy   States and markets   Global links

Tables

The tables include all World Bank member countries (188), and all other economies with populations of more than 30,000 (214 total). Countries and economies are listed alphabetically (except for Hong Kong SAR, China, and Macao SAR, China, which appear after China).

The term country, used interchangeably with economy, does not imply political independence but refers to any territory for which authorities report separate social or economic statistics. When available, aggregate measures for income and regional groups appear at the end of each table.

Aggregate measures for income groups

Aggregate measures for income groups include the 214 economies listed in the tables, plus Taiwan, China, whenever data are available. To maintain consistency in the aggregate measures over time and between tables, missing data are imputed where possible.

Aggregate measures for regions

The aggregate measures for regions cover economies at all income levels, unless otherwise noted.

The country composition of regions may differ from common geographic usage. For regional classifications, see the map on the inside back cover and the list on the back cover flap. For further discussion of aggregation methods, see Sources and methods.

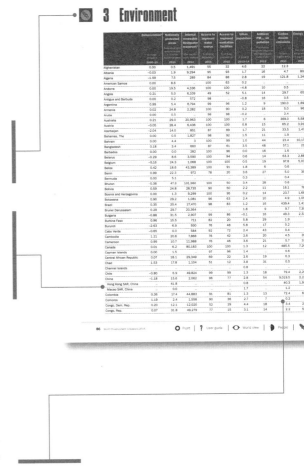

Data presentation conventions

- A blank means not applicable or, for an aggregate, not analytically meaningful.
- A billion is 1,000 million.
- A trillion is 1,000 billion.
- Figures in green italics refer to years or periods other than those specified or to growth rates calculated for less than the full period specified.
- Data for years that are more than three years from the range shown are footnoted.
- The cutoff date for data is February 1, 2016.

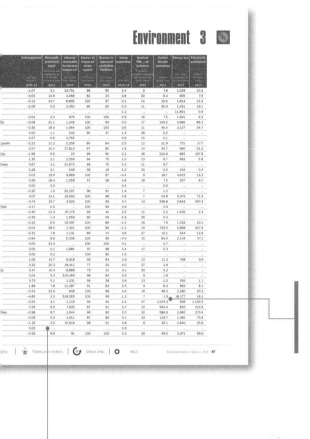

Classification of economies

For operational and analytical purposes the World Bank's main criterion for classifying economies is gross national income (GNI) per capita (converted into U.S. dollars using the *World Bank Atlas* method). Because GNI per capita changes over time, the country composition of income groups may change from one edition of *World Development Indicators* to the next. Once the classification is fixed for an edition, based on GNI per capita in the most recent year for which data are available (2014 in this edition), all historical data presented are based on the same country grouping.

Low-income economies are those with a GNI per capita of $1,045 or less in 2014. Lower middle-income economies are those with a GNI per capita of $1,046–$4,125. Upper middle-income economies are those with a GNI per capita of $4,126–$12,735. High-income economies are those with a GNI per capita of $12,736 or more.

Statistics

Data are shown for economies as they were constituted in 2014, and historical data have been revised to reflect current political arrangements. Exceptions are noted in the tables.

Additional information about the data is provided in *Sources and methods,* which summarizes national and international efforts to improve basic data collection and gives country-level information on primary sources, census years, fiscal years, statistical concepts used, and other background information. *Sources and methods* also provides technical information on calculations used throughout the book.

Country notes
· Data for China do not include data for Hong Kong SAR, China; Macao SAR, China; or Taiwan, China.
· Data for Serbia do not include data for Kosovo or Montenegro.
· Data for Sudan exclude South Sudan unless otherwise noted.

Symbols

..	means that data are not available or that aggregates cannot be calculated because of missing data in the years shown.
0 or 0.0	means zero or small enough that the number would round to zero at the displayed number of decimal places.
/	in dates, as in 2013/14, means that the period of time, usually 12 months, straddles two calendar years and refers to a crop year, a survey year, or a fiscal year.
$	means current U.S. dollars unless otherwise noted.
<	means less than.

User guide to WDI online resources

Visit http://data.worldbank.org/products/wdi to see the many resources available for World Development Indicators, including the time series database, online tables, mobile app, and interactive dashboard for the Sustainable Development Goals.

How to access WDI online tables

Statistical tables that were previously available in the *World Development Indicators* print edition are available online. These reference tables are consistently updated based on revisions to the World Development Indicators database.

To access the WDI online tables, go to http://wdi.worldbank.org/tables. To access a specific WDI online table directly, use the URL http://wdi.worldbank.org/table/ and the table number (for example, http://wdi.worldbank.org/table/1.1 to view the first table in the *World view* section). Each section of this book also lists the indicators

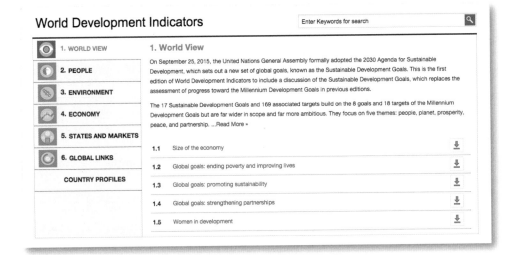

 Front User guide World view People Environment

included by table and by code. To view a specific indicator online, use the URL http://data.worldbank.org/indicator/ and the indicator code (for example, http://data.world bank.org/indicator/SP.POP.TOTL to view a page for total population).

How to use DataBank

DataBank (http://databank.worldbank.org) is a web resource that provides simple and quick access to the World Development Indicators database and other collections of time series data. It has advanced functions for selecting and displaying data, performing customized queries, downloading data, and creating charts and maps. Users can create dynamic custom reports based on their selection of countries, indicators, and years. All these reports can be easily edited, saved, shared, and embedded as widgets on websites or blogs. For more information, see http://databank.worldbank.org/help.

How to download DataFinder

DataFinder is a free mobile app that accesses the full set of data from the World Development Indicators database. Data can be displayed, compared, and saved in a table, chart, or map and shared via email, Facebook, and Twitter. DataFinder works on mobile devices (smartphone or tablet computer) in both offline (no Internet connection) and online (Wi-Fi or 3G/4G connection to the Internet) modes. To download DataFinder, go to http://data.worldbank.org /apps.

How to monitor the Sustainable Development Goals

The World Development Indicators database provides data on trends in Sustainable Development Goals indicators for countries and country groups. An interactive presentation of key indicators for assessing the Sustainable Development Goals is available at http://data.worldbank .org/sdgs.

WORLD
VIEW

On September 25, 2015, the United Nations General Assembly formally adopted the 2030 Agenda for Sustainable Development, which sets out a new set of global goals, known as the Sustainable Development Goals. This is the first edition of *World Development Indicators* to include a discussion of the Sustainable Development Goals, which replaces the assessment of progress toward the Millennium Development Goals in previous editions.

The 17 Sustainable Development Goals and 169 associated targets build on the 8 goals and 18 targets of the Millennium Development Goals but are far wider in scope and far more ambitious. They focus on five themes: people, planet, prosperity, peace, and partnership. Countries have resolved to end poverty and hunger and ensure that all people can fulfill their potential in dignity and equality and in a healthy environment; to protect the planet from degradation and take urgent action on climate change; to ensure that all people can enjoy prosperous and fulfilling lives and that progress takes place in harmony with nature; to foster peaceful, just, and inclusive societies free from fear and violence; and to mobilize the means to implement Agenda 2030, focused on the poorest and most vulnerable, through strong global partnership.

Along with the goals and targets, a global monitoring framework with more than 200 indicators is being developed by UN member states, working closely with UN agencies and other stakeholders. For each goal, *World view* presents recent trends and baselines against key targets, largely using indicators available in the World Development Indicators database and drawing on the specialist knowledge of World Bank staff. Some indicators have been added, and in some cases data have been used from published studies or reports. An interactive presentation of key indicators for assessing the Sustainable Development Goals is available at http://data.worldbank.org/sdgs.

As in previous editions, *World view* also presents indicators that measure progress toward the World Bank Group's twin goals of ending extreme poverty by 2030 and enhancing shared prosperity in every country, which are also central elements of Sustainable Development Goals 1 (end poverty in all its forms everywhere) and 10 (reduce inequality within and among countries). A major change is that the estimates of global and national extreme poverty rates have been updated to the international poverty line of $1.90 a day per person, in 2011 purchasing power parity terms. Estimates of indicators of shared prosperity for 94 countries, including the growth rates of the average income of the bottom 40 percent, are also included.

Measuring and monitoring progress against the Millennium Development Goals were major challenges and required substantial efforts on the part of national statistical agencies and others to improve the quality, frequency, and availability of relevant statistics. With a new, broader set of goals, targets, and indicators, the data requirements are even greater. Baselines and progress for few Sustainable Development Goal targets can be measured completely. Both governments and development partners will need to continue investing in national statistical systems and other relevant public institutions, where much of the data will continue to originate. At the same time, the statistical community needs to strengthen partnerships with the private sector and other emerging actors for advancing new techniques of data collection, analysis, and use.

End poverty in all its forms everywhere

In 2012, 13 percent of the world's population lived below the international poverty line of $1.90 a day, down from 37 percent in 1990. Declines in all regions contributed to the early success of meeting the Millennium Development Goal target of halving extreme poverty globally. Sustainable Development Goal 1 builds on this and proposes ending poverty in all forms by 2030. It also aims to ensure social protection for poor and vulnerable people, to increase access to basic services, and to support people harmed by conflict and climate-related disasters.

Eradicating extreme poverty

Many countries have made dramatic progress in reducing extreme poverty, though the global totals tend to be dominated by reductions in the two largest countries, China and India. In East Asia and Pacific the extreme poverty rate fell from 61 percent in 1990 to 7 percent in 2012, and in South Asia it fell from 51 percent to 19 percent (figure 1a). In contrast, Sub-Saharan Africa's extreme poverty rate did not fall below its 1990 level until 2002. Based on national growth rates over the past 10 years, the global extreme poverty rate is estimated to be below 10 percent in 2015, a drop of more than two-thirds since 1990.

The Sustainable Development Goal target of eliminating extreme poverty in all its forms everywhere by 2030 is very ambitious.

If national growth rates for the past 10 years prevail for the next 15 years, the global extreme poverty rate will fall to 4 percent by 2030, with variations across regions (figure 1b), and if national growth rates for the past 20 years prevail, it will be around 6 percent.[1] Eliminating extreme poverty will require a step change from historical growth rates.

Reducing poverty in all its dimensions according to national definitions

Like the Millennium Development Goals, the Sustainable Development Goals recognize that poverty is defined differently by national authorities. Sustainable Development Goal 1 aims to halve poverty rates based on these national definitions (target 1.2). Some countries define poverty rates using benchmarks based on income;

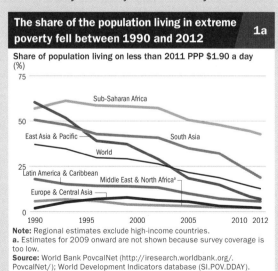

The share of the population living in extreme poverty fell between 1990 and 2012 `1a`

Share of population living on less than 2011 PPP $1.90 a day (%)

Note: Regional estimates exclude high-income countries.
a. Estimates for 2009 onward are not shown because survey coverage is too low.
Source: World Bank PovcalNet (http://iresearch.worldbank.org/. PovcalNet/); World Development Indicators database (SI.POV.DDAY).

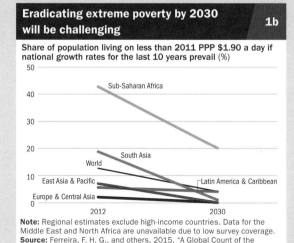

Eradicating extreme poverty by 2030 will be challenging `1b`

Share of population living on less than 2011 PPP $1.90 a day if national growth rates for the last 10 years prevail (%)

Note: Regional estimates exclude high-income countries. Data for the Middle East and North Africa are unavailable due to low survey coverage.
Source: Ferreira, F. H. G., and others, 2015, "A Global Count of the Extreme Poor in 2012: Data Issues, Methodology and Initial Results," Policy Research Working Paper 7432, World Bank, Washington, DC.

while current data are sparse, in the last 15 years both Indonesia and Sri Lanka have halved their income based poverty rate. More recently, some countries—such as Colombia and Mexico —have adopted measures that aim to capture the multidimensional nature of poverty by assessing the extent to which households are deprived in different ways (such as health, education, housing, and labor market opportunities).

Increasing social protection for those most in need

Social protection programs include social assistance, such as cash transfers, school feeding, and targeted food assistance, and social insurance and labor market programs, such as old-age pensions, disability pensions, unemployment insurance, skills training, and wage subsidies. Improving coverage of social protection programs and targeting appropriate schemes to the poor and most vulnerable can further reduce poverty (target 1.3).

Despite progress over the past decade, most poor people remain outside social protection systems, especially in low-income countries. Only one out of five people receives one or more types of social protection benefit in low-income countries, compared with two out of three in upper middle-income countries (figure 1c). The coverage gap is particularly acute in Sub-Saharan Africa and South Asia, where most of the world's extremely poor people live. In Sub-Saharan Africa only 15 percent of people in the bottom income quintile have access to a social protection benefit (figure 1d).

Average social assistance cash benefits account for only 10 percent of poor people's consumption in low-income countries, 21 percent in lower middle-income countries, and 37 percent in upper middle-income countries. Overall, social assistance transfers are not large enough to close the poverty gap in the poorest countries.

Note

1. Ferreira, F. H. G., and others, 2015, "A Global Count of the Extreme Poor in 2012: Data Issues, Methodology and Initial Results," Policy Research Working Paper 7432, World Bank, Washington, DC.

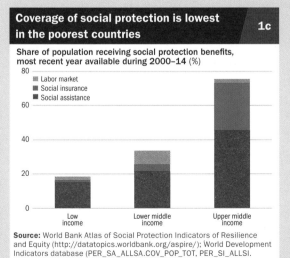

Coverage of social protection is lowest in the poorest countries — 1c

Share of population receiving social protection benefits, most recent year available during 2000–14 (%)

- Labor market
- Social insurance
- Social assistance

Source: World Bank Atlas of Social Protection Indicators of Resilience and Equity (http://datatopics.worldbank.org/aspire/); World Development Indicators database (PER_SA_ALLSA.COV_POP_TOT, PER_SI_ALLSI.COV_POP_TOT, PER_LM_ALLLM.COV_POP_TOT).

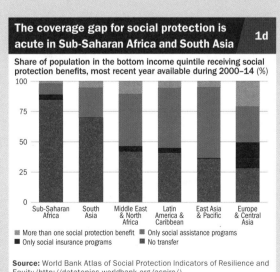

The coverage gap for social protection is acute in Sub-Saharan Africa and South Asia — 1d

Share of population in the bottom income quintile receiving social protection benefits, most recent year available during 2000–14 (%)

- More than one social protection benefit
- Only social assistance programs
- Only social insurance programs
- No transfer

Source: World Bank Atlas of Social Protection Indicators of Resilience and Equity (http://datatopics.worldbank.org/aspire/).

SDG 2 Zero hunger

End hunger, achieve food security and improved nutrition, and promote sustainable agriculture

Over the past 25 years the share of the world's population suffering from hunger has fallen. The prevalence of undernourishment, where food intake does not meet continuous dietary energy requirements, has been almost halved globally, from 19 percent to 11 percent, but remains far higher in low-income countries than elsewhere (figure 2a). Efforts to end hunger by 2030 (target 2.1) will not be successful if current trends continue. Improvements in food security and sustainable agriculture, especially in cereal yields, can help.

Improving nutrition

Consistent with the World Health Assembly's Global Nutrition Targets 2025,[1] Sustainable Development Goal 2 focuses on both childhood malnutrition and the nutritional needs of adolescent girls and pregnant women, along with older people (target 2.2). Anthropometric indices, including stunting (low height for age), wasting (low weight for height), and overweight (high weight for height) in children under age 5, are common indicators of nutrition. The prevalence of child stunting has declined in all income groups since 1990 but remains close to 40 percent in low-income countries and above 30 percent in lower middle-income countries (figure 2b). Sustainable Development Goal 2 aims to reduce the number of children under age 5 who are stunted by 40 percent by 2025

(target 2.2). In countries where the number of children under age 5 is likely to grow, achieving this involves both reducing the number and the prevalence of stunted children.

Supporting food security and sustainable agriculture

Raising the agricultural productivity of poor households will be central to ending hunger by 2030 (targets 2.3 and 2.4). In low-income countries changes in poverty and undernourishment have been closely related to changes in agricultural productivity—and in particular to changes in cereal yields. In periods of stagnant agricultural productivity growth, as experienced by low-income countries from 1990 to 1999, poor people saw little improvement in wealth and nutritional health. But they have seen benefits

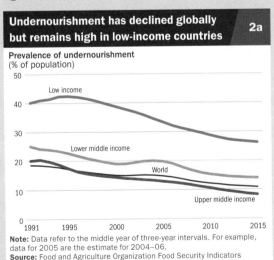

Undernourishment has declined globally but remains high in low-income countries 2a

Prevalence of undernourishment
(% of population)

Note: Data refer to the middle year of three-year intervals. For example, data for 2005 are the estimate for 2004–06.
Source: Food and Agriculture Organization Food Security Indicators database; World Development Indicators database (SN.ITK.DEFC.ZS).

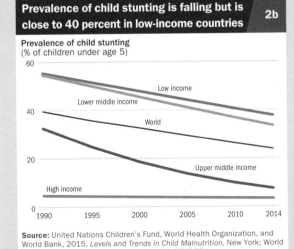

Prevalence of child stunting is falling but is close to 40 percent in low-income countries 2b

Prevalence of child stunting
(% of children under age 5)

Source: United Nations Children's Fund, World Health Organization, and World Bank, 2015, *Levels and Trends in Child Malnutrition*, New York; World Development Indicators database (SH.STA.STNT.ZS).

during more productive periods. Between 2000 and 2012 the average annual growth rate of cereal yields in low-income countries was 2.6 percent; over the same period both poverty and undernourishment fell 2.7 percent a year (figure 2c). A similar directional pattern exists for lower and upper middle-income countries, though the proportional impacts vary.

By 2030, population growth, and hence food demand, is projected to increase the most in the poorest parts of the world. These are also the regions where agricultural productivity is lowest (figure 2d) and where vulnerability to climate change is high. Further gains in agricultural productivity and climate resilience are needed, particularly in low-income countries, to raise poor people's incomes and feed growing populations.

Note

1. World Health Organization Global Targets 2025 (www.who.int/nutrition /global-target-2025/).

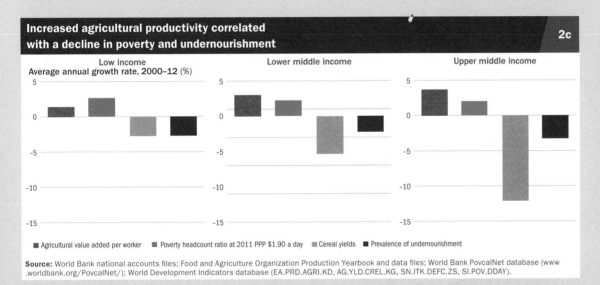

Increased agricultural productivity correlated with a decline in poverty and undernourishment — 2c

Low income
Average annual growth rate, 2000–12 (%)

Lower middle income

Upper middle income

■ Agricultural value added per worker   ■ Poverty headcount ratio at 2011 PPP $1.90 a day   ▨ Cereal yields   ■ Prevalence of undernourishment

Source: World Bank national accounts files; Food and Agriculture Organization Production Yearbook and data files; World Bank PovcalNet database (www .worldbank.org/PovcalNet/); World Development Indicators database (EA.PRD.AGRI.KD, AG.YLD.CREL.KG, SN.ITK.DEFC.ZS, SI.POV.DDAY).

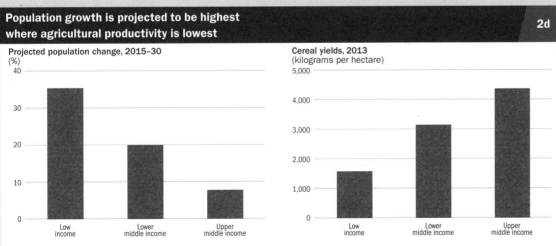

Population growth is projected to be highest where agricultural productivity is lowest — 2d

Projected population change, 2015–30 (%)

Cereal yields, 2013 (kilograms per hectare)

Source: United Nations Population Division (http://esa.un.org/unpd/wup/CD-ROM/WUP2014_XLS_CD_FILES/WUP2014-F05-Total_Population.xls); Food and Agriculture Organization; World Development Indicators database (AG.YLD.CREL.KG, SP.POP.TOTL).

SDG 3 Good health and well-being

Ensure healthy lives and promote well-being for all at all ages

In low-income countries more than half the population dies from communicable diseases or maternal, prenatal, or nutrition conditions. In middle- and high-income countries the pattern is different: More than two-thirds die from noncommunicable diseases. Sustainable Development Goal 3 focuses on improving well-being, especially at the most vulnerable stages of life, providing health services, and improving imbalances between poorer and richer countries.

Targeting a range of health impacts

The Millennium Development Goals focused on improving health conditions in low- and middle-income countries, covering maternal mortality, child mortality, infectious diseases, and sexual and reproductive health. Sustainable Development Goal 3 introduces additional targets for noncommunicable diseases, mental health, substance abuse, injuries, universal health coverage, and pollution.[1]

Reducing maternal mortality

The global maternal mortality ratio declined dramatically between 1990 and 2015, from 385 maternal deaths per 100,000 live births to 216 (figure 3a). Despite this 44 percent decline, the Millennium Development Goal target of reducing the maternal mortality ratio by three-quarters was not met. The decline will need to accelerate considerably for the global maternal mortality ratio to fall below 70 per 100,000 live births by 2030 (target 3.1).

Providing mothers with skilled attendants at delivery and access to hospital treatments is key to treating life-threatening emergencies. Worldwide, the proportion of births attended by skilled health staff increased from 60 percent in 2000 to 68 percent in 2011. However only half of births are attended in low-income countries.

Providing universal access to sexual and reproductive health care

Sustainable Development Goal 3 aims to ensure universal access to sexual and reproductive health care services (target 3.7). One indicator for this is the fertility rate of adolescent women (ages 15–19), as women who give

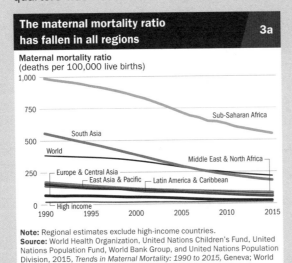

The maternal mortality ratio has fallen in all regions 3a

Maternal mortality ratio
(deaths per 100,000 live births)

Note: Regional estimates exclude high-income countries.
Source: World Health Organization, United Nations Children's Fund, United Nations Population Fund, World Bank Group, and United Nations Population Division, 2015, *Trends in Maternal Mortality: 1990 to 2015*, Geneva; World Development Indicators database (SH.STA.MMRT).

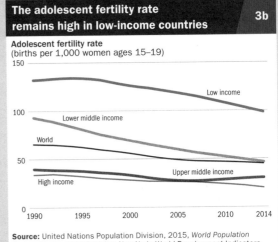

The adolescent fertility rate remains high in low-income countries 3b

Adolescent fertility rate
(births per 1,000 women ages 15–19)

Source: United Nations Population Division, 2015, *World Population Prospects: The 2015 Revision*, New York; World Development Indicators database (SP.ADO.TFRT).

Front | User guide | World view | People | Environment

birth at an early age are likely to bear more children and are at greater risk of death or serious complications from pregnancy. The adolescent fertility rate has been declining worldwide but remains high in low-income countries, at 98 births per 1,000 women ages 15–19 (figure 3b).

Ending preventable childhood deaths

In 2015 the global under-five mortality rate in 2015 was less than half the rate in 1990, falling just short of the Millennium Development Goal target of a two-thirds reduction (figure 3c).[2] Sustainable Development Goal 3 aims to end preventable deaths of newborns and children under age 5 and to reduce the under-five mortality rate in every country to below 25 deaths per 1,000 births (target 3.2). For this to happen, progress needs to accelerate especially in many low-income and lower middle-income countries.

Reducing noncommunicable diseases and injuries

Sustainable Development Goal 3 also aims to reduce deaths and adverse consequences of noncommunicable diseases and injuries (target 3.6). Traffic injuries caused 27 deaths per 100,000 people in low-income countries in 2013, three times more than in high-income countries (figure 3d).

There are challenges for monitoring nearly all the targets. Gaps exist because the key data sources, such as civil registration and vital statistics systems, are weak in many low- and middle-income countries, as are health information systems.

Notes

1. World Health Organization, 2015, *Health in 2015: From MDGs Millennium Development Goals to SDGs Sustainable Development Goals,* Geneva. [www .who.int/gho/publications/mdgs-sdgs/].

2. United Nations Inter-agency Group for Child Mortality Estimation. 2015. *Levels & Trends in Child Mortality. Report 2015.* [http://childmortality.org/]. New York.

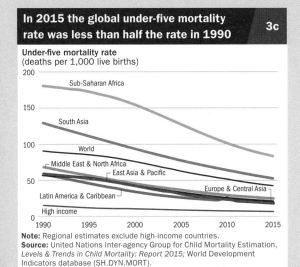

In 2015 the global under-five mortality rate was less than half the rate in 1990 3c

Under-five mortality rate
(deaths per 1,000 live births)

Sub-Saharan Africa
South Asia
World
Middle East & North Africa
East Asia & Pacific
Europe & Central Asia
Latin America & Caribbean
High income

Note: Regional estimates exclude high-income countries.
Source: United Nations Inter-agency Group for Child Mortality Estimation, *Levels & Trends in Child Mortality: Report 2015;* World Development Indicators database (SH.DYN.MORT).

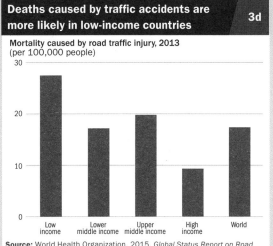

Deaths caused by traffic accidents are more likely in low-income countries 3d

Mortality caused by road traffic injury, 2013
(per 100,000 people)

Low income | Lower middle income | Upper middle income | High income | World

Source: World Health Organization, 2015, *Global Status Report on Road Safety 2015;* World Development Indicators database (SH.STA.TRAF.P5).

SDG 4 Quality education

Ensure inclusive and equitable quality education and promote lifelong learning opportunities for all

Progress has been made toward universal education, with 92 percent of children worldwide completing primary education and 74 percent completing lower secondary education. But the gross tertiary enrollment ratio remains around 30 percent. Increased access to higher education is needed to achieve a productive, talented, and diverse labor force and an empowered citizenry. Sustainable Development Goal 4 also focuses on education quality, proficiency in key subjects at various ages, and access to modern education facilities.

Attending and completing school

Considerable progress has been made since 1990 as more students enroll and finish primary school (target 4.1). The primary completion rate increased from 81 percent in 1990 to 92 percent in 2013 worldwide, and East Asia and Pacific and Europe and Central Asia have achieved or are close to achieving universal primary education. Sub-Saharan Africa still lags behind the rest of the world, despite a substantial increase in the region's primary completion rate to 69 percent in 2013 (figure 4a).

While many children enroll in school, some never attend, attend intermittently, or start but drop out entirely. In 2013, 59 million primary school–age children were not in school, a substantial decrease from the 102 million in 1990 (figure 4b). This reflects great progress considering the number of primary school–age children increased 14 percent over the same period, which placed further pressure on national education systems.

Gross enrollment ratios at all levels of education have risen globally, but wide variations remain between rich and poor countries. For example, children in high-income countries were almost five times more likely than children in low-income countries to have entered pre-primary school in 2013 (target 4.2; figure 4c). The trend is similar for tertiary gross enrollment (target 4.3).

Assessing the quality of education

One challenge of Sustainable Development Goal 4 is how to measure the quality of education and assess learning outcomes. Many types

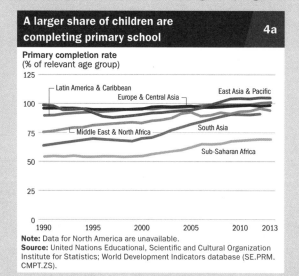

A larger share of children are completing primary school **4a**

Primary completion rate
(% of relevant age group)

Latin America & Caribbean
Europe & Central Asia
East Asia & Pacific
Middle East & North Africa
South Asia
Sub-Saharan Africa

Note: Data for North America are unavailable.
Source: United Nations Educational, Scientific and Cultural Organization Institute for Statistics; World Development Indicators database (SE.PRM.CMPT.ZS).

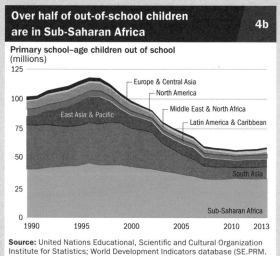

Over half of out-of-school children are in Sub-Saharan Africa **4b**

Primary school–age children out of school
(millions)

Europe & Central Asia
North America
Middle East & North Africa
Latin America & Caribbean
East Asia & Pacific
South Asia
Sub-Saharan Africa

Source: United Nations Educational, Scientific and Cultural Organization Institute for Statistics; World Development Indicators database (SE.PRM.UNER).

 Front   **?** User guide   World view   People   Environment

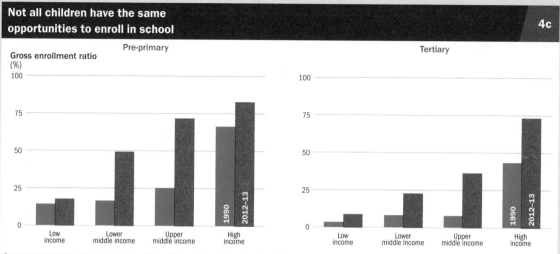

Not all children have the same opportunities to enroll in school

4c

Pre-primary

Gross enrollment ratio (%)

Tertiary

1990   2012–13

Source: United Nations Educational, Scientific and Cultural Organization Institute for Statistics; World Development Indicators database (SE.PRE.ENRR, SE.TER.ENRR).

of learning assessments are available, but different methodologies and coverage of ages, subjects, and years make comparisons across countries difficult.

Students' understanding of core subjects is fundamental to well functioning education systems (targets 4.1 and 4.6), and though not wholly comparable, regional assessments shed light on countries' achievements in these areas. The Programme for the Analysis of Education Systems assessment in Sub-Saharan Africa showed that only half of grade 5 students achieved the minimum learning goal in mathematics. The Trends in International Mathematics and Science Study showed that around 80 percent of grade 4 students in mainly Europe and Central Asia and Middle East and North Africa achieved the low international benchmark for mathematics.

Assessments of adolescents' learning outcomes have shown that around 30 percent of students worldwide fail to achieve minimum mathematics proficiency, according to the Programme for International Student Assessment and the Trends in International Mathematics and Science Study for grade 8 students (figure 4d). Students who do not achieve the lowest level of proficiency by age of 14 or 15 are unlikely to master the skills by the end of schooling and therefore may not be ready for work.

Addressing data challenges

While many indicators and proxies exist to monitor many of the education targets under Sustainable Development Goal 4, more are needed. There is a conceptual challenge in developing global indicators for target 4.4, which stipulates "by 2030, substantially increase the number of youth and adults who have relevant skills, including technical and vocational skills, for employment, decent jobs and entrepreneurship." Countries will need to define relevant skills suitable for their own job market structure and economic situation and set up robust and timely data collection systems to populate these indicators.

Different assessments report varying basic knowledge in mathematics

4d

Students achieving basic knowledge benchmarks in mathematics (%)

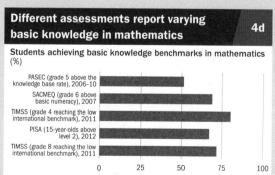

TIMSS is Trends in International Mathematics and Science Study. PISA is Program for International Student Assessment. SACMEQ is Southern and Eastern Africa Consortium for Monitoring Educational Quality. PASEC is Programme for the Analysis of Education Systems.
Source: World Bank EdStats database, Conférence des ministres de l'Éducation des États et gouvernements de la Francophonie (www.confemen .org), Organisation for Economic Co-operation and Development (www.oecd.org /pisa/), Southern and Eastern Africa Consortium for Monitoring Educational Quality (www.sacmeq.org), and TIMSS & PIRLS International Study Center (http://timssandpirls.bc.edu).

SDG 5 Gender equality

Achieve gender equality and empower all women and girls

Despite much progress toward gender equality in recent years, critical gaps between men and women persist. Half of women are economically active, compared with over three-quarters of men. On top of limited economic opportunities, women often have restricted agency—their ability to make decisions about their lives and to act on those decisions. While women and girls usually bear the direct costs of inequalities, gender bias has a cost to all, reducing the pace of development.

Identifying obstacles to equality

Sustainable Development Goal 5 explicitly recognizes gender equality and the empowerment of women and girls and sets ambitious targets for ending all forms of discrimination against women and girls, eliminating all forms of violence and harmful practices, improving economic empowerment and access to productive assets and technologies, and enhancing the female voice and decision-making power beyond the Millennium Development Goal's focus on education.

Empowering women's economic opportunities

Increasing women's income-earning opportunities and their access to productive assets provides a direct pathway out of poverty. Economic empowerment can also give women voice and agency to manage their own money and make decisions for themselves and their family.

Legal frameworks that protect men and women equally are an important first step toward gender equality, but discriminatory laws persist. Around 60 percent of countries lack legislation that ensures equal opportunities in hiring practices, requires equal remuneration for work of equal value, or allows women to perform the same jobs as men. While almost all countries mandate maternity leave, almost half do not guarantee mothers an equivalent position on their return, discriminating against women who become pregnant and want to come back to work after the birth of a child (figure 5a).

Fewer women than men are economically active, and women often occupy less secure and lower paying jobs than men or choose jobs that offer flexible hours, allowing them to balance work and household responsibilities. And more women than men are contributing family

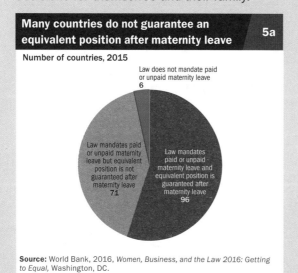

Many countries do not guarantee an equivalent position after maternity leave `5a`

Number of countries, 2015

Law does not mandate paid or unpaid maternity leave
6

Law mandates paid or unpaid maternity leave but equivalent position is not guaranteed after maternity leave
71

Law mandates paid or unpaid maternity leave and equivalent position is guaranteed after maternity leave
96

Source: World Bank, 2016, *Women, Business, and the Law 2016: Getting to Equal*, Washington, DC.

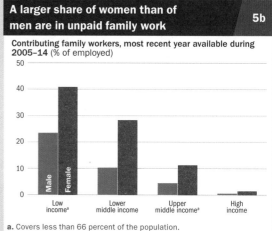

A larger share of women than of men are in unpaid family work `5b`

Contributing family workers, most recent year available during 2005–14 (% of employed)

Male / Female

Low income[a] · Lower middle income · Upper middle income[a] · High income

a. Covers less than 66 percent of the population.
Source: International Labour Organization Key Indicators of the Labour Market database; World Development Indicators database (SL.FAM.WORK. FE.ZS, SL.FAM.WORK.MA.ZS).

 Front | **?** User guide | World view | People | Environment

workers (figure 5b). These jobs are often insecure, do not provide any contractual security or benefits, and offer limited opportunities for career advancement and higher wages.

Firm ownership and management are also dominated by men. Worldwide, 83 percent of firms have a man as a top manager, and 66 percent of firms have no female participation in their ownership (figure 5c).

Access to financial services is another vehicle of economic empowerment, allowing women to borrow and save to start a business, cope with economic shocks, and invest in their family's future. But in many countries women face more barriers than men do in opening a bank account, such as the need for a male family member's permission, a lack of documentation to prove identity, and lack of information. Worldwide, 57 percent of women held their own account at a financial institution in 2014, compared with 64 percent of men.

Ending violence against women and girls
Target 5.2 calls for eliminating all forms of violence against women and girls. Worldwide, an estimated one in three women has experienced physical or sexual violence or both at the hands of a husband, boyfriend, or partner.[1] Rates of violence vary widely across countries, but such violence occurs in all regions, regardless of income or education level.[2] Reliable statistics are hard to collect, and rates are often underestimated.

Eliminating child, early, and forced marriage
Eliminating child, early, and forced marriage is a focus of target 5.3. Child marriage pushes girls into adulthood before they are mature[3]: Young brides often drop out of school, have more children (figure 5d), face higher health risks during pregnancy and childbirth, and suffer more barriers to obtaining a higher paid job and gaining financial independence. All this leads to a lack of voice and agency. Although child marriage is prohibited by law in the majority of countries, one in four women ages 20–24 is married by age 18.[4]

Notes

1. World Bank, 2014, "Gender at Work: A Companion to the World Development Report on Jobs," Washington, DC.
2. United Nations Statistics Division, 2015, *World's Women 2015: Trends and Statistics,* New York.
3. World Bank, 2014, "Voice and Agency: Empowering Women and Girls for Shared Prosperity," Washington, DC.
4. United Nations Children's Fund [http://data.unicef.org/child-protection/child-marriage.html].

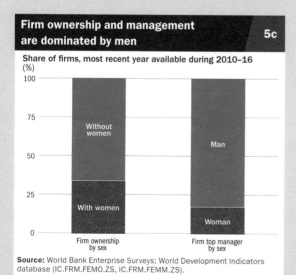

Firm ownership and management are dominated by men   **5c**

Share of firms, most recent year available during 2010–16 (%)

Without women / With women — Firm ownership by sex
Man / Woman — Firm top manager by sex

Source: World Bank Enterprise Surveys; World Development Indicators database (IC.FRM.FEMO.ZS, IC.FRM.FEMM.ZS).

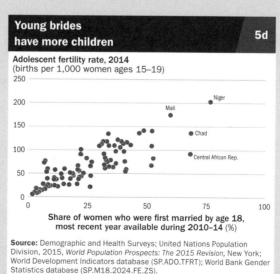

Young brides have more children   **5d**

Adolescent fertility rate, 2014
(births per 1,000 women ages 15–19)

Niger
Mali
Chad
Central African Rep.

Share of women who were first married by age 18, most recent year available during 2010–14 (%)

Source: Demographic and Health Surveys; United Nations Population Division, 2015, *World Population Prospects: The 2015 Revision,* New York; World Development Indicators database (SP.ADO.TFRT); World Bank Gender Statistics database (SP.M18.2024.FE.ZS).

SDG 6 Clean water and sanitation

Ensure availability
and sustainable
management
of water and
sanitation for all

Despite halving the number of people worldwide without access to an improved water source over the past 25 years, the poorest countries are struggling to sustainably provide safe water and adequate sanitation to all. Just over a quarter of people in low-income countries have access to an improved sanitation facility, compared with just over half in lower middle-income countries. Delivery of water supply and sanitation is not just a challenge of service provision; it is intrinsically linked with climate change, water resources management, water scarcity, and water quality.

Ensuring access to an improved water source and improved sanitation facilities

In many countries, economic and population growth as well as urbanization have increased water demand while supply has remained unchanged or even decreased due to climate change. Although 2.6 billion people have gained access to an improved water source since 1990, dwindling supplies of safe drinking water remain a global problem. More than $250 billion in GDP is lost every year in low- and middle-income countries because of inadequate water supply and sanitation services.[1]

Sustainable Development Goal 6 recognizes that sustainably managing water goes beyond simply providing a safe water supply and sanitation to include the environment, human health, food security, disaster resilience, and ultimately economic growth.

Easing access to drinking water

Sustainable Development Goal 6 encompasses a call for drinking water for all (target 6.1). In 2015, 91 percent of the world's population had access to an improved water source, exceeding the Millennium Development Goal target of 88 percent. However, more than 660 million people still lack access to clean water, the majority of them in rural areas, predominantly in Sub-Saharan Africa (figure 6a). Even for those who have access to water, service is often inadequate or unsustainable, and water from an improved source can still be unsafe to drink.[2]

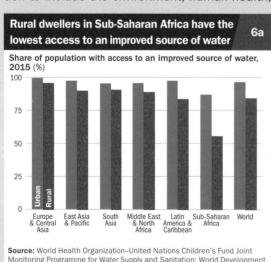

Rural dwellers in Sub-Saharan Africa have the lowest access to an improved source of water 6a

Share of population with access to an improved source of water, 2015 (%)

Source: World Health Organization–United Nations Children's Fund Joint Monitoring Programme for Water Supply and Sanitation; World Development Indicators database (SH.H2O.SAFE.UR.ZS, SH.H2O.SAFE.RU.ZS).

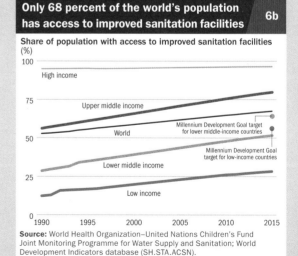

Only 68 percent of the world's population has access to improved sanitation facilities 6b

Share of population with access to improved sanitation facilities (%)

Source: World Health Organization–United Nations Children's Fund Joint Monitoring Programme for Water Supply and Sanitation; World Development Indicators database (SH.STA.ACSN).

 Front | User guide | World view | People | Environment

Improving access to sanitation facilities

Only 68 percent of the world's population has access to improved sanitation facilities, falling short of the Millennium Development Goal target of 77 percent (figure 6b). Sustainable Development Goal 6 aims to ensure adequate sanitation for all and to end open defecation (target 6.2), which contaminates water and spreads diseases such as cholera, diarrhea, and dysentery. Around 842,000 people a year die from diarrhea as a result of unsafe drinking water, sanitation, or hygiene.[3] Seven out of ten people who lack access to safe and hygienic toilet facilities live in rural areas, mostly in Sub-Saharan Africa and South Asia.

Balancing water demand with available resources

Many countries face the threat of water scarcity, prompting calls for efficient water use (target 6.4). Demand for water continues to grow, while global per capita freshwater supplies have been nearly halved over the past 50 years. Today, the Middle East and North Africa and South Asia are classified as water stressed-regions, with less than 1,700 cubic meters of water available per year per person (figure 6c).

Climate change is expected to exacerbate the situation by raising water stress in arid regions and increasing the frequency and magnitude of extreme weather events. In 2030 half the world's population is projected to live in high water-stress regions.[4]

Increasing water withdrawals for agriculture and energy generation will exacerbate competition for water use. The agricultural sector accounts for over 70 percent of global freshwater withdrawals (figure 6d). By 2050 feeding a planet of 9 billion people will require a 15 percent increase in water withdrawals for agriculture.[5] Similarly, water withdrawals for energy generation are projected to grow 20 percent.[6]

Notes

1. World Health Organization, 2012, *Global Costs and Benefits of Drinking-Water Supply and Sanitation Interventions to Reach the MDG Target and Universal Coverage*, Geneva.

2. United Nations Children's Fund, 2015, "The Millennium Development Goal (MDG 7) Drinking Water Target Has Been Met, But Marked Disparities Persist," UNICEF Data: Monitoring the Situation of Children and Women. [http://data.unicef.org/water-sanitation/water.html].

3. World Health Organization, 2015, "Drinking-water", Fact Sheet 391. [www.who.int/mediacentre/factsheets/fs391/en].

4. United Nations, 2014 "International Decade for Action 'Water for Life' 2005–2015." [www.un.org/waterforlifedecade/scarcity.shtml].

5. World Bank, 2013, "Water Resources Management: Sector Results Profile." [www.worldbank.org/en/results/2013/04/15/water-resources-management-results-profile].

6. International Energy Agency, 2012, *World Energy Outlook 2012*, Paris.

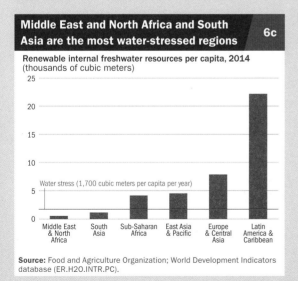

Middle East and North Africa and South Asia are the most water-stressed regions — 6c

Renewable internal freshwater resources per capita, 2014 (thousands of cubic meters)

Water stress (1,700 cubic meters per capita per year)

Source: Food and Agriculture Organization; World Development Indicators database (ER.H2O.INTR.PC).

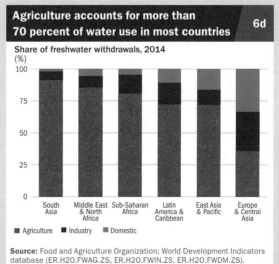

Agriculture accounts for more than 70 percent of water use in most countries — 6d

Share of freshwater withdrawals, 2014 (%)

■ Agriculture ■ Industry ■ Domestic

Source: Food and Agriculture Organization; World Development Indicators database (ER.H2O.FWAG.ZS, ER.H2O.FWIN.ZS, ER.H2O.FWDM.ZS).

SDG 7 Affordable and clean energy

Between 1990 and 2013 worldwide energy use increased about 54 percent, more than the 36 percent increase in the global population. Access to energy is fundamental to development, but as economies evolve, rising incomes and growing populations demand more energy. Meeting Sustainable Development Goal 7 will require increasing access to electricity, the take-up of clean fuels and renewable energies, and energy efficiency.

Ensure access to affordable, reliable, sustainable, and modern energy for all

Achieving universal access

Universal access to affordable, reliable, and modern energy services is critical to sustainable development (target 7.1). Energy, especially electricity, is crucial to improving the standard of living for people in low- and middle-income countries. It is key to providing reliable and efficient lighting, heating, cooking, and mechanical power; to delivering clean water, sanitation, and healthcare; and to operating well functioning transport and telecommunications services. Modern energy services are central to the economic development of a country and to the welfare of its citizens. Without such services, businesses stagnate, and the potential of people to live healthy, productive lives is diminished.

Improvements over the past two decades led to 85 percent of the world enjoying access to electricity in 2012. Nevertheless, around 1.1 billion people are still without. In Sub-Saharan Africa only 35 percent of the population has access to electricity, the lowest among all regions (figure 7a). Almost 40 percent of the world's population relies primarily on wood, coal, charcoal, or animal waste to cook their food, breathing in toxic smoke that causes lung disease and kills nearly 4 million people a year, most of them women and children.[1]

Using renewable energy

While the share of energy use from alternative, cleaner sources has increased since 1970 in all income groups, fossil fuels account for around 81 percent of the world's energy use. Countries need to substantially increase the share of renewable energy in the global energy mix (target 7.2) from its current small share of 18 percent (figure 7b). The largest share of renewable energy comes from traditional uses of biomass

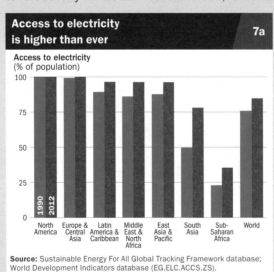

Access to electricity is higher than ever | 7a

Access to electricity
(% of population)

1990 2012

North America · Europe & Central Asia · Latin America & Caribbean · Middle East & North Africa · East Asia & Pacific · South Asia · Sub-Saharan Africa · World

Source: Sustainable Energy For All Global Tracking Framework database; World Development Indicators database (EG.ELC.ACCS.ZS).

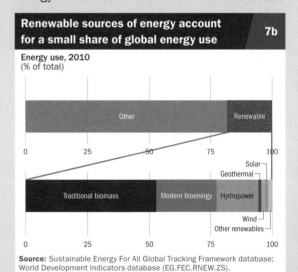

Renewable sources of energy account for a small share of global energy use | 7b

Energy use, 2010
(% of total)

Other · Renewable

Traditional biomass · Modern bioenergy · Hydropower

Solar · Geothermal · Wind · Other renewables

Source: Sustainable Energy For All Global Tracking Framework database; World Development Indicators database (EG.FEC.RNEW.ZS).

 Front | ? User guide | World view | People | Environment

(such as wood and charcoal). Modern biomass and hydropower are important modern renewable energy sources, each accounting for 3–4 percent of total final energy consumption. Other modern renewables (such as biomass, geothermal, wind, and solar)—currently around 1 percent of total consumption—have substantial potential for growth. The share of renewable energy varies widely across the globe. It is falling in lower income regions as they switch from traditional biomass to more modern fuels for cooking and heating. By contrast, higher income regions are gradually shifting toward renewable energy sources, albeit from a low base (figure 7c).

Increasing energy efficiency

Sustainable Development Goal 7 calls on countries to collectively double the global rate of improvement in energy efficiency, and technological progress and a shift away from energy-intensive activities can support this (target 7.3). The energy intensity level of primary energy—the ratio of energy supply to GDP in purchasing power parity terms—indicates energy efficiency, or how much energy is used to produce one unit of economic output. A lower ratio indicates that less energy is used to produce one unit of output. Between 1990 and 2012 the ratio declined 27 percent globally as energy efficiency improved in all income groups (figure 7d), which helped keep total final energy consumption a third lower than it would otherwise have been. The coverage of energy efficiency regulations in industry, buildings, and transport has nearly doubled, from 14 percent of the world's energy consumption in 2005 to 27 percent in 2014. Still much more needs to be done.

Note

1. Sustainable Energy for All (www.se4all.org).

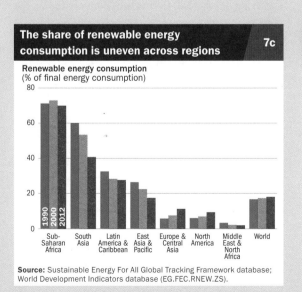

The share of renewable energy consumption is uneven across regions 7c

Renewable energy consumption
(% of final energy consumption)

Source: Sustainable Energy For All Global Tracking Framework database; World Development Indicators database (EG.FEC.RNEW.ZS).

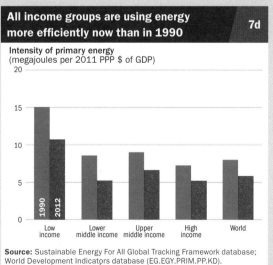

All income groups are using energy more efficiently now than in 1990 7d

Intensity of primary energy
(megajoules per 2011 PPP $ of GDP)

Source: Sustainable Energy For All Global Tracking Framework database; World Development Indicators database (EG.EGY.PRIM.PP.KD).

SDG 8 Productive employment and economic growth

Promote
sustained,
inclusive, and
sustainable
economic
growth, full
and productive
employment,
and decent
work for all

Jobs are the bedrock of both economic and social development. And growth drives development. By leveraging labor, individuals and households have a sustainable pathway out of poverty. Yet more than 200 million people were unemployed in 2015, and many more were underemployed in low-productivity informal sector jobs. Some 600 million new jobs need to be created by 2030, just to keep pace with the rising population.[1] Sustainable Development Goal 8 aims for higher economic productivity and at least 7 percent annual GDP growth in the least developed countries.

Increasing growth in the least developed countries

Of the 48 UN-classified least developed countries in 2015, 23 are classified as fragile by the World Bank. The fragility of a country impacts its growth: Between 2000 and 2014 GDP growth in countries in fragile or conflict situations averaged a little under 4 percent a year, compared with almost 6 percent in the least developed countries as a whole (figures 8a–8c). International efforts to bring peace to countries in fragile or conflict situations and reforms in other least developed countries are needed to achieve at least 7 percent annual GDP growth (target 8.1).

Enhancing economic productivity and value added for labor-intensive sectors

Sustained economic growth is achieved through higher productivity, both within sectors and by

shifting to sectors that generate higher value added and that yield benefits to workers, employers, and the economy. Variation among sectors is higher in countries with low labor productivity, leading to increased inequality. In many lower income countries a large share of working-age adults is not part of the formal labor force, highlighting the importance of the informal sector and the challenge of raising the productivity and quality of such livelihoods. Gender inequalities persist across regions and sectors: Women make up a smaller share of employment in all regions and are disproportionately employed in lower productivity sectors, including agriculture, and in informal sectors (figure 8d).

Creating jobs—led by the private sector

Creating high-quality, sustainable jobs (target 8.3) requires a strong and thriving private sector. In low- and middle-income countries the private sector accounts for up to 90 percent of jobs. Micro, small, and medium-size enterprises, especially in services and agriculture, account for the largest share of new jobs. The formal private sector remains underdeveloped and weakly competitive in many low- and middle-income countries, with the number of formal wage jobs less than the number of new entrants joining the labor force each year. There is a strong correlation between country income and the density of new formal firms. After the

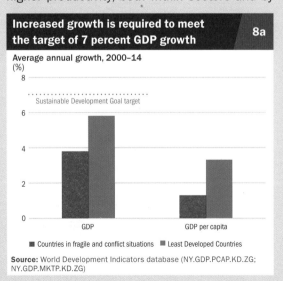

Increased growth is required to meet the target of 7 percent GDP growth | 8a

Average annual growth, 2000–14 (%)

Sustainable Development Goal target

■ Countries in fragile and conflict situations ■ Least Developed Countries

Source: World Development Indicators database (NY.GDP.PCAP.KD.ZG; NY.GDP.MKTP.KD.ZG)

8b

Over 2000–14 the least developed countries averaged 5.8 percent GDP growth …

Average annual GDP growth, 2000–14
(%)

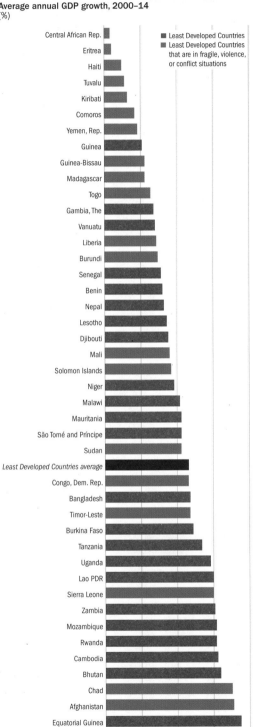

Legend:
- ■ Least Developed Countries
- ■ Least Developed Countries that are in fragile, violence, or conflict situations

Countries (top to bottom): Central African Rep., Eritrea, Haiti, Tuvalu, Kiribati, Comoros, Yemen, Rep., Guinea, Guinea-Bissau, Madagascar, Togo, Gambia, The, Vanuatu, Liberia, Burundi, Senegal, Benin, Nepal, Lesotho, Djibouti, Mali, Solomon Islands, Niger, Malawi, Mauritania, São Tomé and Príncipe, Sudan, *Least Developed Countries average*, Congo, Dem. Rep., Bangladesh, Timor-Leste, Burkina Faso, Tanzania, Uganda, Lao PDR, Sierra Leone, Zambia, Mozambique, Rwanda, Cambodia, Bhutan, Chad, Afghanistan, Equatorial Guinea, Ethiopia

X-axis: 0.0 2.5 5.0 7.5 10.0

Source: World Development Indicators database (NY.GDP.MKTP.KD.ZG).

8c

… and 3.3 percent per capita GDP growth

Average annual per capita GDP growth, 2000–14
(%)

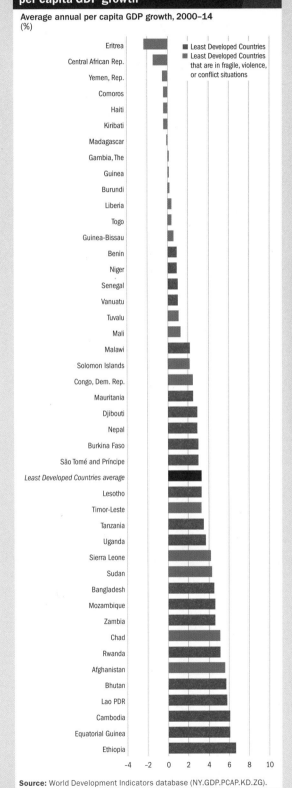

Legend:
- ■ Least Developed Countries
- ■ Least Developed Countries that are in fragile, violence, or conflict situations

Countries (top to bottom): Eritrea, Central African Rep., Yemen, Rep., Comoros, Haiti, Kiribati, Madagascar, Gambia, The, Guinea, Burundi, Liberia, Togo, Guinea-Bissau, Benin, Niger, Senegal, Vanuatu, Tuvalu, Mali, Malawi, Solomon Islands, Congo, Dem. Rep., Mauritania, Djibouti, Nepal, Burkina Faso, São Tomé and Príncipe, *Least Developed Countries average*, Lesotho, Timor-Leste, Tanzania, Uganda, Sierra Leone, Sudan, Bangladesh, Mozambique, Zambia, Chad, Rwanda, Afghanistan, Bhutan, Lao PDR, Cambodia, Equatorial Guinea, Ethiopia

X-axis: -4 -2 0 2 4 6 8 10

Source: World Development Indicators database (NY.GDP.PCAP.KD.ZG).

8

decline in business registration across regions due to the 2008 global economic crisis, most regions—particularly East Asia and Pacific—have seen an uptick in recent years (figure 8e).

Achieving full and productive employment and decent work for all and equal pay

The share of people employed in wage jobs varies by region and gender (figure 8f). Almost two-thirds of people who work in Europe and Central Asia have wage jobs, compared with around a fifth in South Asia, where many jobs are in the informal sector. The Middle East and North Africa has the largest gender gap: Nearly

55 percent of men are in wage jobs, compared with 44 percent of women. The share of women in wage jobs is lowest in Sub-Saharan Africa (14 percent), and the share of men in wage jobs is lowest in South Asia (22 percent). Half of low- and middle-income countries in Europe and Central Asia legally mandate that women receive equal pay for work of equal value (target 8.5), compared with a third of low- and middle-income countries in other regions and only one country in South Asia (Bangladesh; figure 8g).

Empowering young people to work

Sustainable Development Goal 8 focuses on providing opportunities for all, including young people (targets 8.5 and 8.6). Young people not in employment, education, or training represent a missed opportunity and a loss of productive engagement that can have lifelong impacts, including reduced earnings. The Middle East and North Africa and South Asia have the largest shares of young people not in employment, education, or training (figure 8h). Young people often face greater challenges in finding employment due to their lack of experience, their lower access to credit, and their more limited networks that can help identify an employment or entrepreneurial opportunity. Thus youth unemployment rates can be double those of adults.

Women are disproportionately employed in lower productivity sectors — 8d

Labor force status, most recent year available during 2005–14 (% of population ages 15 and older)

[Horizontal bar chart showing Female/Male labor force status for: East Asia & Pacific, Europe & Central Asia, Latin America & Caribbean, Middle East & North Africa, South Asia, Sub-Saharan Africa. X-axis 0 to 100.]

Legend: Employed in agriculture ■ Employed in industry ■ Employed in services ■ Unemployed ■ Not in the labor force

Note: Excludes high-income countries.
Source: International Labour Organization Key Indicators of the Labour Market database.

Most regions have seen an increase in business registration since 2008 — 8e

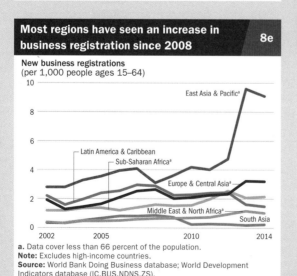

New business registrations (per 1,000 people ages 15–64)

a. Data cover less than 66 percent of the population.
Note: Excludes high-income countries.
Source: World Bank Doing Business database; World Development Indicators database (IC.BUS.NDNS.ZS).

Workers in Sub-Saharan Africa and South Asia are the least likely to be in wage work — 8f

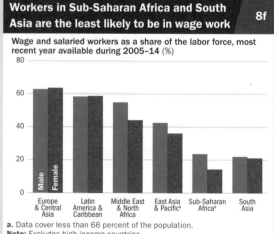

Wage and salaried workers as a share of the labor force, most recent year available during 2005–14 (%)

a. Data cover less than 66 percent of the population.
Note: Excludes high-income countries.
Source: International Labour Organization Key Indicators of the Labour Market database.

○ Front | ? User guide | ◉ World view | 👤 People | 🌿 Environment

Countries differ considerably in which labor protections and regulations they emphasize | 8g

Share of countries with legal framework for equal remuneration for work of equal value, 2015 (%)

Ratio of minimum wage to value added per worker, 2015 (%)

Paid annual leave for a worker with five years of tenure, 2015 (days)

East Asia & Pacific
Europe & Central Asia
Latin America & Caribbean
Middle East & North Africa
South Asia
Sub-Saharan Africa

Note: Excludes high-income countries. For Bangladesh, Brazil, China, India, Indonesia, Mexico, Nigeria, and Pakistan data refer to the largest city.
Source: World Bank Doing Business database.

Where the share of young people not in employment, education, or training is relatively low, as in Sub-Saharan Africa, young people may be engaged in subsistence agriculture and informal sector activities by necessity.

Regulating the labor market

To address the overall goal of productive employment and decent work for all, more jobs are needed, and they need to be better —in terms of working conditions, benefits, and productivity—and more inclusive. Labor market regulations can help address market failures and secure social protection for vulnerable and disadvantaged groups (target 8.8). Good working environments are influenced by many factors. Workers should be able to share in higher productivity, and a minimum wage ensures a basic level of income; however, too high a minimum wage can discourage the creation of wage jobs. There are considerable variations in working conditions and types of benefits across regions (se figure 8g).

Note

1. World Bank, 2012, *World Development Report 2013: Jobs,* Washington, DC.

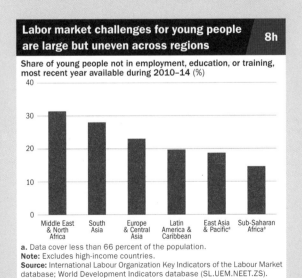

Labor market challenges for young people are large but uneven across regions | 8h

Share of young people not in employment, education, or training, most recent year available during 2010–14 (%)

Middle East & North Africa · South Asia · Europe & Central Asia · Latin America & Caribbean · East Asia & Pacific[a] · Sub-Saharan Africa[a]

a. Data cover less than 66 percent of the population.
Note: Excludes high-income countries.
Source: International Labour Organization Key Indicators of the Labour Market database; World Development Indicators database (SL.UEM.NEET.ZS).

Economy | States and markets | Global links | Back | World Development Indicators 2016 **19**

SDG 9 Industry, innovation, and infrastructure

Since 1990 over $2.5 trillion has been invested in private infrastructure projects around the world.[1] Investments in telecommunications, electricity, and roads form the foundations for industrialization, innovation, and increased productivity.

Build resilient infrastructure, promote inclusive and sustainable industrialization, and foster innovation

Building sustainable and robust infrastructure

Limited access to decent roads can isolate farmers from markets and restrict agricultural production to subsistence levels. It also impacts the ability of rural businesses and enterprises to compete with others in less remote areas. In the short term enhancing rural road connectivity reduces transport costs and improves access to markets and social facilities such as schools and hospitals. In the longer term it elevates agricultural productivity, business profitability, and employment.[2] It also helps strengthen the resilience of rural populations to natural and human-made shocks and disasters by facilitating the movement of people and supplies for faster recovery.

The share of the rural population living within 2 kilometers of a road in good condition is measured through the Rural Access Index[3] and is a useful indicator for governments planning their transport infrastructure (target 9.1). Data availability is limited, but advances in digital technology allow better assessment of population distribution and transport infrastructure location and quality. In Mozambique only an estimated 19 percent of the rural population lives within 2 kilometers of a good road, which means that about 14.5 million rural residents lack access (figure 9a). In Kenya an estimated 57 percent of the rural population lives within 2 kilometers of a good road; about 13.5 million rural residents lack access (figure 9b).

Driving economic growth through industrialization

The industrial sector is vital to economic development, and manufacturing is key to long-term structural change, formal job creation, and the technology and innovation needed for productivity growth.

Manufacturing value added as a share of GDP captures the role of manufacturing in an economy. Worldwide, the share declined from 19 percent in 1997 to 16 percent in 2013 (figure 9c). East Asia and Pacific has historically had the highest share, though it declined from 27 percent in 1990 to 22 percent in 2013,

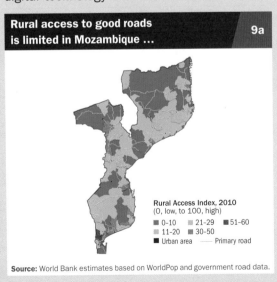

Rural access to good roads is limited in Mozambique ...   9a

Rural Access Index, 2010
(0, low, to 100, high)
- 0–10
- 11–20
- 21–29
- 30–50
- 51–60
- Urban area
- Primary road

Source: World Bank estimates based on WorldPop and government road data.

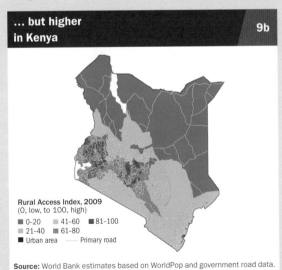

... but higher in Kenya   9b

Rural Access Index, 2009
(0, low, to 100, high)
- 0–20
- 21–40
- 41–60
- 61–80
- 81–100
- Urban area
- Primary road

Source: World Bank estimates based on WorldPop and government road data.

Front | User guide | World view | People | Environment

with China averaging 32 percent and Thailand averaging 28 percent. In South Asia the share has remained fairly constant since 1990; it was about 17 percent in 2014. Between 1990 and 2014 the share increased slightly, from 16 percent to 17 percent, in India, while Bangladesh registered a larger increase, from 13 percent to 17 percent. In the Middle East and North Africa the share was relatively constant between 2001 and 2007, averaging 12 percent. Sub-Saharan Africa has the lowest share, which has been declining over the past 25 years, from 15 percent in 1990 to 11 percent in 2014. North America had the biggest decline in the share, from 17 percent in 1997 to 12 percent in 2013. The share has also been declining in Latin America and the Caribbean, from 22 percent in 1991 to 15 percent in 2014, and in Europe and Central Asia, from 21 percent in 1991 to 15 percent in 2014.

Promoting innovation and research and development

One measure of innovation is the intensity of research and development, measured as expenditure on research and development as a percentage of GDP. Worldwide, it increased slightly from 1.6 percent in 2007 to 1.7 percent in 2013,[4] despite the period's global financial crisis. Asia was the first to recover; in particular China's research and development intensity grew from 1.4 percent in 2007 to 2.0 percent in 2013. In other emerging economies the rise was slower—from 1.1 percent in 2007 to 1.2 percent in 2012 in Brazil—or stagnant—around 0.8 percent in 2007 and 2011 in India. The Russian Federation maintained research and development intensity at pre-crisis levels, averaging around 1.1 percent between 2007 and 2013. Conversely, South Africa saw a substantial drop, from 0.9 percent in 2007 to 0.7 percent in 2012.

Notes

1. World Bank Private Participation in Infrastructure database (http://ppi .worldbank.org).

2. Iimi, A., and A. Diehl, 2015, "A New Measure of Rural Access to Transport: Using GIS Data to Inform Decisions and Attainment of the SDGs," Transport and ICT Connections 23, Washington, DC: World Bank.

3. www.worldbank.org/transport/transportresults/headline/rural-access. html.

4. United Nations Educational, Scientific and Cultural Organization, 2015, *UNESCO Science Report: Towards 2030,* Paris.

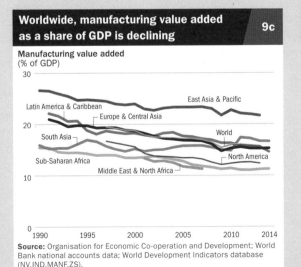

Worldwide, manufacturing value added as a share of GDP is declining 9c

Manufacturing value added (% of GDP)

Source: Organisation for Economic Co-operation and Development; World Bank national accounts data; World Development Indicators database (NV.IND.MANF.ZS).

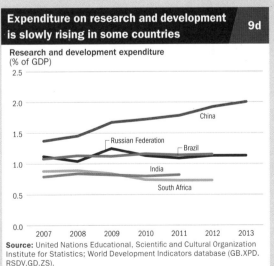

Expenditure on research and development is slowly rising in some countries 9d

Research and development expenditure (% of GDP)

Source: United Nations Educational, Scientific and Cultural Organization Institute for Statistics; World Development Indicators database (GB.XPD. RSDV.GD.ZS).

SDG 10 Reduced inequalities

Reduce inequality within and among countries

The targets of Sustainable Development Goal 10 focus on reducing inequality in a variety of contexts: income inequality within a country and inequality by gender, age, disability, race, class, ethnicity, religion, and opportunity. It also tackles inequality among countries in terms of voice, migration, and international aid.

Reducing inequality within countries

Sustainable Development Goal 10 aims to progressively achieve, by 2030, sustained income growth among the poorest 40 percent of the population at a rate higher than the national average in every country (target 10.1). This echoes the World Bank's goal of promoting shared prosperity, which does not set a specific target for each country but aims to foster income growth among the poorest 40 percent in every country.

In 56 out of 94 countries with data for 2007–12 the per capita income of the poorest 40 percent is growing faster than the national average (countries above the diagonal line in figure 10a). Of those 56, 9 still experienced negative growth (group A in figure 10a), including high-income countries (the United Kingdom and the United States) and middle-income countries (Guatemala and the Kyrgyz Republic). Thus, higher growth among the poorest 40 percent does not necessarily lead to prosperity. Another group of countries experienced relatively strong growth (above 3 percent) over the same period for both the poorest 40 percent and the total population, but in some cases the growth rate for the bottom 40 percent was lower than the national average (China and Vietnam; group B in figure 10a). In these cases the Sustainable Development Goal target would not have been met, even though people on average were better off.

Among countries with data, a larger proportion of low- and middle-income countries than of high-income countries met the target. Specifically, in around two-thirds of low- and middle-income countries the income of the poorest 40 percent grew faster than the national average, compared with half of high-income countries (figure 10b).

Reducing inequality across countries

International aid. Millennium Development Goal 8 focused on the need for high-, middle-, and low-income countries to work together to create

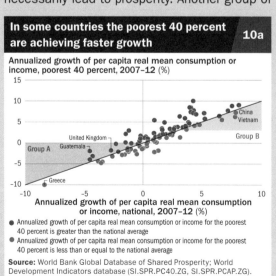

In some countries the poorest 40 percent are achieving faster growth — **10a**

Annualized growth of per capita real mean consumption or income, poorest 40 percent, 2007–12 (%)

Annualized growth of per capita real mean consumption or income, national, 2007–12 (%)

● Annualized growth of per capita real mean consumption or income for the poorest 40 percent is greater than the national average
● Annualized growth of per capita real mean consumption or income for the poorest 40 percent is less than or equal to the national average

Source: World Bank Global Database of Shared Prosperity; World Development Indicators database (SI.SPR.PC40.ZG, SI.SPR.PCAP.ZG).

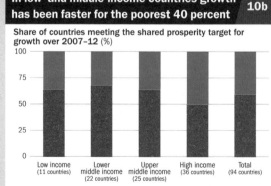

In low- and middle-income countries growth has been faster for the poorest 40 percent — **10b**

Share of countries meeting the shared prosperity target for growth over 2007–12 (%)

Low income (11 countries) · Lower middle income (22 countries) · Upper middle income (25 countries) · High income (36 countries) · Total (94 countries)

■ Annualized growth of per capita real mean consumption or income for the poorest 40 percent is greater than the national average
■ Annualized growth of per capita real mean consumption or income for the poorest 40 percent is less than or equal to the national average

Source: World Bank Global Database of Shared Prosperity; World Development Indicators database (SI.SPR.PC40.ZG, SI.SPR.PCAP.ZG).

○ Front | ? User guide | World view | People | Environment

an environment where rapid sustainable development is possible. The Sustainable Development Goals continue this focus, encouraging official development assistance and financial flows to countries where the need is greatest (target 10.b).

Over 2009–14, nominal inflows of official development assistance grew 27 percent to $161 billion (figure 10c). But meeting target 10.b may require a change in current trends. Increases in inflows to the poorest countries have not kept pace with those to middle-income countries. Official development assistance to Sub-Saharan Africa increased just 4 percent between 2009 and 2014, and official development assistance to the least developed countries increased only 9 percent. The trend was driven primarily by a drop in bilateral aid channeled directly by donors, which accounts for around 75 percent of total net official development assistance. For instance, bilateral aid to the least developed countries fell 16 percent

between 2013 and 2014, a decline explained only partially by the sharp drop in debt relief to Myanmar. Bilateral official development assistance to Sub-Saharan Africa also fell 5 percent in nominal terms from 2013 to 2014.

Migration. People migrate for many reasons, including better employment opportunities and higher wages. Many migrants remit money back to their country of origin, to care for their family, and the amount of such payments is large and has been increasing. Worldwide, personal remittances were estimated at $583 billion in 2014—$436 billion (75 percent) of which went to low- and middle-income countries, up 4.3 percent from 2013.

But it is not cheap to send money across national borders. The cost of sending the equivalent of $200 averaged 8 percent in 2014, down from 10 percent in 2008 but still above the 3 percent called for by 2030 in target 10.c (figure 10d).

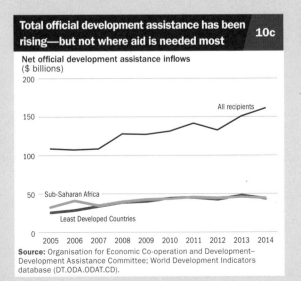

Total official development assistance has been rising—but not where aid is needed most `10c`

Net official development assistance inflows
($ billions)

All recipients

Sub-Saharan Africa

Least Developed Countries

Source: Organisation for Economic Co-operation and Development–Development Assistance Committee; World Development Indicators database (DT.ODA.ODAT.CD).

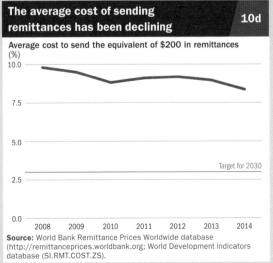

The average cost of sending remittances has been declining `10d`

Average cost to send the equivalent of $200 in remittances
(%)

Target for 2030

Source: World Bank Remittance Prices Worldwide database (http://remittanceprices.worldbank.org; World Development Indicators database (SI.RMT.COST.ZS).

SDG 11 Sustainable cities and communities

An estimated 60 percent of the world's population will live in urban areas by 2030 (figure 11a), and most of the expected 1 billion increase in urban dwellers between 2015 and 2030 will occur in Africa and Asia. This demographic transformation will affect the economic, environmental, social, and political futures of individuals everywhere. Cities are complex systems in which every component affects every other. Sustainable Development Goal 11 focuses on making cities and other human settlements safe, inclusive, resilient, and sustainable.

Improving the quality of housing

Access to adequate, safe, and affordable housing and basic services, in addition to slum upgrading, is critical to sustainable cities (target 11.1). Although there is no consistent definition of slum areas, the United Nations Human Settlements Programme estimates take into consideration the proportion of urban population living in dwellings that lack access to an improved drinking water source, improved sanitation facilities, sufficient living area, durable structure, or security of tenure.

In Sub-Saharan Africa more than half the urban population lives in slum conditions. Countries that have faced civil war report the highest rates: In the Central African Republic, South Sudan, and Sudan more than 90 percent of the urban population lives in slums. Moreover, both

the Central African Republic and Mozambique have seen the number of slum dwellers rise since 1990 (figure 11b). In those countries poor people move from rural areas to cities in search of greater opportunity but often end up even more entrenched in poverty.

Other Sub-Saharan countries have made extraordinary progress in reducing their urban slums. Rwanda lowered the proportion of its urban population living in slums from 96 percent in 1990 to 53 percent in 2014. Mali also saw a large decline, from 94 percent of its urban population to 56 percent.

Reducing the environmental impact of cities

As the world urbanizes, declining air quality in fast-growing regions is placing a growing burden on people's health (target 11.6).

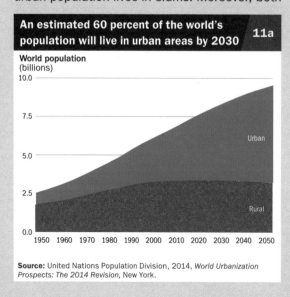

An estimated 60 percent of the world's population will live in urban areas by 2030 — 11a

World population (billions)

Source: United Nations Population Division, 2014, *World Urbanization Prospects: The 2014 Revision*, New York.

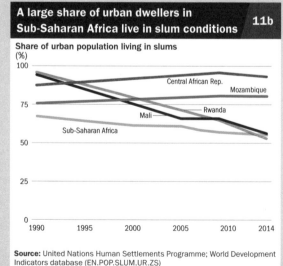

A large share of urban dwellers in Sub-Saharan Africa live in slum conditions — 11b

Share of urban population living in slums (%)

Source: United Nations Human Settlements Programme; World Development Indicators database (EN.POP.SLUM.UR.ZS)

 Front | ? User guide | World view | People | Environment

According to the 2013 Global Burden of Disease study, exposure to outdoor air pollution (as measured by levels of particles less than 2.5 microns in aerodynamic diameter [PM$_{2.5}$]) is responsible for 2.9 million deaths per year, about one every 10 seconds.[1] Outdoor PM$_{2.5}$ levels are highest in East Asia and Pacific (40 micrograms per cubic meter in 2013) and South Asia (45 micrograms per cubic meter, more than four times the guideline value recommended by the World Health Organization; figure 11c). In both regions the levels of outdoor PM$_{2.5}$ have increased from their 1990 levels.

Average pollution levels are estimated by combining satellite observations of airborne particles with models of atmospheric chemistry, which are calibrated against ground-level air quality monitoring data from nearly 3,400 locations and 79 countries. The satellite-based estimates cover both cities and rural areas. While there is no substitute for ground-level monitoring, particularly in densely populated urban areas, large swathes of the globe still do not have this monitoring infrastructure, so remote sensing technologies such as those used for the Global Burden of Disease study continue to be a powerful tool for measuring large-scale exposure to air pollutants.

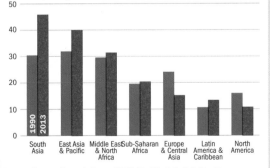

Outdoor air pollution is increasing in East Asia and Pacific and South Asia 11c

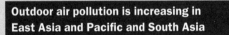
Mean annual concentration of particles less than 2.5 microns in diameter (micrograms per cubic meter)

Source: Brauer, B., and others, 2016, "Ambient Air Pollution Exposure Estimation for the Global Burden of Disease 2013," *Environmental Science & Technology* 50(1): 79–88; World Development Indicators database (EN.ATM.PM25.MC.M3).

Measuring the impact of urbanization

Measuring progress toward the Sustainable Development Goal 11 targets in a consistent way across all countries will be a challenge. For example, the target on transportation systems requires monitoring the proportion of the population with convenient access to public transport. This requires a much more precise understanding of where people live than is currently available. Other targets call for monitoring land consumption and open space, which requires global data on built-up areas.

An even more fundamental challenge is that there is no universal agreement on the definitions of "urban" and "city." Several Sustainable Development Goal targets use terms such as "urban population" and "cities of over 100,000 people." But how large or dense does a settlement need to be in order to be considered a city? Do certain kinds of economic activity need to be present for an area to be considered urban? On the outskirts of a city, where precisely does the urban area end and the rural area begin? Each country defines and measures its urban areas differently, making comparison of trends in urbanization across countries problematic.

Fortunately, new and innovative forms of data can help monitor progress toward Sustainable Development Goal 11, including maps of built-up areas derived from imagery and radar data from satellites. While each country's national definition may be well suited to its national context, global analysis based on these data can be consistent across countries, yielding objective and comparable measures of urbanization. In turn, this can help provide a global picture of the scope and nature of the urbanization challenge and help make cities inclusive, safe, resilient, and sustainable.

Note

1. GBD 2013 Risk Factors Collaborators, 2015, "Global, Regional, and National Comparative Risk Assessment of 79 Behavioral, Environmental, and Occupational, and Metabolic Risks or Clusters of Risks in 188 Countries, 1990–2013: A Systematic Analysis for the Global Burden of Disease Study 2013," *Lancet*.

SDG 12 Responsible consumption and production

A third of the world's energy is consumed by the food sector, but a third of food that is produced is lost or wasted. Saving a quarter of this lost food would be enough to feed 870 million people.[1] Sustainable consumption and production by countries—in essence doing more and better with less —means meeting basic needs of people and promoting a better quality of life while cutting harmful waste and pollution.

Ensure sustainable consumption and production patterns

Managing natural resources efficiently

Adjusted net savings is an indicator of efficient use of natural resources (target 12.2). It measures the difference between national production and consumption—the change in a country's wealth. Adjusted net savings takes into account investment in human capital, depreciation of fixed capital, depletion of natural resources, and pollution damage. Positive savings form the basis for building wealth and future growth. Negative savings rates suggest declining wealth and unsustainable development.

Adjusted net savings is especially useful for gauging whether countries that depend heavily on natural resources are balancing the depletion of their natural resources by investing rents in other forms of productive capital, such as through education. Low- and lower middle-income countries with the highest level of resource dependence also tend to have lower savings rates (figure 12a).

Reducing food loss and waste

Meeting the food needs of a growing global population while reducing food loss and waste (target 12.3) poses a serious challenge. Food loss is defined as a decrease in quantity or quality of food at any stage of the food supply chain, from the point at which it is harvested or made to the point it is eaten. Food waste occurs when edible food reaches the consumer but expires, is thrown away, or is otherwise neglected and not eaten. The extent of food loss varies greatly by income group and region. In the high-income countries of North America and East Asia and Pacific, the equivalent of more than 1,500 calories of food per person per day is lost, mostly through food waste. By contrast, in Sub-Saharan Africa the equivalent of 414 calories

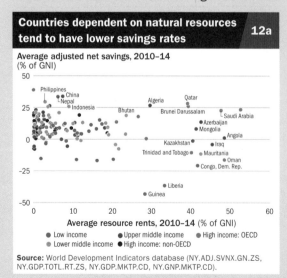

Countries dependent on natural resources tend to have lower savings rates 12a

Average adjusted net savings, 2010–14 (% of GNI)

Average resource rents, 2010–14 (% of GNI)

● Low income ● Upper middle income ● High income: OECD
● Lower middle income ● High income: non-OECD

Source: World Development Indicators database (NY.ADJ.SVNX.GN.ZS, NY.GDP.TOTL.RT.ZS, NY.GDP.MKTP.CD, NY.GNP.MKTP.CD).

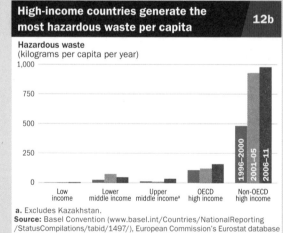

High-income countries generate the most hazardous waste per capita 12b

Hazardous waste (kilograms per capita per year)

a. Excludes Kazakhstan.
Source: Basel Convention (www.basel.int/Countries/NationalReporting /StatusCompilations/tabid/1497/), European Commission's Eurostat database (http://ec.europa.eu/eurostat/tgm/table.do?tab=table&init=1&language=en &pcode=tsdpc250&plugin=1); United Nations Statistics Division Environmental Indicators database (http://unstats.un.org/unsd/environment/hazardous.htm).

○ Front | ? User guide | World view | People | Environment

per person per day is lost, mostly during the process of production, handling, and storage, before food reaches the market.[2]

Minimizing the impact of chemical waste

Sustainable Development Goal 12 aims to reduce the release of chemicals and wastes into the environment and to minimize their adverse impacts on human health (target 12.4). A partial inventory of more than 3,000 toxic sites around the world found that the health of as many as 200 million people living near these sites may be affected.[3]

Per capita generation of hazardous waste nearly doubled worldwide between the late 1990s and the late 2000s. In middle-income countries per capita hazardous waste generation rose from 17 kilograms between 1996 and 2000 to 42 kilograms between 2006 and 2011.[4] However, high-income non–Organisation for Economic Co-operation and Development countries continue to generate the most hazardous waste, 981 kilograms per capita between 2006 and 2011 (figure 12b). Hazardous waste generation by low-income countries was 7 kilograms per capita over the same period.

Reforming fossil fuel subsidies

Sustainable Development Goal 12 calls for rationalizing inefficient fossil-fuel subsidies (target 12.3) though there is some debate over how this should be measured. The International Monetary Fund provides a comprehensive estimate of subsidies by including not only the difference between the final price consumers pay and international market prices, but also the environmental and social costs of local pollution, road traffic, and climate change (figure 12c). Subsidies as a percentage of GDP are highest in upper middle-income countries (nearly 14 percent), followed by lower middle-income and non–Organisation for Economic Co-operation and Development high-income countries (11 percent).

Notes

1. Food and Agriculture Organization, SAVE FOOD: Global Initiative on Food Loss and Waste Reduction, Key Findings. [www.fao.org/save-food /resources/keyfindings/en/].

2. International Energy Agency, 2015, *World Energy Outlook 2015,* Paris; Lipinski, B., and others, 2013, "Reducing Food Loss and Waste," Working Paper, World Resources Institute, Washington, DC.

3. Global Alliance on Health and Pollution, 2013, *The Poisoned Poor: Toxic Chemicals Exposures in Low- and Middle-Income Countries,* New York.

4. Excludes Kazakhstan, which reportedly generated 40.7 tons of hazardous waste per capita in 2010.

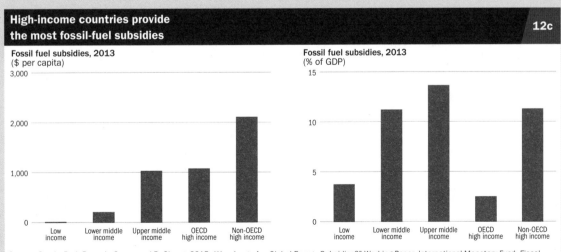

High-income countries provide the most fossil-fuel subsidies 12c

Fossil fuel subsidies, 2013 ($ per capita)

Fossil fuel subsidies, 2013 (% of GDP)

Source: Coady, D., I. Parry, L. Sears, and B. Shang, 2015, "How Large Are Global Energy Subsidies?" Working Paper, International Monetary Fund, Fiscal Affairs Department, Washington, DC.

SDG 13 Climate action

Globally, 2015 was the hottest year on record, according to the World Meteorological Organization. Climate change is already affecting every country on every continent through changing seasons and weather patterns, rising sea levels, and more extreme weather events. Changes in temperature and precipitation pose substantial risks for agriculture, water supplies, food, ecosystems, energy security, and infrastructure.

Take urgent action to combat climate change and its impacts*

Understanding the impacts of climate change

Sustainable Development Goal 13 calls for stronger resilience and capacity to adapt to climate-related hazards and natural disasters; integration of climate change measures into national planning; improved climate-related education, awareness-raising, and capacity building; and mobilization of sustained resources to address the needs of low- and middle-income countries.

Since 1980 both the occurrence and economic impact of weather-related natural disasters such as floods, droughts, and tropical storms have risen.[1] Global climate models indicate that by 2050 low- and middle-income countries are more likely than high-income countries to experience higher temperature increases because of geographic location (figure 13a), possibly leading to more extreme weather-related disasters and associated economic losses.

Addressing climate change

Countries must take steps to strengthen resilience and adaptive capacity to climate-related hazards (target 13.1) and take early action to reduce greenhouse gas emissions.

The Hyogo Framework for Action, which provided a global blueprint for a range of disaster risk reduction efforts for 2005–15, cites climate change as one of the primary factors increasing the severity of future disasters. Under the framework, countries used a 1–5 scale to assess progress on 22 indicators in five areas. Under area 4, which addressed underlying risk factors (including weather, environment, and climate change), the share of countries reporting a score of 4 or higher rose from 13 percent in 2009–11 to 27 percent in 2013–15 (figure 13b).

Integrating climate change measures into national policies, strategies, and planning is critical (target 13.2).[2] The December 2015 Paris

* Acknowledging that the United Nations Framework Convention on Climate Change is the primary international, intergovernmental forum for negotiating the global response to climate change.

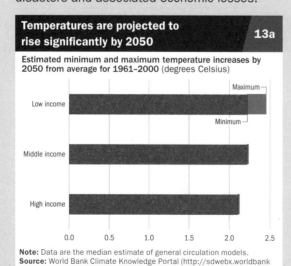

Temperatures are projected to rise significantly by 2050 — 13a

Estimated minimum and maximum temperature increases by 2050 from average for 1961–2000 (degrees Celsius)

Note: Data are the median estimate of general circulation models.
Source: World Bank Climate Knowledge Portal (http://sdwebx.worldbank.org/climateportal/).

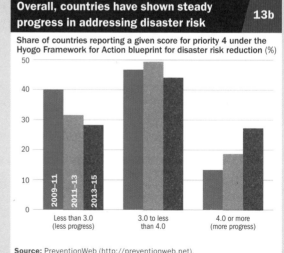

Overall, countries have shown steady progress in addressing disaster risk — 13b

Share of countries reporting a given score for priority 4 under the Hyogo Framework for Action blueprint for disaster risk reduction (%)

Source: PreventionWeb (http://preventionweb.net).

Agreement under the United Nations Framework Convention on Climate Change aims to hold increases in global average temperature to well below 2 degrees Celsius above pre-industrial levels and to reach peak global greenhouse gas emissions as soon as possible. Global emissions of carbon dioxide—a major greenhouse gas and primary driver of climate change—increased from 22.2 billion metric tons in 1990 to 34.6 billion in 2011 and contributed to an increase of about 0.8 degree Celsius in mean global temperature above pre-industrial times (figure 13c).

As of December 2015, 160 nationally determined contributions from 188 countries have been submitted to the United Nations Framework Convention on Climate Change. These commitments include measures to reduce emissions (mitigation), better manage the impacts of change climate on socioeconomic systems and ecosystems (adaptation), and support national policies and planning.[3] The Paris Agreement calls for these contributions to be reviewed and strengthened every five years.

Financing the response to climate change

Sustainable Development Goal 13 also looks at climate finance, in particular the United Nations Framework Convention on Climate Change goal of committing $100 billion a year by 2020 to address the needs of low- and middle-income countries and mobilizing the Green Climate Fund (target 13.a). Organisation for Economic Co-operation and Development data show climate financing from public and private sources, as well as export credits, from high-income to low- and middle-income countries (adjusting for multilateral sources) to be approximately $61.8 billion in 2014, up from $52.2 billion in 2013 (figure 13d). Development is moving toward climate-resilient and low emission pathways in many low- and middle-income countries,[4] which is likely to be enhanced by multilateral development bank commitments to increase support for climate change and disaster risk management, especially in low-income countries. For example, the World Bank includes climate change risks and opportunities in the country partnership frameworks that specify major development challenges in countries and areas of support from partners.

Notes

1. Gitay, H., and others, 2013, *Building Resilience: Integrating Climate and Disaster Risk into Development: The World Bank Group Experience,* Washington, DC: World Bank.
2. Gitay, H., and others, 2013, *Building Resilience: Integrating Climate and Disaster Risk into Development: The World Bank Group Experience,* Washington, DC: World Bank.
3. United Nations Framework Convention on Climate Change, 2015, "Synthesis Report on the Aggregate Effect of the Intended Nationally Determined Contributions," 21st Session, 30 November–11 December, Paris.
4. World Bank, 2015, "2014 Joint Report on Multilateral Development Banks' Climate Finance, Washington, DC.

13

Carbon dioxide emissions are at unprecedented levels `13c`

Carbon dioxide emissions from fossil fuel
(billions of metric tons)

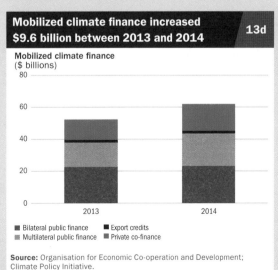

High income

Upper middle income

Low income

Lower middle income

Source: Carbon Dioxide Information Analysis Center; World Development Indicators database (EN.ATM.CO2E.KT).

Mobilized climate finance increased $9.6 billion between 2013 and 2014 `13d`

Mobilized climate finance
($ billions)

■ Bilateral public finance   ■ Export credits
■ Multilateral public finance   ■ Private co-finance

Source: Organisation for Economic Co-operation and Development; Climate Policy Initiative.

SDG 14 Life below water

Fish is the main animal protein for more than 1 billion people. Average worldwide fish consumption is about 20 kilograms per person per year. Yields from the planet's oceans, seas, and marine resources are essential to the food security of much of the world's population. Monitoring progress toward the sustainability of these resources is paramount but creates substantial challenges.

Conserve and sustainably use the oceans, seas, and marine resources for sustainable development

Sustainably capturing and farming seafood

Capture fisheries have dominated the seafood market until recently. Since the 1980s there has been a rise in aquaculture (fish, shellfish, and seaweed farming), which now accounts for nearly half of seafood production (figure 14a). East Asia and Pacific dominates capture fisheries and aquaculture production, where it accounts for over 90 percent of output.

Capture fisheries have generally stagnated since the early 1990s, and many governments have implemented subsidy schemes to protect local fish supplies and employment in the sector. Subsidies to fisheries total approximately $10 billion a year, driving continued fishing despite decreasing catch value and profitability.[1]

Ensuring the effective regulation of fish harvesting along with stopping overfishing and illegal, unreported, and unregulated fishing practices (target 14.4) can support the sustainability of the fishing industry, aquatic habitats, and biodiversity. Based on data for 54 countries and the high seas, illegal and unreported fishers catch 11–26 million tons a year, reducing revenues to legal fishers $10–$23.5 billion a year.[2] Low- and middle-income countries with weak regulatory and enforcement capacity are most at risk from illegal fishing.

Increasing the economic benefits of fish production

Fish production accounts for a substantial share of economic activity in many economies, including Small Island Developing States and countries in Sub-Saharan Africa.[3] Target 14.7 looks to increase the economic benefits to producers from the sustainable use of marine resources. The livelihoods of approximately

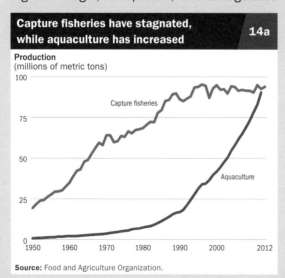

Capture fisheries have stagnated, while aquaculture has increased — 14a

Production (millions of metric tons)

Capture fisheries

Aquaculture

Source: Food and Agriculture Organization.

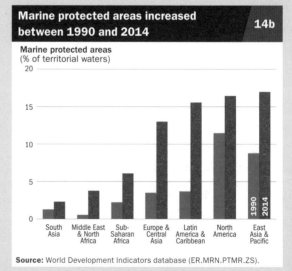

Marine protected areas increased between 1990 and 2014 — 14b

Marine protected areas (% of territorial waters)

South Asia · Middle East & North Africa · Sub-Saharan Africa · Europe & Central Asia · Latin America & Caribbean · North America · East Asia & Pacific

1990 · 2014

Source: World Development Indicators database (ER.MRN.PTMR.ZS).

Front | User guide | World view | People | Environment

60 million full- and part-time workers depend on marine capture fisheries, almost all of them in low- and middle-income countries and half of them women.[4] Fisheries and aquaculture are dominated by small scale, family operations, most of which employ fewer than 10 people.

Protecting and conserving the oceans

Marine protected areas can help rebuild depleting stocks and act as sanctuaries for biodiversity. As of 2014, approximately 2 percent of the global oceans are designated as marine protected areas, with various levels of actual control of access.[5] Target 14.5 seeks the conservation, by 2020, of at least 10 percent of coastal and marine areas. According to the country-level data available, by 2014 South Asia had the lowest share of marine protected areas in its territorial waters. But all regions have achieved at least some progress over the previous two decades (figure 14b).

The condition of marine biodiversity and of the global environment is closely connected with the level of ocean pollution and acidification. The number of dead zones—areas of ocean with too little oxygen for most marine life—has increased by a third between 1995 and 2007, largely as the result of nutrient pollution. Dead zones now rank alongside overfishing, habitat loss, and harmful algal blooms as key stressors of marine ecosystems. There are some 405 dead zones in coastal waters worldwide (figure 14c), affecting an area of 95,000 square miles.[6]

Notes

1. World Bank, 2009, *The Sunken Billions: The Economic Justification for Fisheries Reform,* Washington, DC.

2. Agnew, D. J., and others, 2009, "Estimating the Worldwide Extent of Illegal Fishing," *PLoS ONE* 4(2): e4570.

3. Kelleher, K., 2008, "World Bank Activities in Fisheries," Presentation at High-Level Roundtable on International Cooperation for Sustainable, 25–27 March, Bridgetown.

4. World Bank, 2012, *Hidden Harvest: The Global Contribution of Capture Fisheries,* Report 66469-GLB, Washington, DC; Food and Agriculture Organization, 2014, *The State of World Fisheries and Aquaculture,* Rome.

5. United Nations Environment Programme–World Conservation Monitoring Centre and the International Union for Conservation of Nature.

6. Diaz, R. J., and R. Rosenberg, 2008, "Spreading Dead Zones and Consequences for Marine Ecosystems, *Science* 321(5891): 926–29.

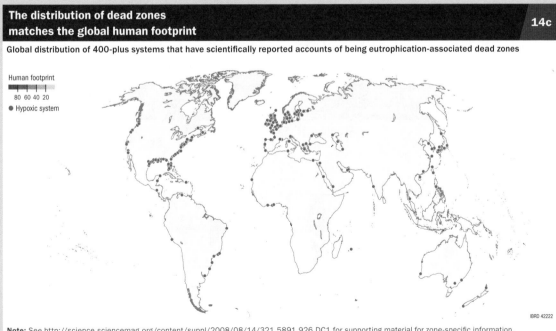

The distribution of dead zones matches the global human footprint 14c

Global distribution of 400-plus systems that have scientifically reported accounts of being eutrophication-associated dead zones

Human footprint
80 60 40 20
● Hypoxic system

IBRD 42222

Note: See http://science.sciencemag.org/content/suppl/2008/08/14/321.5891.926.DC1 for supporting material for zone-specific information.
Source: Diaz, R. J., and R. Rosenberg, 2008, "Spreading Dead Zones and Consequences for Marine Ecosystems, *Science* 321(5891): 926–29.

SDG 15 Life on land

Protect, restore, and promote sustainable use of terrestrial ecosystems, sustainably manage forests, combat desertification, and halt and reverse land degradation and halt biodiversity loss

Forests cover 30 percent of the Earth's land but, despite efforts to protect them, around 13 million hectares vanish each year. Between 1990 and 2015 the world lost more than 129 million hectares—over 3 percent of its forest area. The impact of human activity on the environment directly affects the world's poorest communities, and deforestation, desertification, and loss of biodiversity all pose major challenges to future sustainable development.

Protecting forests

Crucial to the health of the planet, to its diverse species, and to the livelihoods of a fifth of the human population,[1] forests contribute to long-term economic growth, social inclusion, and environmental stability. Despite numerous international engagements to protect forest areas, national and regional afforestation and reforestation efforts need to accelerate in order to ensure the sustainability of forests (target 15.2). While some regions have steadily increased forest coverage, Latin America and the Caribbean has lost 97 million hectares since 1990, and Sub-Saharan Africa has lost 83 million hectares (figure 15a). Over 16 percent of Brazil's original Amazonian forest has disappeared, and the current rate of loss is 2 million hectares a year. Pressures on forests will continue as the world's population grows, urbanization accelerates, and demand for food, fiber, energy, and minerals increases.

Minimizing desertification and land degradation

The loss of potential and existing agricultural land to drought, floods, and land degradation affects vast swathes of the world's poor, many of whom depend on agriculture for their livelihoods and nourishment. Restoring land and soil (target 15.3) helps keep land degradation in check.

Soil degradation affects 52 percent of agricultural land, and arable land is being lost at 30–35 times its historical rate. Drought and desertification have led to losses of 12 million hectares,[2] on which 20 million tons of grain could have been grown, and have further impoverished already vulnerable communities. Degradation in the drylands—zones naturally

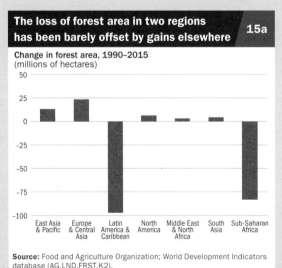

The loss of forest area in two regions has been barely offset by gains elsewhere 15a

Change in forest area, 1990–2015
(millions of hectares)

Source: Food and Agriculture Organization; World Development Indicators database (AG.LND.FRST.K2).

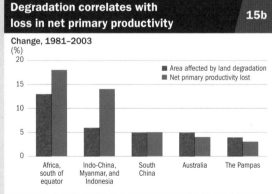

Degradation correlates with loss in net primary productivity 15b

Change, 1981–2003
(%)

■ Area affected by land degradation
■ Net primary productivity lost

Africa, south of equator | Indo-China, Myanmar, and Indonesia | South China | Australia | The Pampas

Source: Bai, Z., and others, 2008, "Global Assessment of Land Degradation and Improvement. 1. Identification by Remote Sensing," Report 2008/01, ISRIC–World Soil Information, Wageningen, Netherlands, as adapted by E. Nkonya and others, 2011, "The Economics of Desertification, Land Degradation, and Drought Toward an Integrated Global Assessment," Discussion Paper on Development Policy 150, Center for Development Research, Bonn, Germany.

predisposed to high aridity and water scarcity —is causing the desertification of 3.6 billion hectares.[3] Degradation and concurrent loss of vegetative cover also lead to a loss in net primary productivity, the rate at which vegetation fixes carbon dioxide from the atmosphere (figure 15b). Implementing sustainable and integrated land and water management practices will help the areas and populations most impacted.

Safeguarding natural habitats and biodiversity

As forests, drylands, and freshwater ecosystems disappear, so does the world's biodiversity. Action to protect and prevent the extinction of threatened species and their habitats will help reverse this (target 15.5). Plants provide humanity with 80 percent of the human diet, and populations throughout Africa, Asia, and Latin America use traditional plant-based medicine to help meet their healthcare needs.

Substantial gains have been made in conserving biodiversity (figure 15c), with roughly 12 percent of global forests now designated as protected areas.

Many species are under threat of extinction due to climate change, poaching, overfishing, pollution, and habitat degradation. Of the 8,300 animal breeds known to humans, 8 percent are extinct, and 22 percent are on the brink of extinction. Among assessed species, the highest number of threatened plants are in Latin America and Caribbean, the highest number of threatened fish are in Sub-Saharan Africa, and the highest number of threatened mammals and birds are in East Asia and Pacific (figure 15d).

Notes

1. Chao, S., 2012, "Forest Peoples: Numbers across the World." Moreton-in-Marsh, United Kingdom: Forest Peoples Program. [www.forestpeoples .org/sites/fpp/files/publication/2012/05/forest-peoples-numbers-across -world-final_0.pdf].
2. www.un.org/sustainabledevelopment/biodiversity/.
3. www.ciesin.columbia.edu/docs/002-217/002-217.html.

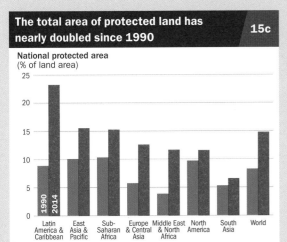

The total area of protected land has nearly doubled since 1990 **15c**

National protected area (% of land area)

Source: United Nations Environmental Program and World Conservation Monitoring Centre, as compiled by the World Resources Institute; World Development Indicators database (ER.LND.PTLD.ZS).

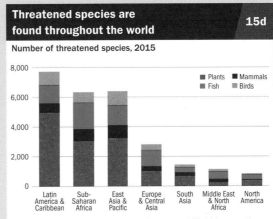

Threatened species are found throughout the world **15d**

Number of threatened species, 2015

Plants Mammals
Fish Birds

Source: United Nations Environmental Program and World Conservation Monitoring Centre; International Union for Conservation of Nature's Red List of Threatened Species; Froese, R., and D. Pauly, eds., 2008, FishBase database (www.fishbase.org); World Development Indicators database (EN.MAM.THRD.NO, EN.BIR.THRD.NO, EN.FSH.THRD.NO, EN.HPT.THRD.NO).

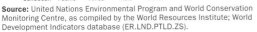

SDG 16 Peace, justice, and strong institutions

Promote peaceful and inclusive societies for sustainable development, provide access to justice for all, and build effective, accountable and inclusive institutions at all levels

Peaceful nations governed with fairness and transparency provide the optimal platforms for implementing development strategies and programs. However, many states are in fragile situations, with citizens and their daily lives compromised by fear, conflict, unjust laws, and opaque governance. The success of the Sustainable Development Goals in such areas depends on achieving livable and calm communities supported by reliable and accountable institutions.

Reducing violence and related deaths

Protecting the lives of people is one of the most important obligations of states (target 16.1). Intentional homicide occurs in every country, but homicide rates vary across and within regions. Latin America and the Caribbean had the highest homicide rate in 2012, 23 per 100,000 people—almost four times the global average of 6 per 100,000 people (figure 16a). Sub-Saharan Africa had 14 homicides per 100,000 people. East Asia and Pacific had the lowest: 2 homicides per 100,000 people.

One measure of peace is the absence of conflict-related deaths. Escalation of several conflicts, coupled with the extreme violence in the Syrian Arab Republic, resulted in 2014 having the highest number of battled-related deaths since 1989. More than 54,000 people were killed in Syria in battle-related deaths in 2014, the most of any country (figure 16b). In the same year, about 12,250 people were killed in Afghanistan, and close to 12,000 were killed in Iraq.

Promoting justice

Strong justice and rule of law systems provide mechanisms for resolving land and natural resource disputes, keeping governments accountable to citizens, and giving businesses the confidence to enter into and enforce contracts (target 16.3).

One monitoring tool is the proportion of the population that has experienced a dispute; accessed a formal, informal, alternative, or traditional dispute resolution mechanism; and feels the process was just. While global coverage is not yet available, appropriate survey methodology has been developed over the past

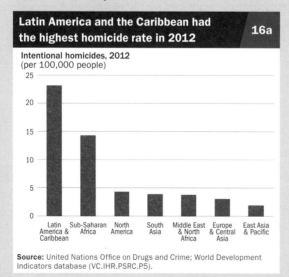

Latin America and the Caribbean had the highest homicide rate in 2012   16a

Intentional homicides, 2012
(per 100,000 people)

Source: United Nations Office on Drugs and Crime; World Development Indicators database (VC.IHR.PSRC.P5).

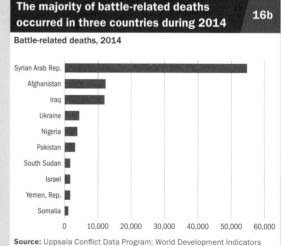

The majority of battle-related deaths occurred in three countries during 2014   16b

Battle-related deaths, 2014

Source: Uppsala Conflict Data Program; World Development Indicators database (VC.BTL.DETH).

○ Front | ？ User guide | ◇ World view | People | Environment

two decades and has been used by national statistical offices in more than 25 countries across all regions.

Strengthening institutions

Building stronger institutions requires efficient, effective, and accountable public spending. Comparing actual primary government expenditure with the original approved budget is one way of analyzing how well government budgets are planned and public financial management is executed. The Public Expenditure and Financial Accountability Program assesses how close 144 national governments come to meeting their proposed targets. Over the past 10 years nearly two-thirds of participating countries were within 10 percentage points of their original budgets, and around half of those were within 5 percentage points (figure 16c). However, more than a tenth of countries deviated by more than 15 percentage points.

Providing legal identity for all

Effective civil registration and vital statistics systems capture key life events, such as births, marriages, and deaths. In seeking legal identity for all, including full birth registration by 2030 (target 16.9), such systems can provide

a crucial tool in a wide range of public policies and programs in health, education, water and sanitation, social protection, food security, and labor and employment.

Globally, many births go unregistered. In 2011 only 72 percent of children under age 5 had their births registered, and in Sub-Saharan Africa fewer than half were registered (figure 16d). In contrast, birth registration is nearly universal in Europe and Central Asia.

Securing the right to information

A citizen's "right to know" reflects a country's commitment to widespread, fair, and transparent sustainable development (target 16.10). Establishing legislative guarantees and mechanisms for public access to information safeguards fundamental freedoms and facilitates public input and review. However, implementation and enforcement of such guarantees and mechanisms are difficult to measure. Measuring both the quality of laws and legislative guarantees and their levels of implementation will be necessary to measure progress toward target 16.10.[1]

Note

1. Trapnell, S. E., and V. L. Lemieux. 2014. "Right to Information: Identifying Drivers of Effectiveness in Implementation." Right to Information Working Paper 2. World Bank, Washington, DC.

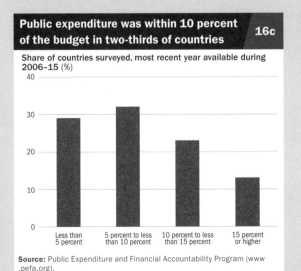

Public expenditure was within 10 percent of the budget in two-thirds of countries 16c

Share of countries surveyed, most recent year available during 2006–15 (%)

Source: Public Expenditure and Financial Accountability Program (www.pefa.org).

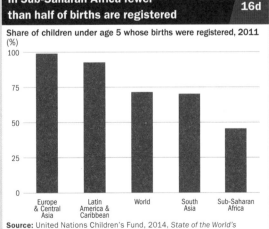

In Sub-Saharan Africa fewer than half of births are registered 16d

Share of children under age 5 whose births were registered, 2011 (%)

Source: United Nations Children's Fund, 2014, *State of the World's Children 2015: Reimagine the Future,* New York; World Development Indicators database (SP.REG.BRTH.ZS).

SDG 17 Partnership for global development

Coordinated global macroeconomic policies, increased aid flows for the poorest countries, effective public-private partnerships, and domestic resource mobilization in low- and middle-income countries are key to achieving development goals.

Strengthen the means of implementation and revitalize the global partnership for sustainable development

Increasing aid flows

Official development assistance from members of the Organisation for Economic Co-operation and Development's Development Assistance Committee (DAC) have increased 66 percent in real terms since 2000, to $137 billion in 2014. Net official development assistance as a share of DAC countries' combined gross national income (GNI) was 0.29 percent, on a par with 2013 (figure 17a). Five DAC members exceeded the UN official development assistance target of 0.7 percent of GNI. The United States was the largest donor by volume: $32 billion in 2014, or 0.19 percent of GNI. Humanitarian aid rose 22 percent in real terms in 2014 and accounted for 10 percent of net official development assistance flows.

Enabling development through remittances

International migration has an important role in economic relations between low- and middle-income countries and high-income countries. An estimated 232 million people, 3.2 percent of the world's population, live and work outside their home country.[1] International remittances, in the form of personal transfers and compensation of employees, have a profound impact on economic outcomes. In 2014 international remittances totaled $528 billion, 72 percent ($378 billion) of which went to low- and middle-income countries (figure 17b). This was equivalent to 1.7 percent of these countries' combined GNI and close to two and a half times the level of official development assistance from DAC donors. For India, the world's largest recipient, international remittances totaled $70 billion in 2014, or 3.4 percent of GNI, only marginally less than the net inflows of debt and foreign direct investment combined.

Supporting the most vulnerable countries

The world's 48 least developed countries, home to 1 billion people, account for only 3 percent of low- and middle-income countries' export earnings. Exports from the least developed countries are highly concentrated: In 2014 Angola, Bangladesh, and Myanmar accounted for

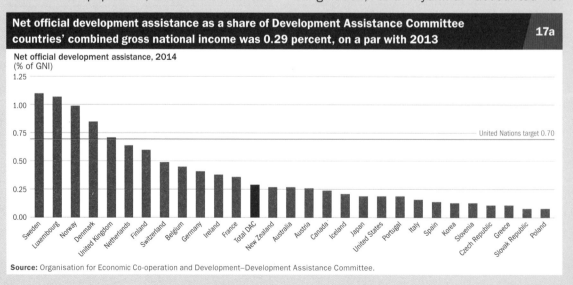

Net official development assistance as a share of Development Assistance Committee countries' combined gross national income was 0.29 percent, on a par with 2013

17a

Net official development assistance, 2014 (% of GNI)

United Nations target 0.70

Sweden, Luxembourg, Norway, Denmark, United Kingdom, Netherlands, Finland, Switzerland, Belgium, Germany, Ireland, France, Total DAC, New Zealand, Australia, Austria, Canada, Iceland, Japan, United States, Portugal, Italy, Spain, Korea, Slovenia, Czech Republic, Greece, Slovak Republic, Poland

Source: Organisation for Economic Co-operation and Development–Development Assistance Committee.

54 percent (figure 17c). Exports were dominated by commodities, notably oil, copper, gold, and natural gas. Between 2009 and 2013 strong global commodity prices drove the least developed countries' export earnings up 63 percent, on a par with the 65 percent increase in those of other low- and middle-income countries. But the least developed countries' lack of diversified export base leaves them vulnerable to global economic trends. In 2014 least developed countries' export earnings fell 13 percent, compared with a 2.6 percent increase in other low- and middle-income countries.

Using public-private partnerships to finance infrastructure

Public-private partnerships have a crucial role in improving efficiency in the delivery of public services and helping governments address infrastructure gaps. From 1990 to 2014 low- and middle-income countries received commitments of $1.44 trillion to finance more than 6,800 infrastructure public-private partnership projects. The pattern of commitments has been uneven, with strong growth prior to the 1997 Asian financial crisis followed by sharp declines before structural reforms, favorable macroeconomic policies, and buoyant global economic conditions sparked a recovery (figure 17d). Commitments

increased sevenfold from 2005 to 2012, to a record $158 billion. Over this period commitments rose 414 percent for energy, 166 percent for transport, and 96 percent for water. Commitments have been flat since 2012, reflecting a slowdown in key emerging markets. In relation to GDP, investment commitments for public-private partnerships in infrastructure remain low, at 0.2–0.6 percent, only half the level recorded prior to the Asian financial crisis.

Note
1. United Nations, 2013, "232 Million International Migrants Living Abroad Worldwide– New Un Global Migration Statistics Reveal," Press release, 11 September, New York. [www.un.org/en/ga/68/meetings/migration/pdf/UN%20press%20release_International%20Migration%20Figures.pdf].

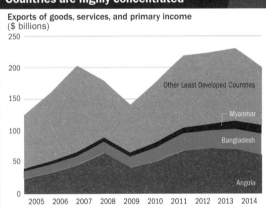

Exports from the Least Developed Countries are highly concentrated **17c**

Exports of goods, services, and primary income ($ billions)

Source: International Monetary Fund; World Development Indicators database (BX.GSR.TOTL.CD).

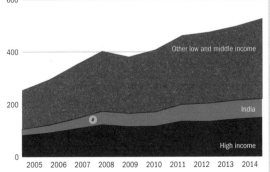

In 2014, 72 percent of personal remittances went to low- and middle-income countries **17b**

Personal remittances (personal transfers and compensation of employees) ($ billions)

Source: International Monetary Fund; World Development Indicators database (BX.TRF.PWKR.CD.DT).

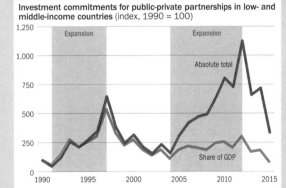

Two expansions, one contraction in public-private partnership investment since 1990 **17d**

Investment commitments for public-private partnerships in low- and middle-income countries (index, 1990 = 100)

a. Predicted based on the first semester of 2015.
Source: World Bank Private Participation in Infrastructure Database (http://ppi.worldbank.org).

Cross-cutting issue
Statistical capacity

Data and statistics

High-quality data and statistics underpin national decision-making processes, guiding resource allocation, private sector investment, program design, and policy formulation. The need for improvements are explicit in targets 17.18 and 17.19 and are a foundation for Agenda 2030: Reliable data are needed to measure progress and support implementation of every one of the Sustainable Development Goals.

For most indicators the best ways to improve data availability are to invest in national statistical capacity and to develop stronger partnerships among international agencies, governments, and civil society. These investments work: Data availability has steadily improved over the last two decades. For instance, the number of countries with enough estimates of poverty incidence to measure a meaningful trend increased from just 2 in 1991 to 53 in 2012 (figure SC1).

Agenda 2030 pledges that no one will be left behind and that the goals and targets will be met by all countries, people, and segments of society. This pledge places new demands on data and statistics and means that disaggregation by sex, income group, age, location, and other dimensions of development takes on new importance. Major investment in appropriate instruments, such as household surveys and civil and vital registration systems, will be required.

The World Bank's Statistical Capacity Indicator is one tool for comparing statistical capacity across countries and over time. Calculated since 2004 using publicly available information, it measures low- and middle-income countries' ability to collect and disseminate statistics about their populations, economies, and societies. The composite indicator combines a variety of different measures to illustrate general trends, but the components can help identify specific areas where progress is being made and where improvements are still needed. For example, Ghana has seen a steady increase in its overall average score, from 51 to 66, because of better statistical methodologies. Notable improvements were a new base year and weights for the consumer price index, rebased national accounts, and better estimates of vaccination coverage.

The average of the Statistical Capacity Indicator has increased in all regions over the last decade (figure SC2), but Sub-Saharan Africa and the Middle East and North Africa have the lowest average. Of the 10 countries with the highest overall indicator value for 2015, 3 were in Latin America and the Caribbean, and 7 were in Europe and Central Asia.

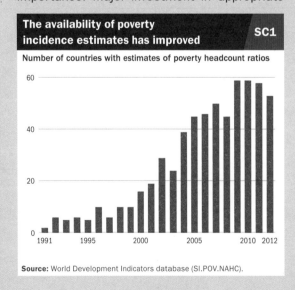

The availability of poverty incidence estimates has improved   SC1

Number of countries with estimates of poverty headcount ratios

Source: World Development Indicators database (SI.POV.NAHC).

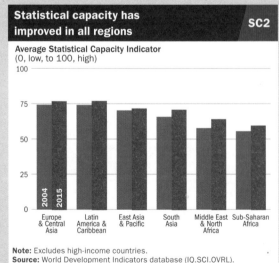

Statistical capacity has improved in all regions   SC2

Average Statistical Capacity Indicator
(0, low, to 100, high)

Note: Excludes high-income countries.
Source: World Development Indicators database (IQ.SCI.OVRL).

Financial inclusion

Access to financial services enables individuals and firms to manage sudden changes in income, smooth cash flow, accumulate assets, and make productive investments. It promotes better use of resources and better access to essential services and enables a higher quality of life. Financial inclusion is an important enabler of development. Improving access to financial services is a cross-cutting target of the Sustainable Development Goals and is explicitly recognized in Sustainable Development Goals 1, 2, 3, 5, 8, and 9.

Financial inclusion means having access to a full range of affordable formal financial products and services, delivered responsibly by sustainable institutions. To manage their financial lives, adults need access to an account or an electronic instrument to securely store money, send payments, and receive deposits. But around 2 billion adults worldwide do not have such an account, and many small businesses cannot access the financial instruments they need. Financial inclusion is a complex concept and is difficult to measure. Important aspects are access to, use of, and quality of services. Moreover, relevant data have been scarce, though recent efforts are improving the situation.

One measure of access to financial services is account ownership. Between 2011 and 2014, 700 million adults became new accountholders, and the share of adults with an account at a financial institution increased from 51 percent to 61 percent. Another 1 percent, while not having an account at a financial institution, reported using mobile money services.

In a select group of 10 low- and middle-income countries with data for 2014, a large share of small and medium-size enterprises have an account at a financial institution, but only a small share obtains financing through loans (figure FI1).

The physical infrastructure of the financial system has been improving. While the number of bank branches per adult remained more or less unchanged worldwide between 2010 and 2014, the number of automated teller machines rose quickly (figure FI2). And innovative ways of accessing financial services are making brick-and-mortar branches less relevant in many cases.

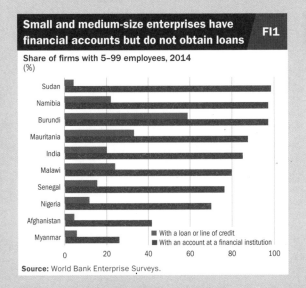

Small and medium-size enterprises have financial accounts but do not obtain loans — FI1

Share of firms with 5–99 employees, 2014 (%)

■ With a loan or line of credit
■ With an account at a financial institution

Source: World Bank Enterprise Surveys.

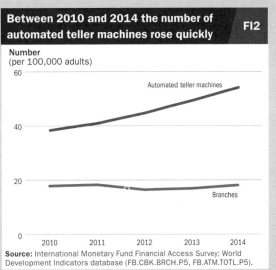

Between 2010 and 2014 the number of automated teller machines rose quickly — FI2

Number (per 100,000 adults)

Automated teller machines

Branches

Source: International Monetary Fund Financial Access Survey; World Development Indicators database (FB.CBK.BRCH.P5, FB.ATM.TOTL.P5).

Cross-cutting issue
Fragility, conflict, and violence

While Sustainable Development Goal 16 is dedicated to promoting peaceful societies, progress toward each Sustainable Development Goal will be severely impacted in regions affected by fragility, conflict, and violence. Episodes of unrest can reverse development efforts and rapidly dismantle achievements built over a long time, along social, political economy, and physical dimensions.

Overall, around a fifth of the world's population is estimated to be in a fragile, conflict, or violent situation, spanning the 35 countries on the World Bank's Harmonized List of Fragile Situations as well as pockets of violence in other countries. The number of forcibly displaced persons—which includes internally displaced people, refugees, and asylum seekers—is estimated to be 60 million, the highest since World War II.

In 2014 the Middle East and North Africa was the region of origin for 4.5 million refugees, 87 percent of whom came from the Syrian Arab Republic, and Sub-Saharan Africa was the region of origin for 4.4 million (figure FCV1). The two regions also lead the world in granting asylum to refugees.

The influx of refugees to host countries presents challenges. Sustainable Development Goals 4 (quality education), 8 (productive employment and economic growth), and 10 (reduce inequalities) will be directly impacted as low- and middle-income countries absorb refugees. Sustainability means that refugees will need to find decent work, their children will need to be educated, and the conflicts and poverty in their home countries will need to be resolved.

Impacting lives and livelihoods
In fragile, conflict, and violent situations individuals and their day-to-day lives are threatened, and their surroundings become dangerous. People flee, and the numbers of internally displaced persons and refugees increase. Fragility, conflict, and violence damage the social fabrics and social contract of countries, impacting behavioral codes and trust in government and aggravating ethnic or religious friction. Fragility, conflict, and violence often disproportionately affect the health and safety of women and children.[1] Combined with the erosion of women's education and rights (including access to reproductive health services), fragility, conflict, and violence often lead to a paradoxical surge in birth rates, increasing pressure on already strained education and health systems.

Eroding institutions and political economy
Governance, rule of law, trust between citizens and governments, justice, and human rights fail when countries become fragile or are affected by conflict or violence. These failures affect the economy by discouraging investments and causing capital flight. In fragile, conflict, and violent situations shadow economies tend to flourish, and the rogue exploitation of mineral and natural resources often finances and fuels conflicts.

Note

1. UN Women: Gender Equality, Development and Peace for the Twenty-first Century, Fact Sheet 5, www.un.org/womenwatch/daw/followup/session/presskit/fs5.htm.

Most refugees are from the Middle East and North Africa and Sub-Saharan Africa FCV1

Number of refugees, 2014 (millions)

■ By region of origin
■ By region of asylum

Middle East & North Africa; Sub-Saharan Africa; South Asia; East Asia & Pacific; Europe & Central Asia; Latin America & Caribbean; North America

Source: United Nations High Commissioner for Refugees Statistical Online Population Database; World Development Indicators database (SM.POP.REFG.OR, SM.POP.REFG).

 Front User guide World view People Environment

Sustainable Development Goals and targets

Goal 1 End poverty in all its forms everywhere

1.1 By 2030, eradicate extreme poverty for all people everywhere, currently measured as people living on less than $1.25 a day

1.2 By 2030, reduce at least by half the proportion of men, women and children of all ages living in poverty in all its dimensions according to national definitions

1.3 Implement nationally appropriate social protection systems and measures for all, including floors, and by 2030 achieve substantial coverage of the poor and the vulnerable

1.4 By 2030, ensure that all men and women, in particular the poor and the vulnerable, have equal rights to economic resources, as well as access to basic services, ownership and control over land and other forms of property, inheritance, natural resources, appropriate new technology and financial services, including microfinance

1.5 By 2030, build the resilience of the poor and those in vulnerable situations and reduce their exposure and vulnerability to climate-related extreme events and other economic, social and environmental shocks and disasters

1.a Ensure significant mobilization of resources from a variety of sources, including through enhanced development cooperation, in order to provide adequate and predictable means for developing countries, in particular least developed countries, to implement programmes and policies to end poverty in all its dimensions

1.b Create sound policy frameworks at the national, regional and international levels, based on pro-poor and gender-sensitive development strategies, to support accelerated investment in poverty eradication actions

Goal 2 End hunger, achieve food security and improved nutrition and promote sustainable agriculture

2.1 By 2030, end hunger and ensure access by all people, in particular the poor and people in vulnerable situations, including infants, to safe, nutritious and sufficient food all year round

2.2 By 2030, end all forms of malnutrition, including achieving, by 2025, the internationally agreed targets on stunting and wasting in children under 5 years of age, and address the nutritional needs of adolescent girls, pregnant and lactating women and older persons

2.3 By 2030, double the agricultural productivity and incomes of small-scale food producers, in particular women, indigenous peoples, family farmers, pastoralists and fishers, including through secure and equal access to land, other productive resources and inputs, knowledge, financial services, markets and opportunities for value addition and non-farm employment

2.4 By 2030, ensure sustainable food production systems and implement resilient agricultural practices that increase productivity and production, that help maintain ecosystems, that strengthen capacity for adaptation to climate change, extreme weather, drought, flooding and other disasters and that progressively improve land and soil quality

2.5 By 2020, maintain the genetic diversity of seeds, cultivated plants and farmed and domesticated animals and their related wild species, including through soundly managed and diversified seed and plant banks at the national, regional and international levels, and promote access to and fair and equitable sharing of benefits arising from the utilization of genetic resources and associated traditional knowledge, as internationally agreed

2.a Increase investment, including through enhanced international cooperation, in rural infrastructure, agricultural research and extension services, technology development and plant and livestock gene banks in order to enhance agricultural productive capacity in developing countries, in particular least developed countries

2.b Correct and prevent trade restrictions and distortions in world agricultural markets, including through the parallel elimination of all forms of agricultural export subsidies and all export measures with equivalent effect, in accordance with the mandate of the Doha Development Round

2.c Adopt measures to ensure the proper functioning of food commodity markets and their derivatives and facilitate timely access to market information, including on food reserves, in order to help limit extreme food price volatility

Goal 3 Ensure healthy lives and promote well-being for all at all ages

3.1 By 2030, reduce the global maternal mortality ratio to less than 70 per 100,000 live births

3.2 By 2030, end preventable deaths of newborns and children under 5 years of age, with all countries aiming to reduce neonatal mortality to at least as low as 12 per 1,000 live births and under-5 mortality to at least as low as 25 per 1,000 live births

3.3 By 2030, end the epidemics of AIDS, tuberculosis, malaria and neglected tropical diseases and combat hepatitis, water-borne diseases and other communicable diseases

3.4 By 2030, reduce by one third premature mortality from non-communicable diseases through prevention and treatment and promote mental health and well-being

3.5 Strengthen the prevention and treatment of substance abuse, including narcotic drug abuse and harmful use of alcohol

3.6 By 2020, halve the number of global deaths and injuries from road traffic accidents

3.7 By 2030, ensure universal access to sexual and reproductive health-care services, including for family planning, information and education, and the integration of reproductive health into national strategies and programmes

3.8 Achieve universal health coverage, including financial risk protection, access to quality essential health-care services and access to safe, effective, quality and affordable essential medicines and vaccines for all

3.9 By 2030, substantially reduce the number of deaths and illnesses from hazardous chemicals and air, water and soil pollution and contamination

3.a Strengthen the implementation of the World Health Organization Framework Convention on Tobacco Control in all countries, as appropriate

3.b Support the research and development of vaccines and medicines for the communicable and non-communicable diseases that primarily affect developing countries, provide access to affordable essential medicines and vaccines, in accordance with the Doha Declaration on the TRIPS Agreement and Public Health, which affirms the right of developing countries to use to the full the provisions in the Agreement on Trade-Related Aspects of Intellectual Property Rights regarding flexibilities to protect public health, and, in particular, provide access to medicines for all

3.c Substantially increase health financing and the recruitment, development, training and retention of the health workforce in developing countries, especially in least developed countries and small island developing States

3.d Strengthen the capacity of all countries, in particular developing countries, for early warning, risk reduction and management of national and global health risks

Goal 4 Ensure inclusive and equitable quality education and promote lifelong learning opportunities for all

4.1 By 2030, ensure that all girls and boys complete free, equitable and quality primary and secondary education leading to relevant and effective learning outcomes

4.2 By 2030, ensure that all girls and boys have access to quality early childhood development, care and pre-primary education so that they are ready for primary education

4.3 By 2030, ensure equal access for all women and men to affordable and quality technical, vocational and tertiary education, including university

4.4 By 2030, substantially increase the number of youth and adults who have relevant skills, including technical and vocational skills, for employment, decent jobs and entrepreneurship

4.5 By 2030, eliminate gender disparities in education and ensure equal access to all levels of education and vocational training for the vulnerable, including persons with disabilities, indigenous peoples and children in vulnerable situations

4.6 By 2030, ensure that all youth and a substantial proportion of adults, both men and women, achieve literacy and numeracy

4.7 By 2030, ensure that all learners acquire the knowledge and skills needed to promote sustainable development, including, among others, through education for sustainable development and sustainable lifestyles, human rights, gender equality, promotion of a culture of peace and non-violence, global citizenship and appreciation of cultural diversity and of culture's contribution to sustainable development

4.a Build and upgrade education facilities that are child, disability and gender sensitive and provide safe, non-violent, inclusive and effective learning environments for all

4.b By 2020, substantially expand globally the number of scholarships available to developing countries, in particular least developed countries, small island developing States and African countries, for enrolment in higher education, including vocational training and information and communications technology, technical, engineering and scientific programmes, in developed countries and other developing countries

4.c By 2030, substantially increase the supply of qualified teachers, including through international cooperation for teacher training in developing countries, especially least developed countries and small island developing States

Goal 5 Achieve gender equality and empower all women and girls

5.1 End all forms of discrimination against all women and girls everywhere

5.2 Eliminate all forms of violence against all women and girls in the public and private spheres, including trafficking and sexual and other types of exploitation

5.3 Eliminate all harmful practices, such as child, early and forced marriage and female genital mutilation

5.4 Recognize and value unpaid care and domestic work through the provision of public services, infrastructure and social protection policies and the promotion of shared responsibility within the household and the family as nationally appropriate

5.5 Ensure women's full and effective participation and equal opportunities for leadership at all levels of decision-making in political, economic and public life

5.6 Ensure universal access to sexual and reproductive health and reproductive rights as agreed in accordance with the Programme of Action of the International Conference on Population and Development and the Beijing Platform for Action and the outcome documents of their review conferences

5.a Undertake reforms to give women equal rights to economic resources, as well as access to ownership and control over land and other forms of property, financial services, inheritance and natural resources, in accordance with national laws

5.b Enhance the use of enabling technology, in particular information and communications technology, to promote the empowerment of women

5.c Adopt and strengthen sound policies and enforceable legislation for the promotion of gender equality and the empowerment of all women and girls at all levels

Goal 6 Ensure availability and sustainable management of water and sanitation for all

6.1 By 2030, achieve universal and equitable access to safe and affordable drinking water for all

6.2 By 2030, achieve access to adequate and equitable sanitation and hygiene for all and end open defecation, paying special attention to the needs of women and girls and those in vulnerable situations

6.3 By 2030, improve water quality by reducing pollution, eliminating dumping and minimizing release of hazardous chemicals and materials, halving the proportion of untreated wastewater and substantially increasing recycling and safe reuse globally

6.4 By 2030, substantially increase water-use efficiency across all sectors and ensure sustainable withdrawals and supply of freshwater to address water scarcity and substantially reduce the number of people suffering from water scarcity

6.5 By 2030, implement integrated water resources management at all levels, including through transboundary cooperation as appropriate

6.6 By 2020, protect and restore water-related ecosystems, including mountains, forests, wetlands, rivers, aquifers and lakes

6.a By 2030, expand international cooperation and capacity-building support to developing countries in water- and sanitation-related activities and programmes, including water harvesting, desalination, water efficiency, wastewater treatment, recycling and reuse technologies

6.b Support and strengthen the participation of local communities in improving water and sanitation management

Goal 7 Ensure access to affordable, reliable, sustainable and modern energy for all

7.1 By 2030, ensure universal access to affordable, reliable and modern energy services

7.2 By 2030, increase substantially the share of renewable energy in the global energy mix

7.3 By 2030, double the global rate of improvement in energy efficiency

7.a By 2030, enhance international cooperation to facilitate access to clean energy research and technology, including renewable energy, energy efficiency and advanced and cleaner fossil-fuel technology, and promote investment in energy infrastructure and clean energy technology

7.b By 2030, expand infrastructure and upgrade technology for supplying modern and sustainable energy services for all in developing countries, in particular least developed countries, small island developing States and landlocked developing countries, in accordance with their respective programmes of support

Goal 8 Promote sustained, inclusive and sustainable economic growth, full and productive employment and decent work for all

8.1 Sustain per capita economic growth in accordance with national circumstances and, in particular, at least 7 percent gross domestic product growth per annum in the least developed countries

8.2 Achieve higher levels of economic productivity through diversification, technological upgrading and innovation, including through a focus on high-value added and labour-intensive sectors

8.3 Promote development-oriented policies that support productive activities, decent job creation, entrepreneurship, creativity and innovation, and encourage the formalization and growth of micro-, small- and medium-sized enterprises, including through access to financial services

8.4 Improve progressively, through 2030, global resource efficiency in consumption and production and endeavour to decouple economic growth from environmental degradation, in accordance with the 10-Year Framework of Programmes on Sustainable Consumption and Production, with developed countries taking the lead

8.5 By 2030, achieve full and productive employment and decent work for all women and men, including for young people and persons with disabilities, and equal pay for work of equal value

8.6 By 2020, substantially reduce the proportion of youth not in employment, education or training

8.7 Take immediate and effective measures to eradicate forced labour, end modern slavery and human trafficking and secure the prohibition and elimination of the worst forms of child labour, including recruitment and use of child soldiers, and by 2025 end child labour in all its forms

8.8 Protect labour rights and promote safe and secure working environments for all workers, including migrant workers, in particular women migrants, and those in precarious employment

8.9 By 2030, devise and implement policies to promote sustainable tourism that creates jobs and promotes local culture and products

8.10 Strengthen the capacity of domestic financial institutions to encourage and expand access to banking, insurance and financial services for all

8.a Increase Aid for Trade support for developing countries, in particular least developed countries, including through the Enhanced Integrated Framework for Trade-related Technical Assistance to least developed countries

8.b By 2020, develop and operationalize a global strategy for youth employment and implement the Global Jobs Pact of the International Labour Organization

Goal 9 Build resilient infrastructure, promote inclusive and sustainable industrialization and foster innovation

9.1 Develop quality, reliable, sustainable and resilient infrastructure, including regional and transborder infrastructure, to support economic development and human well-being, with a focus on affordable and equitable access for all

9.2 Promote inclusive and sustainable industrialization and, by 2030, significantly raise industry's share of employment and gross domestic product, in line with national circumstances, and double its share in least developed countries

9.3 Increase the access of small-scale industrial and other enterprises, in particular in developing countries, to financial services, including affordable credit, and their integration into value chains and markets

9.4 By 2030, upgrade infrastructure and retrofit industries to make them sustainable, with increased resource-use efficiency and greater adoption of clean and environmentally sound technologies and industrial processes, with all countries taking action in accordance with their respective capabilities

9.5 Enhance scientific research, upgrade the technological capabilities of industrial sectors in all countries, in particular developing countries, including, by 2030, encouraging innovation and substantially increasing the number of research and development workers per 1 million people and public and private research and development spending

9.a Facilitate sustainable and resilient infrastructure development in developing countries through enhanced financial, technological and technical support to African countries, least developed countries, landlocked developing countries and small island developing States

9.b Support domestic technology development, research and innovation in developing countries, including by ensuring a conducive policy environment for, inter alia, industrial diversification and value addition to commodities

9.c Significantly increase access to information and communications technology and strive to provide universal and affordable access to the Internet in least developed countries by 2020

Goal 10 Reduce inequality within and among countries

10.1 By 2030, progressively achieve and sustain income growth of the bottom 40 percent of the population at a rate higher than the national average

10.2 By 2030, empower and promote the social, economic and political inclusion of all, irrespective of age, sex, disability, race, ethnicity, origin, religion or economic or other status

10.3 Ensure equal opportunity and reduce inequalities of outcome, including by eliminating discriminatory laws, policies and practices and promoting appropriate legislation, policies and action in this regard

10.4 Adopt policies, especially fiscal, wage and social protection policies, and progressively achieve greater equality

10.5 Improve the regulation and monitoring of global financial markets and institutions and strengthen the implementation of such regulations

10.6 Ensure enhanced representation and voice for developing countries in decision-making in global international economic and financial institutions in order to deliver more effective, credible, accountable and legitimate institutions

10.7 Facilitate orderly, safe, regular and responsible migration and mobility of people, including through the implementation of planned and well-managed migration policies

10.a Implement the principle of special and differential treatment for developing countries, in particular least developed countries, in accordance with World Trade Organization agreements

10.b Encourage official development assistance and financial flows, including foreign direct investment, to States where the need is greatest, in particular least developed countries, African countries, small island developing States and landlocked developing countries, in accordance with their national plans and programmes

10.c By 2030, reduce to less than 3 percent the transaction costs of migrant remittances and eliminate remittance corridors with costs higher than 5 percent

Goal 11 Make cities and human settlements inclusive, safe, resilient and sustainable

11.1 By 2030, ensure access for all to adequate, safe and affordable housing and basic services and upgrade slums

11.2 By 2030, provide access to safe, affordable, accessible and sustainable transport systems for all, improving road safety, notably by expanding public transport, with special attention to the needs of those in vulnerable situations, women, children, persons with disabilities and older persons

11.3 By 2030, enhance inclusive and sustainable urbanization and capacity for participatory, integrated and sustainable human settlement planning and management in all countries

11.4 Strengthen efforts to protect and safeguard the world's cultural and natural heritage

11.5 By 2030, significantly reduce the number of deaths and the number of people affected and substantially decrease the direct economic losses relative to global gross domestic product caused by disasters, including water-related disasters, with a focus on protecting the poor and people in vulnerable situations

11.6 By 2030, reduce the adverse per capita environmental impact of cities, including by paying special attention to air quality and municipal and other waste management

11.7 By 2030, provide universal access to safe, inclusive and accessible, green and public spaces, in particular for women and children, older persons and persons with disabilities

11.a Support positive economic, social and environmental links between urban, peri-urban and rural areas by strengthening national and regional development planning

11.b By 2020, substantially increase the number of cities and human settlements adopting and implementing integrated policies and plans towards inclusion, resource efficiency, mitigation and adaptation to climate change, resilience to disasters, and develop and implement, in line with the Sendai Framework for Disaster Risk Reduction 2015-2030, holistic disaster risk management at all levels

11.c Support least developed countries, including through financial and technical assistance, in building sustainable and resilient buildings utilizing local materials

Sustainable Development Goals and targets (continued)

Goal 12 Ensure sustainable consumption and production patterns

12.1 Implement the 10-Year Framework of Programmes on Sustainable Consumption and Production Patterns, all countries taking action, with developed countries taking the lead, taking into account the development and capabilities of developing countries

12.2 By 2030, achieve the sustainable management and efficient use of natural resources

12.3 By 2030, halve per capita global food waste at the retail and consumer levels and reduce food losses along production and supply chains, including post-harvest losses

12.4 By 2020, achieve the environmentally sound management of chemicals and all wastes throughout their life cycle, in accordance with agreed international frameworks, and significantly reduce their release to air, water and soil in order to minimize their adverse impacts on human health and the environment

12.5 By 2030, substantially reduce waste generation through prevention, reduction, recycling and reuse

12.6 Encourage companies, especially large and transnational companies, to adopt sustainable practices and to integrate sustainability information into their reporting cycle

12.7 Promote public procurement practices that are sustainable, in accordance with national policies and priorities

12.8 By 2030, ensure that people everywhere have the relevant information and awareness for sustainable development and lifestyles in harmony with nature

12.a Support developing countries to strengthen their scientific and technological capacity to move towards more sustainable patterns of consumption and production

12.b Develop and implement tools to monitor sustainable development impacts for sustainable tourism that creates jobs and promotes local culture and products

12.c Rationalize inefficient fossil-fuel subsidies that encourage wasteful consumption by removing market distortions, in accordance with national circumstances, including by restructuring taxation and phasing out those harmful subsidies, where they exist, to reflect their environmental impacts, taking fully into account the specific needs and conditions of developing countries and minimizing the possible adverse impacts on their development in a manner that protects the poor and the affected communities

Goal 13 Take urgent action to combat climate change and its impacts*

13.1 Strengthen resilience and adaptive capacity to climate-related hazards and natural disasters in all countries

13.2 Integrate climate change measures into national policies, strategies and planning

13.3 Improve education, awareness-raising and human and institutional capacity on climate change mitigation, adaptation, impact reduction and early warning

13.a Implement the commitment undertaken by developed-country parties to the United Nations Framework Convention on Climate Change to a goal of mobilizing jointly $100 billion annually by 2020 from all sources to address the needs of developing countries in the context of meaningful mitigation actions and transparency on implementation and fully operationalize the Green Climate Fund through its capitalization as soon as possible

13.b Promote mechanisms for raising capacity for effective climate change-related planning and management in least developed countries and small island developing States, including focusing on women, youth and local and marginalized communities

Goal 14 Conserve and sustainably use the oceans, seas and marine resources for sustainable development

14.1 By 2025, prevent and significantly reduce marine pollution of all kinds, in particular from land-based activities, including marine debris and nutrient pollution

14.2 By 2020, sustainably manage and protect marine and coastal ecosystems to avoid significant adverse impacts, including by strengthening their resilience, and take action for their restoration in order to achieve healthy and productive oceans

14.3 Minimize and address the impacts of ocean acidification, including through enhanced scientific cooperation at all levels

14.4 By 2020, effectively regulate harvesting and end overfishing, illegal, unreported and unregulated fishing and destructive fishing practices and implement science-based management plans, in order to restore fish stocks in the shortest time feasible, at least to levels that can produce maximum sustainable yield as determined by their biological characteristics

14.5 By 2020, conserve at least 10 percent of coastal and marine areas, consistent with national and international law and based on the best available scientific information

14.6 By 2020, prohibit certain forms of fisheries subsidies which contribute to overcapacity and overfishing, eliminate subsidies that contribute to illegal, unreported and unregulated fishing and refrain from introducing new such subsidies, recognizing that appropriate and effective special and differential treatment for developing and least developed countries should be an integral part of the World Trade Organization fisheries subsidies negotiation

14.7 By 2030, increase the economic benefits to small island developing States and least developed countries from the sustainable use of marine resources, including through sustainable management of fisheries, aquaculture and tourism

14.a Increase scientific knowledge, develop research capacity and transfer marine technology, taking into account the Intergovernmental Oceanographic Commission Criteria and Guidelines on the Transfer of Marine Technology, in order to improve ocean health and to enhance the contribution of marine biodiversity to the development of developing countries, in particular small island developing States and least developed countries

14.b Provide access for small-scale artisanal fishers to marine resources and markets

14.c Enhance the conservation and sustainable use of oceans and their resources by implementing international law as reflected in the United Nations Convention on the Law of the Sea, which provides the legal framework for the conservation and sustainable use of oceans and their resources, as recalled in paragraph 158 of "The future we want"

Goal 15 Protect, restore and promote sustainable use of terrestrial ecosystems, sustainably manage forests, combat desertification, and halt and reverse land degradation and halt biodiversity loss

15.1 By 2020, ensure the conservation, restoration and sustainable use of terrestrial and inland freshwater ecosystems and their services, in particular forests, wetlands, mountains and drylands, in line with obligations under international agreements

15.2 By 2020, promote the implementation of sustainable management of all types of forests, halt deforestation, restore degraded forests and substantially increase afforestation and reforestation globally

15.3 By 2030, combat desertification, restore degraded land and soil, including land affected by desertification, drought and floods, and strive to achieve a land degradation-neutral world

15.4 By 2030, ensure the conservation of mountain ecosystems, including their biodiversity, in order to enhance their capacity to provide benefits that are essential for sustainable development

15.5 Take urgent and significant action to reduce the degradation of natural habitats, halt the loss of biodiversity and, by 2020, protect and prevent the extinction of threatened species

* Acknowledging that the United Nations Framework Convention on Climate Change is the primary international, intergovernmental forum for negotiating the global response to climate change.

 Front User guide World view People Environment

15.6 Promote fair and equitable sharing of the benefits arising from the utilization of genetic resources and promote appropriate access to such resources, as internationally agreed .

15.7 Take urgent action to end poaching and trafficking of protected species of flora and fauna and address both demand and supply of illegal wildlife products

15.8 By 2020, introduce measures to prevent the introduction and significantly reduce the impact of invasive alien species on land and water ecosystems and control or eradicate the priority species

15.9 By 2020, integrate ecosystem and biodiversity values into national and local planning, development processes, poverty reduction strategies and accounts

15.a Mobilize and significantly increase financial resources from all sources to conserve and sustainably use biodiversity and ecosystems

15.b Mobilize significant resources from all sources and at all levels to finance sustainable forest management and provide adequate incentives to developing countries to advance such management, including for conservation and reforestation

15.c Enhance global support for efforts to combat poaching and trafficking of protected species, including by increasing the capacity of local communities to pursue sustainable livelihood opportunities

Goal 16 Promote peaceful and inclusive societies for sustainable development, provide access to justice for all and build effective, accountable and inclusive institutions at all levels

16.1 Significantly reduce all forms of violence and related death rates everywhere

16.2 End abuse, exploitation, trafficking and all forms of violence against and torture of children

16.3 Promote the rule of law at the national and international levels and ensure equal access to justice for all

16.4 By 2030, significantly reduce illicit financial and arms flows, strengthen the recovery and return of stolen assets and combat all forms of organized crime

16.5 Substantially reduce corruption and bribery in all their forms

16.6 Develop effective, accountable and transparent institutions at all levels

16.7 Ensure responsive, inclusive, participatory and representative decision-making at all levels

16.8 Broaden and strengthen the participation of developing countries in the institutions of global governance

16.9 By 2030, provide legal identity for all, including birth registration

16.10 Ensure public access to information and protect fundamental freedoms, in accordance with national legislation and international agreements

16.a Strengthen relevant national institutions, including through international cooperation, for building capacity at all levels, in particular in developing countries, to prevent violence and combat terrorism and crime

16.b Promote and enforce non-discriminatory laws and policies for sustainable development

Goal 17 Strengthen the means of implementation and revitalize the Global Partnership for Sustainable Development

17.1 Strengthen domestic resource mobilization, including through international support to developing countries, to improve domestic capacity for tax and other revenue collection

17.2 Developed countries to implement fully their official development assistance commitments, including the commitment by many developed countries to achieve the target of 0.7 per cent of gross national income for official development assistance (ODA/GNI) to developing countries and 0.15 to 0.20 per cent of ODA/GNI to least developed countries; ODA providers are encouraged to consider setting a target to provide at least 0.20 per cent of ODA/GNI to least developed countries

17.3 Mobilize additional financial resources for developing countries from multiple sources

17.4 Assist developing countries in attaining long-term debt sustainability through coordinated policies aimed at fostering debt financing, debt relief and debt restructuring, as appropriate, and address the external debt of highly indebted poor countries to reduce debt distress

17.5 Adopt and implement investment promotion regimes for least developed countries

17.6 Enhance North-South, South-South and triangular regional and international cooperation on and access to science, technology and innovation and enhance knowledge-sharing on mutually agreed terms, including through improved coordination among existing mechanisms, in particular at the United Nations level, and through a global technology facilitation mechanism

17.7 Promote the development, transfer, dissemination and diffusion of environmentally sound technologies to developing countries on favourable terms, including on concessional and preferential terms, as mutually agreed

17.8 Fully operationalize the technology bank and science, technology and innovation capacity-building mechanism for least developed countries by 2017 and enhance the use of enabling technology, in particular information and communications technology

17.9 Enhance international support for implementing effective and targeted capacity-building in developing countries to support national plans to implement all the Sustainable Development Goals, including through North-South, South-South and triangular cooperation

17.10 Promote a universal, rules-based, open, non-discriminatory and equitable multilateral trading system under the World Trade Organization, including through the conclusion of negotiations under its Doha Development Agenda

17.11 Significantly increase the exports of developing countries, in particular with a view to doubling the least developed countries' share of global exports by 2020

17.12 Realize timely implementation of duty-free and quota-free market access on a lasting basis for all least developed countries, consistent with World Trade Organization decisions, including by ensuring that preferential rules of origin applicable to imports from least developed countries are transparent and simple, and contribute to facilitating market access

17.13 Enhance global macroeconomic stability, including through policy coordination and policy coherence

17.14 Enhance policy coherence for sustainable development

17.15 Respect each country's policy space and leadership to establish and implement policies for poverty eradication and sustainable development

17.16 Enhance the Global Partnership for Sustainable Development, complemented by multi-stakeholder partnerships that mobilize and share knowledge, expertise, technology and financial resources, to support the achievement of the Sustainable Development Goals in all countries, in particular developing countries

17.17 Encourage and promote effective public, public-private and civil society partnerships, building on the experience and resourcing strategies of partnerships

17.18 By 2020, enhance capacity-building support to developing countries, including for least developed countries and small island developing States, to increase significantly the availability of high-quality, timely and reliable data disaggregated by income, gender, age, race, ethnicity, migratory status, disability, geographic location and other characteristics relevant in national contexts

17.19 By 2030, build on existing initiatives to develop measurements of progress on sustainable development that complement gross domestic product, and support statistical capacity-building in developing countries

The poverty headcount ratio at $1.90 a day is the share of the population living on less than $1.90 a day in 2011 purchasing power parity (PPP) terms. It is also referred to as the extreme poverty rate. The PPP 2011 $1.90 a day poverty line is the average poverty line of the 15 poorest countries in the world, estimated from household surveys conducted by national statistical offices or by private agencies under the supervision of government or international agencies. Income and consumption data used for estimating poverty are also collected from household surveys. The 2012 estimates are the latest comprehensive update and draw on more than 2 million randomly sampled households, representing 87 percent of the population in 131 low- and middle-income countries (as defined in 1990). This map shows the country-level poverty estimates used to generate the 2012 regional and global poverty estimates. Because 2011 PPPs for Bangladesh, Cabo Verde, Cambodia, Lao PDR, and Jordan require further investigation, estimates for those countries are based on the 2005 PPP $1.25 a day poverty line.

Poverty

Share of population living on less than
2011 PPP $1.90 a day, 2012 (%)

- 50.0 or more
- 25.0–49.9
- 10.0–24.9
- 2.0–9.9
- Less than 2.0
- No data

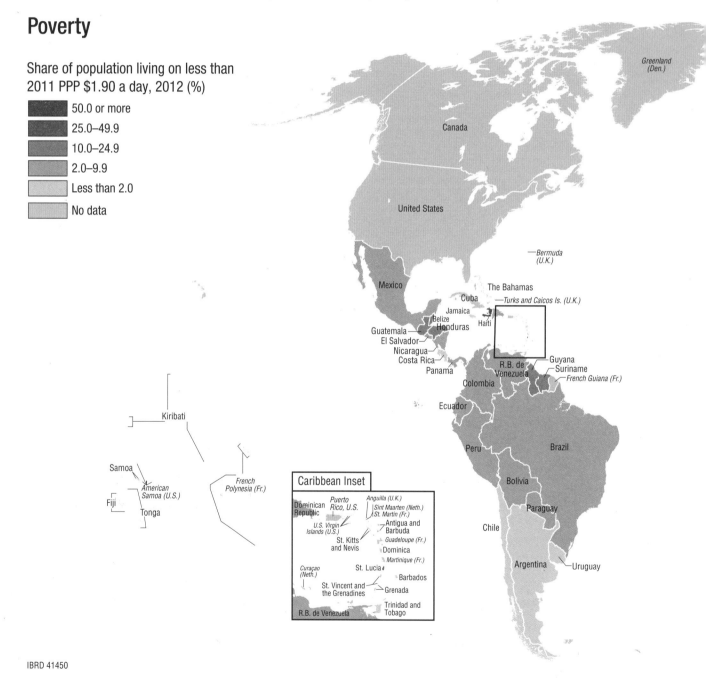

IBRD 41450

Front | User guide | World view | People | Environment

The new poverty line of 2011 PPP $1.90 a day preserves the real purchasing power of the previous line (2005 PPP $1.25 a day) in the world's poorest 15 countries.

The share of people living on less than $1.90 a day in the world fell from 37.0 percent in 1990 to 12.7 percent in 2012.

Between 1990 and 2012 the number of people living on less than $1.90 a day was more than halved, from nearly 2 billion to 897 million.

The share of people living in extreme poverty is projected to fall below 10 percent for the first time by 2015.

Europe Inset

	Population	Surface area	Population density	Urban population	Gross national income				Gross domestic product	
					Atlas method		Purchasing power parity			
	millions	thousand sq. km	people per sq. km	% of total population	$ billions	Per capita $	$ billions	Per capita $	% growth	Per capita % growth
	2014	2014	2014	2014	2014	2014	2014	2014	2013–14	2013–14
Afghanistan	31.6	652.9	48	26	21.4	680	63.2[a]	2,000[a]	1.3	–1.7
Albania	2.9	28.8	106	56	12.9	4,450	31.8	10,980	2.2	2.3
Algeria	38.9	2,381.7	16	70	213.8	5,490	540.5	13,880	3.8	1.8
American Samoa	0.1	0.2	277	87	..	..[b]	..	..	..	..
Andorra	0.1	0.5	155	86	3.3	43,270	..	..	–0.1	4.4
Angola	24.2	1,246.7	19	43	..	..[b]	..	..	..	..
Antigua and Barbuda	0.1	0.4	207	24	1.2	13,300	1.9	21,370	4.8	3.8
Argentina	43.0	2,780.4	16	92	579.2	13,480	..[c]	..[c]	0.5[d]	–0.6[d]
Armenia	3.0	29.7	106	63	12.1	4,020	25.4	8,450	3.5	3.0
Aruba	0.1	0.2	575	42	..	..[e]	..	..	..	..
Australia	23.5	7,741.2	3	89	1,516.2	64,600	1,049.1	44,700	2.5	1.0
Austria	8.5	83.9	104	66	423.9	49,600	404.9	47,380	0.4	–0.4
Azerbaijan	9.5	86.6	115	54	72.4	7,600	161.3	16,920	2.0	0.7
Bahamas, The	0.4	13.9	38	83	8.0	20,980	8.5	22,290	1.0	–0.4
Bahrain	1.4	0.8	1,769	89	28.4	21,060	50.8	37,680	4.5	3.5
Bangladesh	159.1	148.5	1,222	34	171.3	1,080	529.9	3,330	6.1	4.8
Barbados	0.3	0.4	659	32	4.3	15,310	4.3	15,190	0.2	–0.1
Belarus	9.5	207.6	47	76	69.5	7,340	166.8	17,610	1.6	1.5
Belgium	11.2	30.5	371	98	530.6	47,240	495.2	44,090	1.3	0.9
Belize	0.4	23.0	15	44	1.5	4,350	2.6	7,590	3.6	1.4
Benin	10.6	114.8	94	44	9.5	890	21.4	2,020	6.5	3.8
Bermuda	0.1	0.1	1,304	100	6.9	106,140	4.3	66,560	–2.5	–2.8
Bhutan	0.8	38.4	20	38	1.8	2,370	5.6	7,280	5.5	4.0
Bolivia	10.6	1,098.6	10	68	30.3	2,870	66.4	6,290	5.5	3.8
Bosnia and Herzegovina	3.8	51.2	75	40	18.5	4,840	40.3	10,550	1.1	1.2
Botswana	2.2	581.7	4	57	16.1	7,240	35.6	16,030	4.4	2.4
Brazil	206.1	8,515.8	25	85	2,429.7	11,790	3,209.4	15,570	0.1	–0.8
Brunei Darussalam	0.4	5.8	79	77	15.1	37,320	29.3	72,190	–2.3	–3.7
Bulgaria	7.2	111.0	67	74	55.0	7,620	121.6	16,840	1.6	2.1
Burkina Faso	17.6	274.2	64	29	12.3	700	28.2	1,600	4.0	1.0
Burundi	10.8	27.8	421	12	2.9	270	8.3	770	4.7	1.3
Cabo Verde	0.5	4.0	128	65	1.8	3,450	3.2	6,200	2.8	1.5
Cambodia	15.3	181.0	87	21	15.6	1,020	47.2	3,080	7.1	5.3
Cameroon	22.8	475.4	48	54	30.8	1,350	67.1	2,950	5.9	3.3
Canada	35.5	9,984.7	4	82	1,835.1	51,630	1,576.5	44,350	2.4	1.3
Cayman Islands	0.1	0.3	247	100	..	..[e]	..	..	..	..
Central African Republic	4.8	623.0	8	40	1.6	320	2.9	600	1.0	–1.0
Chad	13.6	1,284.0	11	22	13.3	980	28.2	2,070	7.3	3.8
Channel Islands	0.2	0.2	857	31	..	..[e]	..	..	..	..
Chile	17.8	756.1	24	89	264.8	14,910	378.7	21,320	1.9	0.8
China	1,364.3	9,562.9	145	54	10,097.0	7,400	17,966.9	13,170	7.3	6.7
Hong Kong SAR, China	7.2	1.1	6,897	100	292.0	40,320	409.7	56,570	2.5	1.7
Macao SAR, China	0.6	0.0[f]	19,073	100	44.1	76,270	69.4	120,140	–0.4	–2.1
Colombia	47.8	1,141.7	43	76	381.0	7,970	616.9	12,910	4.6	3.6
Comoros	0.8	1.9	414	28	0.6	790	1.1	1,430	2.1	–0.4
Congo, Dem. Rep.	74.9	2,344.9	33	42	28.7	380	48.8	650	9.0	5.7
Congo, Rep.	4.5	342.0	13	65	12.3	2,720	23.4	5,200	6.8	4.2

	Population	Surface area	Population density	Urban population	Gross national income				Gross domestic product	
					Atlas method		Purchasing power parity			
	millions	thousand sq. km	people per sq. km	% of total population	$ billions	Per capita $	$ billions	Per capita $	% growth	Per capita % growth
	2014	2014	2014	2014	2014	2014	2014	2014	2013–14	2013–14
Costa Rica	4.8	51.1	93	76	48.1	10,120	68.6	14,420	3.5	2.4
Côte d'Ivoire	22.2	322.5	70	53	32.2	1,450	69.4	3,130	8.5	5.9
Croatia	4.2	56.6	76	59	55.0	12,980	88.6	20,910	−0.4	0.0
Cuba	11.4	109.9	107	77	..	..[b]	..	..	2.7	2.5
Curaçao	0.2	0.4	351	89	..	..[e]	..	..	..	..
Cyprus	1.2	9.3	125	67	22.5[g]	26,370[g]	24.9[g]	29,190[g]	−2.3[g]	−1.4[g]
Czech Republic	10.5	78.9	136	73	193.1	18,350	302.5	28,740	2.0	1.9
Denmark	5.6	43.1	133	88	345.8	61,330	264.2	46,850	1.1	0.7
Djibouti	0.9	23.2	38	77	..	..[h]	..	..	6.0	4.6
Dominica	0.1	0.8	96	69	0.5	6,930	0.8	10,480	3.9	3.4
Dominican Republic	10.4	48.7	215	78	62.9	6,040	131.1	12,600	7.3	6.1
Ecuador	15.9	256.4	64	64	96.8	6,090	178.0	11,190	3.7	2.1
Egypt, Arab Rep.	89.6	1,001.5	90	43	287.7	3,210	920.7	10,280	2.2	0.0
El Salvador	6.1	21.0	295	66	23.9	3,920	48.9	8,000	2.0	1.7
Equatorial Guinea	0.8	28.1	29	40	8.4	10,210[i]	14.5	17,660	−0.3	−3.2
Eritrea	5.1	117.6	51	22	..	..[j]	..	..	..	..
Estonia	1.3	45.2	31	68	25.0	19,010	36.1	27,490	2.9	3.2
Ethiopia	97.0	1,104.3	97	19	53.6	550	145.0	1,500	10.3	7.5
Faroe Islands	0.0[k]	1.4	35	42	..	..[e]	..	..	..	..
Fiji	0.9	18.3	49	53	4.3	4,870	7.5	8,410	6.9	6.2
Finland	5.5	338.4	18	84	264.6	48,440	221.9	40,630	−0.4	−0.8
France	66.2	549.1	121	79	2,844.3	42,950	2,655.5	40,100	0.2	−0.3
French Polynesia	0.3	4.0	76	56	..	..[e]	..	..	..	..
Gabon	1.7	267.7	7	87	16.4	9,720	29.0	17,200	4.3	2.0
Gambia, The	1.9	11.3	191	59	0.9	460	3.0	1,580	0.9	−2.3
Georgia	3.7[l]	69.7	79[l]	53	16.7[l]	4,490[l,m]	33.8[l]	9,080[l]	4.8[l]	6.1[l]
Germany	81.0	357.2	232	75	3,853.6	47,590	3,843.2	47,460	1.6	3.1
Ghana	26.8	238.5	118	53	42.7	1,590	104.5	3,900	4.0	1.6
Greece	10.9	132.0	84	78	250.1	22,810	296.6	27,050	0.7	1.5
Greenland	0.1	410.5[n]	0[o]	86	..	..[e]	..	..	..	..
Grenada	0.1	0.3	313	36	0.8	7,910	1.2	11,720	5.7	5.2
Guam	0.2	0.5	310	94	..	..[e]	..	..	..	..
Guatemala	16.0	108.9	149	51	55.0	3,430	116.1	7,250	4.2	2.1
Guinea	12.3	245.9	50	37	5.8	470	13.9	1,130	0.4	−2.3
Guinea-Bissau	1.8	36.1	64	49	1.0	550	2.5	1,380	2.5	0.1
Guyana	0.8	215.0	4	28	3.0	3,940	5.3[a]	6,940[a]	5.2	4.9
Haiti	10.6	27.8	384	57	8.7	820	18.3	1,730	2.7	1.4
Honduras	8.0	112.5	71	54	18.1	2,270	36.4	4,570	3.1	1.6
Hungary	9.9	93.0	109	71	131.6	13,340	236.3	23,960	3.7	4.0
Iceland	0.3	103.0	3	94	15.0	46,350	13.5	41,800	1.8	0.7
India	1,295.3	3,287.3	436	32	2,028.0	1,570	7,292.8	5,630	7.3	6.0
Indonesia	254.5	1,910.9	140	53	923.7	3,630	2,592.3	10,190	5.0	3.7
Iran, Islamic Rep.	78.1	1,745.2	48	73	549.0	7,120	1,280.2	16,590	4.3	3.0
Iraq	34.8	435.2	80	69	227.3	6,530	525.6	15,100	−2.1	−5.0
Ireland	4.6	70.3	67	63	214.7	46,520	197.7	42,830	5.2	4.8
Isle of Man	0.1	0.6	153	52	..	..[e]	..	..	..	..
Israel	8.2	22.1	380	92	290.2	35,320	273.6	33,300	2.6	0.6

	Population	Surface area	Population density	Urban population	Gross national income				Gross domestic product	
					Atlas method		Purchasing power parity			
	millions	thousand sq. km	people per sq. km	% of total population	$ billions	Per capita $	$ billions	Per capita $	% growth	Per capita % growth
	2014	2014	2014	2014	2014	2014	2014	2014	2013–14	2013–14
Italy	60.8	301.3	207	69	2,102.2	34,580	2,155.2	35,450	–0.4	–1.4
Jamaica	2.7	11.0	251	55	14.0	5,150	23.5	8,640	0.7	0.5
Japan	127.1	378.0	349	93	5,339.1	42,000	4,846.7	38,120	–0.1	0.1
Jordan	6.6	89.3	74	83	34.1	5,160	78.7	11,910	3.1	0.8
Kazakhstan	17.3	2,724.9	6	53	204.8	11,850	375.3	21,710	4.4	2.9
Kenya	44.9	580.4	79	25	58.1	1,290	131.8	2,940	5.3	2.6
Kiribati	0.1	0.8	136	44	0.3	2,950	0.4[a]	3,340[a]	3.7	1.9
Korea, Dem. People's Rep.	25.0	120.5	208	61	..	..[j]	..	..	..	..
Korea, Rep.	50.4	100.3	517	82	1,365.8	27,090	1,697.0	33,650	3.3	2.9
Kosovo	1.8	10.9	167	..	7.3	3,990	17.0[a]	9,300[a]	1.2	0.9
Kuwait	3.8	17.8	211	98	185.0	49,300	299.7	79,850	–1.6	–5.8
Kyrgyz Republic	5.8	199.9	30	36	7.3	1,250	18.8	3,220	3.6	1.5
Lao PDR	6.7	236.8	29	38	11.1	1,660	33.8	5,060	7.5	5.8
Latvia	2.0	64.5	32	67	30.4	15,250	46.6	23,360	2.4	3.3
Lebanon	4.5	10.5	444	88	45.6	10,030	80.0[a]	17,590[a]	2.0	0.8
Lesotho	2.1	30.4	69	27	2.8	1,330	6.6	3,150	3.6	2.4
Liberia	4.4	111.4	46	49	1.6	370	3.1	700	0.7	–1.7
Libya	6.3	1,759.5	4	78	49.0	7,820	100.1[a]	16,000[a]	–24.0	–23.9
Liechtenstein	0.0[k]	0.2	233	14	..	..[e]	..	..	..	..
Lithuania	2.9	65.3	47	67	45.2	15,410	77.4	26,390	3.0	3.9
Luxembourg	0.6	2.6	215	90	42.3	75,960	36.5	65,570	4.1	1.6
Macedonia, FYR	2.1	25.7	82	57	10.7	5,150	27.3	13,170	3.8	3.6
Madagascar	23.6	587.3	41	34	10.4	440	33.0	1,400	3.3	0.5
Malawi	16.7	118.5	177	16	4.2	250	13.2	790	5.7	2.5
Malaysia	29.9	330.8	91	74	332.5	11,120	740.8	24,770	6.0	4.4
Maldives	0.4	0.3	1,337	44	2.6	6,410	4.4	10,920	6.5	4.4
Mali	17.1	1,240.2	14	39	11.0	650	25.8	1,510	7.2	4.1
Malta	0.4	0.3	1,336	95	*8.9*	*21,000*	*11.6*	*27,390*	*2.9*	*1.9*
Marshall Islands	0.1	0.2	294	72	0.2	4,390	0.2[a]	4,700[a]	–1.0	–1.2
Mauritania	4.0	1,030.7	4	59	5.0	1,270	14.7	3,710	6.4	3.8
Mauritius	1.3	2.0	621	40	12.1	9,630	22.9	18,150	3.6	3.4
Mexico	125.4	1,964.4	65	79	1,237.5	9,870	2,111.2	16,840	2.2	0.9
Micronesia, Fed. Sts.	0.1	0.7	149	22	0.3	3,200	0.4[a]	3,590[a]	–3.4	–3.7
Moldova	3.6[p]	33.9	124[p]	45	9.1[p]	2,560[p]	19.6[p]	5,500[p]	4.6[p]	4.7[p]
Monaco	0.0[k]	0.0[f]	18,812	100	..	..[e]	..	..	..	..
Mongolia	2.9	1,564.1	2	71	12.5	4,280	32.4	11,120	7.8	5.9
Montenegro	0.6	13.8	46	64	4.5	7,320	9.5	15,250	1.8	1.7
Morocco	33.9	446.6	76	60	105.8[q]	3,070[q]	251.5[q]	7,290[q]	2.4[q]	1.0[q]
Mozambique	27.2	799.4	35	32	16.4	600	30.3	1,120	7.2	4.3
Myanmar	53.4	676.6	82	34	68.1	1,270	..	..	8.5	7.6
Namibia	2.4	824.3	3	46	13.5	5,630	23.6	9,810	6.4	3.9
Nepal	28.2	147.2	197	18	20.6	730	68.0	2,410	5.4	4.1
Netherlands	16.9	41.5	501	90	874.6	51,860	824.1	48,860	1.0	0.6
New Caledonia	0.3	18.6	15	70	..	..[e]	..	..	..	..
New Zealand	4.5	267.7	17	86	185.2	41,070	163.3	36,200	3.0	1.5
Nicaragua	6.0	130.4	50	58	11.3	1,870	28.8	4,790	4.7	3.5
Niger	19.1	1,267.0	15	18	7.8	410	17.4	910	6.9	2.7

	Population	Surface area	Population density	Urban population	Gross national income				Gross domestic product	
					Atlas method		Purchasing power parity			
	millions	thousand sq. km	people per sq. km	% of total population	$ billions	Per capita $	$ billions	Per capita $	% growth	Per capita % growth
	2014	2014	2014	2014	2014	2014	2014	2014	2013–14	2013–14
Nigeria	177.5	923.8	195	47	526.5	2,970	1,013.7	5,710	6.3	3.5
Northern Mariana Islands	0.1	0.5	119	89	..	..[e]	..	..	..	..
Norway	5.1	385.2	14	80	532.3	103,620	344.7	67,100	2.2	1.1
Oman	4.2	309.5	14	77	*65.9*	*16,870*	*131.6*	*33,690*	2.9	−5.1
Pakistan	185.0	796.1	240	38	258.3	1,400	941.1	5,090	4.7	2.6
Palau	0.0[k]	0.5	46	86	0.2	11,110	0.3[a]	14,280[a]	8.0	7.0
Panama	3.9	75.4	52	66	43.1	11,130	77.1	19,930	6.2	4.5
Papua New Guinea	7.5	462.8	16	13	16.7	2,240	20.8[a]	2,790[a]	8.5	6.3
Paraguay	6.6	406.8	16	59	28.8	4,400	55.5	8,470	4.7	3.3
Peru	31.0	1,285.2	24	78	196.9	6,360	354.2	11,440	2.4	1.0
Philippines	99.1	300.0	332	44	347.5	3,500	837.6	8,450	6.1	4.5
Poland	38.0	312.7	124	61	520.1	13,680	928.4	24,430	3.3	3.4
Portugal	10.4	92.2	114	63	222.1	21,360	295.1	28,370	0.9	1.5
Puerto Rico	3.5	8.9	400	94	*69.4*	*19,310*	*86.2[a]*	*23,960[a]*	*−0.6*	*0.7*
Qatar	2.2	11.6	187	99	200.3	92,200	292.0	134,420	4.0	0.6
Romania	19.9	238.4	87	54	189.5	9,520	397.1	19,950	2.8	3.2
Russian Federation	143.8	17,098.3	9	74	1,930.6	13,220	3,237.4	22,160	0.6	−1.1
Rwanda	11.3	26.3	460	28	7.9	700	18.5	1,630	7.0	4.5
Samoa	0.2	2.8	68	19	0.8	4,060	1.1[a]	5,610[a]	1.2	0.4
San Marino	0.0[k]	0.1	527	94	..	..[e]	..	..	..	..
São Tomé and Príncipe	0.2	1.0	194	65	0.3	1,670	0.6	3,140	4.5	2.3
Saudi Arabia	30.9	2,149.7[r]	14	83	*759.3*	*25,140*	*1,549.8*	*51,320*	3.6	1.3
Senegal	14.7	196.7	76	43	15.4	1,050	33.8	2,300	4.7	1.5
Serbia	7.1	88.4	82	55	41.5	5,820	93.0	13,040	−1.8	−1.3
Seychelles	0.1	0.5	201	54	1.3	14,120	2.3	24,810	3.3	1.6
Sierra Leone	6.3	72.3	87	40	4.4	700	11.2	1,770	4.6	2.3
Singapore	5.5	0.7	7,737	100	301.6	55,150	439.0	80,270	2.9	1.6
Sint Maarten	0.0[k]	0.0[f]	1,108	100	..	..[e]	..	..	..	..
Slovak Republic	5.4	49.0	113	54	96.2	17,750	148.5	27,410	2.5	2.4
Slovenia	2.1	20.3	102	50	48.6	23,580	62.6	30,360	3.0	2.9
Solomon Islands	0.6	28.9	20	22	1.0	1,830	1.2[a]	2,020[a]	1.5	−0.5
Somalia	10.5	637.7	17	39	..	..[j]	..	..	..	..
South Africa	54.0	1,219.1	45	64	367.2	6,800	685.7	12,700	1.5	0.0
South Sudan	11.9	644.3	..	19	11.6	970	21.4[a]	1,800[a]	3.4	−0.6
Spain	46.5	505.9	93	79	1,366.0	29,390	1,556.6	33,490	1.4	1.7
Sri Lanka	20.8	65.6	331	18	71.4	3,440	214.0	10,300	4.5	3.5
St. Kitts and Nevis	0.1	0.3	211	32	0.8	14,920	1.2	22,600	6.9	5.6
St. Lucia	0.2	0.6	301	18	1.3	7,260	1.9	10,540	0.5	−0.3
St. Martin	0.0[k]	0.1	580	..	..	..[e]	..	..	..	..
St. Vincent & the Grenadines	0.1	0.4	280	50	0.7	6,610	1.2	10,730	0.6	0.6
Sudan	39.4	1,879.4	22[s]	34	67.3	1,710	154.4	3,920	3.1	0.9
Suriname	0.5	163.8	3	66	5.4	9,950	9.2	17,040	1.8	0.9
Swaziland	1.3	17.4	74	21	4.5	3,550	10.0	7,880	2.5	1.0
Sweden	9.7	447.4	24	86	596.9	61,570	454.4	46,870	2.3	1.3
Switzerland	8.2	41.3	207	74	693.7	84,720	484.4	59,160	1.9	0.7
Syrian Arab Republic	22.2	185.2	121	57	..	..[h]	..	..	..	..
Tajikistan	8.3	142.6	59	27	8.9	1,080	22.1	2,660	6.7	4.3

	Population	Surface area	Population density	Urban population	Gross national income				Gross domestic product	
					Atlas method		Purchasing power parity			
	millions	thousand sq. km	people per sq. km	% of total population	$ billions	Per capita $	$ billions	Per capita $	% growth	Per capita % growth
	2014	2014	2014	2014	2014	2014	2014	2014	2013–14	2013–14
Tanzania	51.8	947.3	59	31	46.4[t]	920[t]	126.3[t]	2,510[t]	7.0[t]	3.6[t]
Thailand	67.7	513.1	133	49	391.7	5,780	1,006.9	14,870	0.9	0.5
Timor-Leste	1.2	14.9	82	32	3.2	2,680	6.2[a]	5,080[a]	7.0	4.2
Togo	7.1	56.8	131	39	4.0	570	9.2	1,290	5.7	2.9
Tonga	0.1	0.8	147	24	0.4	4,260	0.6[a]	5,270[a]	2.1	1.7
Trinidad and Tobago	1.4	5.1	264	9	27.2	20,070	43.3	31,970	0.8	0.4
Tunisia	11.0	163.6	71	67	46.5	4,230	121.2	11,020	2.7	1.7
Turkey	75.9	783.6	99	73	822.4	10,830	1,485.2	19,560	2.9	1.7
Turkmenistan	5.3	488.1	11	50	42.5	8,020	77.1[a]	14,520[a]	10.3	8.9
Turks and Caicos Islands	0.0[k]	1.0	36	92	..	..[e]	..	..	..	..
Tuvalu	0.0[k]	0.0[f]	330	59	0.1	5,720	0.1[a]	5,410[a]	2.0	1.8
Uganda	37.8	241.6	188	16	25.3	670	65.0	1,720	4.8	1.5
Ukraine	45.4	603.6	78	69	152.1	3,560	366.2	8,560	−6.8	−0.8
United Arab Emirates	9.1	83.6	109	85	405.2	44,600	615.3	67,720	4.6	4.0
United Kingdom	64.6	243.6	267	82	2,801.5	43,390	2,550.1	39,500	2.9	2.3
United States	318.9	9,831.5	35	81	17,611.5	55,230	17,823.2	55,900	2.4	1.6
Uruguay	3.4	176.2	20	95	55.9	16,350	69.1	20,220	3.5	3.1
Uzbekistan	30.8	447.4	72	36	64.3	2,090	179.4[a]	5,830[a]	8.1	6.3
Vanuatu	0.3	12.2	21	26	0.8	3,160	0.8[a]	3,030[a]	2.3	0.0
Venezuela, RB	30.7	912.1	35	89	373.3	12,500[i]	535.7	17,700	−4.0	−5.3
Vietnam	90.7	331.0	293	33	171.9	1,890	485.2	5,350	6.0	4.9
Virgin Islands (U.S.)	0.1	0.4	298	95	..	..[e]	..	..	..	..
West Bank and Gaza	4.3	6.0	713	75	13.1	3,060	21.5	5,000	−1.5	−4.3
Yemen, Rep.	26.2	528.0	50	34	33.3	1,300	93.3	3,650	4.2	1.5
Zambia	15.7	752.6	21	40	26.4	1,680	57.9	3,690	6.0	2.8
Zimbabwe	15.2	390.8	39	33	12.8	840	25.2	1,650	3.8	1.5
World	**7,259.7 s**	**134,325.3 s**	**56 w**	**53 w**	**78,399.9 t**	**10,799 w**	**108,477.1 t**	**14,942 w**	**2.5 w**	**1.3 w**
East Asia & Pacific	2,264.1	24,825.2	93	56	22,032.5	9,731	33,741.6	14,903	3.6	2.9
Europe & Central Asia	902.0	28,460.4	33	71	22,932.5	25,425	26,001.8	28,827	1.4	1.2
Latin America & Caribbean	626.3	20,425.3	31	80	6,207.5	9,912	9,535.7	15,226	1.3	0.2
Middle East & North Africa	417.5	11,370.8	37	64	3,570.2	8,722	7,267.2	17,754	2.5	0.5
North America	354.5	19,816.2	19	81	19,452.6	54,879	19,406.4	54,748	2.4	1.6
South Asia	1,721.2	5,136.2	361	33	2,575.3	1,496	9,118.9	5,298	6.9	5.5
Sub-Saharan Africa	974.3	24,291.1	41	37	1,603.7	1,646	3,309.3	3,396	4.4	1.6
Low income	622.0	14,455.8	47	30	390.3	628	977.0	1,571	6.3	3.5
Lower middle income	2,878.5	20,523.3	142	39	5,807.5	2,018	17,275.3	6,002	5.7	4.1
Upper middle income	2,360.8	41,620.9	58	62	18,712.6	7,926	33,583.2	14,225	4.5	3.7
High income	1,398.4	57,725.3	25	81	53,561.2	38,301	56,961.0	40,732	1.7	1.3

a. Based on regression; others are extrapolated from the 2011 International Comparison Program benchmark estimates. b. Estimated to be upper middle income ($4,126–$12,735). c. Data series will be calculated once ongoing revisions to official statistics reported by the National Statistics and Censuses Institute of Argentina have been finalized. d. Data are officially reported statistics by the National Statistics and Censuses Institute of Argentina. On February 1, 2013, the International Monetary Fund (IMF) issued a declaration of censure and in December 2013 called on Argentina to implement specific actions to address the quality of its official GDP data according to a specified timetable. On June 3, 2015, the IMF Executive Board recognized the material progress in remedying the inaccurate provision of data since 2013 but found that some actions called for by the end of February 2015 had not yet been completely implemented. The IMF Executive Board will review this issue again by July 15, 2016. e. Estimated to high income ($12,736 or more). f. Greater than 0 but less than 50. g. Data are for the area controlled by the government of Cyprus. h. Estimated to be lower middle income ($1,046–$4,125). i. Included in the aggregates for high-income economies based on earlier data. j. Estimated to be low income ($1,045 or less). k. Greater than 0 but less than 50,000. l. Excludes Abkhazia and South Ossetia. m. Included in the aggregates for lower middle-income economies based on earlier data. n. Refers to area free from ice. o. Greater than 0 but less than 0.5. p. Excludes Transnistria. q. Includes Former Spanish Sahara. r. Provisional estimate. s. Includes South Sudan. t. Covers mainland Tanzania only.

About the data

Population, land area, income (as measured by gross national income, GNI), and output (as measured by gross domestic product, GDP) are basic measures of the size of an economy. They also provide a broad indication of actual and potential resources and are therefore used throughout *World Development Indicators* to normalize other indicators.

Population

Population estimates are usually based on national population censuses. Estimates for the years before and after the census are interpolations or extrapolations based on demographic models. Errors and undercounting occur even in high-income countries; in some low- and middle-income countries errors may be substantial because of limits in the transport, communications, and other resources required to conduct and analyze a full census.

The quality and reliability of official demographic data are also affected by public trust in the government, government commitment to full and accurate enumeration, confidentiality and protection against misuse of census data, and census agencies' independence from political influence. Moreover, comparability of population indicators is limited by differences in the concepts, definitions, collection procedures, and estimation methods used by national statistical agencies and other organizations that collect the data.

More countries conducted a census in the 2010 census round (2005–14) than in previous rounds. As of December 2014 (the end of the 2010 census round), about 93 percent of the estimated world population has been enumerated in a census. The currentness of a census and the availability of complementary data from surveys or registration systems are important indicators of demographic data quality. See *Sources and methods* for the most recent census or survey year and for the completeness of registration.

Current population estimates for low- and middle-income countries that lack recent census data and pre- and post-census estimates for countries with census data are provided by the United Nations Population Division and other agencies. The cohort component method—a standard method for estimating and projecting population—requires fertility, mortality, and net migration data, often collected from sample surveys, which can be small or limited in coverage. Population estimates are derived from demographic modeling and so are susceptible to biases and errors from shortcomings in the model and in the data. In the UN estimates, because the five-year age group is the cohort unit and five-year period data are used, interpolations to obtain annual data or single age structure may not reflect actual events or age composition.

Surface area

Surface area includes inland bodies of water and some coastal waterways and thus differs from land area, which excludes bodies of water, and from gross area, which may include offshore territorial waters. It is particularly important for understanding an economy's agricultural capacity and the environmental effects of human activity. Innovations in satellite mapping and computer databases have resulted in more precise measurements of land and water areas.

Urban population

There is no consistent and universally accepted standard for distinguishing urban from rural areas, in part because of the wide variety of situations across countries. Most countries use an urban classification related to the size or characteristics of settlements. Some define urban areas based on the presence of certain infrastructure and services. And other countries designate urban areas based on administrative arrangements. Because the estimates in the table are based on national definitions of what constitutes a city or metropolitan area, cross-country comparisons should be made with caution.

Size of the economy

GNI measures total domestic and foreign value added claimed by residents. GNI comprises GDP plus net receipts of primary income (compensation of employees and property income) from nonresident sources. GDP is the sum of gross value added by all resident producers in the economy plus any product taxes (less subsidies) not included in the valuation of output. GNI is calculated without deducting for depreciation of fabricated assets or for depletion and degradation of natural resources. Value added is the net output of an industry after adding up all outputs and subtracting intermediate inputs. The World Bank uses GNI per capita in U.S. dollars to classify countries for analytical purposes and to determine borrowing eligibility. For definitions of the income groups in *World Development Indicators,* see *User guide.*

When calculating GNI in U.S. dollars from GNI reported in national currencies, the World Bank follows the *World Bank Atlas* conversion method, using a three-year average of exchange rates to smooth the effects of transitory fluctuations in exchange rates. (For further discussion of the *World Bank Atlas* method, see *Sources and methods*.)

Because exchange rates do not always reflect differences in price levels between countries, the table also converts GNI and GNI per capita estimates into international dollars using purchasing power parity (PPP) rates. PPP rates provide a standard measure allowing comparison of real levels of expenditure between countries, just as conventional price indexes allow comparison of real values over time.

PPP rates are calculated by simultaneously comparing the prices of similar goods and services among a large number of countries. In the most recent round of price surveys by the International Comparison Program (ICP) in 2011, 177 countries and territories fully participated and 22 partially participated. PPP rates for 47 high- and upper middle-income countries are from Eurostat and the Organisation for Economic Co-operation and Development (OECD); PPP estimates incorporate new price data collected since 2011. For the remaining 2011 ICP economies PPP rates are extrapolated from the 2011 ICP benchmark results, which account for relative price changes between each economy and the United States. For countries that did not participate in the 2011 ICP round, PPP rates are imputed using a statistical model. More information on the results of the 2011 ICP is available at http://icp.worldbank.org.

Growth rates of GDP and GDP per capita are calculated using constant price data in local currency. Constant price U.S. dollar series are used to calculate regional and income group growth rates. Growth rates in the table are annual averages (see *Sources and methods*).

Definitions

• **Population** is based on the de facto definition of population, which counts all residents regardless of legal status or citizenship—except for refugees not permanently settled in the country of asylum, who are generally considered part of the population of their country of origin. The values shown are midyear estimates. • **Surface area** is a country's total area, including areas under inland bodies of water and some coastal waterways. • **Population density** is midyear population divided by land area. • **Urban population** is the midyear population of areas defined as urban in each country and obtained by the United Nations Population Division. • **Gross national income, *Atlas* method,** is the sum of value added by all resident producers plus any product taxes (less subsidies) not included in the valuation of output plus net receipts of primary income (compensation of employees and property income) from abroad. Data are in current U.S. dollars converted using the *World Bank Atlas* method (see *Sources and methods*). • **Gross national income, purchasing power parity,** is GNI converted to international dollars using PPP rates. An international dollar has the same purchasing power over GNI that a U.S. dollar has in the United States. • **Gross national income per capita** is GNI divided by midyear population. • **Gross domestic product** is the sum of value added by all resident producers plus any product taxes (less subsidies) not included in the valuation of output. Growth is calculated from constant price GDP data in local currency. • **Gross domestic product per capita** is GDP divided by midyear population.

Data sources

The World Bank's population estimates are compiled and produced by its Development Data Group in consultation with its Health Global Practice, operational staff, and country offices. The United Nations Population Division (2015) is a source of the demographic data for more than half the countries, most of them low- and middle-income countries. Other important sources are census reports and other statistical publications from national statistical offices, Eurostat's Population database, the United Nations Statistics Division's *Population and Vital Statistics Report,* and the U.S. Bureau of the Census's International Data Base. Data on surface and land area are from the Food and Agriculture Organization, which gathers these data from national agencies through annual questionnaires and by analyzing the results of national agricultural censuses. Data on urban population shares are from United Nations Population Division (2014). GNI, GNI per capita, GDP growth, and GDP per capita growth are estimated by World Bank staff based on national accounts data collected by World Bank staff during economic missions or reported by national statistical offices to other international organizations such as the OECD. PPP conversion factors are estimates by Eurostat/OECD and by World Bank staff based on data collected by the ICP.

References

Eurostat. n.d. *Population database.* [http://ec.europa.eu/eurostat/]. Luxembourg.

OECD (Organisation for Economic Co-operation and Development). n.d. OECD.StatExtracts database. [http://stats.oecd.org/]. Paris.

United Nations Population Division. 2014. *World Urbanization Prospects: The 2014 Revision.* [http://esa.un.org/unpd/wup/]. New York.

———. 2015. *World Population Prospects: The 2015 Revision.* [http://esa.un.org/unpd/wpp/]. New York.

United Nations Statistics Division. Various years. *Population and Vital Statistics Report.* New York.

To access the World Development Indicators online tables, use the URL http://wdi.worldbank.org/table/ and the table number (for example, http://wdi.worldbank.org/table/1.1). To view a specific indicator online, use the URL http://data.worldbank.org/indicator/ and the indicator code (for example, http://data.worldbank.org /indicator/SP.POP.TOTL).

1.1 Size of the economy

Population ♀♂	SP.POP.TOTL
Surface area	AG.SRF.TOTL.K2
Population density	EN.POP.DNST
Gross national income, *Atlas* method	NY.GNP.ATLS.CD
Gross national income per capita, *Atlas* method	NY.GNP.PCAP.CD
Purchasing power parity gross national income	NY.GNP.MKTP.PP.CD
Purchasing power parity gross national income, Per capita	NY.GNP.PCAP.PP.CD
Gross domestic product	NY.GDP.MKTP.KD.ZG
Gross domestic product, Per capita	NY.GDP.PCAP.KD.ZG

1.2 Global goals: ending poverty and improving lives

Share of poorest quintile in national consumption or income	SI.DST.FRST.20
Prevalence of stunting ♀♂	SH.STA.STNT.ZS
Maternal mortality ratio, Modeled estimate	SH.STA.MMRT
Under-five mortality rate ♀♂	SH.DYN.MORT
Prevalence of HIV	SH.DYN.AIDS.ZS
Incidence of tuberculosis	SH.TBS.INCD
Mortality caused by road traffic injury	SH.STA.TRAF.P5
Primary completion rate ♀♂	SE.PRM.CMPT.ZS
Contributing family workers, Male ♀♂	SL.FAM.WORK.MA.ZS
Contributing family workers, Female ♀♂	SL.FAM.WORK.FE.ZS
GDP per person employed, % growth	..[a]

1.3 Global goals: promoting sustainability

Access to an improved water source	SH.H2O.SAFE.ZS
Access to improved sanitation facilities	SH.STA.ACSN
Access to electricity	EG.ELC.ACCS.ZS
Renewable energy consumption	EG.FEC.RNEW.ZS
Research and development expenditure	GB.XPD.RSDV.GD.ZS

Urban population living in slums	EN.POP.SLUM.UR.ZS
Ambient PM 2.5 air pollution	EN.ATM.PM25.MC.M3
Adjusted net savings	NY.ADJ.SVNG.GN.ZS
Carbon dioxide emissions per capita	EN.ATM.CO2E.PC
Nationally protected terrestrial and marine areas	ER.PTD.TOTL.ZS
Intentional homicides (per 100,000 people)	VC.IHR.PSRC.P5
Internet users	IT.NET.USER.P2

1.4 Global goals: strengthening partnership

This table provides data on net official development assistance by donor, least developed countries' access to high-income markets, and the Debt Initiative for Heavily Indebted Poor Countries. ..[b]

1.5 Women in development

Life expectancy at birth, Male ♀♂	SP.DYN.LE00.MA.IN
Life expectancy at birth, Female ♀♂	SP.DYN.LE00.FE.IN
Women ages 20–24 first married by age 18	SP.M18.2024.FE.ZS
Account at a financial institution, Male ♀♂	WP_time_01.2
Account at a financial institution, Female ♀♂	WP_time_01.3
Wage and salaried workers, Male ♀♂	SL.EMP.WORK.MA.ZS
Wage and salaried workers, Female ♀♂	SL.EMP.WORK.FE.ZS
Female part-time employment ♀♂	SL.TLF.PART.TL.FE.ZS
Firms with female participation in ownership	IC.FRM.FEMO.ZS
Female legislators, senior officials, and managers	SG.GEN.LSOM.ZS
Women in parliaments	SG.GEN.PARL.ZS
Nondiscrimination clause mentions gender in the constitution	SG.NOD.CONS

♀♂ Data disaggregated by sex are available in the World Development Indicators database.
a. Derived from data elsewhere in the World Development Indicators database.
b. Available online only as part of the table, not as an individual indicator.

Poverty rates

	International poverty line in local currency		Population below international poverty lines[a]									
	$1.90 a day	$3.10 a day	Reference year[b]	Population below $1.90 a day %	Poverty gap at $1.90 a day %	Population below $3.10 a day %	Poverty gap at $3.10 a day %	Reference year[b]	Population below $1.90 a day %	Poverty gap at $1.90 a day %	Population below $3.10 a day %	Poverty gap at $3.10 a day %
	2011	2011										
Albania	110.5	180.3	2008	<2.0	<0.5	6.1	0.9	2012	<2.0	<0.5	6.8	1.4
Angola	140.3	228.9		..	..	..	..	2008	30.1	9.6	54.5	22.5
Argentina	5.3	8.6	2012[c,d]	<2.0	0.8	3.7	1.5	2013[c,d]	<2.0	1.0	3.6	1.6
Armenia	349.2	569.7	2012	<2.0	<0.5	17.4	3.5	2013	2.4	0.6	17.0	3.7
Azerbaijan	0.6	1.0	2004	<2.0	<0.5	<2.0	<0.5	2005	<2.0	<0.5	<2.0	<0.5
Bangladesh	31.9[e]	51.0[e]	2005	51.6	14.2	81.5	35.5	2010	43.7	11.2	77.6	31.4
Belarus	3,481.6	5,680.5	2011	<2.0	<0.5	<2.0	<0.5	2012	<2.0	<0.5	<2.0	<0.5
Belize	2.2[f]	3.7[f]	1998[c]	14.4	5.9	32.6	12.7	1999[c]	13.9	6.2	26.0	11.5
Benin	427.3	697.2	2003	48.9	16.3	77.2	35.3	2011	53.1	19.0	75.6	37.2
Bhutan	32.2	52.6	2007	8.0	1.6	28.9	8.0	2012	2.2	<0.5	13.5	3.0
Bolivia	5.5	9.0	2012[c]	9.1	4.9	15.8	7.7	2013[c]	7.7	3.8	13.4	6.4
Bosnia and Herzegovina	1.6	2.7	2004	<2.0	<0.5	<2.0	<0.5	2007	<2.0	<0.5	<2.0	<0.5
Botswana	8.4	13.8	2002	29.8	11.4	49.0	22.6	2009	18.2	5.8	35.7	14.0
Brazil	3.2	5.1	2012[c]	4.6	2.5	9.3	4.1	2013[c]	4.9	2.8	9.1	4.3
Bulgaria	1.5	2.4	2011[c]	2.2	0.9	4.7	1.9	2012[c]	2.0	0.8	4.7	1.7
Burkina Faso	422.3	689.0	2003	57.3	23.7	79.3	41.8	2009	55.3	19.9	80.5	39.3
Burundi	925.9	1,510.7	1998	84.1	44.8	95.0	62.8	2006	77.7	32.9	92.2	53.6
Cabo Verde	97.7[e]	156.4[e]	2001	28.2	9.3	50.8	21.2	2007	17.6	4.7	39.3	14.1
Cambodia	2,019.1[e]	3,230.6[e]	2011	8.9	1.5	43.3	10.7	2012	6.2	1.0	37.0	8.8
Cameroon	437.7	714.2	2001	23.1	6.1	50.9	18.4	2007	29.3	8.3	54.3	21.7
Central African Republic	509.0	830.4	2003	64.8	30.3	84.2	48.0	2008	66.3	33.1	82.3	49.5
Chad	477.5	779.0	2003	62.9	26.7	84.6	45.7	2011	38.4	15.3	64.8	29.7
Chile	744.1	1,214.1	2011[c]	<2.0	0.5	2.9	1.1	2013[c]	<2.0	<0.5	2.1	0.8
China[g]	7.0	11.5	2008[h]	14.7	3.9	33.0	11.6	2010[h]	11.2	2.7	27.2	9.1
Colombia	2,274.2	3,710.5	2012[c]	7.1	2.9	16.2	6.2	2013[c]	6.1	2.5	13.8	5.3
Comoros	419.1	683.8		..	..	..	..	2004	13.5	3.7	32.3	11.1
Congo, Dem. Rep.	1,021.7	1,667.0	2004	91.2	59.3	96.9	73.0	2012	77.2	39.3	90.7	57.0
Congo, Rep.	563.4	919.2	2005	50.2	19.9	71.8	36.4	2011	28.7	9.6	52.9	21.9
Costa Rica	653.2[f]	1,065.7[f]	2012[c]	<2.0	0.7	4.1	1.5	2013[c]	<2.0	0.6	4.0	1.4
Croatia	8.3	13.5	2010	<2.0	<0.5	<2.0	<0.5	2011[c]	<2.0	0.5	<2.0	<0.5
Czech Republic	28.3	46.2	2011[c]	<2.0	<0.5	<2.0	<0.5	2012[c]	<2.0	<0.5	<2.0	<0.5
Côte d'Ivoire	447.8	730.6	2002	23.0	7.1	54.8	19.5	2008	29.0	10.3	55.1	23.2
Djibouti	192.8	314.6	2002	20.6	6.0	46.1	16.7	2012	18.3	7.9	37.0	15.5
Dominican Republic	39.4[f]	64.3[f]	2012[c]	2.6	0.7	10.2	2.8	2013[c]	2.3	0.6	9.1	2.4
Ecuador	1.0	1.7	2012[c]	5.9	2.5	14.0	5.2	2013[c]	4.4	1.7	11.6	4.0
El Salvador	1.0[f]	1.6[f]	2012[c]	4.2	1.0	13.6	3.8	2013[c]	3.3	0.7	11.5	3.2
Estonia	1.2	1.9	2011[c]	<2.0	1.2	<2.0	<0.5	2012[c]	<2.0	1.2	<2.0	<0.5
Ethiopia	10.3	16.9	2004	36.3	8.3	76.2	27.5	2010	33.5	9.0	71.3	26.5
Fiji	2.3	3.8	2002	5.1	0.9	20.2	5.4	2008	3.6	0.7	17.0	4.1
Gabon	682.5	1,113.6		..	..	..	..	2005	8.0	1.9	24.4	7.2
Gambia, The	20.6	33.6	1998	73.8	38.2	86.9	55.0	2003	45.3	17.7	68.0	33.4
Georgia	1.6	2.6	2012	15.5	5.0	34.6	12.8	2013	11.5	3.4	28.6	9.8
Ghana	1.5	2.4	1998	33.9	11.3	60.5	25.5	2005	25.2	8.4	49.0	19.6
Guatemala	7.4[f]	12.0[f]	2006[c]	11.5	3.9	23.7	9.3	2011[c]	11.5	4.0	26.5	9.8
Guinea	4,887.4	7,974.3	2007	59.7	23.7	81.2	42.4	2012	35.3	10.3	68.7	27.1
Guinea-Bissau	471.6	769.5	2002	53.9	18.6	80.9	38.3	2010	67.1	30.5	83.6	48.5
Guyana	253.2[f]	413.1[f]	1992[c]	33.2	12.5	58.6	25.7	1998[c]	14.0	5.0	28.3	11.2

 Front User guide World view People Environment

	International poverty line in local currency		Population below international poverty lines[a]									
	$1.90 a day	$3.10 a day	Reference year[b]	Population below $1.90 a day %	Poverty gap at $1.90 a day %	Population below $3.10 a day %	Poverty gap at $3.10 a day %	Reference year[b]	Population below $1.90 a day %	Poverty gap at $1.90 a day %	Population below $3.10 a day %	Poverty gap at $3.10 a day %
	2011	2011										
Haiti	39.3[f]	64.2[f]	2001[c]	55.6	28.0	73.4	42.5	2012[c]	53.9	28.9	71.0	42.2
Honduras	19.2[f]	31.2[f]	2012[c]	21.4	9.3	37.3	17.1	2013[c]	18.9	7.7	34.6	15.2
Hungary	262.0	427.4	2011[c]	<2.0	<0.5	<2.0	<0.5	2012[c]	<2.0	<0.5	<2.0	<0.5
India[g]	28.5	46.4	2009[h]	31.4	7.0	67.9	24.4	2011	21.3	4.3	58.0	18.5
Indonesia[g]	7,774.7	12,685.0	2008	21.3	4.3	54.5	17.6	2010	15.9	2.9	46.3	14.2
Iran, Islamic Rep.	5,158.2	8,415.9	2009[h]	<2.0	<0.5	3.1	0.5	2013[h]	<2.0	<0.5	<2.0	<0.5
Jamaica	120.4[f]	196.4[f]	2002	2.8	0.7	10.6	2.9	2004	<2.0	<0.5	8.2	2.0
Jordan	0.6[e]	1.0[e]	2008	<2.0	<0.5	3.0	<0.5	2010	<2.0	<0.5	<2.0	<0.5
Kazakhstan	158.9	259.2	2012	<2.0	<0.5	<2.0	<0.5	2013	<2.0	<0.5	<2.0	<0.5
Kenya	67.3	109.8	1997	21.5	5.6	45.9	16.6	2005	33.6	11.7	58.9	25.5
Kiribati	2.0[f]	3.3[f]		..	..	..	..	2006	14.1	4.6	34.7	12.2
Kosovo	0.7[f]	1.1[f]	2012	<2.0	<0.5	<2.0	<0.5	2013	<2.0	<0.5	<2.0	<0.5
Kyrgyz Republic	33.3	54.4	2011	<2.0	<0.5	19.3	3.5	2012	2.9	0.7	20.0	4.2
Lao PDR	4,677.0[e]	7,483.2[e]	2007	36.3	9.5	69.3	27.1	2012	30.0	7.8	63.3	23.3
Latvia	0.8	1.2	2011[c]	<2.0	1.0	<2.0	<0.5	2012[c]	<2.0	1.0	<2.0	<0.5
Lesotho	7.3	12.0	2002	61.3	32.0	78.9	47.1	2010	59.7	31.8	77.3	46.6
Liberia	1.1	1.8		..	..	..	..	2007	68.6	28.1	89.6	48.6
Lithuania	3.4	5.5	2011[c]	<2.0	0.8	<2.0	<0.5	2012[c]	<2.0	0.8	<2.0	<0.5
Macedonia, FYR	43.6	71.1	2006	2.7	0.6	8.3	2.4	2008	<2.0	<0.5	8.7	2.0
Madagascar	1,339.3	2,185.2	2005	74.1	31.7	89.9	51.8	2010	81.8	40.3	92.9	59.0
Malawi	148.2	241.9	2004	73.6	31.7	90.1	51.7	2010	70.9	33.3	87.6	51.8
Malaysia	3.0	4.9	2007[i]	<2.0	<0.5	2.7	<0.5	2009[c]	<2.0	<0.5	2.7	<0.5
Maldives	20.3	33.1	2004[h]	2.4	<0.5	15.0	3.4	2009	5.6	1.1	17.9	5.0
Mali	421.5	687.8	2006	50.6	17.5	76.1	36.0	2009	49.3	15.2	77.7	34.6
Mauritania	214.3	349.7	2004	14.4	3.6	40.3	12.9	2008	10.9	2.9	32.5	10.1
Mauritius	34.7	56.7	2006	<2.0	<0.5	3.0	0.6	2012	<2.0	<0.5	3.0	0.7
Mexico	17.0	27.7	2010	3.8	1.0	11.9	3.5	2012	2.7	0.7	10.3	2.7
Micronesia, Fed. Sts.	1.9[f]	3.1[f]		..	..	..	..	2000[c,d]	50.4	28.5	66.7	40.4
Moldova	10.4	16.9	2012	<2.0	<0.5	2.9	0.5	2013	<2.0	<0.5	<2.0	<0.5
Mongolia	1,121.6	1,830.0	2011	<2.0	<0.5	6.2	1.1	2012	<2.0	<0.5	4.0	0.7
Montenegro	0.9	1.4	2012	<2.0	0.5	2.1	1.0	2013	<2.0	<0.5	3.9	1.4
Morocco	8.0	13.0	2000	6.2	1.3	25.6	6.7	2007	3.1	0.6	15.5	3.7
Mozambique	29.5	48.1	2002	80.4	41.5	92.0	59.3	2008	68.7	31.4	87.5	50.2
Namibia	9.7	15.9	2003	31.5	10.2	54.7	23.4	2009	22.6	6.7	45.7	17.7
Nepal	48.9	79.9	2003	47.1	14.8	74.4	33.2	2010	15.0	3.0	48.4	14.7
Nicaragua	17.4[f]	28.4[f]	2005	15.6	3.6	39.4	12.9	2009[c]	10.8	3.6	25.2	9.1
Niger	434.6	709.1	2007	72.0	28.8	90.1	49.8	2011	50.3	13.9	81.8	35.2
Nigeria	151.1	246.5	2003	53.5	21.9	78.5	39.5	2009	53.5	21.8	76.5	39.1
Pakistan	48.3	78.8	2007	13.3	2.1	53.2	14.3	2010	8.3	1.2	45.0	10.8
Panama	1.1[f]	1.7[f]	2012[c]	4.4	1.4	9.9	3.6	2013[c]	2.9	0.8	8.0	2.6
Papua New Guinea	4.1[f]	6.6[f]	1996	53.2	28.1	70.2	41.4	2009	39.3	15.9	64.7	30.4
Paraguay	4,387.9	7,159.2	2012[c]	3.7	1.2	9.7	3.3	2013[c]	2.2	0.9	6.3	2.2
Peru	3.0	4.9	2012[c]	4.1	1.1	10.8	3.6	2013[c]	3.7	0.9	9.7	3.1
Philippines	35.9	58.5	2009	12.0	2.4	36.5	11.0	2012	13.1	2.7	37.6	11.7
Poland	3.7	6.0	2011	<2.0	<0.5	<2.0	<0.5	2012	<2.0	<0.5	<2.0	<0.5
Romania	3.8	6.2	2011	<2.0	<0.5	4.5	0.7	2012	<2.0	<0.5	4.1	0.7
Russian Federation	31.9	52.0	2011	<2.0	<0.5	<2.0	<0.5	2012	<2.0	<0.5	<2.0	<0.5

	International poverty line in local currency		Population below international poverty lines[a]									
	$1.90 a day 2011	$3.10 a day 2011	Reference year[b]	Population below $1.90 a day %	Poverty gap at $1.90 a day %	Population below $3.10 a day %	Poverty gap at $3.10 a day %	Reference year[b]	Population below $1.90 a day %	Poverty gap at $1.90 a day %	Population below $3.10 a day %	Poverty gap at $3.10 a day %
Rwanda	469.0	765.2	2005	68.0	31.1	84.1	49.1	2010	60.3	23.7	80.7	42.6
Samoa	3.6[f]	5.9[f]	..	..	..	..	..	2008	<2.0	<0.5	8.4	1.7
São Tomé and Príncipe	19,370.1	31,603.9	2000	29.5	7.7	61.7	22.8	2010	33.9	9.1	69.2	26.4
Senegal	467.6	762.9	2005	37.6	12.4	65.8	28.2	2011	38.0	12.8	66.3	28.4
Serbia	86.2	140.6	2009	<2.0	<0.5	<2.0	<0.5	2010	<2.0	<0.5	<2.0	<0.5
Seychelles	15.0[f]	24.5[f]	1999	<2.0	<0.5	2.4	0.7	2006	<2.0	<0.5	<2.0	<0.5
Sierra Leone	3,357.7	5,478.3	2003	58.6	21.8	80.9	41.1	2011	52.3	16.7	80.0	36.7
Slovak Republic	1.1	1.8	2011[c]	<2.0	<0.5	<2.0	<0.5	2012[c]	<2.0	<0.5	<2.0	<0.5
Slovenia	1.3	2.1	2011[c]	<2.0	<0.5	<2.0	<0.5	2012[c]	<2.0	<0.5	<2.0	<0.5
Solomon Islands	13.5[f]	22.1[f]	..	..	..	..	..	2005	45.6	17.4	69.3	33.6
South Africa	9.6	15.7	2008	15.1	4.2	33.3	12.1	2011	16.6	4.9	34.7	13.1
Sri Lanka	80.2	130.9	2009	2.4	<0.5	16.8	3.5	2012	<2.0	<0.5	14.0	2.8
St. Lucia	4.1[f]	6.6[f]	..	..	..	..	..	1995[c]	35.8	13.2	61.8	27.3
Sudan	2.8	4.6	..	..	..	..	..	2009	14.9	4.0	38.9	12.8
Suriname	3.6[f]	5.8[f]	..	..	..	..	..	1999[c]	23.4	16.5	40.2	23.0
Swaziland	7.7	12.6	2000	48.4	17.5	70.2	34.2	2009	42.0	16.6	63.1	31.1
Tajikistan	3.6	5.8	2007	10.4	3.8	32.7	10.1	2009	4.7	0.9	23.4	5.5
Tanzania	1,112.5	1,815.1	2007	52.7	19.0	77.9	37.6	2011	46.6	14.4	76.1	33.6
Thailand	24.4	39.8	2011	<2.0	<0.5	<2.0	<0.5	2012	<2.0	<0.5	<2.0	<0.5
Timor-Leste	1.1[f]	1.7[f]	2001	44.2	13.5	72.8	31.4	2007	46.8	12.1	80.1	32.9
Togo	441.2	719.9	2006	55.6	21.1	76.7	39.1	2011	54.2	23.2	74.5	39.5
Tonga	3.1[f]	5.1[f]	..	..	..	..	..	2009	<2.0	<0.5	8.2	1.8
Trinidad and Tobago	8.8[f]	14.3[f]	1988[i]	<2.0	<0.5	7.7	1.6	1992[i]	3.4	0.9	12.2	3.4
Tunisia	1.3	2.2	2005	3.1	0.7	13.3	3.4	2010	<2.0	<0.5	8.4	2.1
Turkey	2.2	3.6	2011	<2.0	<0.5	4.0	0.7	2012	<2.0	<0.5	3.1	0.6
Turkmenistan	2.9[f]	4.7[f]	1993[i]	80.9	39.5	94.2	58.7	1998[h]	42.3	14.5	69.1	31.0
Uganda	1,799.1	2,935.4	2009	41.5	13.2	69.4	30.2	2012	33.2	10.1	63.0	25.6
Ukraine	6.3	10.3	2012	<2.0	<0.5	<2.0	<0.5	2013	<2.0	<0.5	<2.0	<0.5
Uruguay	31.2	50.9	2012[c]	<2.0	<0.5	<2.0	<0.5	2013[c]	<2.0	<0.5	<2.0	<0.5
Uzbekistan	1,207.8[f]	1,970.7[f]	2002	65.6	22.4	44.4	25.8	2003	66.8	25.3	87.8	46.4
Vanuatu	220.1[f]	359.1[f]	..	..	..	..	..	2010	15.4	3.7	38.8	12.8
Venezuela, RB	5.5	9.0	2005[c]	17.0	12.5	24.0	15.5	2006[c]	9.2	6.8	14.9	8.8
Vietnam	14,487.4	23,637.4	2010	4.8	1.0	18.1	4.9	2012	3.2	0.6	13.9	3.5
West Bank and Gaza	4.8[f]	7.8[f]	2007	<2.0	<0.5	7.4	1.9	2009	<2.0	<0.5	2.6	0.5
Zambia	4,760.1	7,766.6	2006	60.5	30.1	76.9	45.4	2010	64.4	31.6	78.9	47.5

a. Based on nominal per capita consumption averages and distributions estimated parametrically from unit-record household survey data, unless otherwise noted. b. Refers to the period of reference of a survey. For surveys in which the period of reference covers multiple years, it is the first year. c. Estimated nonparametrically from nominal income per capita distributions based on unit-record household survey data. d. Covers urban areas only. e. Because the 2011 purchasing power parity (PPP) estimate needs to be further analyzed, the 2005 estimate is used. Thus data listed for the $1.90 a day poverty line refer to the $1.25 a day poverty line, and data listed for the $3.10 a day poverty line refer to the $2 a day poverty line. f. Based on PPP dollars imputed using regression. g. Based on benchmark national PPP estimate rescaled to account for cost-of-living differences in urban and rural areas. The national estimates are the population-weighted average of urban and rural estimates. h. Estimated nonparametrically from nominal consumption per capita distributions based on grouped household survey data. i. Based on per capita income averages and distribution data estimated parametrically from grouped household survey data.

Global and regional trends in poverty indicators at the poverty line of 2011 PPP $1.90 a day

Region	1990	1993	1996	1999	2002	2005	2008	2011	2012	Trend, 1990–2012
Poverty rate (% of population)										
Low and middle income	44.4	41.2	35.2	34.3	31.0	24.7	21.9	16.5	14.9	
East Asia & Pacific	60.6	52.0	39.3	37.5	29.2	18.6	15.0	8.5	7.2	
Europe & Central Asia	1.9	5.2	7.0	7.8	6.2	5.5	3.1	2.4	2.1	
Latin America & Caribbean	17.8	15.0	14.1	13.9	13.2	9.9	7.1	5.9	5.6	
Middle East & North Africa	6.0	7.0	6.1	4.2	a	3.3	2.7	a	a	
South Asia	50.6	47.9	42.8	a	40.8	35.0	32.1	22.2	18.8	
Sub-Saharan Africa	56.8	61.1	58.5	58.0	57.1	50.5	47.8	44.4	42.7	
World	37.1	34.7	29.7	29.1	26.3	21.6	18.7	14.1	12.7	
Number of poor people (millions)										
Low and middle income	1,959	1,917	1,716	1,751	1,645	1,401	1,254	983	897	
East Asia & Pacific	996	891	699	689	553	367	297	173	147	
Europe & Central Asia	9	24	33	37	29	26	15	11	10	
Latin America & Caribbean	78	69	69	71	70	56	41	35	34	
Middle East & North Africa	14	17	16	11	a	10	9	a	a	
South Asia	575	579	550	a	583	539	501	362	309	
Sub-Saharan Africa	288	336	349	375	399	402	392	394	389	
World	1,959	1,917	1,716	1,751	1,645	1,401	1,254	983	897	
Share of total poor population living in each region (low- and middle-income countries only, %)										
East Asia and Pacific	50.8	46.5	40.7	39.4	33.6	26.2	23.7	17.6	16.4	
Europe and Central Asia	0.4	1.3	1.9	2.1	1.8	1.8	1.2	1.2	1.1	
Latin America & Caribbean	4.0	3.6	4.0	4.1	4.3	4.0	3.3	3.6	3.8	
Middle East & North Africa	0.7	0.9	0.9	0.6	a	0.7	0.7	a	a	
South Asia	29.3	30.2	32.1	a	35.4	38.5	40.0	36.8	34.5	
Sub-Saharan Africa	14.7	17.5	20.4	21.4	24.3	28.7	31.2	40.0	43.4	
Survey coverage (% of total population represented by surveys conducted within five years of the reference year)										
Low and middle income	86.6	89.5	91.7	67.9	87.2	90.2	92.1	88.6	86.8	
East Asia & Pacific	92.3	93.1	93.5	93.3	93.3	91.6	93.7	93.6	91.8	
Europe & Central Asia	81.5	87.2	97.1	93.9	96.7	97.0	93.2	90.1	90.0	
Latin America & Caribbean	94.6	91.6	95.7	97.5	97.3	93.4	95.3	92.1	91.2	
Middle East & North Africa	77.3	65.8	82.0	69.8	22.7	82.4	48.2	38.6	37.4	
South Asia	97.3	98.7	98.5	19.9	98.5	95.6	98.3	98.2	98.2	
Sub-Saharan Africa	45.9	68.8	68.0	53.3	59.9	73.1	81.2	75.2	68.7	

Note: Income groups are based on how countries were classified in 1990.
a. Estimates not shown due to very low population coverage of available survey data.
Source: World Bank PovcalNet (http://iresearch.worldbank.org/PovcalNet/).

Poverty rates

The World Bank produced its first global poverty estimates for *World Development Report 1990: Poverty* (World Bank 1990) using household survey data for 22 countries (Ravallion, Datt, and van de Walle 1991). Since then there has been considerable expansion in the number of countries that field household income and expenditure surveys. The World Bank's Development Research Group maintains a database that updates regional and global aggregates annually. The database incorporates country-level updates as soon as new survey data become available.

The latest comprehensive revision took place in October 2015 and incorporate many revisions. The two most notable ones were the 2011 purchasing power parity (PPP) conversion factors and the new international poverty line at $1.90 a day. As differences in the cost of living across the world evolve, the global poverty line has to be periodically updated to reflect changes in prices. The previous change was in 2008, when 2005 PPP $1.25 a day was adopted as the global line. The latest revision is based on the national poverty lines of the same 15 poorest countries from the 2008 revision and thus preserves the real purchasing power of the previous line in the world's poorest countries (World Bank 2016).

Based on the new poverty line of 2011 PPP $1.90 a day, the World Bank revised the entire series of global poverty, from 1981 to 2012, using the latest household income and consumption survey data. For five countries (Bangladesh, Cabo Verde, Cambodia, Jordan, and Lao PDR), the poverty estimates are still measured at 2005 PPP $1.25 a day because price data (both consumer price indexes and 2011 PPPs) need to be further analyzed before being used to estimate poverty.

PovcalNet (http://iresearch.worldbank.org/PovcalNet) is an interactive computational tool that allows users to replicate these internationally comparable $1.90 and $3.10 a day poverty estimates for countries, regions, and custom country groupings and for different poverty lines. The Poverty and Equity Data portal (http://poverty data.worldbank.org/poverty/home) provides access to the database and user-friendly dashboards with graphs and interactive maps that visualize trends in key poverty and inequality indicators for different regions and countries. The country dashboards display trends in poverty measures based on the national poverty lines (see online table 2.7) alongside the internationally comparable estimates in the table produced from PovcalNet.

Data availability

The World Bank's internationally comparable poverty monitoring database draws on income or detailed consumption data from more than 1,000 household surveys across 131 low- and middle-income countries and 21 high-income countries (as defined in 1990). For high-income countries, estimates are available for inequality and income distribution only. The 2012 estimates use more than 2 million randomly sampled households, representing 87 percent of the population in low- and middle-income countries. Despite progress in the last decade, the challenges of measuring poverty remain. The timeliness, frequency, accessibility, quality, and comparability of household surveys need to increase substantially, particularly in the poorest countries. The availability and quality of poverty monitoring data remain low in small states, countries in fragile situations, low-income countries, and even some middle-income countries.

The lack of frequent, timely, and comparable data available in some countries creates uncertainty over the magnitude of poverty reduction. The table on trends in poverty indicators reports the percentage of the regional and global population represented by household survey samples collected during the reference year or during the two preceding or two subsequent years (in other words, within a five-year window centered on the reference year). Data coverage in Sub-Saharan Africa and the Middle East and North Africa remains low and variable. The need to improve household survey programs for monitoring poverty is clearly urgent. But institutional, political, and financial obstacles continue to limit data collection, analysis, and public access.

Data quality

Other data quality issues arise in measuring household living standards. Surveys ask detailed questions on sources of income and how it was spent, which must be carefully recorded by trained personnel. Income is difficult to measure accurately, and consumption comes closer to the notion of living standards. Moreover, income can vary over time even if living standards do not. But consumption data are not always available: the latest estimates reported here use consumption for about two-thirds of countries.

Similar surveys may not be strictly comparable because of differences in timing, sampling frames, or the quality and training of enumerators. Comparisons of countries at different levels of development also pose problems because of differences in the relative importance of the consumption of nonmarket goods. The local market value of all consumption in kind (including own production, particularly important in poor rural economies) should be included in total consumption expenditure, but in practice are often not. Most survey data now include valuations for consumption or income from own production, but valuation methods vary.

The statistics reported here are based on consumption data or, when unavailable, on income data. Analysis of some 20 countries for which both consumption and income data were available from the same surveys found income to yield a higher mean than consumption but also higher inequality. When poverty measures based on consumption and income were compared, the two effects roughly cancelled each other out: there was no significant statistical difference.

Invariably some sampled households do not participate in surveys because they refuse to do so or because nobody is at home during the interview visit. This is referred to as "unit nonresponse" and is distinct from "item nonresponse," which occurs when some of the sampled respondents participate but refuse to answer certain questions, such as those pertaining to income or consumption. To the extent that survey nonresponse is random, there is no concern regarding biases in survey-based inferences; the sample will still be representative of the population. However, households with different incomes may not be equally likely to respond. Richer households may be less likely to participate because of the high opportunity cost of their time or because of privacy concerns. It is conceivable that the poorest can likewise be underrepresented; some are homeless or nomadic and hard to reach in standard household survey designs, and some may be physically or socially isolated and thus less likely to be interviewed. This can bias both poverty and inequality measurement if not corrected for (Korinek, Mistiaen, and Ravallion 2007).

International poverty lines

International comparisons of poverty estimates entail both conceptual and practical problems. Countries have different definitions of poverty, and consistent comparisons across countries can be difficult. National poverty lines tend to have higher purchasing power in rich countries, where more generous standards are used, than in poor countries. Poverty measures based on an international poverty line attempt to hold the real value of the poverty line constant across countries, as is done when making comparisons over time. Since *World Development Report 1990* the World Bank has aimed to apply a common standard in measuring extreme poverty, anchored to what *poverty* means in the world's poorest countries. The welfare of people living in different countries can be measured on a common scale by adjusting for differences in the purchasing power of currencies. The commonly used $1 a day standard, measured in 1985 international prices and adjusted to local currency using PPPs, was chosen for *World Development Report 1990* because it was typical of the poverty lines in low-income countries at the time.

Early editions of *World Development Indicators* used PPPs from the Penn World Tables to convert values in local currency to equivalent purchasing power measured in U.S dollars. Later editions used 1993 consumption PPP estimates produced by the World Bank. International poverty lines were revised following the release of PPPs compiled in the 2005 round and the 2011 round of the International Comparison Program, along with data from an expanded set of household income and expenditure surveys. The current extreme poverty line is set at $1.90 a day in 2011 PPP terms, which represents the mean of the poverty lines found in the poorest 15 countries ranked by per capita consumption. This poverty line maintains the same standard for extreme poverty—the poverty line typical of the poorest countries in the world—but updates it using the latest information on the cost of living in low- and middle-income countries (World Bank 2015).

PPP exchange rates are used to estimate global poverty because they take into account the local prices of goods and services not traded internationally. But PPP rates were designed for comparing aggregates from national accounts, not for making international poverty comparisons. As a result, there is no certainty that an international poverty line measures the same degree of need or deprivation across countries. So-called poverty PPPs, designed to compare the consumption of the poorest people in the world, might provide a better basis for comparison of poverty across countries. Work on these measures is ongoing.

Definitions

• **International poverty line in local currency** is the international poverty lines of $1.90 and $3.10 a day in 2011 prices, converted to local currency using the PPP conversion factors estimated by the International Comparison Program. • **Reference year** is the period of reference of a survey. For surveys in which the period of reference covers multiple years, it is the first year. • **Population below $1.90 a day** and **population below $3.10 a day** are the percentages of the population living on less than $1.90 a day and $3.10 a day at 2011 international prices. As a result of revisions in PPP exchange rates, consumer price indexes, or welfare aggregates, poverty rates for individual countries cannot be compared with poverty rates reported in earlier editions. The PovcalNet online database and tool (http://iresearch.worldbank.org/PovcalNet) always contain the most recent full time series of comparable country data. • **Poverty gap** is the mean shortfall from the poverty line (counting the nonpoor as having zero shortfall), expressed as a percentage of the poverty line. This measure reflects the depth of poverty as well as its incidence.

Data sources

The poverty measures are prepared by the World Bank's Development Research Group. The international poverty lines are based on nationally representative primary household surveys conducted by national statistical offices or by private agencies under the supervision of government or international agencies and obtained from government statistical offices and World Bank Group country departments. For details on data sources and methods used in deriving the World Bank's latest estimates, see http://iresearch.worldbank .org/povcalnet.

References

Korinek, A., J. A. Mistiaen, and M. Ravallion. 2007. "An Econometric Method of Correcting for Unit Nonresponse Bias in Surveys." *Journal of Econometrics* 136: 213–35.

Ravallion, M., G. Datt, and D. van de Walle. 1991. "Quantifying Absolute Poverty in the Developing World." *Review of Income and Wealth* 37(4): 345–61.

World Bank. 1990. *World Development Report 1990: Poverty.* Washington, DC.

———. 2015. *A Measured Approach to Ending Poverty and Boosting Shared Prosperity: Concepts, Data, and the Twin Goals.* Policy Research Report. Washington, DC.

———. 2016. *Global Monitoring Report 2015/2016: Development Goals in an Era of Demographic Change.* Washington, DC: World Bank.

Shared prosperity

	Period		Annualized growth in mean income or consumption per capita		Mean income or consumption per capita[a]			
			%		2011 PPP $ a day			
			Bottom 40% of the population	Total population	Bottom 40% of the population		Total population	
	Baseline year	Most recent year			Baseline	Most recent	Baseline	Most recent
Albania	2008	2012	−1.2	−1.3	4.3	4.1	7.8	7.4
Argentina[b]	2007	2012	6.4	3.1	5.6	7.7	18.2	21.2
Armenia	2008	2013	−1.5	−1.1	3.4	3.2	6.3	6.0
Australia	2003	2010	4.4	4.7	0.8	0.9	1.6	1.7
Austria	2007	2012	0.4	0.4	27.8	28.3	52.7	53.7
Bangladesh	2005	2010	1.7	1.4	0.8[c]	0.9[c]	1.6[c]	1.7[c]
Belarus	2006	2011	9.1	8.1	6.5	10.1	11.7	17.2
Belgium	2007	2012	1.1	0.4	25.8	27.3	46.9	47.9
Bhutan	2007	2012	6.5	6.5	2.6	3.5	5.9	8.0
Bolivia	2007	2012	10.1	4.3	2.3	3.7	9.8	12.1
Brazil	2007	2012	6.9	4.5	3.4	4.8	14.0	17.5
Bulgaria	2007	2012	1.3	1.4	6.8	7.2	14.7	15.7
Cambodia	2007	2012	8.5	4.1	1.1[c]	1.7[c]	2.4[c]	2.9[c]
Canada	2004	2010	2.1	1.9	2.1	2.7	8.8	10.4
Chile	2006	2011	3.9	2.8	5.5	6.6	18.1	20.9
China	2005	2010	7.2	7.9	3.2	4.2	10.6	14.4
Colombia	2008	2012	6.0	3.6	2.8	3.5	11.6	13.3
Congo, Dem. Rep.	2004	2012	7.8	7.2	0.3	0.6	0.9	1.5
Congo, Rep.	2005	2011	7.2	4.3	1.0	1.5	3.0	3.8
Costa Rica	2010	2013	1.3	3.1	6.6	6.9	20.3	22.3
Croatia	2004	2010	1.6	0.3	11.7	12.8	21.9	22.2
Cyprus	2007	2012	−2.8	−1.6	27.1	23.6	50.8	46.9
Czech Republic	2007	2012	0.2	0.4	15.7	15.8	25.8	26.3
Denmark	2007	2012	−0.8	0.3	28.6	27.6	48.3	49.1
Dominican Republic	2007	2012	1.8	−0.2	3.8	4.2	11.9	11.8
Ecuador	2007	2012	5.5	1.0	2.9	3.8	10.7	11.3
El Salvador	2007	2012	0.2	−1.5	3.6	3.6	9.9	9.2
Estonia	2007	2012	−2.1	−1.2	12.8	11.6	24.6	23.1
Ethiopia	2004	2010	−1.5	−0.1	1.5	1.4	2.7	2.7
Finland	2007	2012	1.6	1.1	26.7	28.9	46.8	49.4
France	2007	2012	0.2	0.4	26.6	26.8	51.5	52.5
Georgia	2008	2013	2.9	2.6	2.1	2.5	5.3	6.1
Germany	2006	2011	1.4	0.1	26.5	28.4	52.4	52.8
Greece	2007	2012	−10.0	−8.4	16.3	9.6	34.7	22.4
Guatemala	2006	2011	−1.8	−4.6	2.7	2.5	10.9	8.6
Honduras	2007	2012	−3.2	−2.7	2.1	1.8	8.9	7.8
Hungary	2007	2012	−1.9	−0.7	10.9	9.9	19.3	18.7
Iceland	2007	2012	−3.9	−4.6	33.1	27.2	58.7	46.5
India	2004	2011	3.2	3.7	1.5	1.8	2.8	3.6
Indonesia	2011	2014	3.8	3.4	2.1	4.8	5.4	6.3
Iran, Islamic Rep.	2009	2013	3.1	−1.2	2.6	3.0	17.4	16.6
Iraq	2007	2012	0.3	1.0	0.4	0.6	1.2	1.5
Ireland	2007	2012	−4.4	−3.9	26.2	20.9	50.0	41.0
Italy	2007	2012	−2.9	−1.8	21.2	18.4	43.5	39.7
Jordan	2006	2010	2.7	2.6	3.2[c]	3.6[c]	6.4[c]	7[c]
Kazakhstan	2009	2013	8.9	7.6	5.1	7.1	9.0	12.0
Kyrgyz Republic	2008	2012	−0.1	−2.4	3.3	3.3	6.6	6.0

Shared prosperity

	Period		Annualized growth in mean income or consumption per capita		Mean income or consumption per capita[a]			
			%		2011 PPP $ a day			
			Bottom 40% of		Bottom 40% of the population		Total population	
	Baseline year	Most recent year	the population	Total population	Baseline	Most recent	Baseline	Most recent
Lao PDR	2007	2012	1.2	2.0	1.0	1.0	2.0	2.2
Latvia	2007	2012	−3.0	−4.3	9.7	8.3	22.4	17.9
Lithuania	2007	2012	−1.8	−1.2	10.1	9.3	21.0	19.8
Luxembourg	2007	2012	−2.7	−0.5	38.3	33.4	72.8	70.8
Madagascar	2005	2010	−4.5	−3.5	0.8	0.6	1.7	1.5
Malawi	2004	2010	−1.8	1.3	0.8	0.7	1.8	1.9
Mali	2006	2009	2.2	−1.5	1.1	1.2	2.5	2.4
Mauritania	2008	2014	3.3	1.6	2.4	5.5	1.5	1.7
Mauritius	2006	2012	0.8	0.9	5.3	5.5	11.0	11.6
Mexico	2008	2012	1.1	−0.2	3.4	3.5	11.3	11.2
Moldova	2008	2013	5.0	1.8	4.2	5.4	8.8	9.6
Montenegro	2008	2013	−4.8	−3.6	8.9	6.9	16.4	13.6
Nepal	2003	2010	7.5	4.1	1.2	2.0	3.0	3.9
Netherlands	2007	2012	0.0	−1.0	28.1	28.0	51.7	49.2
Nigeria	2003	2009	0.1	1.1	0.9	0.9	2.3	2.5
Norway	2007	2012	3.2	2.4	33.4	39.0	58.4	65.8
Pakistan	2004	2010	3.8	2.7	1.8	2.3	3.4	4.0
Panama	2008	2012	4.1	3.6	4.6	5.4	17.2	19.8
Paraguay	2007	2012	7.2	5.2	3.4	4.8	11.8	15.1
Peru	2007	2012	8.6	4.0	3.1	4.6	11.2	13.6
Philippines	2006	2012	1.1	0.4	2.1	2.2	5.6	5.7
Poland	2007	2012	2.0	1.4	7.6	8.4	15.2	16.3
Portugal	2007	2012	−2.0	−2.1	12.9	11.7	28.0	25.1
Romania	2008	2013	0.6	−0.3	4.8	5.0	8.9	8.8
Russian Federation	2007	2012	5.9	5.3	7.6	10.1	19.4	25.1
Rwanda	2005	2010	5.0	3.9	0.7	0.9	2.3	2.8
Senegal	2005	2011	−0.2	0.3	1.3	1.3	3.1	3.2
Serbia	2007	2010	−1.8	−1.3	7.3	6.9	13.4	12.8
Slovak Republic	2007	2012	5.5	6.7	12.5	16.3	20.3	28.0
Slovenia	2007	2012	−0.8	−0.3	20.6	19.8	33.4	33.0
South Africa	2006	2011	4.1	4.4	1.7	2.1	9.5	11.8
Spain	2007	2012	−1.3	0.0	17.1	16.0	36.2	36.3
Sri Lanka	2006	2012	2.2	1.7	3.0	3.4	6.8	7.5
Sweden	2007	2012	2.0	2.3	26.2	29.0	45.1	50.5
Switzerland	2007	2012	2.4	0.9	30.5	34.4	63.2	66.2
Tanzania	2007	2011	3.5	1.6	1.0	1.2	2.4	2.6
Thailand	2008	2012	4.8	3.9	5.2	6.2	12.5	14.5
Togo	2006	2011	−2.2	0.9	1.0	0.9	2.5	2.6
Tunisia	2005	2010	3.5	2.6	3.7	4.4	8.4	9.6
Turkey	2007	2012	4.3	4.8	5.4	6.7	12.9	16.3
Uganda	2009	2012	3.9	2.9	1.2	1.4	3.1	3.4
Ukraine	2008	2013	3.5	2.3	6.8	8.1	11.6	13.0
United Kingdom	2007	2012	−1.7	−2.8	23.9	22.0	51.1	44.4
United States	2007	2013	−0.2	−0.4				
Uruguay	2007	2012	7.9	4.3	6.0	8.8	18.6	23.0
Vietnam	2004	2010	6.2	7.8	2.1	3.1	5.0	7.9

a. For some countries means are not reported because of grouped or confidential data. b. Covers urban areas only. c. Based on 2005 purchasing power parity rates.

Shared prosperity

The World Bank Group released the Global Database of Shared Prosperity in October 2014, a year and half after announcing its new twin goals of ending extreme poverty and promoting shared prosperity around the world. The database was updated and expanded in October 2015 to include estimates for 94 countries, including high-income countries. The period of growth assessed was updated from around 2006–11 to around 2007–12 (World Bank 2015b).

Promoting shared prosperity is defined as fostering income growth of the bottom 40 percent of the welfare distribution in every country and is measured by calculating the annualized growth of mean per capita real income or consumption of the bottom 40 percent. The choice of the bottom 40 percent as the target population is one of practical compromise. The bottom 40 percent differs across countries depending on the welfare distribution, and it can change over time within a country. Because boosting shared prosperity is a country-specific goal, there is no numerical target defined globally. And at the country level the shared prosperity goal is unbounded (World Bank 2015a).

Improvements in shared prosperity require both a growing economy and a consideration of equity. Shared prosperity explicitly recognizes that while growth is necessary for improving economic welfare in a society, progress is measured by how those gains are shared with its poorest members. Moreover, in an inclusive society, it is not sufficient to raise everyone above an absolute minimum standard of living; economic growth must increase prosperity among poor people over time.

The decision to measure shared prosperity based on income or consumption was not taken to ignore the many other dimensions of welfare. It is motivated by the need for an indicator that is easy to understand, communicate, and measure—though measurement challenges exist. Indeed, shared prosperity comprises many dimensions of well-being of the less well-off, and when analyzing shared prosperity in the context of a country, it is important to consider a wide range of indicators of welfare.

To generate measures of shared prosperity that are reasonably comparable across countries, the World Bank Group has a standardized approach for choosing time periods, data sources, and other relevant parameters. The Global Database of Shared Prosperity is the result of these efforts. Its purpose is to allow for cross-country comparison and benchmarking, but users should consider alternative choices for surveys and time periods when cross-country comparison is not the primary consideration.

World Development Indicators includes the following shared prosperity indicators: survey mean per capita real income or consumption of the bottom 40 percent, survey mean per capita real income or consumption of the total population, annualized growth of survey mean per capita real income or consumption of the bottom 40 percent, and annualized growth of survey mean per capita real income or consumption of the total population. Related information, such as survey years defining the growth period and the type of welfare aggregate used to calculate the growth rates, are provided in the footnotes.

In the latest update of the database, survey means of income or consumption are updated with the 2011 purchasing power parity (PPP) rates for all countries except Bangladesh, Cambodia, Iraq, and Lao PDR, for which survey means are presented in 2005 PPP terms because price data, both consumer price indexes and 2011 PPPs, require further investigation.

The World Bank Group is committed to updating the shared prosperity indicators every year. Given that new household surveys are not available for every year for most countries, updated estimates will be reported for only a subset of countries each year.

Calculation of growth rates

Growth rates are calculated as annualized average growth rates over a roughly five-year period. Since many countries do not conduct surveys on a precise five-year schedule, the following rules guide selection of the survey years used to calculate the growth rates in the 2015 update: the final year of the growth period (T_1) is the most recent year of a survey but no earlier than 2010, and the initial year (T_0) is as close to $T_1 - 5$ as possible, within a two-year band. Thus the gap between initial and final survey years ranges from three to seven years. If two surveys are equidistant from $T_1 - 5$, other things being equal, the more recent survey year is selected as T_0. The comparability of welfare aggregates (income or consumption) for the years chosen for T_0 and T_1 is assessed for every country. If comparability across the two surveys is a major concern, the selection criteria are re-applied to select the next best survey year.

Once two surveys are selected for a country, the annualized growth of mean per capita real income or consumption is computed by first estimating the mean per capita real income or consumption of the bottom 40 percent of the welfare distribution in years T_0 and T_1 and then computing the annual average growth rate between those years using a compound growth formula. Growth of mean per capita real income or consumption of the total population is computed in the same way using data for the total population.

Data availability

This edition of World Development Indicators includes estimates of shared prosperity for 71 low- and middle-income countries and 23 high-income countries. While all countries are encouraged to estimate the annualized growth of mean per capita real income or consumption of the bottom 40 percent, the Global Database of Shared Prosperity includes only a subset of countries that meet certain criteria. The first important consideration is comparability across time and across countries. Household surveys are infrequent in most countries and are rarely aligned across countries in terms of timing. Consequently, comparisons across countries or over time should be made with a high degree of caution.

Lack of household survey data is even more problematic for monitoring shared prosperity than for monitoring poverty. To monitor shared prosperity, two surveys of a country have to be conducted within five years or so during a chosen period—in this case around 2007–12. They have to be reasonably comparable in both survey design and construction of the welfare aggregates. Thus, not every survey that can generate poverty estimates can generate shared prosperity estimates.

The second consideration is the coverage of countries, with data that are as recent as possible. Since shared prosperity must be estimated and used at the country level, there are good reasons for obtaining a wide coverage of countries, regardless of the size of their population. Moreover, for policy purposes it is important to have indicators for the most recent period possible for each country. The selection of survey years and countries needs to be made consistently and transparently, achieving a balance among matching the time period as closely as possible across all countries, including the most recent data, and ensuring the widest possible coverage of countries, across regions and income levels. In practice, this means that time periods will not match perfectly across countries. This is a compromise: While it introduces a degree of incomparability, it also creates a database that includes a larger set of countries than would be possible otherwise.

Data quality

Like poverty rates, estimates of annualized growth of mean per capita real income or consumption of the bottom 40 percent are based on income or consumption data collected in household surveys, and the same quality issues apply. See the discussion in the *Poverty rates* section.

Definitions

• **Period** is the period of reference of a survey. For surveys in which the period of reference covers multiple years, it is the first year.
• **Annualized growth in mean income or consumption per capita** is the annualized growth in mean per capita real income consumption from household surveys over a roughly five-year period. It is calculated for the bottom 40 percent of a country's population and for the total population of a country. • **Mean income or consumption per capita** is the mean income or consumption per capita from

household surveys used in calculating the welfare growth rate, expressed in PPP-adjusted dollars per day at 2011 prices. It is calculated for the bottom 40 percent of a country's population and for the total population of a country.

Data sources

The Global Database of Shared Prosperity was prepared by the Global Poverty Working Group, which comprises poverty measurement specialists of different departments of the World Bank Group. The database's primary source of data is the World Bank Group's PovcalNet database, an interactive computational tool that allows users to replicate the World Bank Group's official poverty estimates measured at international poverty lines ($1.90 or $3.10 per day per capita). The datasets included in PovcalNet are provided and reviewed by the members of the Global Poverty Working Group. The choice of consumption or income to measure shared prosperity for a country is consistent with the welfare aggregate used to estimate extreme poverty rates in PovcalNet, unless there are strong arguments for using a different welfare aggregate. The practice adopted by the World Bank Group for estimating global and regional poverty rates is, in principle, to use per capita consumption expenditure as the welfare measure wherever available and to use income as the welfare measure for countries for which consumption data are unavailable. However, in some cases data on consumption may be available but are outdated or not shared with the World Bank Group for recent survey years. In these cases, if data on income are available, income is used for estimating shared prosperity.

References

World Bank. 2015a. *A Measured Approach to Ending Poverty and Boosting Shared Prosperity: Concepts, Data, and the Twin Goals*. Policy Research Report. Washington, DC.

———. 2015b. Global Database of Shared Prosperity. [www.worldbank.org/en/topic/poverty/brief/global-database-of-shared-prosperity]. Washington, DC.

———. Various years. PovcalNet. [http://iresearch.worldbank.org/PovcalNet/]. Washington, DC.

PEOPLE

People presents indicators of education, health, jobs, social protection, and gender. Together with the indicators in *World view,* such as population, poverty, and shared prosperity, they provide a multidimensional portrait of the progress of societies across the world. As with the Millennium Development Goals, people is one of the key themes of the new Sustainable Development Goals.

Data for estimating the indicators in the *People* section have been collected and compiled by national authorities and various international development agencies, including the World Bank. In many cases, thematic interagency and expert collaboration helps ensure that estimates are robust, reliable, and timely.

For example, estimates of child mortality used to vary by data source and by methodology, making interpretation for global monitoring difficult. The United Nations Inter-agency Group for Child Mortality Estimation, established in 2004, has addressed this issue by compiling all available data, assessing data quality, and fitting an appropriate statistical model to generate a smooth trend curve. This effort has improved accuracy, transparency, and comparability of estimates of neonatal, infant, and under-five mortality rates that span more than 50 years. Similar interagency efforts have also improved maternal mortality estimates. For gender statistics the World Bank is helping develop methodologies to collect data on asset ownership and entrepreneurship. The World Bank also leads data collection efforts in such areas as financial inclusion and employment law and business regulations from a gender perspective.

Alongside interagency collaboration, a close working relationship with countries and national statistical offices and investment in improving national statistical capacity help advance data quality at both the national and subnational levels. The Sustainable Development Goals call for disaggregated indicators, and some estimates presented in *People* are now available by subnational location, including those for malnutrition, poverty, and population (see http://data.worldbank.org /wdi/sub-national). These data highlight disparities within countries, and *World Development Indicators* will continue to expand its subnational coverage, wherever data sources permit.

An important update this year is an adjustment to the international poverty line to reflect the new update to purchasing power parity rates from the 2011 round of the International Comparison Program. The international poverty line has been set at $1.90 a day per person in 2011 purchasing power parity (PPP) terms, replacing the previous line of $1.25 a day per person in 2005 PPP terms. The entire series of global poverty rates—from 1981 to 2012—has been revised based on these new data. For more information, see the *About the data* for poverty rates in *World view.* Other indicators have also been added this year, many of them related to the Sustainable Development Goals, including prevalence of anemia among all women of reproductive age, contraceptive prevalence (modern methods), share of deaths that are registered, demand for family planning satisfied by modern methods, share of the population practicing open defecation, prevalence of road traffic injuries, risk of catastrophic expenditure for surgical care, risk of impoverishing expenditure for surgical care, size of the specialist surgical workforce, number of surgical procedures performed, indicators of financial inclusion, prevalence of violence against women, prevalence of child marriage, prevalence of female genital mutilation or cutting, women's agency, and a wider range of education indicators.

The primary completion rate is the proportion of new entrants in the last grade of primary education among the total population at the entrance age for the last grade of primary education. The rate can exceed 100 percent because new entrants may include over-age and underage children. It reflects both the coverage of the education system and the educational attainment of students. Although the rate does not always ensure that expected learning outcomes occur, since some students finish school without acquiring adequate literacy and numeracy skills, it is a good indicator of the quality and efficiency of the school system. Worldwide, the primary completion rate reached 92 percent in 2013. However, progress has been stagnant in recent years, and there are large regional differences in achievement. Many children drop out of school before completion because of cost, distance, physical danger, and failure to advance.

Education for all

Primary completion rate, most recent year available during 2010–15 (% of relevant age group)

- 95 or more
- 85–94
- 70–84
- 50–69
- Less than 50
- No data

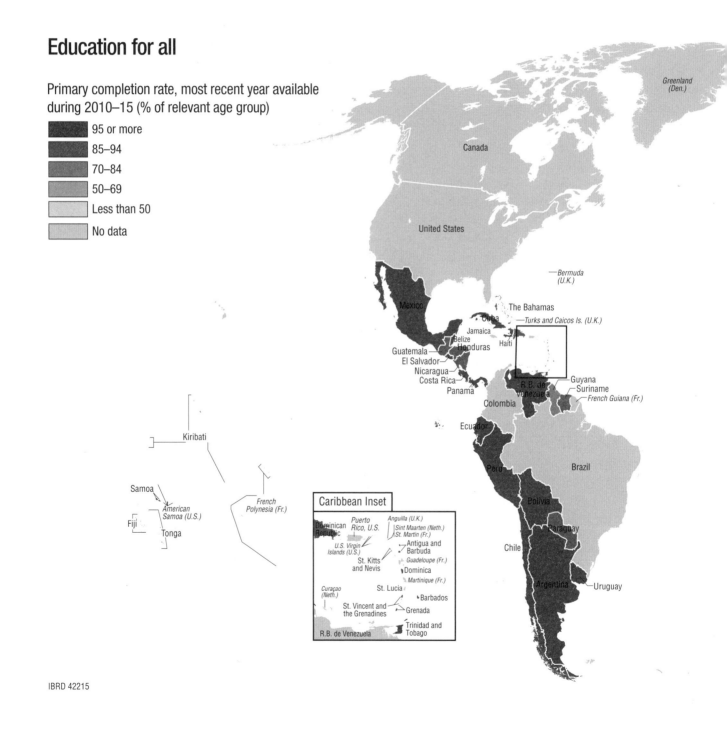

IBRD 42215

In the Middle East and North Africa the primary completion rate increased from 76 percent in 1990 to 94 percent in 2013.

Sub-Saharan Africa, which has the lowest primary completion rate, showed the most rapid progress during the past decade: The primary completion rate increased 15 percent, to 69 percent in 2013.

In Latin America and the Caribbean the primary completion rate reached 101 percent in 2013, and in East Asia and Pacific it reached 105 percent.

Over the past two decades three countries have quadrupled their primary completion rate: Benin (19 percent in 1990 to 76 percent in 2014), Ethiopia (14 percent in 1994 to 54 percent in 2014), and Bhutan (24 percent in 1993 to 97 percent in 2014).

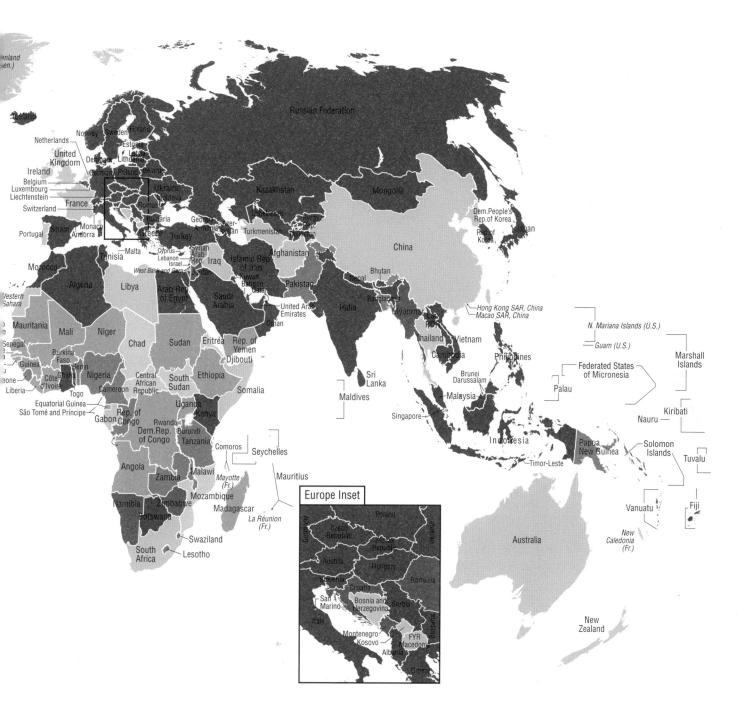

2 People

	Prevalence of child malnutrition, stunting % of children under age 5 2008–14[a]	Under-five mortality rate per 1,000 live births 2015	Maternal mortality ratio Modeled estimate per 100,000 live births 2015	Adolescent fertility rate births per 1,000 women ages 15–19 2014	Prevalence of HIV % of population ages 15–49 2014	Primary completion rate % of relevant age group 2010–14[a]	Youth literacy rate % of population ages 15–24 2005–14[a]	Labor force participation rate Modeled ILO estimate % of population ages 15 and older 2014	Vulnerable employment % of total employment 2010–14[a]	Unemployment Modeled ILO estimate % of total labor force 2014	Female legislators, senior officials, and managers % of total 2010–14[a]
Afghanistan	..	91	396	77	<0.1	..	47	48	..	9	..
Albania	23.1	14	29	21	..	108	99	55	58	16	..
Algeria	11.7	26	140	11	<0.1	109	..	44	27	10	11
American Samoa	..	..	..	..	..	..	..	..	..	..	..
Andorra	..	3	..	..	..	..	..	..	..	..	..
Angola	..	157	477	167	2.4	50	73	70	..	7	..
Antigua and Barbuda	..	8	..	46	..	102	..	..	..	..	..
Argentina	..	13	52	64	0.5	101	99	61	21	8	..
Armenia	20.8	14	25	24	0.2	..	100	64	42	17	..
Aruba	..	16	..	23	..	95	99	..	4	..	43
Australia	..	4	6	14	..	..	..	65	..	6	..
Austria	..	4	4	7	..	99	98	61	9	5	27
Azerbaijan	18.0	32	25	59	0.1	98	100	67	56	5	..
Bahamas, The	..	12	80	31	..	93	..	74	..	15	52
Bahrain	..	6	15	14	..	..	98	70	2	4	..
Bangladesh	36.1	38	176	83	<0.1	74	81	71	58	4	5
Barbados	7.7	13	27	42	..	96	..	71	..	12	48
Belarus	..	5	4	19	0.5	98	100	56	..	6	..
Belgium	..	4	7	8	..	90	..	53	11	9	30
Belize	19.3	17	28	67	1.2	102	..	66	..	12	..
Benin	34.0	100	405	85	1.1	76	..	73	88	1	..
Bermuda	..	..	..	..	..	79	..	..	8	..	44
Bhutan	33.6	33	148	23	..	97	..	73	53	3	17
Bolivia	27.2	38	206	71	0.3	96	99	73	54	3	..
Bosnia and Herzegovina	8.9	5	11	9	..	..	100	45	25	28	..
Botswana	..	44	129	34	25.2	100	98	77	13	18	39
Brazil	..	16	44	67	..	..	99	70	23	7	37
Brunei Darussalam	19.7	10	23	21	..	101	99	64	..	4	34
Bulgaria	..	10	11	39	..	99	98	53	9	12	37
Burkina Faso	35.1	89	371	110	0.9	61	..	83	..	3	..
Burundi	57.5	82	712	29	1.1	67	89	83	94	7	..
Cabo Verde	..	25	42	74	1.1	100	98	68	..	9	..
Cambodia	32.4	29	161	51	0.6	96	87	83	64	0	..
Cameroon	32.6	88	596	107	4.8	72	81	70	74	4	..
Canada	..	5	7	10	..	..	..	66	..	7	36
Cayman Islands	..	..	..	..	..	..	..	..	4	..	..
Central African Republic	40.7	130	882	93	4.3	44	36	79	..	7	..
Chad	38.7	139	856	137	2.5	38	50	72	..	7	..
Channel Islands	..	9	..	7	..	..	..	59	..	..	..
Chile	1.8	8	22	48	0.3	97	99	62	..	6	..
China	9.4	11	27	7	..	..	100	71	..	5	..
Hong Kong SAR, China	..	2	..	3	..	99	..	59	7	3	32
Macao SAR, China	..	4	..	3	..	..	100	72	4	2	32
Colombia	12.7	16	64	52	0.4	..	98	68	48	10	53
Comoros	32.1	74	335	70	..	74	87	58	..	7	..
Congo, Dem. Rep.	42.6	98	693	123	1.0	67	84	72	..	8	..
Congo, Rep.	25.0	45	442	119	2.8	74	81	71	..	7	..

	Prevalence of child malnutrition, stunting	Under-five mortality rate	Maternal mortality ratio	Adolescent fertility rate	Prevalence of HIV	Primary completion rate	Youth literacy rate	Labor force participation rate	Vulnerable employment	Unemployment	Female legislators, senior officials, and managers
			Modeled estimate	births per 1,000			% of population	Modeled ILO estimate		Modeled	
				women ages	% of		ages	% of population		ILO estimate	
	% of children under age 5	per 1,000 live births	per 100,000 live births	15–19	population ages 15–49	% of relevant age group	15–24	ages 15 and older	% of total employment	% of total labor force	% of total
	2008–14[a]	2015	2015	2014	2014	2010–14[a]	2005–14[a]	2014	2010–14[a]	2014	2010–14[a]
Costa Rica	5.6	10	25	57	0.3	99	99	63	21	8	35
Côte d'Ivoire	29.6	93	645	135	3.5	57	48	67	79	4	..
Croatia	..	4	8	10	..	92	100	51	10	17	25
Cuba	..	6	39	46	0.3	98	100	57	..	3	..
Curaçao	..	11	..	34	..	..	..	..	..	..	..
Cyprus	..	3	7	5	..	100	100	64	14	16	14
Czech Republic	..	3	4	10	..	100	..	60	15	6	26
Denmark	..	4	6	4	0.2	99	..	62	5	7	28
Djibouti	33.5	65	229	22	1.6	64[b]	..	52	..	..	..
Dominica	..	21	..	..	..	107	..	..	..	..	..
Dominican Republic	7.1	31	92	98	1.0	91	97	65	42	15	37
Ecuador	25.2	22	64	76	0.3	113	99	69	39	5	40
Egypt, Arab Rep.	22.3	24	33	52	<0.1	104	92	49	26	13	7
El Salvador	20.6	17	54	66	0.5	107	97	62	38	6	37
Equatorial Guinea	26.2	94	342	110	6.2	51	98	87	..	8	..
Eritrea	50.3	47	501	56	0.7	37	92	85	..	7	..
Estonia	..	3	9	14	..	107	100	62	6	8	36
Ethiopia	40.4	59	353	60	1.2	54	..	84	89	5	22
Faroe Islands	..	..	..	..	..	..	..	..	..	..	..
Fiji	..	22	30	44	0.1	103	..	55	..	8	..
Finland	..	2	3	7	..	99	..	59	10	9	32
France	..	4	8	9	..	..	..	56	7	10	39
French Polynesia	..	6	..	36	..	..	..	56	..	..	..
Gabon	17.5	51	291	102	3.9	..	89	61	31	20	..
Gambia, The	25.0	69	706	114	1.8	67	71	77	61	7	..
Georgia	11.3	12	36	41	0.3	116	100	65	60	13	..
Germany	..	4	6	7	..	101	..	60	6	5	30
Ghana	18.8	62	319	68	1.5	101[b]	86	70	77	2	..
Greece	..	5	3	8	..	97	99	53	30	26	23
Greenland	..	..	..	..	..	..	..	..	..	..	..
Grenada	..	12	27	31	..	95	..	..	..	..	..
Guam	..	10	..	49	..	..	..	63	..	..	..
Guatemala	48.0	29	88	81	0.5	87	92	68	45	3	..
Guinea	35.8	94	679	142	1.6	50	31	72	90	2	..
Guinea-Bissau	27.6	93	549	91	3.7	62	75	73	..	7	..
Guyana	12.0	39	229	88	1.8	84	93	61	..	11	..
Haiti	21.9	69	359	40	1.9	108	..	66	..	7	..
Honduras	22.7	20	129	66	0.4	91	96	63	53	4	..
Hungary	..	6	17	18	..	99	99	52	6	8	40
Iceland	..	2	3	6	..	97	..	74	9	5	40
India	..	48	174	26	..	96	86	54	81	4	14
Indonesia	36.4	27	126	50	0.5	101	99	68	33	6	23
Iran, Islamic Rep.	..	16	25	27	0.1	102	98	45	41	13	..
Iraq	22.6	32	50	83	..	..	82	42	..	16	..
Ireland	..	4	8	11	0.3	..	..	60	13	12	33
Isle of Man	..	..	..	..	..	..	..	..	..	..	..
Israel	..	4	5	10	..	102	..	63	..	6	..

2 People

	Prevalence of child malnutrition, stunting % of children under age 5 2008–14ᵃ	Under-five mortality rate per 1,000 live births 2015	Maternal mortality ratio Modeled estimate per 100,000 live births 2015	Adolescent fertility rate births per 1,000 women ages 15–19 2014	Prevalence of HIV % of population ages 15–49 2014	Primary completion rate % of relevant age group 2010–14ᵃ	Youth literacy rate % of population ages 15–24 2005–14ᵃ	Labor force participation rate Modeled ILO estimate % of population ages 15 and older 2014	Vulnerable employment % of total employment 2010–14ᵃ	Unemployment Modeled ILO estimate % of total labor force 2014	Female legislators, senior officials, and managers % of total 2010–14ᵃ
Italy	..	4	4	6	..	100	100	49	18	13	25
Jamaica	5.7	16	89	61	1.6	..	96	63	38	13	..
Japan	7.1	3	5	4	..	102	..	59	..	4	..
Jordan	7.8	18	58	24	..	86	99	42	10	11	..
Kazakhstan	13.1	14	12	29	0.2	113ᵇ	100	73	29	4	..
Kenya	26.0	49	510	92	5.3	104	..	67	..	9	..
Kiribati	..	56	90	18	..	112	..	..	53	..	36
Korea, Dem. People's Rep.	27.9	25	82	1	..	..	100	78	..	4	..
Korea, Rep.	2.5	3	11	2	..	103	..	61	..	4	..
Kosovo	..	..	..	..	..	..	..	..	17	..	15
Kuwait	5.8	9	4	10	..	103	99	69	2	3	..
Kyrgyz Republic	12.9	21	76	40	0.3	105	100	68	42	8	..
Lao PDR	43.8	67	197	65	0.3	100	..	78	84	1	..
Latvia	..	8	18	14	..	111	100	61	8	10	45
Lebanon	..	8	15	13	<0.1	78	..	48	..	6	..
Lesotho	33.2	90	487	92	23.4	76	83	66	..	26	..
Liberia	32.1	70	725	111	1.2	59	..	62	79	4	..
Libya	..	13	9	6	..	..	100	53	..	19	..
Liechtenstein	..	..	..	..	..	102ᵇ	..	..	..	..	..
Lithuania	..	5	10	12	..	97	100	61	10	11	38
Luxembourg	..	2	10	6	..	82	..	57	6	6	24
Macedonia, FYR	4.9	6	8	18	..	..	99	55	23	28	28
Madagascar	49.2	50	353	117	0.3	69	65	88	86	4	25
Malawi	42.4	64	634	137	10.0	79	72	83	..	8	..
Malaysia	..	7	40	13	0.5	103	98	60	21	2	25
Maldives	20.3	9	68	7	..	..	..	67	19	12	..
Mali	..	115	587	175	1.4	53	47	66	..	8	..
Malta	..	6	9	17	..	92	99	52	9	6	23
Marshall Islands	..	36	..	..	..	100	..	..	..	..	..
Mauritania	22.0	85	602	79	0.7	68	..	54	..	31	..
Mauritius	..	14	53	29	0.9	97	98	59	17	8	..
Mexico	13.6	13	38	63	0.2	103	99	62	..	5	..
Micronesia, Fed. Sts.	..	35	100	16	..	..	..	..	..	..	..
Moldova	6.4	16	23	23	0.6	93	100	41	32	3	44
Monaco	..	4	..	..	..	..	..	..	..	..	..
Mongolia	10.8	22	44	16	..	110	98	63	51	5	..
Montenegro	9.4	5	7	12	..	93ᵇ	99	50	..	19	30
Morocco	14.9	28	121	32	0.1	102	82	51	51	10	..
Mozambique	43.1	79	489	143	10.6	48	67	84	..	23	..
Myanmar	35.1	50	178	17	0.7	85	96	79	..	3	..
Namibia	23.1	45	265	77	16.0	86	..	60	8	19	43
Nepal	40.5	36	258	73	0.2	106ᵇ	85	83	..	3	..
Netherlands	..	4	7	4	..	..	..	64	13	7	30
New Caledonia	..	13	..	19	..	..	100	57	..	..	..
New Zealand	..	6	11	24	..	..	..	68	..	6	..
Nicaragua	..	22	150	90	0.3	85	..	64	47	5	..
Niger	43.0	96	553	204	0.5	59	24	65	..	5	..

Front | User guide | World view | People | Environment

	Prevalence of child malnutrition, stunting	Under-five mortality rate	Maternal mortality ratio	Adolescent fertility rate	Prevalence of HIV	Primary completion rate	Youth literacy rate	Labor force participation rate	Vulnerable employment	Unemployment	Female legislators, senior officials, and managers
			Modeled estimate	births per 1,000			% of population ages 15–24	Modeled ILO estimate % of population ages 15 and older		Modeled ILO estimate	
	% of children under age 5	per 1,000 live births	per 100,000 live births	women ages 15–19	% of population ages 15–49	% of relevant age group			% of total employment	% of total labor force	% of total
	2008–14[a]	2015	2015	2014	2014	2010–14[a]	2005–14[a]	2014	2010–14[a]	2014	2010–14[a]
Nigeria	32.9	109	814	112	3.2	76	66	56	..	8	..
Northern Mariana Islands	..	..	..	..	..	..	..	..	..	..	..
Norway	..	3	5	6	0.2	101	..	65	5	3	31
Oman	9.8	12	17	9	0.2	109	99	66	..	7	..
Pakistan	45.0	81	178	39	<0.1	74	73	55	..	5	..
Palau	..	16	..	..	..	96	100	..	..	..	..
Panama	19.1	17	94	75	0.6	102	98	66	30	4	46
Papua New Guinea	49.5	57	215	55	0.7	79	72	72	..	3	..
Paraguay	10.9	21	132	58	0.4	89	99	70	38	5	34
Peru	18.4	17	68	50	0.4	96	99	76	46	4	30
Philippines	33.6	28	114	61	<0.1	101	98	65	38	7	..
Poland	..	5	3	14	<0.1	98	100	57	17	9	38
Portugal	..	4	10	10	..	..	99	60	15	14	33
Puerto Rico	..	6	14	43	..	..	99	43	..	14	..
Qatar	..	8	13	11	..	94	99	87	0	0	12
Romania	..	11	31	35	..	94	99	57	31	7	31
Russian Federation	..	10	25	24	..	101	100	64	6	5	38
Rwanda	44.3	42	290	27	2.8	67	82	86	78	1	..
Samoa	..	18	51	26	..	100	99	42	31	..	36
San Marino	..	3	..	..	..	95	..	..	..	..	..
São Tomé and Príncipe	31.6	47	156	85	0.8	92[b]	80	61	..	..	24
Saudi Arabia	..	15	12	9	..	111	99	55	..	6	7
Senegal	19.4	47	315	80	0.5	59	56	77	58	10	..
Serbia	6.0	7	17	19	..	102	99	53	29	22	33
Seychelles	7.9	14	..	58	..	112	99	..	10	..	..
Sierra Leone	37.9	120	1,360	120	1.4	70	64	67	..	3	..
Singapore	..	3	10	4	..	..	100	68	9	3	34
Sint Maarten	..	..	..	..	..	..	..	..	..	..	..
Slovak Republic	..	7	6	20	<0.1	96	..	60	12	13	31
Slovenia	..	3	9	4	<0.1	98	100	58	15	10	38
Solomon Islands	..	28	114	49	..	87	..	66	..	4	..
Somalia	25.3	137	732	105	0.5	..	..	56	..	7	..
South Africa	23.9	41	138	47	18.9	..	99	53	9	25	31
South Sudan	31.1	93	789	68	2.7	37	37	..	..	..	..
Spain	..	4	5	9	..	100	100	59	13	25	30
Sri Lanka	14.7	10	30	15	<0.1	98	98	55	43	5	28
St. Kitts and Nevis	..	11	..	..	..	82	..	..	..	..	..
St. Lucia	2.5	14	48	54	..	..	..	69	..	..	..
St. Martin	..	..	..	..	..	..	..	..	..	..	..
St. Vincent & the Grenadines	..	18	45	52	..	101	..	67	..	..	..
Sudan	38.2	70	311	76	0.2	56	88	54	..	15	..
Suriname	8.8	21	155	47	1.0	94	98	55	13	6	36
Swaziland	31.0	61	389	74	27.7	79	94	58	..	22	..
Sweden	..	3	4	6	0.2	102	..	64	7	8	35
Switzerland	..	4	5	3	..	97	..	68	9	5	33
Syrian Arab Republic	27.5	13	68	40	<0.1	69	96	44	33	11	9
Tajikistan	26.8	45	32	38	0.4	100[b]	100	68	..	11	..

	Prevalence of child malnutrition, stunting % of children under age 5 2008–14ᵃ	Under-five mortality rate per 1,000 live births 2015	Maternal mortality ratio Modeled estimate per 100,000 live births 2015	Adolescent fertility rate births per 1,000 women ages 15–19 2014	Prevalence of HIV % of population ages 15–49 2014	Primary completion rate % of relevant age group 2010–14ᵃ	Youth literacy rate % of population ages 15–24 2005–14ᵃ	Labor force participation rate Modeled ILO estimate % of population ages 15 and older 2014	Vulnerable employment % of total employment 2010–14ᵃ	Unemployment Modeled ILO estimate % of total labor force 2014	Female legislators, senior officials, and managers % of total 2010–14ᵃ
Tanzania	34.8	49	398	119	5.3	74	86	89	74	3	..
Thailand	16.3	12	20	45	1.1	..	97	72	56	1	25
Timor-Leste	57.7	53	215	48	..	98	80	38	70	5	10
Togo	27.5	78	368	92	2.4	85	80	81	..	7	..
Tonga	8.1	17	124	15	..	111	99	64	..	..	..
Trinidad and Tobago	..	20	63	32	..	95	100	64	16	4	..
Tunisia	10.1	14	62	7	<0.1	97	97	48	22	13	..
Turkey	9.5	14	16	28	..	100	99	49	29	9	10
Turkmenistan	..	51	42	17	..	..	100	62	..	11	..
Turks and Caicos Islands	..	..	..	..	..	..	..	..	..	..	..
Tuvalu	..	27	..	..	..	93	..	..	..	..	..
Uganda	33.7	55	343	115	7.3	56	84	77	79	4	..
Ukraine	..	9	24	25	1.2	110	100	60	18	8	38
United Arab Emirates	..	7	6	29	..	103	..	81	..	4	..
United Kingdom	..	4	9	15	..	..	..	62	13	6	34
United States	2.1	7	14	24	..	..	..	62	..	6	43
Uruguay	11.7	10	15	57	0.7	104	99	66	23	7	44
Uzbekistan	..	39	36	18	0.2	96	100	62	..	11	..
Vanuatu	28.5	28	78	43	..	94	95	71	..	..	..
Venezuela, RB	13.4	15	95	80	0.6	96	98	65	30	9	..
Vietnam	19.4	22	54	38	0.5	106	97	78	63	2	..
Virgin Islands (U.S.)	..	10	..	44	..	..	..	62	..	..	..
West Bank and Gaza	7.4	21	45	59	..	97	99	41	26	26	..
Yemen, Rep.	46.8	42	385	62	<0.1	69	88	49	30	17	5
Zambia	40.0	64	224	93	12.4	81	..	79	79	13	..
Zimbabwe	27.6	71	443	110	16.7	89	91	87	66	5	..
World	**23.8 w**	**43 w**	**216 w**	**45 w**	**0.8 w**	**92 w**	**91 w**	**63 w**	**.. w**	**6 w**	**..**
East Asia & Pacific	11.3ᶜ	17	59	21	..	105	99	70	..	5	..
Europe & Central Asia	10.0ᶜ	11	16	18	..	98	100	59	14	9	..
Latin America & Caribbean	10.7ᶜ	18	67	65	..	101	98	66	32	7	..
Middle East & North Africa	17.2ᶜ	23	81	39	0.1	94	93	49	31	11	..
North America	..	6	13	23	..	..	..	63	..	6	..
South Asia	37.2	53	182	35	..	91	83	56	77	4	..
Sub-Saharan Africa	35.7ᶜ	83	547	103	4.5	69	71	70	..	8	..
Low income	37.6	76	495	98	2.9	71	68	78	..	6	..
Lower middle income	33.5	53	253	47	..	91	86	59	66	5	..
Upper middle income	7.5	19	55	31	..	103	99	67	..	6	..
High income	3.3	7	17	20	..	99	100	61	..	7	..

a. Data are for the most recent year available during the period specified. b. Data are for 2015. c. Excludes high-income countries.

About the data

Though not included in the table due to space limitations, many indicators in this section are available disaggregated by sex, place of residence, wealth, and age in the World Development Indicators database.

Child malnutrition

Good nutrition is the cornerstone for survival, health, and development. Well-nourished children perform better in school, grow into healthy adults, and in turn give their children a better start in life. Well-nourished women face fewer risks during pregnancy and childbirth, and their children set off on firmer developmental paths, both physically and mentally. Undernourished children have lower resistance to infection and are more likely to die from common childhood ailments such as diarrheal diseases and respiratory infections. Frequent illness saps the nutritional status of those who survive, locking them into a vicious cycle of recurring sickness and faltering growth.

With underweight children (low weight for age) a less prominent problem today than in the Millennium Development Goals era, both the World Health Assembly's Global Nutrition Targets 2025 and the Sustainable Development Goals have shifted focus to stunting (low height for age), wasting (low weight for height), and overweight (high weight for height) in children under age 5. Estimates of wasting and severe wasting can show large fluctuations across surveys within countries. Better estimates would be based on annual incidence, but such data do not exist at national or regional level. Estimates of stunting are more stable, and thus reliable trends can be derived. Childhood stunting is a largely irreversible outcome of inadequate nutrition and repeated bouts of infection during the first 1,000 days of a child's life. Stunting has long-term effects on individuals and societies, including diminished cognitive and physical development, reduced productive capacity and poor health, and increased risk of degenerative diseases such as diabetes.

Under-five mortality

Mortality rates for children and others are important indicators of health status. When data on the incidence and prevalence of diseases are unavailable, mortality rates may be used to identify vulnerable populations. And they are among the indicators most frequently used to compare socioeconomic development across countries.

The main sources of mortality data are vital registration systems and direct or indirect estimates based on sample surveys or censuses. A complete vital registration system—covering at least 90 percent of vital events in the population—is the best source of age-specific mortality data. But complete vital registration systems are fairly uncommon in low- and middle-income countries. Thus estimates must be obtained from sample surveys or derived by applying indirect estimation techniques to registration, census, or survey data (see *Sources and methods*). Survey data are subject to recall error.

To make estimates comparable and to ensure consistency across estimates by different agencies, the UN Inter-agency Group for Child Mortality Estimation, which comprises UNICEF, the WHO, the United Nations Population Division, the World Bank, and other universities and research institutes, has developed and adopted a statistical method that uses all available information to reconcile differences. Trend lines are obtained by fitting a country-specific regression model of mortality rates against their reference dates. (For further discussion of childhood mortality estimates, see UN Inter-agency Group for Child Mortality Estimation [2015]; for detailed background data and for a graphic presentation, see www.childmortality.org).

Maternal mortality

Measurements of maternal mortality are subject to many types of errors. In countries with incomplete vital registration systems, deaths of women of reproductive age or their pregnancy status may not be reported, or the cause of death may not be known. Even in high-income countries with reliable vital registration systems, misclassification of maternal deaths has been found to lead to serious underestimation. Surveys and censuses can be used to measure maternal mortality by asking respondents about survivorship of sisters. But these estimates are retrospective, referring to a period approximately five years before the survey, and may be affected by recall error. Further, they reflect pregnancy-related deaths (deaths while pregnant or within 42 days of pregnancy termination, irrespective of the cause of death) and need to be adjusted to conform to the strict definition of maternal death.

Maternal mortality ratios in the table are modeled estimates based on work by the WHO, UNICEF, the United Nations Population Fund (UNFPA), the World Bank, and the United Nations Population Division, and include country-level time series data. For countries without complete registration data but with other types of data and for countries with no data, maternal mortality is estimated with a multilevel regression model using available national maternal mortality data and socioeconomic information, including fertility, birth attendants, and gross domestic product. The methodology differs from that used for previous estimates, so data presented here should not be compared across editions (WHO and others 2015).

Adolescent fertility

Reproductive health is a state of physical and mental well-being in relation to the reproductive system and its functions and processes. Means of achieving reproductive health include education and services during pregnancy and childbirth, safe and effective contraception, and prevention and treatment of sexually transmitted diseases. Complications of pregnancy and childbirth are the leading cause of death and disability among women of reproductive age in low- and middle-income countries.

Adolescent pregnancies are high risk for both mother and child. They are more likely to result in premature delivery, low birthweight, delivery complications, and death. Many adolescent pregnancies are unintended, but young girls may continue their pregnancies, giving up opportunities for education and employment, or seek unsafe

2 People

abortions. Estimates of adolescent fertility rates are based on vital registration systems or, in their absence, censuses or sample surveys and are generally considered reliable measures of fertility in the recent past. Where no empirical information on age-specific fertility rates is available, a model is used to estimate the share of births to adolescents. For countries without vital registration systems fertility rates are generally based on extrapolations from trends observed in censuses or surveys from earlier years.

Prevalence of HIV

HIV prevalence rates reflect the rate of HIV infection in each country's population. Low national prevalence rates can be misleading, however. They often disguise epidemics that are initially concentrated in certain localities or population groups and threaten to spill over into the wider population. In many low- and middle-income countries most new infections occur in young adults, with young women especially vulnerable.

Data on HIV prevalence are from the Joint United Nations Programme on HIV/AIDS. Changes in procedures and assumptions for estimating the data and better coordination with countries have resulted in improved estimates. The models, which are updated annually, track the course of HIV epidemics and their impacts, making full use of information on HIV prevalence trends from surveillance data as well as survey data. The models take into account reduced infectivity among people receiving antiretroviral therapy (which is having a larger impact on HIV prevalence and allowing HIV-positive people to live longer) and allow for changes in urbanization over time in generalized epidemics (important because prevalence is higher in urban areas and because many countries have seen rapid urbanization over the past two decades). The estimates include plausibility bounds, available at http://data.worldbank.org, which reflect the certainty associated with each of the estimates.

Primary completion

Many governments publish statistics that indicate how their education systems are working and developing—statistics on enrollment, graduates, financial and human resources, and efficiency indicators such as repetition rates, pupil–teacher ratios, and cohort progression. Primary completion, measured by the gross intake ratio to last grade of primary education, is a core indicator of an education system's performance. It reflects an education system's coverage and the educational attainment of students.

The indicator reflects the primary cycle, which typically lasts six years (with a range of four to seven years), as defined by the International Standard Classification of Education (ISCED2011). It is a proxy that should be taken as an upper estimate of the actual primary completion rate, since data limitations preclude adjusting for students who drop out during the final year of primary education.

There are many reasons why the primary completion rate may exceed 100 percent. The numerator may include late entrants and overage children who have repeated one or more grades of primary education as well as children who entered school early, while the denominator is the number of children at the entrance age for the last grade of primary education.

Youth literacy

The youth literacy rate for ages 15–24 is a standard measure of recent progress in student achievement. It reflects the accumulated outcomes of primary and secondary education by indicating the proportion of the population that has acquired basic literacy and numeracy skills over the previous 10 years or so.

Conventional literacy statistics that divide the population into two groups—literate and illiterate—are widely available and useful for tracking global progress toward universal literacy. In practice, however, literacy is difficult to measure. Estimating literacy rates requires census or survey measurements under controlled conditions. Many countries report the number of literate or illiterate people from self-reported data. Some use educational attainment data as a proxy but apply different lengths of school attendance or levels of completion. And there is a trend among recent national and international surveys toward using a direct reading test of literacy skills. Because definitions and methods of data collection differ across countries, data should be used cautiously. Generally, literacy encompasses numeracy, the ability to make simple arithmetic calculations.

Data on youth literacy are compiled by the United Nations Educational, Scientific and Cultural Organization (UNESCO) Institute for Statistics based on national censuses and household surveys and, for countries without recent literacy data, using the Global Age-Specific Literacy Projection Model. For detailed information, see www.uis.unesco.org.

Labor force participation

The labor force is the supply of labor available for producing goods and services in an economy. It includes people who are currently employed, people who are unemployed but seeking work, and first-time job-seekers. Not everyone who works is included, however. There are variations in the treatment of contributing family workers and unemployed and not looking for work by country, and some countries do not count members of the armed forces. Labor force size tends to vary during the year as seasonal workers enter and leave.

Data on the labor force are compiled by the International Labour Organization (ILO) from labor force surveys, censuses, and establishment censuses and surveys and from administrative records such as employment exchange registers and unemployment insurance schemes. Labor force surveys are the most comprehensive source for internationally comparable labor force data. Labor force data from population censuses are often based on a limited number of questions on the economic characteristics of individuals, with little scope to probe. Establishment censuses and surveys provide data on the employed population only, not unemployed workers, workers in small establishments, or workers in the informal sector.

 Front | User guide | World view | People | Environment

Besides the data sources, there are other important factors that affect data comparability, such as census or survey reference period, definitions, and geographic coverage.

The labor force participation rates in the table are modeled estimates from the ILO's Key Indicators of the Labour Market, 9th edition, database. These harmonized estimates use strict data selection criteria and enhanced methods to ensure comparability across countries and over time to avoid the inconsistencies mentioned above. Estimates are based mainly on labor force surveys, with other sources (population censuses and nationally reported estimates) used only when no survey data are available. National estimates of labor force participation rates are available in the World Development Indicators online database.

Vulnerable employment

The proportion of contributing family workers and own-account workers in total employment is derived from information on status in employment. Each group faces different economic risks, and contributing family workers and own-account workers are the most vulnerable—and therefore the most likely to fall into poverty. They are the least likely to have formal work arrangements, are the least likely to have social protection and safety nets to guard against economic shocks, and are often incapable of generating enough savings to offset these shocks. A high proportion of contributing family workers in a country indicates weak development, little job growth, and often a large rural economy.

Data on vulnerable employment are drawn from labor force and general household surveys, censuses, and official estimates. Besides the limitation mentioned for calculating labor force participation rates, there are other reasons to limit comparability. For example, covering only civilian employment can result in an underestimation of "employees" and "workers not classified by status," especially in countries with large armed forces. While the categories of contributing family workers and own-account workers would not be affected, their relative shares would be.

Unemployment

The ILO defines the unemployed as members of the working-age population who are without work but available for and seeking work, including people who have lost their jobs or who have voluntarily left work. Some unemployment is unavoidable. At any time some workers are temporarily unemployed—between jobs as employers look for the right workers and workers search for better jobs. Such unemployment, often called frictional unemployment, results from the normal operation of labor markets.

Changes in unemployment over time may reflect changes in the demand for and supply of labor, but they may also reflect changes in reporting practices. In countries without unemployment or welfare benefits people eke out a living in the informal economy or in informal work arrangements. In countries with well developed safety nets workers can afford to wait for suitable or desirable jobs. But high and sustained unemployment indicates serious inefficiencies in resource allocation.

The criteria for people considered to be seeking work, and the treatment of people temporarily laid off or seeking work for the first time, vary across countries. In many cases it is especially difficult to measure employment and unemployment in agriculture. The timing of a survey can maximize the effects of seasonal unemployment in agriculture. And informal sector employment is difficult to quantify where informal activities are not tracked.

Data on unemployment are drawn from labor force surveys and general household surveys, censuses, and official estimates. Administrative records, such as social insurance statistics and employment office statistics, are also included but limited to registered unemployment only.

Women tend to be excluded from the unemployment count for various reasons. Women suffer more from discrimination and from structural, social, and cultural barriers that impede them from seeking work. Also, women are often responsible for the care of children and the elderly and for household affairs. They may not be available for work during the short reference period, as they need to make arrangements before starting work. Further, women are considered to be employed when they are working part-time or in temporary jobs, despite the instability of these jobs or their active search for more secure employment.

The unemployment rates in the table are modeled estimates from the ILO's Key Indicators of the Labour Market, 9th edition, database. National estimates of unemployment are available in the World Development Indicators online database.

Female legislators, senior officials, and managers

Despite much progress in recent decades, gender inequalities remain pervasive in many dimensions of life. While gender inequalities exist throughout the world, they are most prevalent in low-income countries. Inequalities in the allocation of education, health care, nutrition, and political voice matter because of their strong association with well-being, productivity, and economic growth. These patterns of inequality begin at an early age, with boys usually receiving a larger share of education and health spending than girls, for example. The share of women in high-skilled occupations such as legislators, senior officials, and managers indicates women's status and role in the labor force and society at large. Women are vastly underrepresented in decision-making positions in government, although there is some evidence of recent improvement.

Data on female legislators, senior officials, and managers are based on the employment by occupation estimates, classified according to the International Standard Classification of Occupations 1988. Data are drawn mostly from labor force surveys, supplemented in limited cases with other household surveys, population censuses, and official estimates. Countries could apply different practice whether or where the armed forces are included. Armed forces constitute a separate major group, but in some countries they are included in the most closely matching civilian occupation or in nonclassifiable workers. For country-level information on classification, source, reference period, or definition, consult the footnotes in the World Development Indicators database or the ILO's Key Indicators of the Labour Market, 9th edition, database.

Definitions

• **Prevalence of child malnutrition, stunting** is the percentage of children under age 5 whose height for age is more than two standard deviations below the median for the international reference population ages 0–59 months. Data are based on the WHO child growth standards released in 2006. • **Under-five mortality rate** is the probability of a child born in a specific year dying before reaching age 5, if subject to the age-specific mortality rates of that year. The probability is expressed as a rate per 1,000 live births. • **Maternal mortality ratio,** modeled estimate, is the number of women who die from pregnancy-related causes while pregnant or within 42 days of pregnancy termination, per 100,000 live births. • **Adolescent fertility rate** is the number of births per 1,000 women ages 15–19. • **Prevalence of HIV** is the percentage of people ages 15–49 who are infected with HIV. • **Primary completion rate,** or gross intake ratio to the last grade of primary education, is the number of new entrants (enrollments minus repeaters) in the last grade of primary education, regardless of age, divided by the population at the entrance age for the last grade of primary education. Data limitations preclude adjusting for students who drop out during the final year of primary education. • **Youth literacy rate** is the percentage of people ages 15–24 who can both read and write with understanding a short simple statement about their everyday life. • **Labor force participation rate** is the proportion of the population ages 15 and older that engages actively in the labor market, by either working or looking for work during a reference period. Data are modeled ILO estimates. • **Vulnerable employment** is contributing family workers and own-account workers as a percentage of total employment. • **Unemployment** is the share of the labor force without work but available for and seeking employment. Definitions of labor force and unemployment may differ by country. Data are modeled ILO estimates. • **Female legislators, senior officials, and managers** are the percentage of legislators, senior officials, and managers (International Standard Classification of Occupations–88 category 1) who are female.

Data sources

Data on prevalence of stunting are from the WHO's Global Database on Child Growth and Malnutrition (www.who.int/nutgrowthdb). Data on under-five mortality rates are from the UN Inter-agency Group for Child Mortality Estimation (www.childmortality.org) and are based mainly on household surveys, censuses, and vital registration data. Modeled estimates of maternal mortality ratios are from the UN Maternal Mortality Estimation Inter-agency Group (www.who.int/reproductivehealth/publications/monitoring/maternal-mortality-2015/). Data on adolescent fertility rates are from United Nations Population Division (2015), with annual data linearly interpolated by the World Bank's Development Data Group. Data on HIV prevalence are from UNAIDS (2015). Data on primary completion rates and youth literacy rates are from the UNESCO Institute for Statistics (www.uis.unesco.org). Data on labor force participation rates, vulnerable employment, unemployment, and female legislators, senior officials, and managers are from the ILO's Key Indicators of the Labour Market, 9th edition, database.

References

ILO (International Labour Organization). Various years. *Key Indicators of the Labour Market.* Geneva: International Labour Office.

UNAIDS (Joint United Nations Programme on HIV/AIDS). 2015. *How AIDS Changed Everything.* [www.unaids.org/en/resources/documents/2015/MDG6_15years-15lessonsfromtheAIDSresponse]. Geneva.

UNICEF (United Nations Children's Fund), WHO (World Health Organization), and the World Bank. 2015. *Joint Child Malnutrition Estimates—Levels and Trends (2015 Edition).* [www.who.int/nutgrowthdb/estimates2014/]. New York: UNICEF.

UN Inter-agency Group for Child Mortality Estimation. 2015. *Levels and Trends in Child Mortality: Report 2015.* [http://childmortality.org/files_v20/download/IGME%20report%202015%20child%20mortality%20final.pdf]. New York.

United Nations Population Division. 2015. *World Population Prospects: The 2015 Revision.* [http://esa.un.org/unpd/wpp/]. New York: United Nations, Department of Economic and Social Affairs.

WHO (World Health Organization), UNICEF (United Nations Children's Fund), UNFPA (United Nations Population Fund), World Bank Group, and the United Nations Population Division. 2015. *Trends in Maternal Mortality: 1990 to 2015.* [www.who.int/reproductivehealth/publications/monitoring/maternal-mortality-2015/]. Geneva: WHO.

To access the World Development Indicators online tables, use the URL http://wdi.worldbank.org/table/ and the table number (for example, http://wdi.worldbank.org/table/2.1). To view a specific indicator online, use the URL http://data.worldbank.org/indicator/ and the indicator code (for example, http://data.worldbank.org/indicator/SP.POP.TOTL).

2.1 Population dynamics

Population ♀♂	SP.POP.TOTL
Population growth	SP.POP.GROW
Population ages 0–14 ♀♂	SP.POP.0014.TO.ZS
Population ages 15–64 ♀♂	SP.POP.1564.TO.ZS
Population ages 65+ ♀♂	SP.POP.65UP.TO.ZS
Dependency ratio, Young	SP.POP.DPND.YG
Dependency ratio, Old	SP.POP.DPND.OL
Crude death rate	SP.DYN.CDRT.IN
Crude birth rate	SP.DYN.CBRT.IN

2.2 Labor force structure

Labor force participation rate, Male ♀♂	SL.TLF.CACT.MA.ZS
Labor force participation rate, Female ♀♂	SL.TLF.CACT.FE.ZS
Labor force, Total ♀♂	SL.TLF.TOTL.IN
Labor force, Female ♀♂	SL.TLF.TOTL.FE.ZS
Labor force, Average annual growth	..a,b

2.3 Employment by sector

Agriculture, Male ♀♂	SL.AGR.EMPL.MA.ZS
Agriculture, Female ♀♂	SL.AGR.EMPL.FE.ZS
Industry, Male ♀♂	SL.IND.EMPL.MA.ZS
Industry, Female ♀♂	SL.IND.EMPL.FE.ZS
Services, Male ♀♂	SL.SRV.EMPL.MA.ZS
Services, Female ♀♂	SL.SRV.EMPL.FE.ZS

2.4 Decent work and productive employment

Employment to population ratio, Total ♀♂	SL.EMP.TOTL.SP.ZS
Employment to population ratio, Youth ♀♂	SL.EMP.1524.SP.ZS
Vulnerable employment, Male ♀♂	SL.EMP.VULN.MA.ZS
Vulnerable employment, Female ♀♂	SL.EMP.VULN.FE.ZS
GDP per person employed,% growth	..a

2.5 Unemployment

Unemployment, Male ♀♂	SL.UEM.TOTL.MA.ZS
Unemployment, Female ♀♂	SL.UEM.TOTL.FE.ZS
Youth unemployment, Male ♀♂	SL.UEM.1524.MA.ZS
Youth unemployment, Female ♀♂	SL.UEM.1524.FE.ZS
Long-term unemployment, Total ♀♂	SL.UEM.LTRM.ZS
Long-term unemployment, Male ♀♂	SL.UEM.LTRM.MA.ZS
Long-term unemployment, Female ♀♂	SL.UEM.LTRM.FE.ZS
Unemployment by educational attainment, Primary ♀♂	SL.UEM.PRIM.ZS
Unemployment by educational attainment, Secondary ♀♂	SL.UEM.SECO.ZS
Unemployment by educational attainment, Tertiary ♀♂	SL.UEM.TERT.ZS

2.6 Children at work

Children in employment, Total ♀♂	SL.TLF.0714.ZS
Children in employment, Male ♀♂	SL.TLF.0714.MA.ZS
Children in employment, Female ♀♂	SL.TLF.0714.FE.ZS
Work only ♀♂	SL.TLF.0714.WK.ZS
Study and work ♀♂	SL.TLF.0714.SW.ZS
Employment in agriculture ♀♂	SL.AGR.0714.ZS
Employment in manufacturing ♀♂	SL.MNF.0714.ZS
Employment in services ♀♂	SL.SRV.0714.ZS
Self-employed ♀♂	SL.SLF.0714.ZS
Wage workers ♀♂	SL.WAG.0714.ZS
Unpaid family workers ♀♂	SL.FAM.0714.ZS

2.7 Poverty rates at national poverty lines

Poverty headcount ratio, Rural	SI.POV.RUHC
Poverty headcount ratio, Urban	SI.POV.URHC
Poverty headcount ratio, National	SI.POV.NAHC
Poverty gap, Rural	SI.POV.RUGP
Poverty gap, Urban	SI.POV.URGP
Poverty gap, National	SI.POV.NAGP

2.8 Poverty rates at international poverty lines

Population living below 2011 PPP $1.90 a day	SI.POV.DDAY
Poverty gap at 2011 PPP $1.90 a day	SI.POV.2DAY
Population living below 2011 PPP $3.10 a day	SI.POV.GAPS
Poverty gap at 2011 PPP $3.10 a day	SI.POV.GAP2

2.9 Distribution of income or consumption

Gini index	SI.POV.GINI
Share of consumption or income, Lowest 10% of population	SI.DST.FRST.10
Share of consumption or income, Lowest 20% of population	SI.DST.FRST.20
Share of consumption or income, Second 20% of population	SI.DST.02ND.20
Share of consumption or income, Third 20% of population	SI.DST.03RD.20
Share of consumption or income, Fourth 20% of population	SI.DST.04TH.20

2 People

Share of consumption or income, Highest
20% of population — SI.DST.05TH.20

Share of consumption or income, Highest
10% of population — SI.DST.10TH.10

2.9.2 Shared prosperity

Annualized growth in mean consumption or
income per capita, bottom 40% — SI.SPR.PC40.ZG

Annualized growth in mean consumption or
income per capita, total population — SI.SPR.PCAP.ZG

Mean consumption or income per capita,
bottom 40% — SI.SPR.PC40

Mean consumption or income per capita,
total population — SI.SPR.PCAP

2.10 Education inputs

Government expenditure per student, Primary — SE.XPD.PRIM.PC.ZS

Government expenditure per student,
Secondary — SE.XPD.SECO.PC.ZS

Government expenditure per student, Tertiary — SE.XPD.TERT.PC.ZS

Government expenditure on education,
% of GDP — SE.XPD.TOTL.GD.ZS

Government expenditure on education,
% of total government expenditure — SE.XPD.TOTL.GB.ZS

Trained teachers in primary education ♀♂ — SE.PRM.TCAQ.ZS

Trained teachers in secondary education ♀♂ — SE.SEC.TCAQ.ZS

Primary school pupil-teacher ratio — SE.PRM.ENRL.TC.ZS

Secondary school pupil-teacher ratio — SE.SEC.ENRL.TC.ZS

2.11 Participation in education

Gross enrollment ratio, Preprimary ♀♂ — SE.PRE.ENRR

Gross enrollment ratio, Primary ♀♂ — SE.PRM.ENRR

Gross enrollment ratio, Secondary ♀♂ — SE.SEC.ENRR

Gross enrollment ratio, Tertiary ♀♂ — SE.TER.ENRR

Net enrollment rate, Primary ♀♂ — SE.PRM.NENR

Net enrollment rate, Secondary ♀♂ — SE.SEC.NENR

Adjusted net enrollment rate, Primary, Male ♀♂ — SE.PRM.TENR.MA

Adjusted net enrollment rate, Primary, Female ♀♂ — SE.PRM.TENR.FE

Primary school-age children out of school,
Male ♀♂ — SE.PRM.UNER.MA

Primary school-age children out of school,
Female ♀♂ — SE.PRM.UNER.FE

2.12 Education efficiency

Gross intake ratio in first grade of primary
education, Male ♀♂ — SE.PRM.GINT.MA.ZS

Gross intake ratio in first grade of primary
education, Female ♀♂ — SE.PRM.GINT.FE.ZS

Cohort survival rate, Reaching grade 5,
Male ♀♂ — SE.PRM.PRS5.MA.ZS

Cohort survival rate, Reaching grade 5,
Female ♀♂ — SE.PRM.PRS5.FE.ZS

Cohort survival rate, Reaching last grade of
primary education, Male ♀♂ — SE.PRM.PRSL.MA.ZS

Cohort survival rate, Reaching last grade of
primary education, Female ♀♂ — SE.PRM.PRSL.FE.ZS

Repeaters in primary education, Male ♀♂ — SE.PRM.REPT.MA.ZS

Repeaters in primary education, Female ♀♂ — SE.PRM.REPT.FE.ZS

Transition rate to secondary education, Male ♀♂ — SE.SEC.PROG.MA.ZS

Transition rate to secondary education,
Female ♀♂ — SE.SEC.PROG.FE.ZS

2.13 Education completion and outcomes

Primary completion rate, Male ♀♂ — SE.PRM.CMPT.MA.ZS

Primary completion rate, Female ♀♂ — SE.PRM.CMPT.FE.ZS

Lower secondary completion rate, Male ♀♂ — SE.SEC.CMPT.LO.MA.ZS

Lower secondary completion rate, Female ♀♂ — SE.SEC.CMPT.LO.FE.ZS

Youth literacy rate, Male ♀♂ — SE.ADT.1524.LT.MA.ZS

Youth literacy rate, Female ♀♂ — SE.ADT.1524.LT.FE.ZS

Adult literacy rate, Male ♀♂ — SE.ADT.LITR.MA.ZS

Adult literacy rate, Female ♀♂ — SE.ADT.LITR.FE.ZS

Students at lowest proficiency on PISA,
Mathematics — ..[b]

Students at lowest proficiency on PISA,
Reading — ..[b]

Students at lowest proficiency on PISA,
Science — ..[b]

2.14 Education gaps by income, gender, and area

This table provides education survey data
for the poorest and richest quintiles. — ..[b]

2.15 Health systems

Total health expenditure — SH.XPD.TOTL.ZS

Public health expenditure — SH.XPD.PUBL

Out-of-pocket health expenditure — SH.XPD.OOPC.TO.ZS

External resources for health — SH.XPD.EXTR.ZS

Health expenditure per capita, $ — SH.XPD.PCAP

Health expenditure per capita, PPP $ — SH.XPD.PCAP.PP.KD

Physicians — SH.MED.PHYS.ZS

Nurses and midwives — SH.MED.NUMW.P3

Hospital beds — SH.MED.BEDS.ZS

Completeness of birth registration — SP.REG.BRTH.ZS

Completeness of death registration — SP.REG.DTHS.ZS

2.16 Disease prevention coverage and quality

Access to an improved water source — SH.H2O.SAFE.ZS

Access to improved sanitation facilities — SH.STA.ACSN

Child immunization rate, Measles — SH.IMM.MEAS

Child immunization rate, DTP3 — SH.IMM.IDPT

Children with acute respiratory infection
taken to health provider — SH.STA.ARIC.ZS

Children with diarrhea who received oral rehydration and continuous feeding	SH.STA.ORCF.ZS
Children sleeping under treated bed nets	SH.MLR.NETS.ZS
Children with fever receiving antimalarial drugs	SH.MLR.TRET.ZS
Tuberculosis treatment success rate	SH.TBS.CURE.ZS
Tuberculosis case detection rate	SH.TBS.DTEC.ZS

2.17 Reproductive health

Total fertility rate	SP.DYN.TFRT.IN
Adolescent fertility rate	SP.ADO.TFRT
Unmet need for contraception	SP.UWT.TFRT
Contraceptive prevalence rate	SP.DYN.CONU.ZS
Pregnant women receiving prenatal care	SH.STA.ANVC.ZS
Births attended by skilled health staff	SH.STA.BRTC.ZS
Maternal mortality ratio, National estimate	SH.STA.MMRT.NE
Maternal mortality ratio, Modeled estimate	SH.STA.MMRT
Lifetime risk of maternal mortality	SH.MMR.RISK

2.18 Nutrition and growth

Prevalence of undernourishment	SN.ITK.DEFC.ZS
Prevalence of underweight, Male ♀♂	SH.STA.MALN.MA.ZS
Prevalence of underweight, Female ♀♂	SH.STA.MALN.FE.ZS
Prevalence of stunting, Male ♀♂	SH.STA.STNT.MA.ZS
Prevalence of stunting, Female ♀♂	SH.STA.STNT.FE.ZS
Prevalence of wasting, Male ♀♂	SH.STA.WAST.MA.ZS
Prevalence of wasting, Female ♀♂	SH.STA.WAST.FE.ZS
Prevalence of severe wasting, Male ♀♂	SH.SVR.WAST.MA.ZS
Prevalence of severe wasting, Female ♀♂	SH.SVR.WAST.FE.ZS
Prevalence of overweight children, Male ♀♂	SH.STA.OWGH.MA.ZS
Prevalence of overweight children, Female ♀♂	SH.STA.OWGH.FE.ZS

2.19 Nutrition intake and supplements

Low-birthweight babies	SH.STA.BRTW.ZS
Exclusive breastfeeding	SH.STA.BFED.ZS
Consumption of iodized salt	SN.ITK.SALT.ZS
Vitamin A supplementation	SN.ITK.VITA.ZS
Prevalence of anemia among children under age 5	SH.ANM.CHLD.ZS

Prevalence of anemia among pregnant women	SH.PRG.ANEM
Prevalence of anemia among nonpregnant women	SH.ANM.NPRG.ZS

2.20 Health risk factors and future challenges

Prevalence of smoking, Male ♀♂	SH.PRV.SMOK.MA
Prevalence of smoking, Female ♀♂	SH.PRV.SMOK.FE
Incidence of tuberculosis	SH.TBS.INCD
Prevalence of diabetes	SH.STA.DIAB.ZS
Prevalence of HIV, Total	SH.DYN.AIDS.ZS
Women's share of population ages 15+ living with HIV ♀♂	SH.DYN.AIDS.FE.ZS
Prevalence of HIV, Youth male ♀♂	SH.HIV.1524.MA.ZS
Prevalence of HIV, Youth female ♀♂	SH.HIV.1524.FE.ZS
Antiretroviral therapy coverage	SH.HIV.ARTC.ZS
Death from communicable diseases and maternal, prenatal, and nutrition conditions	SH.DTH.COMM.ZS
Death from non-communicable diseases	SH.DTH.NCOM.ZS
Death from injuries	SH.DTH.INJR.ZS

2.21 Mortality

Life expectancy at birth ♀♂	SP.DYN.LE00.IN
Neonatal mortality rate	SH.DYN.NMRT
Infant mortality rate ♀♂	SP.DYN.IMRT.IN
Under-five mortality rate, Total ♀♂	SH.DYN.MORT
Under-five mortality rate, Male ♀♂	SH.DYN.MORT.MA
Under-five mortality rate, Female ♀♂	SH.DYN.MORT.FE
Adult mortality rate, Male ♀♂	SP.DYN.AMRT.MA
Adult mortality rate, Female ♀♂	SP.DYN.AMRT.FE

2.22 Health gaps by income

This table provides health survey data for the poorest and richest quintiles.	..b

♀♂ Data disaggregated by sex are available in the World Development Indicators database.
a. Derived from data elsewhere in the World Development Indicators database.
b. Available online only as part of the table, not as an individual indicator.

The indicators presented in the *Environment* section measure the use of resources and the way human activities affect both the natural and the built environment. They include measures of environmental goods (forest, water, cultivable land) and of degradation (pollution, deforestation, loss of habitat, and loss of biodiversity).

The adoption of the Sustainable Development Goals in 2015 is recognition that economic growth, poverty eradication, and environmental sustainability are intertwined; viable and long-lasting development can be ensured only by protecting the environment and using its resources wisely. These global goals draw attention to a wide array of the environmental conditions that need to be closely monitored.

Growing populations and expanding economies have placed greater demands on land, water, forests, minerals, and energy resources. Efforts to reduce poverty and promote sustainable economic growth are undermined by the degradation of soils, the increasing scarcity of freshwater, the overexploitation of coastal ecosystems and fisheries, the loss of forest cover, long-term changes in the Earth's climate, and the loss of biological diversity. People in extreme poverty—the roughly 700 million living on less than $1.90 a day in purchasing power parity terms in 2015—are disproportionately affected by these adverse environmental conditions.

Economic growth and greater energy use are positively correlated. Access to electricity and the use of energy are vital to raising standards of living. But economic growth often has negative environmental consequences, with disproportionate impacts on the poorest communities. Recognizing this, the World Bank Group has joined the United Nations Sustainable Energy for All initiative, which calls on governments, businesses, and civil societies to achieve three goals by 2030: providing universal access to electricity and clean cooking fuels, doubling the share of the world's energy supply from renewable sources, and doubling the rate of improvement in energy efficiency. New indicators from the Global Tracking Framework database cover these three goals and go beyond to include primary energy intensity, renewable energy consumption, renewable electricity output, access to electricity, and access to non-solid fuels.

Other indicators in this section cover greenhouse gas emissions, ambient air pollution, energy (production, use, dependency, efficiency), electricity production and sources, agriculture and food production, forests and biodiversity, threatened species, water resources, climate variability, exposure to impact, resilience, urbanization, and natural resources rents. Where possible, estimates of the indicators have been drawn from international sources and have been standardized to facilitate comparisons across countries. But ecosystems span national boundaries, and access to natural resources may vary within countries. For example, water may be abundant in some parts of a country but scarce in others, and countries often share water resources. Greenhouse gas emissions and climate change are measured globally, but their effects are experienced locally.

Global demand for energy is surging. The share of energy production from alternative sources has increased slightly since 1990, but fossil fuels, such as coal, oil, and natural gas, supplied more than 81 percent of the world's total energy production in 2013. Fossil fuels are the primary source of carbon dioxide emissions, which, along with the other greenhouse gases, are believed to be the principal cause of global climate change. Producing the energy needed for growth while mitigating its effects on the world's climate is a global challenge. Because commercial energy is widely traded, its production and use need to be distinguished.

Energy use

Energy use per capita, 2013
(kilograms of oil equivalent)

- 5,000 or more
- 2,500–4,999
- 1,000–2,499
- 500–999
- Less than 500
- No data

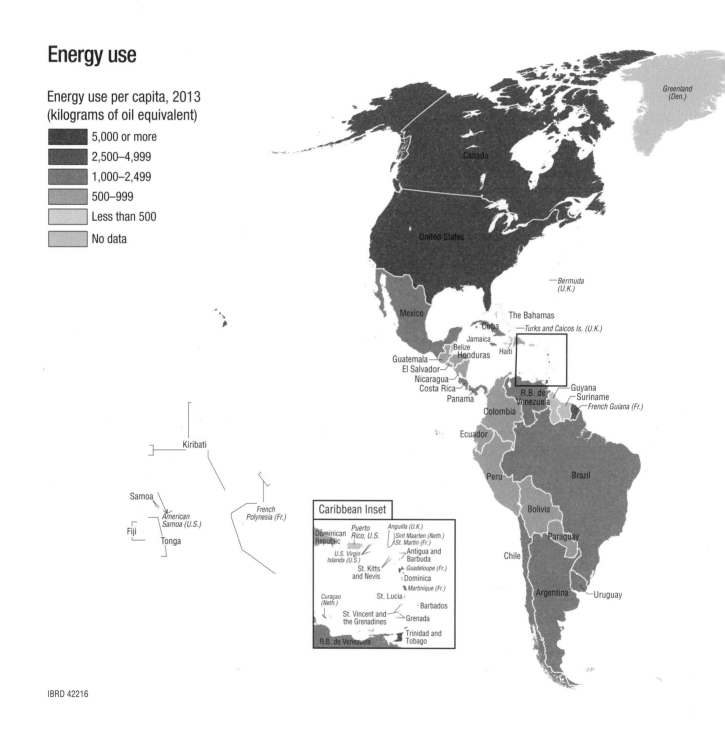

IBRD 42216

Total energy use worldwide increased 54 percent between 1990 and 2013, to 13.2 billion metric tons of oil equivalent.

High-income economies used 6.5 billion metric tons of energy in 2013—half the world's total energy use.

North America has the highest energy use per capita, more than twice that of Europe and Central Asia, more than 10 times that of Sub-Saharan Africa, and nearly 13 times that of South Asia.

Almost 40 percent of the world's people rely primarily on wood, coal, charcoal, or animal waste to cook their food, which forces them to breathe in toxic smoke that causes lung diseases and kills nearly 4 million people a year—most of them women and children.

Europe Inset

3 Environment

	Deforestation[a]	Nationally protected areas	Internal renewable freshwater resources[b]	Access to improved water source	Access to improved sanitation facilities	Urban population	Ambient PM$_{2.5}$ air pollution	Carbon dioxide emissions	Energy use	Electricity production
	average annual %	Terrestrial and marine areas % of total territorial area	Per capita cubic meters	% of total population	% of total population	% growth	Population-weighted exposure micrograms per cubic meter	million metric tons	Per capita kilograms of oil equivalent	billion kilowatt hours
	2000–15	2014	2014	2015	2015	2013–14	2013	2011	2013	2013
Afghanistan	0.00	0.5	1,491	55	32	4.6	22	12.3	..	..
Albania	−0.03	1.9	9,294	95	93	1.7	16	4.7	800	7.0
Algeria	−1.59	7.5	289	84	88	2.8	19	121.8	1,246	59.9
American Samoa	0.00	8.6	..	100	63	0.2	..	..	..	..
Andorra	0.00	19.5	4,336	100	100	−4.8	10	0.5	..	..
Angola	0.21	5.0	6,109	49	52	5.1	14	29.7	655	6.0
Antigua and Barbuda	0.00	0.2	572	98	..	−0.8	16	0.5	..	..
Argentina	0.99	5.4	6,794	99	96	1.2	9	190.0	1,895	139.2
Armenia	0.02	24.8	2,282	100	90	0.2	18	5.0	969	7.7
Aruba	0.00	0.5	..	98	98	−0.2	..	2.4	..	..
Australia	0.21	29.0	20,963	100	100	1.7	6	369.0	5,586	249.0
Austria	−0.05	28.4	6,436	100	100	0.8	15	65.2	3,918	64.5
Azerbaijan	−2.04	14.0	851	87	89	1.7	21	33.5	1,474	23.4
Bahamas, The	0.00	0.5	1,827	98	92	1.5	11	1.9	..	..
Bahrain	0.00	4.4	3	100	99	1.0	44	23.4	10,172	25.9
Bangladesh	0.18	3.4	660	87	61	3.5	48	57.1	216	53.0
Barbados	0.00	0.0	282	100	96	0.0	16	1.6	..	..
Belarus	−0.29	8.6	3,590	100	94	0.6	14	63.3	2,882	31.5
Belgium	−0.16	24.3	1,068	100	100	0.5	19	97.8	5,039	82.1
Belize	0.42	18.6	43,389	100	91	1.8	6	0.6	..	..
Benin	0.99	22.3	972	78	20	3.6	27	5.0	393	0.2
Bermuda	0.00	5.1	..	..	..	0.3	..	0.4	..	..
Bhutan	−0.38	47.3	101,960	100	50	3.4	28	0.6	..	..
Bolivia	0.59	24.8	28,735	90	50	2.2	11	16.1	786	8.1
Bosnia and Herzegovina	0.00	1.3	9,299	100	95	0.2	14	23.7	1,688	17.5
Botswana	0.90	29.2	1,081	96	63	2.4	10	4.9	1,098	0.9
Brazil	0.35	20.4	27,470	98	83	1.2	16	439.4	1,438	570.3
Brunei Darussalam	0.29	29.7	20,364	..	..	1.8	9	9.7	7,393	4.4
Bulgaria	−0.88	31.5	2,907	99	86	−0.1	16	49.3	2,327	43.1
Burkina Faso	0.96	15.5	711	82	20	5.8	29	1.9	..	..
Burundi	−2.63	6.9	930	76	48	5.8	17	0.2	..	..
Cabo Verde	−0.65	0.0	584	92	72	2.4	43	0.4	..	..
Cambodia	1.21	20.6	7,868	76	42	2.6	20	4.5	396	1.8
Cameroon	0.99	10.7	11,988	76	46	3.6	21	5.7	331	6.8
Canada	0.01	6.2	80,183	100	100	1.3	12	485.5	7,202	651.8
Cayman Islands	0.00	1.5	..	97	96	1.4	..	0.6	..	..
Central African Republic	0.07	18.1	29,349	69	22	2.6	19	0.3	..	..
Chad	1.53	17.8	1,104	51	12	3.8	31	0.5	..	..
Channel Islands	..	..	..	..	..	0.8	..	..	..	..
Chile	−0.80	6.9	49,824	99	99	1.3	18	79.4	2,201	73.1
China	−1.18	15.6	2,062	96	77	2.8	54	9,019.5	2,226	5,422.2
Hong Kong SAR, China	..	41.8	..	..	..	0.8	..	40.3	1,938	39.2
Macao SAR, China	..	0.0	..	..	..	1.7	..	1.2	..	..
Colombia	0.36	17.4	44,883	91	81	1.3	13	72.4	669	64.7
Comoros	1.19	2.4	1,558	90	36	2.7	7	0.2	..	..
Congo, Dem. Rep.	0.20	12.1	12,020	52	29	4.4	18	3.4	292	8.6
Congo, Rep.	0.07	31.8	49,279	77	15	3.1	14	2.2	556	1.8

	Deforestation[a]	Nationally protected areas	Internal renewable freshwater resources[b]	Access to improved water source	Access to improved sanitation facilities	Urban population	Ambient PM$_{2.5}$ air pollution	Carbon dioxide emissions	Energy use	Electricity production
		Terrestrial and marine areas % of total territorial area	Per capita cubic meters	% of total population	% of total population		Population-weighted exposure micrograms per cubic meter	million metric tons	Per capita kilograms of oil equivalent	billion kilowatt hours
	average annual % 2000–15	2014	2014	2015	2015	% growth 2013–14	2013	2011	2013	2013
Costa Rica	−1.07	3.1	23,751	98	95	2.4	9	7.8	1,029	10.2
Côte d'Ivoire	−0.05	14.9	3,468	82	23	3.8	20	6.4	605	7.6
Croatia	−0.13	23.7	8,895	100	97	0.1	14	20.6	1,814	13.3
Cuba	−2.09	5.0	3,350	95	93	0.3	11	35.9	1,031	19.1
Curaçao	..	..	..	..	..	1.2	..	..	11,801	0.9
Cyprus	−0.04	2.0	676	100	100	0.9	16	7.5	1,691	4.3
Czech Republic	−0.08	21.1	1,249	100	99	0.0	17	109.5	3,990	86.2
Denmark	−0.30	18.0	1,064	100	100	0.6	11	40.4	3,107	34.7
Djibouti	0.00	1.1	342	90	47	1.4	28	0.5	..	..
Dominica	0.57	0.6	2,765	..	..	0.9	15	0.1	..	..
Dominican Republic	−2.23	11.2	2,258	85	84	2.5	12	21.9	731	17.7
Ecuador	0.57	15.4	27,819	87	85	1.9	14	35.7	980	23.3
Egypt, Arab Rep.	−1.58	9.6	20	99	95	2.3	36	220.8	885	167.8
El Salvador	1.35	2.1	2,559	94	75	1.0	13	6.7	693	5.8
Equatorial Guinea	0.67	2.1	31,673	48	75	3.3	11	6.7	..	..
Eritrea	0.28	3.1	548	58	16	4.2	25	0.5	164	0.4
Estonia	0.03	19.9	9,669	100	97	−0.4	9	18.7	4,623	13.3
Ethiopia	0.59	18.4	1,258	57	28	4.8	18	7.5	507	8.7
Faroe Islands	0.00	0.0	..	..	..	0.4	..	0.6	..	..
Fiji	−0.25	1.0	32,207	96	91	1.4	7	1.2	..	..
Finland	0.07	14.1	19,592	100	98	0.6	7	54.8	6,075	71.3
France	−0.74	25.7	3,020	100	99	0.7	14	338.8	3,843	567.4
French Polynesia	−3.17	0.0	..	100	99	0.9	..	0.9	..	..
Gabon	−0.30	12.3	97,175	93	42	2.5	11	2.2	1,435	2.4
Gambia, The	−0.39	1.4	1,556	90	59	4.3	35	0.4	..	..
Georgia	−0.15	6.5	15,597	100	86	−1.0	16	7.9	1,032	10.1
Germany	−0.04	38.5	1,321	100	99	−1.2	15	729.5	3,868	627.4
Ghana	−0.32	7.8	1,131	89	15	3.6	27	10.1	344	12.9
Greece	−0.84	8.6	5,336	100	99	−0.4	15	84.0	2,134	57.1
Greenland	0.00	22.4	..	100	100	0.1	..	0.7	..	..
Grenada	0.00	0.1	1,881	97	98	0.4	17	0.3	..	..
Guam	0.00	5.2	..	100	90	1.5	..	..	..	..
Guatemala	1.06	15.7	6,818	93	64	2.9	12	11.3	768	9.9
Guinea	0.52	20.3	18,411	77	20	4.0	27	2.6	..	..
Guinea-Bissau	0.47	10.4	8,886	79	21	4.1	30	0.2	..	..
Guyana	0.04	5.3	315,489	98	84	0.6	9	1.8	..	..
Haiti	0.73	0.1	1,231	58	28	3.6	13	2.2	393	1.1
Honduras	1.88	7.8	11,387	91	83	2.5	9	8.4	662	8.1
Hungary	−0.53	22.6	608	100	98	0.4	16	48.5	2,280	30.3
Iceland	−4.60	2.3	519,265	100	99	1.2	7	1.9	18,177	18.1
India	−0.54	3.1	1,116	94	40	2.4	47	2,074.3	606	1,193.5
Indonesia	0.56	6.0	7,935	87	61	2.7	15	564.0	850	215.6
Iran, Islamic Rep.	−0.98	6.7	1,644	96	90	2.0	32	586.6	2,960	270.4
Iraq	−0.06	0.4	1,011	87	86	3.1	33	133.7	1,481	73.6
Ireland	−1.25	3.5	10,616	98	91	0.8	8	36.1	2,840	25.8
Isle of Man	0.00	..	..	..	..	0.9	..	..	..	..
Israel	−0.52	8.6	91	100	100	2.0	26	69.5	2,971	59.9

3 Environment

	Deforestation[a]	Nationally protected areas	Internal renewable freshwater resources[b]	Access to improved water source	Access to improved sanitation facilities	Urban population	Ambient PM$_{2.5}$ air pollution	Carbon dioxide emissions	Energy use	Electricity production
	average annual %	Terrestrial and marine areas % of total territorial area	Per capita cubic meters	% of total population	% of total population	% growth	Population-weighted exposure micrograms per cubic meter	million metric tons	Per capita kilograms of oil equivalent	billion kilowatt hours
	2000–15	2014	2014	2015	2015	2013–14	2013	2011	2013	2013
Italy	−0.74	13.3	3,002	100	100	1.1	18	398.0	2,579	287.9
Jamaica	0.12	1.4	3,977	94	82	0.6	11	7.8	1,084	4.2
Japan	−0.02	2.1	3,382	100	100	0.4	16	1,187.7	3,570	1,038.5
Jordan	0.00	2.1	103	97	99	2.5	26	22.3	1,196	17.3
Kazakhstan	0.11	3.3	3,722	93	98	1.3	14	261.8	4,787	95.4
Kenya	−1.60	10.6	461	63	30	4.3	11	13.6	492	8.9
Kiribati	0.00	11.8	..	67	40	2.0	7	0.1	..	..
Korea, Dem. People's Rep.	1.83	1.3	2,677	100	82	0.8	24	73.6	581	19.5
Korea, Rep.	0.11	2.6	1,286	98	100	0.5	29	589.4	5,253	537.9
Kosovo	..	..	..	..	..	..	..	..	1,297	6.5
Kuwait	−1.33	11.0	0	99	100	4.4	49	91.0	9,757	61.0
Kyrgyz Republic	1.72	6.9	8,385	90	93	2.3	18	6.6	690	14.0
Lao PDR	−0.90	16.7	28,463	76	71	4.6	27	1.2	..	..
Latvia	−0.24	17.8	8,396	99	88	−4.1	12	7.8	2,159	6.2
Lebanon	−0.31	0.9	1,056	99	81	1.3	24	20.5	1,573	18.2
Lesotho	−1.11	0.5	2,480	82	30	3.2	11	2.2	..	..
Liberia	0.65	0.8	45,490	76	17	3.2	23	0.9	..	..
Libya	0.00	0.3	112	..	97	0.1	28	39.0	2,711	30.3
Liechtenstein	0.00	44.3	..	..	..	0.5	..	0.1	..	..
Lithuania	−0.53	16.3	5,272	97	92	−0.9	14	13.7	2,357	4.2
Luxembourg	0.00	34.6	1,798	100	98	2.7	15	10.8	7,310	1.8
Macedonia, FYR	−0.28	9.7	2,602	99	91	0.2	17	9.3	1,349	6.1
Madagascar	0.28	2.0	14,297	52	12	4.6	6	2.4	..	..
Malawi	0.78	16.8	967	90	41	4.1	9	1.2	..	..
Malaysia	−0.19	8.0	19,397	98	96	2.5	14	225.7	3,020	138.3
Maldives	0.00	0.1	75	99	98	4.5	16	1.1	..	..
Mali	1.34	8.4	3,512	77	25	4.9	36	1.3	..	..
Malta	0.00	0.5	118	100	100	1.1	14	2.5	1,735	2.3
Marshall Islands	0.00	0.2	..	95	77	0.6	8	0.1	..	..
Mauritania	1.93	1.4	101	58	40	3.5	70	2.3	..	..
Mauritius	0.48	0.0	2,182	100	93	−0.2	10	3.9	1,095	2.9
Mexico	0.18	6.0	3,262	96	85	1.7	12	466.5	1,546	297.1
Micronesia, Fed. Sts.	0.00	0.0	..	89	57	0.5	4	0.1	..	..
Moldova	−1.75	3.8	456	88	76	0.0	17	5.0	863	4.5
Monaco	0.00	99.7	..	100	100	0.3	..	..	..	..
Mongolia	−0.48	17.2	11,959	64	60	3.0	8	19.1	1,826	5.0
Montenegro	−2.14	2.7	..	100	96	0.4	15	2.6	1,651	3.9
Morocco	−0.85	20.1	855	85	77	2.2	17	56.5	564	27.9
Mozambique	0.53	10.9	3,685	51	21	3.6	7	3.3	407	14.9
Myanmar	1.11	4.1	18,770	81	80	2.5	29	10.4	313	11.9
Namibia	0.92	23.2	2,564	91	34	4.6	8	2.8	742	1.3
Nepal	0.45	22.9	7,035	92	46	3.2	46	4.3	370	3.6
Netherlands	−0.30	18.1	652	100	98	1.1	17	168.0	4,605	100.9
New Caledonia	0.00	91.0	..	99	100	2.3	..	3.9	..	..
New Zealand	−0.01	29.8	72,510	100	..	1.5	9	31.2	4,392	43.3
Nicaragua	1.22	22.0	25,973	87	68	1.7	7	4.9	594	4.2
Niger	0.93	17.6	183	58	11	5.4	38	1.4	152	0.4

 Front User guide World view People Environment

	Deforestation[a] average annual % 2000–15	Nationally protected areas Terrestrial and marine areas % of total territorial area 2014	Internal renewable freshwater resources[b] Per capita cubic meters 2014	Access to improved water source % of total population 2015	Access to improved sanitation facilities % of total population 2015	Urban population % growth 2013–14	Ambient PM2.5 air pollution Population-weighted exposure micrograms per cubic meter 2013	Carbon dioxide emissions million metric tons 2011	Energy use Per capita kilograms of oil equivalent 2013	Electricity production billion kilowatt hours 2013
Nigeria	3.12	11.8	1,245	69	29	4.5	30	88.0	773	29.0
Northern Mariana Islands	0.63	26.3	..	98	80	1.2	..	..	..	..
Norway	0.00	9.1	74,364	100	98	1.5	6	45.5	6,439	133.7
Oman	0.00	4.0	330	93	97	8.7	30	64.9	6,232	26.2
Pakistan	2.03	8.6	297	91	64	3.3	46	163.5	475	97.8
Palau	0.00	0.2	..	..	100	1.6	..	0.2	..	..
Panama	0.34	5.2	35,320	95	75	2.1	7	9.7	1,057	9.0
Papua New Guinea	0.01	0.7	107,321	40	19	2.2	6	5.2	..	..
Paraguay	1.39	6.5	17,856	98	89	1.7	14	5.3	764	60.4
Peru	0.19	19.4	52,981	87	76	1.7	13	53.1	708	43.4
Philippines	−0.96	2.4	4,832	92	74	1.3	9	82.0	457	75.3
Poland	−0.28	29.3	1,410	98	97	−0.2	17	317.3	2,565	164.0
Portugal	0.32	1.9	3,653	100	100	0.4	10	49.7	2,083	50.5
Puerto Rico	−0.68	0.6	2,001	..	99	−1.4	..	..	..	..
Qatar	0.00	1.2	26	100	98	3.4	38	83.9	19,120	34.7
Romania	−0.52	22.1	2,129	100	79	−0.1	17	84.8	1,592	58.5
Russian Federation	−0.05	8.8	29,989	97	72	0.3	14	1,808.1	5,093	1,057.6
Rwanda	−2.64	9.4	838	76	62	5.9	17	0.7	..	..
Samoa	0.00	0.2	..	99	92	−0.2	7	0.2	..	..
San Marino	..	0.0	..	..	..	0.7	..	..	..	..
São Tomé and Príncipe	0.24	0.0	11,699	97	35	3.1	7	0.1	..	..
Saudi Arabia	0.00	28.2	78	97	100	2.5	54	520.3	6,363	284.0
Senegal	0.47	14.5	1,758	79	48	3.9	41	7.9	261	3.7
Serbia	−0.70	6.8	1,179	99	96	−0.3	16	49.2	2,078	39.2
Seychelles	0.00	0.1	..	96	98	2.3	7	0.6	..	..
Sierra Leone	−0.28	3.8	25,334	63	13	3.1	24	0.9	..	..
Singapore	0.00	3.4	110	100	100	1.3	17	22.4	4,833	48.0
Sint Maarten	..	..	..	..	..	2.9	..	..	..	..
Slovak Republic	−0.07	36.6	2,325	100	99	−0.3	16	34.4	3,178	28.5
Slovenia	−0.08	54.0	9,054	100	99	0.0	14	15.4	3,323	15.8
Solomon Islands	0.24	0.2	78,123	81	30	4.1	5	0.2	..	..
Somalia	1.02	0.3	570	..	..	3.6	10	0.6	..	..
South Africa	0.00	10.2	830	93	66	2.4	14	477.2	2,658	253.2
South Sudan	0.00	20.8	2,183	59	7	5.0	16	..	59	0.5
Spain	−0.57	10.2	2,393	100	100	0.0	12	270.7	2,504	279.3
Sri Lanka	0.37	2.6	2,542	96	95	1.0	17	15.2	488	12.0
St. Kitts and Nevis	0.00	0.3	437	98	..	1.4	..	0.3	..	..
St. Lucia	0.32	0.7	1,634	96	91	0.8	16	0.4	..	..
St. Martin	0.00	..	..	..	..	..	..	..	..	..
St. Vincent & the Grenadines	−0.26	0.5	914	95	..	0.7	14	0.2	..	..
Sudan	0.80	1.7[c]	102	56	24	2.6	27	16.6[c]	375	10.3
Suriname	0.03	8.6	183,930	95	79	0.8	11	1.9	..	..
Swaziland	−0.88	4.0	2,080	74	58	1.4	10	1.0	..	..
Sweden	0.02	13.0	17,636	100	99	1.2	7	52.1	5,132	153.0
Switzerland	−0.34	9.9	4,934	100	100	1.3	18	36.6	3,304	68.8
Syrian Arab Republic	−0.91	0.7	322	90	96	2.4	24	57.7	592	25.9
Tajikistan	−0.03	21.9	7,650	74	95	2.5	20	2.8	303	17.1

	Deforestation[a] average annual % 2000–15	Nationally protected areas Terrestrial and marine areas % of total territorial area 2014	Internal renewable freshwater resources[b] Per capita cubic meters 2014	Access to improved water source % of total population 2015	Access to improved sanitation facilities % of total population 2015	Urban population % growth 2013–14	Ambient PM$_{2.5}$ air pollution Population-weighted exposure micrograms per cubic meter 2013	Carbon dioxide emissions million metric tons 2011	Energy use Per capita kilograms of oil equivalent 2013	Electricity production billion kilowatt hours 2013
Tanzania	0.75	26.1	1,621	56	16	5.5	9	7.3	470	5.6
Thailand	0.24	12.5	3,315	98	93	2.9	22	303.4	1,988	165.7
Timor-Leste	1.31	2.1	6,777	72	41	4.7	6	0.2	..	..
Togo	4.09	19.8	1,616	63	12	3.9	25	2.1	463	0.1
Tonga	0.00	1.5	..	100	91	0.7	7	0.1	..	..
Trinidad and Tobago	0.00	2.6	2,835	95	92	−0.9	9	49.6	14,538	9.5
Tunisia	−1.62	3.7	381	98	92	1.3	16	25.6	956	18.4
Turkey	−1.00	0.2	2,990	100	95	1.9	17	320.8	1,553	240.2
Turkmenistan	0.00	3.2	265	..	..	2.0	42	62.2	5,012	18.9
Turks and Caicos Islands	0.00	3.6	..	..	..	2.3	..	0.2	..	..
Tuvalu	0.00	0.0	..	98	83	1.8	..	..	..	..
Uganda	3.09	16.0	1,032	79	19	5.4	18	3.8	..	..
Ukraine	−0.10	3.9	1,215	96	96	0.0	15	286.2	2,553	193.7
United Arab Emirates	−0.28	16.1	17	100	98	0.8	41	178.5	7,691	106.2
United Kingdom	−0.43	13.8	2,246	100	99	1.0	11	448.2	2,978	356.3
United States	−0.14	14.8	8,838	99	100	1.0	11	5,305.6	6,914	4,286.9
Uruguay	−2.31	1.7	26,963	100	96	0.5	7	7.8	1,351	11.7
Uzbekistan	−0.02	3.4	531	87	100	1.9	26	114.9	1,419	54.2
Vanuatu	0.00	2.3	..	95	58	3.4	7	0.1	..	..
Venezuela, RB	0.33	36.7	26,227	93	94	1.4	13	188.8	2,271	123.2
Vietnam	−1.73	2.5	3,961	98	78	3.0	25	173.2	668	127.0
Virgin Islands (U.S.)	0.67	2.8	..	100	96	−0.4	..	..	..	..
West Bank and Gaza	0.00	..	189	58	92	3.3	26	2.2	..	..
Yemen, Rep.	0.00	0.6	80	55	53	4.2	36	22.3	324	8.5
Zambia	0.33	37.9	5,101	65	44	4.2	12	3.0	631	13.3
Zimbabwe	1.70	26.6	804	77	37	1.8	9	9.9	758	9.5
World	**0.09 w**	**12.8 w**	**5,925 s**	**91 w**	**68 w**	**2.1 w**	**32 w**	**34,649.5[d] w**	**1,894 w**	**23,342.6 w**
East Asia & Pacific	−0.17	18.0	4,525	94	77	2.4	40	13,002.8	2,073	8,424.5
Europe & Central Asia	−0.10	9.6	7,866	98	93	0.5	15	6,735.1	3,216	5,305.3
Latin America & Caribbean	0.36	16.1	22,162	95	83	1.4	14	1,776.6	1,373	1,565.6
Middle East & North Africa	−0.88	10.0	554	93	91	2.5	32	2,343.4	2,190	1,323.4
North America	−0.06	10.5	15,993	99	100	1.0	11	5,791.4	6,943	4,940.8
South Asia	−0.37	4.5	1,152	92	45	2.7	46	2,328.4	550	1,370.4
Sub-Saharan Africa	0.48	13.5	3,987	68	30	4.2	21	746.2	671	453.8
Low income	0.44	14.0	4,777	66	28	4.2	20	155.4	..	..
Lower middle income	0.38	8.7	3,065	90	52	2.7	36	4,153.0	636	2,482.8
Upper middle income	0.03	12.9	6,594	95	80	2.3	39	13,166.2	2,015	8,203.9
High income	−0.03	13.9	11,319	99	96	0.7	15	15,233.6	4,656	12,556.2

a. Negative values indicate an increase in forest area. b. River flows from other countries are not included because of data unreliability. c. Includes South Sudan. d. Includes emissions not allocated to specific countries.

About the data

Environmental resources are needed to promote economic growth and reduce poverty, but growth can create new stresses on the environment. Deforestation, loss of biologically diverse habitat, depletion of water resources, pollution, urbanization, and increasing demand for energy production are some of the factors that must be considered when shaping development strategies.

Loss of forests

Forests provide habitat for many species and act as carbon sinks. If properly managed they also provide a livelihood for people who manage and use forest resources. FAO (2015) provides information on forest cover in 2015 and adjusted estimates of forest cover in 1990, 2000, and 2010. Data presented here do not distinguish natural forests from plantations, a breakdown the FAO provides only for low- and middle-income countries. Thus, data may underestimate the rate at which natural forest is disappearing in some countries.

Habitat protection and biodiversity

Deforestation is a major cause of loss of biodiversity, and habitat conservation is vital for stemming this loss. Conservation efforts have focused on protecting areas of high biodiversity. The World Conservation Monitoring Centre (WCMC) and the United Nations Environment Programme (UNEP) compile data on protected areas. Differences in definitions, reporting practices, and reporting periods limit cross-country comparability. Nationally protected areas are defined using the six International Union for Conservation of Nature (IUCN) categories for areas of at least 1,000 hectares—scientific reserves and strict nature reserves with limited public access, national parks of national or international significance and not materially affected by human activity, natural monuments and natural landscapes with unique aspects, managed nature reserves and wildlife sanctuaries, protected landscapes (which may include cultural landscapes), and areas managed mainly for the sustainable use of natural systems to ensure long-term protection and maintenance of biological diversity—as well as terrestrial protected areas not assigned to an IUCN category. Designating an area as protected does not mean that protection is in force. For small countries with protected areas smaller than 1,000 hectares, the size limit in the definition leads to underestimation of protected areas. Due to variations in consistency and methods of collection, data quality is highly variable across countries. Some countries update their information more frequently than others, some have more accurate data on the extent of coverage, and many underreport the number or extent of protected areas.

Freshwater resources

The data on freshwater resources are derived from estimates of runoff into rivers and recharge of groundwater. These estimates are derived from different sources and refer to different years, so cross-country comparisons should be made with caution. Data are collected intermittently and may hide substantial year-to-year variations in total renewable water resources. Data do not distinguish between seasonal and geographic variations in water availability within countries. Data for small countries and countries in arid and semiarid zones are less reliable than data for larger countries and countries with greater rainfall.

Water and sanitation

A reliable supply of safe drinking water and sanitary disposal of excreta are two of the most important means of improving human health and protecting the environment. Improved sanitation facilities prevent human, animal, and insect contact with excreta.

Data on access to an improved water source measure the percentage of the population with ready access to water for domestic purposes and are estimated by the World Health Organization (WHO)/United Nations Children's Fund (UNICEF) Joint Monitoring Programme for Water Supply and Sanitation based on surveys and censuses. The coverage rates are based on information from service users on household use rather than on information from service providers, which may include nonfunctioning systems. Access to drinking water from an improved source does not ensure that the water is safe or adequate, as these characteristics are not tested at the time of survey. While information on access to an improved water source is widely used, it is extremely subjective; terms such as "safe," "improved," "adequate," and "reasonable" may have different meanings in different countries despite official WHO definitions (see *Definitions*). Even in high-income countries treated water may not always be safe to drink. Access to an improved water source is equated with connection to a supply system; it does not account for variations in the quality and cost of the service.

Urbanization

There is no consistent and universally accepted standard for distinguishing urban from rural areas and, by extension, calculating their populations. Most countries use a classification related to the size or characteristics of settlements. Some define areas based on the presence of certain infrastructure and services. Others designate areas based on administrative arrangements. Because data are based on national definitions, cross-country comparisons should be made with caution.

Air pollution

Air pollution places a major burden on world health. Almost 40 percent of the world's people rely on wood, charcoal, dung, crop waste, or coal to meet basic energy needs. In both cities and rural areas exposure to air pollution is the main environmental threat to health, responsible for 5.5 million deaths per year, about one every 2 seconds. Cooking with solid fuels creates harmful smoke and particulates that fill homes and the surrounding environment. Long-term exposure to high levels of fine particulates in the air contributes to a range of health effects, including respiratory diseases, lung cancer, and heart disease. Not only does exposure to air pollution endanger people's health, it also carries huge economic costs and represents a drag on development, particularly for low- and middle-income countries and vulnerable segments of the population such as children and the elderly.

Data on exposure to ambient air pollution are derived from estimates of annual concentrations of very fine particulates produced for the Global Burden of Disease study, an international scientific effort led by the Institute for Health Metrics and Evaluation at the University of Washington. Estimates of annual concentrations are generated by combining data from atmospheric chemistry transport models and satellite observations of aerosols in the atmosphere. Modeled concentrations are calibrated against observations from ground-level monitoring of particulates at some 3,400 locations in 79 countries. Exposure to concentrations of particulates in both urban and rural areas is weighted by population and is aggregated at the national level.

Pollutant concentrations are sensitive to local conditions, and even monitoring sites in the same city may register different levels. Direct monitoring of ambient $PM_{2.5}$ is still rare in many parts of the world, and measurement protocols and standards are not the same for all countries. These data should be considered only a general indication of air quality, intended for cross-country comparisons of the relative risk of particulate matter pollution.

Carbon dioxide emissions

Carbon dioxide emissions are the primary source of greenhouse gases, which contribute to global warming, threatening human and natural habitats. Fossil fuel combustion and cement manufacturing are the primary sources of anthropogenic carbon dioxide emissions, which the U.S. Department of Energy's Carbon Dioxide Information Analysis Center (CDIAC) calculates using data from the United Nations Statistics Division's World Energy Data Set and the U.S. Bureau of Mines's Cement Manufacturing Data Set. Carbon dioxide emissions, often calculated and reported as elemental carbon, were converted to actual carbon dioxide mass by multiplying them by 3.667 (the ratio of the mass of carbon to that of carbon dioxide). Although estimates of global carbon dioxide emissions are probably accurate within 10 percent (as calculated from global average fuel chemistry and use), country estimates may have larger error bounds. Trends estimated from a consistent time series tend to be more accurate than individual values. Each year the CDIAC recalculates the entire time series since 1949, incorporating recent findings and corrections. Estimates exclude fuels supplied to ships and aircraft in international transport because of the difficulty of apportioning the fuels among benefiting countries.

Energy use

In most economies growth in energy use is closely related to growth in the modern sectors—industry, motorized transport, and urban areas—but also reflects climatic, geographic, and economic factors. Energy use has been growing rapidly in low- and middle-income economies, but high-income economies still use more than four times as much energy per capita.

Total energy use refers to the use of primary energy before transformation to other end-use fuels (such as electricity and refined petroleum products). It includes energy from combustible renewables and waste—solid biomass and animal products, gas and liquid from biomass, and industrial and municipal waste. Biomass is any plant matter used directly as fuel or converted into fuel, heat, or electricity. Data for combustible renewables and waste are often based on small surveys or other incomplete information and thus give only a broad impression of developments and are not strictly comparable across countries. The International Energy Agency (IEA) reports include country notes that explain some of these differences (see *Data sources*). All forms of energy—primary energy and primary electricity—are converted into oil equivalents. A notional thermal efficiency of 33 percent is assumed for converting nuclear electricity into oil equivalents and 100 percent efficiency for converting hydroelectric power.

Electricity production

Use of energy is important in improving people's standard of living. But electricity generation also can damage the environment. Whether such damage occurs depends largely on how electricity is generated. For example, burning coal releases twice as much carbon dioxide—a major contributor to global warming—as does burning an equivalent amount of natural gas. Nuclear energy does not generate carbon dioxide emissions, but it produces other dangerous waste products.

The IEA compiles data on energy inputs used to generate electricity. Data for countries that are not members of the Organisation for Economic Co-operation and Development (OECD) are based on national energy data adjusted to conform to annual questionnaires completed by OECD member governments. In addition, estimates are sometimes made to complete major aggregates from which key data are missing, and adjustments are made to compensate for differences in definitions. The IEA makes these estimates in consultation with national statistical offices, oil companies, electric utilities, and national energy experts. It occasionally revises its time series to reflect political changes. For example, the IEA has constructed historical energy statistics for countries of the former Soviet Union. In addition, energy statistics for other countries have undergone continuous changes in coverage or methodology in recent years as more detailed energy accounts have become available. Breaks in series are therefore unavoidable.

Definitions

• **Deforestation** is the permanent conversion of natural forest area to other uses, including agriculture, ranching, settlements, and infrastructure. Deforested areas do not include areas logged but intended for regeneration or areas degraded by fuelwood gathering, acid precipitation, or forest fires. • **Nationally protected areas** are terrestrial and marine protected areas as a percentage of total territorial area and include all nationally designated protected areas with known location and extent. All overlaps between different designations and categories, buffered points, and polygons are removed, and all undated protected areas are dated. • **Internal renewable freshwater resources** are the average annual flows of rivers and groundwater from rainfall in the country. Natural incoming flows originating outside a country's borders and overlapping water resources between surface runoff and groundwater recharge are excluded. • **Access to an improved water source** is the percentage of the population using an improved drinking water source. An improved drinking water source includes piped water on premises (piped household water connection located inside the user's dwelling, plot, or yard), public taps or standpipes, tube wells, or boreholes, protected dug wells, protected springs, and rainwater collection. • **Access to improved sanitation facilities** is the percentage of the population using improved sanitation facilities. Improved sanitation facilities are likely to ensure hygienic separation of human excreta from human contact. They include flush/pour flush toilets (to piped sewer system, septic tank, or pit latrine), ventilated improved pit latrines, pit latrines with slab, and composting toilets. • **Urban population** growth is the annual rate of change of urban population assuming exponential change. Urban population is the proportion of midyear population of areas defined as urban in each country, which is obtained by the United Nations, multiplied by the World Bank estimate of total population. • **Ambient PM$_{2.5}$ air pollution** is defined as exposure to fine suspended particulates of less than 2.5 microns in aerodynamic diameter that are capable of penetrating deep into the respiratory tract and causing severe health damage. Data are aggregated at the national level and include both rural and urban areas. Exposure is calculated by weighting mean annual concentrations of PM$_{2.5}$ by population. • **Carbon dioxide emissions** are emissions from the burning of fossil fuels and the manufacture of cement and include carbon dioxide produced during consumption of solid, liquid, and gas fuels and gas flaring. • **Energy use** refers to the use of primary energy before transformation to other end use fuels, which equals indigenous production plus imports and stock changes, minus exports and fuels supplied to ships and aircraft engaged in international transport. • **Electricity production** is measured at the terminals of all alternator sets in a station. In addition to hydropower, coal, oil, gas, and nuclear power generation, it covers generation by geothermal, solar, wind, and tide and wave energy as well as that from combustible renewables and waste. Production includes the output of electric plants designed to produce electricity only, as well as that of combined heat and power plants.

Data sources

Data on deforestation are from FAO (2015) and the FAO's website. Data on protected areas, derived from the UNEP and WCMC online databases, are based on data from national authorities, national legislation, and international agreements. Data on freshwater resources are from the FAO's AQUASTAT database. Data on access to water and sanitation are from the WHO/UNICEF Joint Monitoring Programme for Water Supply and Sanitation. Data on urban population are from the United Nations Population Division (2014). Data on particulate matter concentrations are from the Global Burden of Disease 2013 study (www.healthdata.org/gbd/data) by the Institute for Health Metrics and Evaluation (see GBD 2013 Risk Factors Collaborators 2015). See Brauer and others (2016) for the data and methods used to estimate ambient PM$_{2.5}$ exposure. Data on carbon dioxide emissions are from CDIAC online databases. Data on energy use and electricity production are from IEA online databases and its annual *Energy Statistics of Non-OECD Countries, Energy Balances of Non-OECD Countries, Energy Statistics of OECD Countries,* and *Energy Balances of OECD Countries.*

References

Brauer, M., G. Freedman, J. Frostad, A. van Donkelaar, R. V. Martin, et al. 2016. "Ambient Air Pollution Exposure Estimation for the Global Burden of Disease 2013." *Environmental Science & Technology* 50(1): 79–88.

CDIAC (Carbon Dioxide Information Analysis Center). n.d. Online database. [http://cdiac.ornl.gov/home.html]. Oak Ridge National Laboratory, Environmental Science Division, Oak Ridge, TN.

FAO (Food and Agriculture Organization of the United Nations). 2015. *Global Forest Resources Assessment 2015.* Rome.

———. n.d. AQUASTAT. Online database. [www.fao.org/nr/water/aquastat/data/query/index.html]. Rome.

GBD 2013 Risk Factors Collaborators. 2015. "Global, Regional, and National Comparative Risk Assessment of 79 Behavioral, Environmental, and Occupational, and Metabolic Risks or Clusters of Risks in 188 Countries, 1990–2013: A Systematic Analysis for the Global Burden of Disease Study 2013." *Lancet.*

IEA (International Energy Agency). Various years. *Energy Balances of Non-OECD Countries.* Paris.

———.Various years. *Energy Balances of OECD Countries.* Paris.

———. Various years. *Energy Statistics of Non-OECD Countries.* Paris.

———.Various years. *Energy Statistics of OECD Countries.* Paris.

UNEP (United Nations Environment Programme) and WCMC (World Conservation Monitoring Centre). 2013. Online databases. [www.unep-wcmc.org/datasets-tools–reports_15.html?&types=Data,Website,Tool&ctops=]. Cambridge, UK.

United Nations Population Division. 2014. *World Urbanization Prospects: The 2014 Revision.* [http://esa.un.org/unpd/wup/]. New York: United Nations, Department of Economic and Social Affairs.

WHO (World Health Organization)–UNICEF (United Nations Children's Fund) Joint Monitoring Programme for Water Supply and Sanitation. 2015. Online databases. [www.wssinfo.org].

3 Environment

To access the World Development Indicators online tables, use the URL http://wdi.worldbank.org/table/ and the table number (for example, http://wdi.worldbank.org/table/3.1). To view a specific indicator online, use the URL http://data.worldbank.org/indicator/ and the indicator code (for example, http://data.worldbank.org /indicator/SP.RUR.TOTL.ZS).

3.1 Rural environment and land use

Rural population	SP.RUR.TOTL.ZS
Rural population growth	SP.RUR.TOTL.ZG
Land area	AG.LND.TOTL.K2
Forest area	AG.LND.FRST.ZS
Permanent cropland	AG.LND.CROP.ZS
Arable land, % of land area	AG.LND.ARBL.ZS
Arable land, hectares per person	AG.LND.ARBL.HA.PC

3.2 Agricultural inputs

Agricultural land, % of land area	AG.LND.AGRI.ZS
Agricultural land, % irrigated	AG.LND.IRIG.AG.ZS
Average annual precipitation	AG.LND.PRCP.MM
Land under cereal production	AG.LND.CREL.HA
Fertilizer consumption, % of fertilizer production	AG.CON.FERT.PT.ZS
Fertilizer consumption, kilograms per hectare of arable land	AG.CON.FERT.ZS
Agricultural employment	SL.AGR.EMPL.ZS
Tractors	AG.LND.TRAC.ZS

3.3 Agricultural output and productivity

Crop production index	AG.PRD.CROP.XD
Food production index	AG.PRD.FOOD.XD
Livestock production index	AG.PRD.LVSK.XD
Cereal yield	AG.YLD.CREL.KG
Agriculture value added per worker	EA.PRD.AGRI.KD

3.4 Deforestation and biodiversity

Forest area	AG.LND.FRST.K2
Average annual deforestation	..[a,b]
Threatened species, Mammals	EN.MAM.THRD.NO
Threatened species, Birds	EN.BIR.THRD.NO
Threatened species, Fishes	EN.FSH.THRD.NO
Threatened species, Higher plants	EN.HPT.THRD.NO
Terrestrial protected areas	ER.LND.PTLD.ZS
Marine protected areas	ER.MRN.PTMR.ZS

3.5 Freshwater

Internal renewable freshwater resources	ER.H2O.INTR.K3
Internal renewable freshwater resources, Per capita	ER.H2O.INTR.PC
Annual freshwater withdrawals, cu. m	ER.H2O.FWTL.K3
Annual freshwater withdrawals, % of internal resources	ER.H2O.FWTL.ZS

Annual freshwater withdrawals, % for agriculture	ER.H2O.FWAG.ZS
Annual freshwater withdrawals, % for industry	ER.H2O.FWIN.ZS
Annual freshwater withdrawals, % of domestic	ER.H2O.FWDM.ZS
Water productivity, GDP/water use	ER.GDP.FWTL.M3.KD
Access to an improved water source, % of rural population	SH.H2O.SAFE.RU.ZS
Access to an improved water source, % of urban population	SH.H2O.SAFE.UR.ZS

3.6 Energy production and use

Energy production	EG.EGY.PROD.KT.OE
Energy use	EG.USE.COMM.KT.OE
Energy use, Average annual growth	..[a,b]
Energy use, Per capita	EG.USE.PCAP.KG.OE
Fossil fuel	EG.USE.COMM.FO.ZS
Combustible renewable and waste	EG.USE.CRNW.ZS
Alternative and nuclear energy production	EG.USE.COMM.CL.ZS

3.7 Electricity production, sources, and access

Electricity production	EG.ELC.PROD.KH
Coal sources	EG.ELC.COAL.ZS
Natural gas sources	EG.ELC.NGAS.ZS
Oil sources	EG.ELC.PETR.ZS
Hydropower sources	EG.ELC.HYRO.ZS
Renewable sources	EG.ELC.RNWX.ZS
Nuclear power sources	EG.ELC.NUCL.ZS
Access to electricity	EG.ELC.ACCS.ZS

3.8 Energy dependency, efficiency and carbon dioxide emissions

Net energy imports	EG.IMP.CONS.ZS
GDP per unit of energy use	EG.GDP.PUSE.KO.PP.KD
Carbon dioxide emissions, Total	EN.ATM.CO2E.KT
Carbon dioxide emissions, Carbon intensity	EN.ATM.CO2E.EG.ZS
Carbon dioxide emissions, Per capita	EN.ATM.CO2E.PC
Carbon dioxide emissions, kilograms per 2011 PPP $ of GDP	EN.ATM.CO2E.PP.GD.KD

3.9 Trends in greenhouse gas emissions

Greenhouse gas emissions, Total	EN.ATM.GHGT.KT.CE
Greenhouse gas emissions, % change	EN.ATM.GHGT.ZG
Methane emissions, Total	EN.ATM.METH.KT.CE
Methane emissions, % change	EN.ATM.METH.ZG

Methane emissions, From energy processes	EN.ATM.METH.EG.ZS
Methane emissions, Agricultural	EN.ATM.METH.AG.ZS
Nitrous oxide emissions, Total	EN.ATM.NOXE.KT.CE
Nitrous oxide emissions, % change	EN.ATM.NOXE.ZG
Nitrous oxide emissions, From energy processes	EN.ATM.NOXE.EG.ZS
Nitrous oxide emissions, Agricultural	EN.ATM.NOXE.AG.ZS
Other greenhouse gas emissions, Total	EN.ATM.GHGO.KT.CE
Other greenhouse gas emissions, % change	EN.ATM.GHGO.ZG

3.10 Carbon dioxide emissions by sector

Electricity and heat production	EN.CO2.ETOT.ZS
Manufacturing industries and construction	EN.CO2.MANF.ZS
Residential buildings and commercial and public services	EN.CO2.BLDG.ZS
Transport	EN.CO2.TRAN.ZS
Other sectors	EN.CO2.OTHX.ZS

3.11 Climate variability, exposure to impact, and resilience

Land area where elevation is below 5 meters	AG.LND.EL5M.ZS
Urban land area where elevation is below 5 meters	AG.LND.EL5M.UR.ZS
Rural land area where elevation is below 5 meters	AG.LND.EL5M.RU.ZS
Population living in areas where elevation is below 5 meters	EN.POP.EL5M.ZS
Urban population living in areas where elevation is below 5 meters	EN.POP.EL5M.UR.ZS
Rural population living in areas where elevation is below 5 meters	EN.POP.EL5M.RU.ZS
Population affected by droughts, floods, and extreme temperatures	EN.CLC.MDAT.ZS
Disaster risk reduction progress score	EN.CLC.DRSK.XQ

3.12 Urbanization.

Urban population	SP.URB.TOTL
Urban population, % of total population	SP.URB.TOTL.IN.ZS
Urban population, Average annual growth	SP.URB.GROW
Population in urban agglomerations of more than 1 million	EN.URB.MCTY.TL.ZS
Population in the largest city	EN.URB.LCTY.UR.ZS
Access to improved sanitation facilities, % of urban population	SH.STA.ACSN.UR
Access to improved sanitation facilities, % of rural population	SH.STA.ACSN.RU

3.13 Sustainable energy for all

Access to electricity, % of population	EG.ELC.ACCS.ZS
Access to electricity, % of urban population	EG.ELC.ACCS.UR.ZS
Access to electricity, % of rural population	EG.ELC.ACCS.RU.ZS
Access to non-solid fuel, % of population	EG.NSF.ACCS.ZS
Access to non-solid fuel, % of urban population	EG.NSF.ACCS.UR.ZS
Access to non-solid fuel, % of rural population	EG.NSF.ACCS.RU.ZS
Energy intensity level of primary energy	EG.EGY.PRIM.PP.KD
Renewable energy consumption	EG.FEC.RNEW.ZS
Renewable electricity output	EG.ELC.RNEW.ZS

3.14 Contribution of natural resources to gross domestic product

Total natural resources rents	NY.GDP.TOTL.RT.ZS
Oil rents	NY.GDP.PETR.RT.ZS
Natural gas rents	NY.GDP.NGAS.RT.ZS
Coal rents	NY.GDP.COAL.RT.ZS
Mineral rents	NY.GDP.MINR.RT.ZS
Forest rents	NY.GDP.FRST.RT.ZS

a. Derived from data elsewhere in the World Development Indicators database.
b. Available online only as part of the table, not as an individual indicator.

ECONOMY

The *Economy* section provides a picture of the global economy and the economic activity of more than 200 countries and territories. It includes measures of macroeconomic performance and stability as well as broader measures of income and savings adjusted for pollution, depreciation, and resource depletion.

Global real gross domestic product grew 2.4 percent in 2015, to about $74 trillion in current prices, and is projected to grow 2.9 percent in 2016. Low- and middle-income economies accounted for 33 percent of the global economy in 2015, an increase of 1 percentage point. They grew an estimated 4.3 percent in 2015 and are projected to grow 4.8 percent in 2016. Expected growth in high-income economies has been revised from earlier forecasts to 1.6 percent in 2015 and 2.1 percent in 2016.

The adjusted net savings indicator has been updated this year with new data on the health impacts of air pollution from the Global Burden of Disease 2013, an international scientific effort led by the Institute for Health Metrics and Evaluation at the University of Washington, Seattle. Damages include the costs of premature mortality due to exposure to ambient particulate matter, household air pollution due to cooking with solid fuels, and ambient ozone pollution.

In August 2015 the International Monetary Fund began using the Government Finance Statistics Manual (GFSM) 2014 framework for its *Government Finance Statistics Yearbook* and database. Affected series have been adjusted from 1990 onward. Historical series based on the previous (2001) framework, with data up to 2012, can be accessed through the World Development Indicators archives (http://databank.worldbank.org/data/source/WDI-Archives).

GFSM 2014 provides comprehensive fiscal data through accrual reporting and allows data inconsistencies to be detected and fiscal transparency to be improved. In turn, fiscal analyses by end-users will be more detailed and robust. The new framework emphasizes economically meaningful fiscal indicators and allows for the phased implementation of accrual accounting while supporting needed improvements in the compilation of cash-based fiscal statistics for the public and general government sectors and subsectors. It also harmonizes the system used to report fiscal statistics with other macroeconomic statistical systems—most notably the System of National Accounts and the European System of Accounts.

A key feature of GFSM 2014 is its distinction between transactions and other economic flows. Transactions cover all exchanges or transfers that take place by mutual agreement and the consumption of fixed capital (the economic equivalent of "depreciation"). Mutual agreement does not mean that transactions have to be entered into voluntarily (the payment of taxes is treated as a transaction despite being compulsory). Additionally, transactions cover monetary exchanges and in-kind activity (such as the receipt of commodity grants and noncash remuneration). Other economic flows are the result of events that affect the value of nonfinancial assets, financial assets, and liabilities but that are not exchanges or transfers. These flows can reflect either price changes (including exchange rate movements) or volume changes due to one-off events (such as mineral discoveries or natural disasters).

For more information, see http://www.imf.org/external/Pubs/FT/GFS/Manual/2014/gfsfinal.pdf.

Economic growth reduces poverty. As a result, fast-growing middle-income economies are closing the income gap with high-income economies. But growth must be sustained over the long term, and gains must be shared to make lasting improvements to the well-being of all people. The 2007 financial crisis spread from high-income to low-income economies in 2008. A year later it became the most severe global recession in 50 years and affected sustained development around the world. Average annual per capita GDP growth in low- and middle-income countries slowed from 5 percent over 2000–09 (the pre-crisis period) to 4.3 percent over 2009–14 (the post-crisis period), which was still faster than in high-income countries. High-income countries grew an average of 1.2 percent a year after the crisis, down from 1.5 percent before the crisis. The low- and middle-income countries in Middle East and North Africa saw the largest drop: Average annual per capita GDP growth fell 3.4 percentage points, from 3.1 percent in the pre-crisis period to –0.3 percent in the post-crisis period.

Economic growth

Average annual growth of
per capita GDP, 2009–14 (%)

- 6.0 or more
- 4.0–5.9
- 2.0–3.9
- 0.0–1.9
- Less than 0.0
- No data

IBRD 41453

Front | ? User guide | World view | People | Environment

Turkmenistan saw the highest average per capita GDP growth over 2009–14 among low- and middle-income countries: 9.9 percent. This rapid growth was driven by the well planned development of the hydrocarbon sector and considerable government spending on infrastructure.

China's economy has been slowing down: Average annual per capita GDP growth dropped from 10.2 percent pre-crisis to 7.9 percent post-crisis. This is attributable to the slowdown in property investment and shrinking exports from the manufacturing industry.

Sri Lanka is the fastest growing country in South Asia, with average annual per capita GDP growth of 6.7 percent in the post-crisis period, thanks to the end of three decades of civil conflict in 2009. The whole economy has been rejuvenated, with its main sectors encompassing tourism, tea export, apparel, textile, and rice production.

After a decade of civil war, Sierra Leone has been steadily growing. Average annual per capita GDP growth reached 8.5 percent over 2009–14, compared with 3.3 percent before the crisis, supported by mineral exploration and diamond exports.

4 Economy

	Gross domestic product			Gross savings	Adjusted net savings	Current account balance	Central government cash surplus or deficit	Central government debt	Consumer price index	Broad money
	average annual % growth			% of GDP	% of GNI	% of GDP	% of GDP	% of GDP	% growth	% of GDP
	1990–2000	2000–09	2009–14	2014	2014ᵃ	2014	2013	2013	2014	2014
Afghanistan	..	8.5	6.8	–4.8	–18.3	–20.1	–0.6	..	4.6	34.9
Albania	3.6	5.7	2.0	11.8	–1.6	–12.9	..	..	1.6	85.8
Algeria	1.9	4.2	3.2	43.5	26.9	–4.5	–0.3	..	2.9	79.4
American Samoa	..	..	..	..	..	..	..	..	..	..
Andorra	3.2	4.3	–3.1	..	..	..	..	..	..	..
Angola	..	..	..	29.5	..	6.0	6.1	..	7.3	32.9
Antigua and Barbuda	3.5	4.9	0.1	9.1	..	–17.0	–1.3	..	1.1	97.9
Argentina	4.3	4.9ᵇ	4.1ᵇ	17.7	10.1	–1.1	..	..	..	26.6
Armenia	–1.9	10.6	4.5	13.8	0.4	–7.3	–1.3	..	3.0	34.6
Aruba	3.9	–0.1	..	..	..	..	..	..	0.4	..
Australia	3.6	3.3	2.7	23.9	8.5	–3.0	–1.5	38.3	2.5	109.5
Austriaᶜ	2.5	1.9	1.2	24.9	11.8	1.9	–1.4	83.4	1.6	..
Azerbaijan	–6.3	17.9	2.9	39.3	17.8	13.6	6.1	..	..	36.6
Bahamas, The	2.6	1.0	1.1	6.3	2.3	–18.0	..	..	1.5	74.4
Bahrain	5.0	6.0	3.9	24.7	–2.0	3.3	–0.5	35.6	2.8	76.6
Bangladesh	4.7	5.7	6.2	37.7	25.2	–1.0	–0.8	..	7.0	63.2
Barbados	1.7	1.9	0.3	–1.0	–0.3	–5.8	–12.2	131.6	1.9	..
Belarus	–1.6	8.2	3.3	26.5	17.3	–6.8	0.1	25.2	..	30.8
Belgiumᶜ	2.2	1.9	1.0	23.8	9.8	–0.2	–2.4	101.5	0.3	..
Belize	4.5	4.2	2.8	9.9	–5.5	–8.0	–0.2	74.5	0.9	78.6
Benin	4.6	4.0	4.7	16.2	12.3	–7.4	2.7	..	–1.1	42.7
Bermuda	2.9	2.3	–3.4	54.2	..	15.1	..	..	..	..
Bhutan	5.2	8.4	6.0	34.8	14.7	–24.7	..	..	8.2	62.7
Bolivia	4.0	4.0	5.4	20.8	8.3	0.0	..	..	5.8	84.5
Bosnia and Herzegovina	28.5	5.3	0.8	10.9	..	–7.8	–1.7	46.0	–0.9	63.2
Botswana	4.9	4.7	6.6	47.7	34.8	15.8	1.4	18.7	4.4	39.3
Brazil	2.8	3.7	3.1	16.2	7.3	–4.3	–1.8	..	6.3	89.2
Brunei Darussalam	2.1	1.4	0.6	58.3	25.8	27.8	..	..	–0.2	67.5
Bulgaria	–0.4	5.8	0.9	22.3	10.7	1.2	–0.8	17.2	–1.4	81.3
Burkina Faso	5.5	6.2	5.7	..	..	..	–3.9	..	–0.2	32.8
Burundi	–2.9	3.3	4.2	17.8	–8.6	–9.3	..	..	4.4	21.8
Cabo Verde	12.1	7.3	2.0	..	..	–8.6	..	..	–0.2	95.0
Cambodia	7.0	9.2	7.1	15.5	3.1	–9.9	–3.1	..	3.9	63.0
Cameroon	1.8	3.3	4.7	10.2	–2.3	–3.8	..	..	1.9	21.9
Canada	3.1	2.1	2.5	21.4	7.0	–2.1	–0.6	48.8	1.9	..
Cayman Islands	..	..	..	..	..	..	..	..	..	..
Central African Republic	1.8	2.3	–7.6	..	..	..	0.7	..	1.5	28.7
Chad	2.2	11.4	6.5	..	..	..	..	..	1.7	15.7
Channel Islands	..	0.5	..	..	..	..	..	..	..	..
Chile	6.6	4.2	4.8	20.2	4.0	–1.2	–0.6	..	4.4	83.3
China	10.6	10.9	8.5	49.3	34.5	2.1	..	..	2.0	193.1
Hong Kong SAR, China	3.6	4.8	3.5	25.9	..	1.2	..	..	4.4	362.0
Macao SAR, China	2.2	11.9	13.2	57.3	..	38.0	24.1	..	6.0	110.0
Colombia	2.8	4.6	4.9	18.4	3.3	–5.2	–5.5	58.6	2.9	46.8
Comoros	1.6	2.0	2.8	10.9	–2.2	–7.5	..	..	..	42.0
Congo, Dem. Rep.	–4.9	5.1	7.7	10.0	–26.6	–9.2	..	..	1.6	12.9
Congo, Rep.	1.0	4.0	4.7	..	..	..	..	..	0.1	36.1

 Front | User guide | World view | People | Environment

	Gross domestic product			Gross savings	Adjusted net savings	Current account balance	Central government cash surplus or deficit	Central government debt	Consumer price index	Broad money
	average annual % growth			% of GDP	% of GNI	% of GDP	% of GDP	% of GDP	% growth	% of GDP
	1990–2000	2000–09	2009–14	2014	2014[a]	2014	2013	2013	2014	2014
Costa Rica	5.3	5.1	4.4	14.3	14.7	–4.4	–5.2	..	4.5	52.1
Côte d'Ivoire	3.1	1.0	5.2	15.8	13.0	–2.0	–2.3	..	0.5	37.5
Croatia	3.1	3.7	–1.2	18.9	3.0	0.7	–3.4	..	–0.2	69.9
Cuba	–0.7	6.4	2.8	..	..	..	..	..	..	..
Curaçao	..	..	..	..	..	..	..	..	..	..
Cyprus[c,d]	4.2	3.6	–1.9	8.8	0.3	–4.5	–4.6	145.8	–1.4	..
Czech Republic	1.4	4.1	0.7	23.9	5.7	0.7	–2.3	40.8	0.3	78.2
Denmark	2.8	1.2	0.4	25.8	14.5	6.3	–1.2	46.6	0.6	65.2
Djibouti	–2.0	4.0	4.8	..	..	–21.2	..	..	2.9	83.1
Dominica	2.0	3.1	0.5	0.5	..	–14.2	–11.8	..	0.8	96.4
Dominican Republic	6.3	5.1	4.6	18.4	14.6	–3.2	–3.2	..	3.0	35.0
Ecuador	2.2	4.5	5.3	27.8	11.2	–0.6	..	..	3.6	42.8
Egypt, Arab Rep.	4.4	4.9	2.5	12.0	2.4	–2.0	–10.1	..	10.1	76.5
El Salvador	4.8	2.4	1.9	8.8	0.5	–4.8	–1.4	55.9	1.1	43.3
Equatorial Guinea	36.7	17.7	–0.3	..	..	..	..	..	6.4	20.3
Eritrea	6.5	0.2	..	..	..	..	..	..	..	..
Estonia[c]	5.7	5.2	4.2	29.1	16.5	1.0	0.0	0.6	–0.1	..
Ethiopia	3.8	8.5	10.5	31.1	14.5	–6.9	–1.3	..	7.4	..
Faroe Islands	..	..	..	..	..	..	..	..	..	..
Fiji	2.7	1.6	2.3	..	..	–13.4	..	..	0.5	73.9
Finland[c]	2.9	2.4	0.3	19.0	6.3	–0.9	–2.6	53.7	1.0	..
France[c]	2.0	1.5	1.0	20.0	6.6	–1.0	–3.2	88.5	0.5	..
French Polynesia	..	..	..	..	..	..	..	..	..	..
Gabon	2.3	1.0	6.2	..	..	..	..	..	4.7	23.5
Gambia, The	3.0	3.2	2.6	27.9	8.3	6.4	..	..	5.9	54.9
Georgia	–7.1[e]	7.4[e]	5.6[e]	20.0[e]	9.4[e]	–10.5	–0.5	32.5	3.1	38.3
Germany[c]	1.7	1.0	1.8	26.9	13.3	7.2	–0.2	52.3	0.9	..
Ghana	4.3	5.7	8.9	18.5	1.6	–9.6	–3.9	..	15.5	33.1
Greece[c]	2.4	3.1	–5.4	10.8	–5.8	–2.1	–14.6	181.9	–1.3	..
Greenland	1.9	1.7	..	..	..	..	..	..	..	..
Grenada	3.2	3.1	1.1	–6.1	..	–25.3	–5.5	..	–0.9	88.4
Guam	..	..	..	..	..	..	..	..	..	..
Guatemala	4.2	3.7	3.6	11.6	2.6	–2.1	–2.3	24.3	3.4	47.2
Guinea	4.2	2.7	2.8	–17.1	–47.8	–18.6	..	..	9.7	..
Guinea-Bissau	0.6	2.4	2.5	3.8	–19.3	–5.5	..	..	–1.5	48.3
Guyana	5.4	2.3	5.0	3.3	–10.4	–12.4	..	..	1.8	66.8
Haiti	..	0.7	2.5	23.2	16.6	–6.9	..	..	4.6	44.9
Honduras	3.2	4.9	3.5	14.8	10.4	–7.5	–6.1	..	6.1	55.2
Hungary	1.9	2.8	1.0	24.3	10.9	2.2	–5.4	94.5	–0.2	58.3
Iceland	2.8	4.3	1.4	20.1	11.2	3.2	–1.6	103.2	2.0	84.3
India	6.0	7.6	6.9	31.3	19.0	–1.3	–3.8	50.3	6.4	77.4
Indonesia	4.2	5.3	5.8	31.4	26.3	–3.1	–1.8	25.0	6.4	39.6
Iran, Islamic Rep.	2.4	5.5	0.2	..	..	..	..	..	17.2	..
Iraq	10.3	3.9	7.3	27.0	–2.6	13.6	..	..	2.2	35.5
Ireland[c]	7.7	4.0	1.7	23.9	16.1	3.6	–5.7	133.0	0.2	..
Isle of Man	6.4	6.2	..	..	..	..	..	..	..	..
Israel	5.7	3.5	3.8	23.7	15.3	4.2	–4.6	..	0.5	85.4

4 Economy

	Gross domestic product			Gross savings	Adjusted net savings	Current account balance	Central government cash surplus or deficit	Central government debt	Consumer price index	Broad money
	average annual % growth			% of GDP	% of GNI	% of GDP	% of GDP	% of GDP	% growth	% of GDP
	1990–2000	2000–09	2009–14	2014	2014[a]	2014	2013	2013	2014	2014
Italy[c]	1.6	0.6	–0.8	18.3	3.5	1.9	–3.0	134.7	0.2	..
Jamaica	1.6	1.3	0.2	14.1	10.9	–7.8	0.8	..	8.3	56.5
Japan	1.0	0.9	1.4	22.4	3.4	0.5	–7.2	201.1	2.7	251.3
Jordan	5.0	7.1	2.7	21.2	15.7	–6.8	–8.3	66.8	2.8	125.3
Kazakhstan	–4.1	8.8	6.0	26.3	3.0	2.1	..	..	6.7	32.8
Kenya	2.2	4.3	5.8	9.6	4.0	–10.4	–3.8	..	6.9	42.9
Kiribati	4.0	1.5	2.5	..	..	26.8	..	..	..	..
Korea, Dem. People's Rep.	..	..	..	..	..	..	..	..	..	..
Korea, Rep.	6.2	4.4	3.5	34.9	18.7	6.0	1.7	..	1.3	139.9
Kosovo	..	5.3	3.2	18.1	..	–7.6	..	..	0.4	..
Kuwait	4.9	7.2	3.5	48.8	18.7	33.0	..	..	2.9	72.2
Kyrgyz Republic	–4.1	4.6	4.2	9.9	–5.8	–24.2	–6.5	..	7.5	32.7
Lao PDR	6.4	7.0	8.1	16.7	–4.1	–3.4	–0.8	..	4.1	..
Latvia[c]	5.4	6.6	2.9	20.8	0.2	–2.0	0.5	41.6	0.6	..
Lebanon	5.3	5.3	2.6	4.1	–7.7	–26.7	–10.6	..	0.7	256.9
Lesotho	3.8	3.6	4.9	39.1	29.2	–10.5	..	..	5.3	38.0
Liberia	4.2	0.3	6.9	4.4	–27.9	–60.2	..	..	9.8	37.3
Libya	..	5.8	–9.8	..	..	–0.2	..	..	2.6	127.5
Liechtenstein	6.2	2.5	..	..	..	..	..	..	..	..
Lithuania[c]	4.8	6.2	3.8	18.7	20.1	3.5	–1.3	43.8	0.1	..
Luxembourg[c]	4.4	3.2	2.7	19.2	12.5	5.6	–0.6	20.1	0.6	..
Macedonia, FYR	–0.8	3.7	2.0	29.3	13.5	–0.9	–3.9	..	–0.3	59.4
Madagascar	2.0	3.6	2.1	5.4	–5.3	–5.9	–1.7	..	6.1	24.4
Malawi	3.7	4.5	4.4	15.2	1.8	–25.3	..	..	24.4	34.1
Malaysia	7.0	5.1	5.6	29.3	12.0	4.3	–4.4	51.6	3.1	137.1
Maldives	..	8.4	5.5	..	..	–4.1	–7.7	64.9	2.1	57.6
Mali	3.9	5.3	2.8	29.5	14.8	–3.4	–1.4	..	0.9	33.0
Malta[c]	5.2	1.8	2.2	..	..	3.8	–2.6	88.3	0.3	..
Marshall Islands	0.4	1.4	1.7	..	..	–10.7	..	..	..	..
Mauritania	2.9	6.1	5.4	18.0	–16.4	–29.1	..	..	3.5	28.9
Mauritius	5.2	3.8	3.5	7.6	2.7	–5.5	–4.1	50.1	3.2	102.8
Mexico	3.3	2.2	3.3	19.5	7.9	–1.9	..	..	4.0	51.8
Micronesia, Fed. Sts.	1.8	–0.3	–0.4	..	..	–10.0	..	..	..	..
Moldova	–9.6[f]	5.6[f]	5.0[f]	19.4[f]	13.8[f]	–7.1	–2.0	24.3	5.1	59.0
Monaco	1.9	4.2	..	..	..	..	..	..	..	..
Mongolia	1.0	7.5	11.7	23.8	7.2	–11.7	–7.1	..	13.0	48.7
Montenegro	..	4.7	1.4	5.0	..	–15.2	..	..	–0.7	..
Morocco	2.9[g]	5.0[g]	3.9[g]	25.8[g]	16.6[g]	–7.3	–7.4	58.2	0.4	118.0
Mozambique	8.6	8.2	7.1	15.4	8.5	–36.4	–2.6	..	2.6	49.4
Myanmar	..	..	..	..	..	–2.6	..	..	5.5	39.3
Namibia	3.3	5.3	5.5	19.4	16.9	–10.6	–11.9	35.5	5.4	52.7
Nepal	4.9	3.7	4.4	41.3	32.7	2.5	1.5	..	8.4	86.7
Netherlands[c]	3.3	1.7	0.3	29.0	16.9	10.6	–0.8	68.3	1.0	..
New Caledonia	..	..	..	..	..	..	..	..	..	..
New Zealand	3.4	2.9	2.3	21.2	13.8	–3.2	–0.6	60.2	0.9	..
Nicaragua	3.7	3.4	4.9	19.4	11.7	–7.1	0.5	..	6.0	37.1
Niger	2.4	4.1	6.7	21.3	5.7	–15.0	..	..	–0.8	27.4

 Front **?** User guide World view  People Environment

	Gross domestic product			Gross savings	Adjusted net savings	Current account balance	Central government cash surplus or deficit	Central government debt	Consumer price index	Broad money
	average annual % growth			% of GDP	% of GNI	% of GDP	% of GDP	% of GDP	% growth	% of GDP
	1990–2000	2000–09	2009–14	2014	2014[a]	2014	2013	2013	2014	2014
Nigeria	1.9	10.0	5.5	22.2	11.0	0.2	*–1.3*	*10.4*	8.1	20.2
Northern Mariana Islands	..	..	..	..	..	..	..	..	..	..
Norway	3.9	2.0	1.5	37.9	21.0	9.4	11.6	21.0	2.0	..
Oman	4.5	2.8	3.5	*20.5*	*–20.1*	5.0	*–0.4*	..	1.0	42.2
Pakistan	3.8	5.1	3.4	22.8	14.1	–1.5	–5.2	..	7.2	52.0
Palau	*2.0*	0.4	3.9	..	..	..	..	..	..	..
Panama	4.7	6.8	8.7	*25.2*	*24.3*	–11.4	..	..	2.6	..
Papua New Guinea	3.8	3.8	8.1	..	..	14.1	..	..	5.2	44.9
Paraguay	3.0	3.2	6.3	17.0	10.0	–0.4	*–1.0*	..	5.0	50.6
Peru	4.5	5.9	5.9	22.2	13.2	–4.0	*2.0*	*19.2*	3.2	43.0
Philippines	3.3	4.9	6.1	46.3	28.7	3.8	*–1.9*	*51.5*	4.1	71.6
Poland	4.7	4.3	2.8	18.1	10.0	–2.0	–3.5	55.6	0.1	61.6
Portugal[c]	2.8	0.8	–1.3	14.9	2.4	0.5	–5.4	138.0	–0.3	..
Puerto Rico	3.6	0.3	*–2.0*	..	..	..	..	..	..	..
Qatar	..	13.5	8.6	58.3	29.6	23.6	..	..	3.1	65.9
Romania	0.0	5.8	1.5	22.3	21.6	–0.5	–2.8	41.5	1.1	39.3
Russian Federation	–4.7	6.0	2.9	23.4	11.9	3.1	0.7	13.6	7.8	60.3
Rwanda	–0.2	7.7	7.2	15.5	4.8	–13.3	–3.0	..	1.3	..
Samoa	2.6	3.6	1.2	..	..	–6.1	*0.0*	..	–0.4	43.9
San Marino	5.8	*3.2*	..	..	..	..	..	..	1.1	..
São Tomé and Príncipe	..	5.6	4.5	..	..	–30.7	*–12.1*	..	7.0	40.3
Saudi Arabia	2.1	5.9	5.4	*44.1*	*20.0*	10.2	..	..	2.7	61.8
Senegal	3.0	4.3	3.6	..	..	..	–5.3	..	–1.1	45.0
Serbia	*0.7*	5.5	0.5	10.7	..	–6.0	*–6.1*	..	2.1	48.1
Seychelles	4.4	2.4	6.2	16.3	..	–21.8	*4.8*	*73.0*	1.4	64.8
Sierra Leone	–3.0	7.2	11.0	..	..	–18.8	..	..	7.3	20.9
Singapore	7.2	6.0	5.8	46.7	36.9	19.1	*8.6*	*109.7*	1.0	131.4
Sint Maarten	..	..	..	..	..	..	..	..	..	..
Slovak Republic[c]	*4.5*	5.8	2.4	19.8	1.3	0.2	–2.3	63.2	–0.1	..
Slovenia[c]	*4.3*	3.7	–0.2	26.8	10.8	7.0	*–3.5*	..	0.2	..
Solomon Islands	3.4	3.9	6.0	..	..	–4.3	..	..	5.2	42.5
Somalia	..	..	..	..	..	..	..	..	..	..
South Africa	2.1	4.0	2.5	14.9	2.1	–5.5	–4.3	..	6.4	71.0
South Sudan	..	..	..	..	..	..	..	..	..	..
Spain[c]	2.7	2.9	–1.1	20.7	6.6	0.9	–4.8	96.5	–0.1	..
Sri Lanka	5.3	5.5	6.8	..	..	–2.6	*–5.3*	*68.7*	3.3	37.7
St. Kitts and Nevis	4.6	3.4	1.9	*23.7*	..	–8.0	*11.2*	..	0.8	155.7
St. Lucia	3.5	3.0	–0.3	*11.6*	..	*–7.5*	–6.5	..	3.5	89.5
St. Martin	..	..	..	..	..	..	..	..	..	..
St. Vincent & the Grenadines	3.3	4.1	0.2	*–4.7*	..	*–29.2*	..	..	0.2	77.8
Sudan	5.5[h]	7.5[h]	0.6[i]	9.8	6.1	–6.6	..	..	36.9	18.4
Suriname	0.8	5.2	3.6	..	..	–7.4	*–1.2*	..	3.3	55.4
Swaziland	3.2	2.5	2.3	..	..	3.3	..	..	5.7	24.3
Sweden	2.3	2.4	2.0	29.2	18.8	5.7	–1.2	42.0	–0.2	66.9
Switzerland	1.2	2.2	1.8	31.5	15.0	7.3	*0.1*	*24.2*	0.0	188.6
Syrian Arab Republic	5.1	*5.0*	..	..	..	..	..	..	*36.7*	..
Tajikistan	–10.4	8.5	7.2	*17.2*	*14.3*	–3.8	..	..	..	19.9

4 Economy

	Gross domestic product			Gross savings	Adjusted net savings	Current account balance	Central government cash surplus or deficit	Central government debt	Consumer price index	Broad money
	average annual % growth			% of GDP	% of GNI	% of GDP	% of GDP	% of GDP	% growth	% of GDP
	1990–2000	2000–09	2009–14	2014	2014ᵃ	2014	2013	2013	2014	2014
Tanzaniaʲ	3.0	6.9	6.7	20.5	15.1	–10.4	–5.3	..	6.1	23.4
Thailand	4.1	4.8	3.9	27.4	12.0	3.8	–0.8	29.2	1.9	127.8
Timor-Leste	..	3.4	6.8	195.7	..	78.1	..	..	0.4	42.3
Togo	3.5	2.2	5.2	–5.8	–19.5	–13.1	–4.6	..	0.2	49.0
Tonga	2.6	0.7	0.9	29.4	..	–7.5	..	..	2.5	48.3
Trinidad and Tobago	4.6	7.4	0.9	..	..	..	..	..	5.7	55.4
Tunisia	4.7	4.6	2.1	12.3	–2.7	–8.8	–5.1	44.6	4.9	66.6
Turkey	3.9	4.9	5.2	14.7	10.7	–5.8	–0.8	38.0	8.9	60.6
Turkmenistan	–3.2	8.0	11.3	..	..	..	..	..	..	..
Turks and Caicos Islands	..	..	..	..	..	..	..	..	..	..
Tuvalu	3.2	1.2	2.1	..	..	17.8	..	..	..	..
Uganda	7.0	7.8	5.5	19.0	3.1	–9.9	–2.1	33.2	4.3	22.3
Ukraine	–9.3	5.7	0.8	10.0	–2.7	–3.5	–4.1	33.7	12.2	61.1
United Arab Emirates	4.8	5.3	4.8	..	..	..	0.2	1.9	2.3	77.8
United Kingdom	3.0	2.1	1.9	12.4	3.6	–5.1	–5.5	98.3	1.5	138.7
United States	3.6	2.1	2.2	18.4	6.4	–2.2	–1.4	96.2	1.6	89.8
Uruguay	3.9	3.2	4.8	16.3	8.1	–4.4	–2.0	43.3	8.9	47.1
Uzbekistan	–0.2	6.9	8.2	..	..	..	..	..	..	..
Vanuatu	3.4	3.9	1.7	28.9	..	2.4	–2.3	..	0.8	73.8
Venezuela, RB	1.6	5.1	1.9	25.6	14.4	2.9	..	..	62.2	52.9
Vietnam	7.9	6.8	5.8	30.3	14.9	5.1	..	..	4.1	127.5
Virgin Islands (U.S.)	..	..	..	..	..	..	..	..	..	..
West Bank and Gaza	14.3	2.7	4.4	7.8	..	–10.9	0.3	..	1.7	17.6
Yemen, Rep.	5.6	4.0	–2.7	..	..	–4.3	..	..	..	39.1
Zambia	1.6	7.2	7.0	..	..	–1.4	4.1	..	7.8	21.0
Zimbabwe	2.5	–7.2	8.6	..	..	..	..	..	..	..
World	**2.9 w**	**2.9 w**	**2.7 w**	**22.8 w**	**12.7 w**					
East Asia & Pacific	3.3	4.2	4.5	30.9	22.7					
Europe & Central Asia	1.9	2.2	1.2	21.5	9.5					
Latin America & Caribbean	3.2	3.5	3.5	18.1	7.7					
Middle East & North Africa	3.8	5.4	3.6	36.4	16.3					
North America	3.6	2.1	2.2	18.7	6.5					
South Asia	5.6	7.1	6.5	30.6	18.9					
Sub-Saharan Africa	2.4	5.4	4.3	16.8	5.6					
Low income	2.3	5.4	6.4	17.0	0.8					
Lower middle income	3.5	6.4	5.7	28.1	17.2					
Upper middle income	4.7	6.5	5.7	31.6	23.7					
High income	2.6	2.1	1.8	21.3	8.4					

a. Includes data on pollution damage for 2010, the most recent year available. b. Data are officially reported statistics from the National Statistics and Censuses Institute of Argentina. On February 1, 2013, the International Monetary Fund (IMF) issued a declaration of censure and in December 2013 called on Argentina to implement specific actions to address the quality of its official GDP data on a specified timetable. On June 3, 2015, the IMF Executive Board recognized the material progress in remedying the inaccurate provision of data since 2013 but found that some actions called for by the end of February 2015 had not been completely implemented. The IMF Executive Board will review this issue again by July 15, 2016. c. As members of the European Monetary Union, these countries share a single currency, the euro. d. Refers to the area controlled by the government of the Republic of Cyprus. e. Excludes Abkhazia and South Ossetia. f. Excludes Transnistria. g. Includes Former Spanish Sahara. h. Includes South Sudan. i. Includes South Sudan until July 9, 2011. j. Covers mainland Tanzania only.

About the data

Economic data are organized by several different accounting conventions: the system of national accounts, the balance of payments, government finance statistics, and international finance statistics. There has been progress in unifying the concepts in the system of national accounts, balance of payments, and government finance statistics, but there are many national variations in the implementation of these standards. For example, even though the United Nations recommends using the 2008 System of National Accounts (2008 SNA) methodology in compiling national accounts, many are still using earlier versions, some as old as 1968. The International Monetary Fund (IMF) has recently published a new balance of payments methodology (BPM6), but many countries are still using the previous version. Similarly, the standards and definitions for government finance statistics were updated in 2014, but several countries still report using the 1986 or 2001 version. For individual country information about methodology used, refer to *Sources and methods*.

Economic growth

An economy's growth is measured by the change in the volume of its output or in the real incomes of its residents. The 2008 SNA offers three plausible indicators for calculating growth: the volume of gross domestic product (GDP), real gross domestic income, and real gross national income. Only growth in GDP is reported here.

Growth rates of GDP and its components are calculated using the least squares method and constant price data in the local currency for countries and using constant price U.S. dollar series for regional and income groups. Local currency series are converted to constant U.S. dollars using an exchange rate in the common reference year. The growth rates are average annual and compound growth rates. Methods of computing growth are described in *Sources and methods*. Forecasts of growth rates come from World Bank (2016).

Rebasing national accounts

Rebasing of national accounts can alter the measured growth rate of an economy and lead to breaks in series that affect the consistency of data over time. When countries rebase their national accounts, they update the weights assigned to various components to better reflect current patterns of production or uses of output. The new base year should represent normal operation of the economy—it should be a year without major shocks or distortions. Some countries have not rebased their national accounts for many years. Using an old base year can be misleading because implicit price and volume weights become progressively less relevant and useful.

To obtain comparable series of constant price data for computing aggregates, the World Bank rescales GDP and value added by industrial origin to a common reference year.

Rescaling may result in a discrepancy between the rescaled GDP and the sum of the rescaled components. To avoid distortions in the growth rates, the discrepancy is left unallocated. As a result, the weighted average of the growth rates of the components generally does not equal the GDP growth rate.

Adjusted net savings

Adjusted net savings measure the change in a country's real wealth after accounting for the depreciation and depletion of a full range of assets in the economy. If a country's adjusted net savings are positive and the accounting includes a sufficiently broad range of assets, economic theory suggests that the present value of social welfare is increasing. Conversely, persistently negative adjusted net savings indicate that the present value of social welfare is decreasing, suggesting that an economy is on an unsustainable path.

Adjusted net savings are derived from standard national accounting measures of gross savings by making four adjustments. First, estimates of fixed capital consumption of produced assets are deducted to obtain net savings. Second, current public expenditures on education are added to net savings (in standard national accounting these expenditures are treated as consumption). Third, estimates of the depletion of a variety of natural resources are deducted to reflect the decline in asset values associated with their extraction and harvest. And fourth, deductions are made for damages from carbon dioxide emissions and local air pollution. Damages from local air pollution include damages from exposure to household air pollution from cooking with solid fuels, ambient concentrations of very fine particulate matter with an aerodynamic diameter of less than 2.5 microns, and ambient ozone pollution. By accounting for the depletion of natural resources and the degradation of the environment, adjusted net savings go beyond the definition of savings or net savings in the SNA.

Balance of payments

The balance of payments records an economy's transactions with the rest of the world. Balance of payments accounts are divided into two groups: the current account, which records transactions in goods, services, primary income, and secondary income, and the capital and financial account, which records capital transfers, acquisition or disposal of nonproduced, nonfinancial assets, and transactions in financial assets and liabilities. The current account balance is a more analytically useful indicator of an external imbalance.

Where to draw the line for analytical purposes requires a judgment concerning the imbalance that best indicates the need for adjustment. There are a number of definitions in common use for this and related analytical purposes. The trade balance is the difference between exports and imports of goods. From an analytical view it is arbitrary to distinguish goods from services. For example, a unit of foreign exchange earned by a freight company strengthens the balance of payments to the same extent as the foreign exchange earned by a goods exporter. Even so, the trade balance is useful because it is often the most timely indicator of trends in the current account balance. Customs authorities are typically able to provide data on trade in goods long before data on trade in services are available.

Beginning in August 2012, the International Monetary Fund implemented the Balance of Payments Manual 6 (BPM6) framework in its major statistical publications. The World Bank implemented BPM6 in its online databases and publications in April 2013. Balance of payments data for 2005 onward are presented in accord with the BPM6. The historical BPM5 data series will end with data for 2008, which can be accessed through the World Development Indicators archives (http://databank.worldbank.org/data/source/WDI-Archives).

The complete balance of payments methodology can be accessed at www.imf.org/external/np/sta/bop/bop.htm.

Government finance

In August 2015 the International Monetary Fund began using the Government Finance Statistics Manual (GFSM) 2014 framework for its *Government Finance Statistics Yearbook* and database. The 2014 framework will be implemented in World Development Indicators from April 2016 onward; affected series will be adjusted from 1990 onward. Historical series based on the previous (2001) framework, with data up to 2012, can be accessed through the World Development Indicators archives.

The GFSM 2014 framework addresses the measurement of important international economic developments that have taken place in recent years, including through improved recording and methodological treatment of various types of events. The changes include methodological changes in the 2008 SNA, clarifications of existing methodological guidelines, presentational changes, and editorial changes. It aims to harmonize, to the extent possible, the guidelines with the 2008 SNA, the BPM6, and the Monetary and Financial Statistics Manual. For debt-related issues GFSM 2014 is supplemented with the Public Sector Debt Statistics: Guide for Compilers and Users. Furthermore, efforts to harmonize statistical reporting and financial reporting, and new developments in the International Public Sector Accounting Standards, have led to additional changes.

Some differences remain between GFSM 2014 and the SNA, particularly in how some government production activities are treated, because they serve different analytic purposes. GFSM 2014 measures the impact of economic events such as taxing, spending, borrowing, and lending on government finances and on the remainder of the economy. The SNA measures production and consumption of goods and services and the savings and investment created in doing so. As a result, the treatment of some government production activities differs in GFSM 2014 from the treatment of those activities in the 2008 SNA. The complete GFSM 2014 can be accessed at www.imf.org/external/Pubs/FT/GFS /Manual/2014/gfsfinal.pdf.

For most countries central government finance data have been consolidated into one account, but for others only budgetary central government accounts are available. Countries reporting budgetary data are noted in *Sources and methods.* Because budgetary accounts may not include all central government units (such as social security funds), they usually provide an incomplete picture.

In federal states the central government accounts provide an incomplete view of total public finance.

Data on government revenue and expense are collected by the IMF through questionnaires to member countries and by the Organisation for Economic Co-operation and Development (OECD). Despite IMF efforts to standardize data collection, statistics are often incomplete, untimely, and not comparable across countries.

Government finance statistics are reported in local currency. The indicators here are shown as percentages of GDP. Many countries report government finance data by fiscal year; see *Sources and methods* for information on fiscal year end by country.

Financial accounts

Money and the financial accounts that record the supply of money lie at the heart of a country's financial system. There are several commonly used definitions of the money supply. The narrowest, M1, encompasses currency held by the public and demand deposits with banks. M2 includes M1 plus time and savings deposits with banks that require prior notice for withdrawal. M3 includes M2 as well as various money market instruments, such as certificates of deposit issued by banks, bank deposits denominated in foreign currency, and deposits with financial institutions other than banks. However defined, money is a liability of the banking system, distinguished from other bank liabilities by the special role it plays as a medium of exchange, a unit of account, and a store of value.

A general and continuing increase in an economy's price level is called inflation. The increase in the average prices of goods and services in the economy should be distinguished from a change in the relative prices of individual goods and services. Generally accompanying an overall increase in the price level is a change in the structure of relative prices, but it is only the average increase, not the relative price changes, that constitutes inflation. A commonly used measure of inflation is the consumer price index, which measures the prices of a representative basket of goods and services purchased by a typical household. The consumer price index is usually calculated on the basis of periodic surveys of consumer prices. Other price indices are derived implicitly from indexes of current and constant price series.

Consumer price indexes are produced more frequently and so are more current. They are constructed explicitly, using surveys of the cost of a defined basket of consumer goods and services. Nevertheless, consumer price indexes should be interpreted with caution. The definition of a household, the basket of goods, and the geographic (urban or rural) and income group coverage of consumer price surveys can vary widely by country. In addition, weights are derived from household expenditure surveys, which, for budgetary reasons, tend to be conducted infrequently in the poorest countries, impairing comparability over time. Although useful for measuring consumer price inflation within a country, consumer price indexes are of less value in comparing countries.

Definitions

• **Gross domestic product (GDP)** at purchaser prices is the sum of gross value added by all resident producers in the economy plus any product taxes (less subsidies) not included in the valuation of output. It is calculated without deducting for depreciation of fabricated capital assets or for depletion and degradation of natural resources. Value added is the net output of an industry after adding up all outputs and subtracting intermediate inputs. • **Gross savings** are the difference between gross national income and public and private consumption, plus net current transfers. • **Adjusted net savings** measure the change in value of a specified set of assets, excluding capital gains. They are net savings plus education expenditure minus energy depletion, mineral depletion, net forest depletion, and carbon dioxide and local air pollution damage. • **Current account balance** is the sum of net exports of goods and services, net primary income, and net secondary income. • **Central government cash surplus or deficit** is revenue (including grants) minus expense, minus net acquisition of nonfinancial assets. This cash surplus or deficit is close to the earlier overall budget balance (still missing is lending minus repayments, which are included as a financing item under net acquisition of financial assets). • **Central government debt** is the entire stock of direct government fixed-term contractual obligations to others outstanding on a particular date. It includes domestic and foreign liabilities such as currency and money deposits, securities other than shares, and loans. It is the gross amount of government liabilities reduced by the amount of equity and financial derivatives held by the government. Because debt is a stock rather than a flow, it is measured as of a given date, usually the last day of the fiscal year. • **Consumer price index** reflects changes in the cost to the average consumer of acquiring a basket of goods and services that may be fixed or may change at specified intervals, such as yearly. The Laspeyres formula is generally used. • **Broad money** (IFS line 35L..ZK) is the sum of currency outside banks; demand deposits other than those of the central government; the time, savings, and foreign currency deposits of resident sectors other than the central government; bank and traveler's checks; and other securities such as certificates of deposit and commercial paper.

Data sources

Data on GDP for most countries are collected from national statistical organizations and central banks by visiting and resident World Bank missions; data for selected high-income economies are from the OECD. Data on gross savings are from World Bank national accounts data files. Data on adjusted net savings are based on a conceptual underpinning by Hamilton and Clemens (1999). Data on consumption of fixed capital are from the United Nations Statistics Division's National Accounts Statistics: Main Aggregates and Detailed Tables, the OECD's National Accounts Statistics database, and the Penn World Table (Feenstra, Inklaar, and Timmler 2013), with missing data estimated by World Bank staff. Data on education expenditure are from the United Nations Educational, Scientific and Cultural Organization Institute for Statistics, with missing data estimated by World Bank

staff. Data on forest, energy, and mineral depletion are based on the sources and methods described in World Bank (2011). Additional data on energy commodity production and reserves are from the United States Energy Information Administration. Estimates of damages from carbon dioxide emissions follow the method of Fankhauser (1994) using data from the International Energy Agency's CO_2 Emissions from Fuel Combustion Statistics database. Data on exposure to household air pollution, ambient particulate matter pollution, and ambient ozone are from the Institute for Health Metrics and Evaluation's Global Burden of Disease 2013 study. Data on current account balances are from the IMF's Balance of Payments Statistics Yearbook and International Financial Statistics. Data on central government finances are from the IMF's Government Finance Statistics database. Data on the consumer price index are from the IMF's International Financial Statistics. Data on broad money are from the IMF's monthly International Financial Statistics and annual International Financial Statistics Yearbook.

References

De la Torre, A., E. L. Yeyati, and S. Pienknagura. 2013. *Latin America's Deceleration and the Exchange Rate Buffer.* Semiannual Report, Office of the Chief Economist. Washington, DC: World Bank.

Fankhauser, S. 1994. "The Social Costs of Greenhouse Gas Emissions: An Expected Value Approach." *Energy Journal* 15 (2): 157–84.

Feenstra, R. C., R. Inklaar, and M. P. Timmer. 2013. "The Next Generation of the Penn World Table." [www.ggdc.net/pwt].

Hamilton, K., and M. Clemens. 1999. "Genuine Savings Rates in Developing Countries." *World Bank Economic Review* 13 (2): 333–56.

IMF (International Monetary Fund). 2014. *Government Finance Statistics Manual.* Washington, DC.

———. Various issues. *International Financial Statistics.* Washington, DC.

———. Various years. *Balance of Payments Statistics Yearbook. Parts 1 and 2.* Washington, DC.

Institute for Health Metrics and Evaluation. 2016. Global Burden of Disease 2013 data. University of Washington, Seattle. [www.healthdata.org/gbd/data].

International Energy Agency. Various years. CO_2 Emissions from Fuel Combustion Statistics database. [http://dx.doi.org/10.1787/co2-data-en]. Paris.

Organisation for Economic Co-operation and Development. Various years. National Accounts Statistics database. [http://dx.doi.org/10.1787/na-data-en]. Paris.

United Nations Statistics Division. Various years. *National Accounts Statistics: Main Aggregates and Detailed Tables. Parts 1 and 2.* New York: United Nations.

United States Energy Information Administration. Various years. International Energy Statistics database. [www.eia.gov/cfapps/ipdbproject/IEDIndex3.cfm]. Washington, DC.

World Bank. 2011. *The Changing Wealth of Nations: Measuring Sustainable Development for the New Millennium.* Washington, DC.

———. 2016. *Global Economic Prospects: Spillovers and Weak Growth.* Washington, DC.

4 Economy

Online tables and indicators

To access the World Development Indicators online tables, use the URL http://wdi.worldbank.org/table/ and the table number (for example, http://wdi.worldbank.org/table/4.1). To view a specific indicator online, use the URL http://data.worldbank.org/indicator/ and the indicator code (for example, http://data.worldbank.org /indicator/NY.GDP.MKTP.KD.ZG).

4.1 Growth of output

Gross domestic product	NY.GDP.MKTP.KD.ZG
Agriculture	NV.AGR.TOTL.KD.ZG
Industry	NV.IND.TOTL.KD.ZG
Manufacturing	NV.IND.MANF.KD.ZG
Services	NV.SRV.TETC.KD.ZG

4.2 Structure of output

Gross domestic product	NY.GDP.MKTP.CD
Agriculture	NV.AGR.TOTL.ZS
Industry	NV.IND.TOTL.ZS
Manufacturing	NV.IND.MANF.ZS
Services	NV.SRV.TETC.ZS

4.3 Structure of manufacturing

Manufacturing value added	NV.IND.MANF.CD
Food, beverages and tobacco	NV.MNF.FBTO.ZS.UN
Textiles and clothing	NV.MNF.TXTL.ZS.UN
Machinery and transport equipment	NV.MNF.MTRN.ZS.UN
Chemicals	NV.MNF.CHEM.ZS.UN
Other manufacturing	NV.MNF.OTHR.ZS.UN

4.4 Structure of merchandise exports

Merchandise exports	TX.VAL.MRCH.CD.WT
Food	TX.VAL.FOOD.ZS.UN
Agricultural raw materials	TX.VAL.AGRI.ZS.UN
Fuels	TX.VAL.FUEL.ZS.UN
Ores and metals	TX.VAL.MMTL.ZS.UN
Manufactures	TX.VAL.MANF.ZS.UN

4.5 Structure of merchandise imports

Merchandise imports	TM.VAL.MRCH.CD.WT
Food	TM.VAL.FOOD.ZS.UN
Agricultural raw materials	TM.VAL.AGRI.ZS.UN
Fuels	TM.VAL.FUEL.ZS.UN
Ores and metals	TM.VAL.MMTL.ZS.UN
Manufactures	TM.VAL.MANF.ZS.UN

4.6 Structure of service exports

Commercial service exports	TX.VAL.SERV.CD.WT
Transport	TX.VAL.TRAN.ZS.WT
Travel	TX.VAL.TRVL.ZS.WT
Insurance and financial services	TX.VAL.INSF.ZS.WT
Computer, information, communications, and other commercial services	TX.VAL.OTHR.ZS.WT

4.7 Structure of service imports

Commercial service imports	TM.VAL.SERV.CD.WT
Transport	TM.VAL.TRAN.ZS.WT
Travel	TM.VAL.TRVL.ZS.WT
Insurance and financial services	TM.VAL.INSF.ZS.WT
Computer, information, communications, and other commercial services	TM.VAL.OTHR.ZS.WT

4.8 Structure of demand

Household final consumption expenditure	NE.CON.PETC.ZS
General government final consumption expenditure	NE.CON.GOVT.ZS
Gross capital formation	NE.GDI.TOTL.ZS
Exports of goods and services	NE.EXP.GNFS.ZS
Imports of goods and services	NE.IMP.GNFS.ZS
Gross savings	NY.GNS.ICTR.ZS

4.9 Growth of consumption and investment

Household final consumption expenditure	NE.CON.PRVT.KD.ZG
Household final consumption expenditure, Per capita	NE.CON.PRVT.PC.KD.ZG
General government final consumption expenditure	NE.CON.GOVT.KD.ZG
Gross capital formation	NE.GDI.TOTL.KD.ZG
Exports of goods and services	NE.EXP.GNFS.KD.ZG
Imports of goods and services	NE.IMP.GNFS.KD.ZG

4.10 Toward a broader measure of national income

Gross domestic product, $	NY.GDP.MKTP.CD
Gross domestic product, % growth	NY.GDP.MKTP.KD.ZG
Gross national income, $	NY.GNP.MKTP.CD
Gross national income, % growth	NY.GNP.MKTP.KD.ZG
Consumption of fixed capital	NY.ADJ.DKAP.GN.ZS
Natural resource depletion	NY.ADJ.DRES.GN.ZS
Adjusted net national income, $	NY.ADJ.NNTY.CD
Adjusted net national income, % growth	NY.ADJ.NNTY.KD.ZG

4.11 Toward a broader measure of savings

Gross savings	NY.ADJ.ICTR.GN.ZS
Consumption of fixed capital	NY.ADJ.DKAP.GN.ZS
Education expenditure	NY.ADJ.AEDU.GN.ZS
Net forest depletion	NY.ADJ.DFOR.GN.ZS
Energy depletion	NY.ADJ.DNGY.GN.ZS
Mineral depletion	NY.ADJ.DMIN.GN.ZS
Carbon dioxide damage	NY.ADJ.DCO2.GN.ZS
Local pollution damage	NY.ADJ.DPEM.GN.ZS
Adjusted net savings	NY.ADJ.SVNG.GN.ZS

4.12 Central government finances

Revenue	GC.REV.XGRT.GD.ZS
Expense	GC.XPN.TOTL.GD.ZS
Cash surplus or deficit	GC.BAL.CASH.GD.ZS
Net incurrence of liabilities, Domestic	GC.FIN.DOMS.GD.ZS
Net incurrence of liabilities, Foreign	GC.FIN.FRGN.GD.ZS
Debt and interest payments, Total debt	GC.DOD.TOTL.GD.ZS
Debt and interest payments, Interest	GC.XPN.INTP.RV.ZS

4.13 Central government expenditure

Goods and services	GC.XPN.GSRV.ZS
Compensation of employees	GC.XPN.COMP.ZS
Interest payments	GC.XPN.INTP.ZS
Subsidies and other transfers	GC.XPN.TRFT.ZS
Other expense	GC.XPN.OTHR.ZS

4.14 Central government revenues

Taxes on income, profits and capital gains	GC.TAX.YPKG.RV.ZS
Taxes on goods and services	GC.TAX.GSRV.RV.ZS
Taxes on international trade	GC.TAX.INTT.RV.ZS
Other taxes	GC.TAX.OTHR.RV.ZS
Social contributions	GC.REV.SOCL.ZS
Grants and other revenue	GC.REV.GOTR.ZS

4.15 Monetary indicators

Broad money	FM.LBL.BMNY.ZG
Claims on domestic economy	FM.AST.DOMO.ZG.M3
Claims on central governments	FM.AST.CGOV.ZG.M3
Interest rate, Deposit	FR.INR.DPST
Interest rate, Lending	FR.INR.LEND
Interest rate, Real	FR.INR.RINR

4.16 Exchange rates and price

Official exchange rate	PA.NUS.FCRF
Purchasing power parity (PPP) conversion factor	PA.NUS.PPP
Ratio of PPP conversion factor to market exchange rate	PA.NUS.PPPC.RF
Real effective exchange rate	PX.REX.REER
GDP implicit deflator	NY.GDP.DEFL.KD.ZG
Consumer price index	FP.CPI.TOTL.ZG
Wholesale price index	FP.WPI.TOTL

4.17 Balance of payments current account

Goods and services, Exports	BX.GSR.GNFS.CD
Goods and services, Imports	BM.GSR.GNFS.CD
Balance on primary income	BN.GSR.FCTY.CD
Balance on secondary income	BN.TRF.CURR.CD
Current account balance	BN.CAB.XOKA.CD
Total reserves	FI.RES.TOTL.CD

 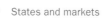

STATES AND MARKETS

States and markets indicators encompass private investment and performance, the public sector's role in nurturing investment and growth, and the quality and availability of infrastructure essential for growth. These indicators measure the business environment, government functions, financial system development, infrastructure, information and communication technology, science and technology, government and policy performance, and conditions in fragile countries with weak institutions.

This year, stock market data from the World Federation of Exchanges replaces estimates from Standard and Poor's, which discontinued the *Global Stock Markets Factbook* in 2013, for indicators of listed companies, market capitalization, the value of shares traded, and the turnover ratio. Time series go back to 1975 where available; additional data, including indicators on fixed income and derivatives and equity markets can be found on the World Federation of Exchanges website (www.world-exchanges.org).

Stock market size can be measured in various ways, and each produces a different ranking of countries. Both number of listed companies and market capitalization measure market size and are positively correlated with the ability to mobilize capital and diversify risk. Market liquidity is measured by the value of shares traded, which represents the transfer of ownership effected automatically through the exchange's electronic order book. Finally, turnover velocity is the ratio between the electronic order book turnover of domestic shares, and their market capitalization; only domestic shares are used in order to be consistent between exchanges.

The data for market capitalization and listed domestic companies are provided for each exchange, and *World Development Indicators* uses two approaches to calculate country-level estimates. When there is only one reported exchange in a country, its data was used to represent that country. When there are several exchanges in a country, care was taken to avoid double-counting; for example, where companies are listed on more than one exchange in the country, the exchange that provided the most comprehensive data set was used. When different companies are listed on the exchanges, the data for number of listed companies and domestic market capitalization have been aggregated to obtain country-level figures.

States and markets also includes the latest updates to data on business regulations and the business environment, from the Doing Business initiative and Enterprise Surveys. This year, there are new measures of regulatory quality in registering property, dealing with construction permits, obtaining electricity, and enforcing contracts.

A new indicator of public-private partnerships has also been added to complement existing data on private participation in telecommunications, energy, transport, and water and sanitation infrastructure projects. Public-private partnership projects refer to brownfield concessions, greenfield projects, and management and leases but excludes merchants where private parties assume the risks without government guarantee. Public-private partnership projects help determine the gap between infrastructure demand and available resources, thus making important contributions to improving the efficiency of public services in infrastructure and extending delivery to poor people. As in previous editions, the latest trend data on various indicators related to information and communications technology are also presented, including goods trade, telecommunications revenue, mobile subscriptions, and Internet use.

The digital and information revolution has changed the way the world learns, communicates, does business, and treats illnesses. Information and communication technologies offer vast opportunities for progress in all walks of life in all countries—opportunities for economic growth, improved health, better service delivery, learning through distance education, and social and cultural advances. The Internet delivers information to schools and hospitals, improves public and private services, and increases productivity and participation. Through mobile phones, Internet access is expanding in low- and middle-income countries. The mobility, ease of use, flexible deployment, and declining rollout costs of wireless technologies enable mobile communications to reach rural populations. According to the International Telecommunication Union, by the end of 2015 the number of Internet users worldwide reached 3.2 billion.

Internet users

Individuals using the Internet, 2014 (% of population)

- 80 or more
- 60–79
- 40–59
- 20–39
- Less than 20
- No data

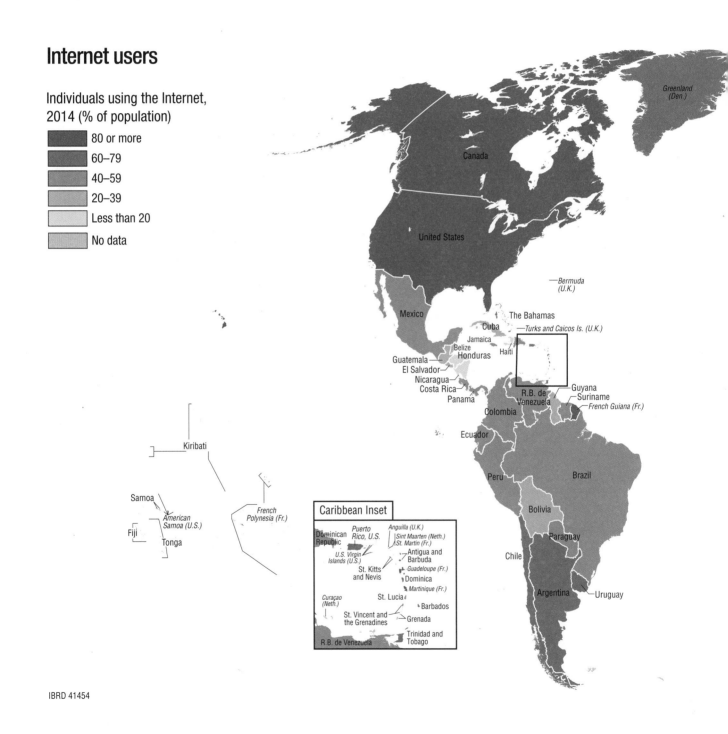

IBRD 41454

The worldwide Internet penetration rate has increased almost sixfold, from 7 percent in 2000 to 41 percent in 2014.

In South Asia 17 percent of the population was online at the end of 2014, the lowest Internet penetration rate among all regions.

In 2014 more than 680 million people were using the Internet in China, followed by 282 million in the United States and 228 million in India. But the Internet penetration rate shows disparity—49 percent in China, 87 percent in the United States, and 18 percent in India.

The Internet penetration rate nearly quadrupled in the Middle East and North Africa, from 10 percent in 2005 to 38 percent in 2014.

5 States and markets

	Business entry density per 1,000 people ages 15–64 2014	Time required to start a business days June 2015	Stock market capitalization % of GDP 2014	Domestic credit provided by financial sector % of GDP 2014	Tax revenue collected by central government % of GDP 2013	Military expenditures % of GDP 2014	Mobile cellular subscriptions[a] per 100 people 2014	Individuals using the Internet[a] % of population 2014	High-technology exports % of manufactured exports 2014	Overall statistical capacity (0, low, to 100, high) 2015
Afghanistan	0.15	7	..	−2.3	7.5	1.3	75	6	..	51.1
Albania	1.11	6	..	68.1	..	1.0	105	60	0.1	72.2
Algeria	0.58	20	..	18.0	37.2	5.6	93	18	0.2	53.3
American Samoa	..	..	..	..	..	..	..	..	..	..
Andorra	..	..	..	..	..	..	83	96	..	..
Angola	..	36	..	16.9	17.3	4.4	63	21	..	47.8
Antigua and Barbuda	3.53	21	..	84.6	18.6	..	132	64	0.0	57.8
Argentina	0.43	25	11.2	35.6	..	0.8	159	65	6.7	95.6
Armenia	1.52	3	1.2	51.3	17.5	4.0	116	46	2.7	93.3
Aruba	..	..	..	..	..	..	135	84	5.4	..
Australia	14.91	3	88.6	165.9	22.2	1.8	131	85	13.6	..
Austria	0.73	22	22.2	126.9	26.2	0.7	152	81	13.9	..
Azerbaijan	0.99	3	..	33.8	13.0	4.8	111	61	7.0	67.8
Bahamas, The	..	29	..	102.6	..	..	82	77	0.0	..
Bahrain	..	9	65.6	75.1	1.1	4.2	173	91	1.5	..
Bangladesh	0.09	20	20.1	58.6	8.7	1.2	80	10	..	76.7
Barbados	..	18	61.6	..	25.2	..	129	77	16.4	..
Belarus	1.05	3	..	42.8	15.1	1.3	123	59	3.9	87.8
Belgium	2.05	4	71.2	116.0	25.5	1.0	114	85	12.8	..
Belize	3.08	43	..	57.7	22.6	1.0	51	39	0.0	54.4
Benin	..	12	..	20.4	15.5	1.0	100	5	4.1	66.7
Bermuda	..	..	26.3	..	..	..	91	97	27.8	..
Bhutan	0.06	15	..	47.3	..	..	82	34	0.0	68.9
Bolivia	0.57	50	16.4	55.2	..	1.5	96	39	8.1	78.9
Bosnia and Herzegovina	0.83	67	..	60.3	19.8	1.1	91	61	2.4	67.8
Botswana	13.11	48	..	8.5	26.7	1.9	167	19	0.2	45.6
Brazil	2.88	83	34.9	105.1	14.1	1.3	139	58	10.6	65.6
Brunei Darussalam	..	14	..	25.5	..	3.1	110	69	7.8	..
Bulgaria	8.86	18	9.7	62.5	18.6	1.5	138	55	6.9	84.4
Burkina Faso	0.15	13	..	28.8	16.6	1.3	72	9	10.6	67.8
Burundi	..	4	..	23.4	..	2.0	30	1	1.3	55.6
Cabo Verde	..	10	..	84.6	..	0.6	122	40	0.0	66.7
Cambodia	..	87	..	47.2	11.9	1.7	133	9	0.2	76.7
Cameroon	..	15	..	16.3	..	1.3	76	11	4.9	55.6
Canada	1.28	2	117.3	..	11.7	1.0	81	87	14.8	..
Cayman Islands	..	..	..	..	..	..	154	74	..	..
Central African Republic	..	22	..	33.6	9.5	..	25	4	0.0	52.2
Chad	..	60	..	11.0	..	..	40	3	..	65.6
Channel Islands	..	..	..	..	..	..	..	..	..	..
Chile	8.03	6	90.4	120.3	17.5	2.0	133	72	6.2	95.6
China	..	31	58.0	169.3	10.4	2.1[b]	92	49	25.4	70.0
Hong Kong SAR, China	31.30	2	1,111.4	236.5	..	..	234	75	42.9	..
Macao SAR, China	..	..	..	−4.1	37.0	..	323	70	0.2	..
Colombia	2.00	11	38.8	71.1	13.4	3.5	113	53	7.7	84.4
Comoros	..	15	..	29.2	..	..	51	7	0.1	42.2
Congo, Dem. Rep.	0.05	11	..	8.6	..	1.4	53	3	..	57.8
Congo, Rep.	..	53	..	0.8	..	5.0	108	7	2.0	50.0

States and markets 5

	Business entry density per 1,000 people ages 15–64 2014	Time required to start a business days June 2015	Stock market capitalization % of GDP 2014	Domestic credit provided by financial sector % of GDP 2014	Tax revenue collected by central government % of GDP 2013	Military expenditures % of GDP 2014	Mobile cellular subscriptions[a] per 100 people 2014	Individuals using the Internet[a] % of population 2014	High-technology exports % of manufactured exports 2014	Overall statistical capacity (0, low, to 100, high) 2015
Costa Rica	1.10	24	..	63.0	13.9	..	144	49	*43.3*	84.4
Côte d'Ivoire	..	7	34.1	29.2	14.5	*1.5*	106	15	3.7	58.9
Croatia	4.63	12	*38.6*	90.8	*19.6*	1.5	104	69	8.4	80.0
Cuba	..	..	..	..	..	3.5	22	30	..	..
Curaçao	..	..	..	..	..	..	122	..	..	..
Cyprus	13.70	8	17.4	307.8	23.5	1.8	96	69	6.2	..
Czech Republic	3.42	15	..	73.5	*13.5*	1.0	130	80	14.9	..
Denmark	4.36	3	224.9	35.1	1.3	126	96	14.4	..
Djibouti	..	14	..	33.2	..	..	32	11	..	46.7
Dominica	..	12	..	60.1	*23.1*	..	127	63	*8.8*	52.2
Dominican Republic	1.20	15	..	50.4	13.8	0.6	79	50	3.7	78.9
Ecuador	..	51	..	31.7	..	2.7	104	43	4.8	72.2
Egypt, Arab Rep.	..	8	23.2	88.2	*12.5*	1.7	114	32	1.3	91.1
El Salvador	0.52	17	*45.1*	73.4	15.4	1.0	144	30	4.8	91.1
Equatorial Guinea	..	135	..	4.7	..	1.1	66	19	..	42.2
Eritrea	..	84	..	..	..	..	6	1	..	27.8
Estonia	16.05	4	*10.1*	4.5	1.0	1.9	161	84	11.5	..
Ethiopia	..	19	..	..	*9.2*	0.7	32	3	8.1	68.9
Faroe Islands	..	..	..	..	..	..	124	95	..	..
Fiji	..	58	*11.4*	113.1	..	1.1	99	42	2.1	61.1
Finland	3.43	14	..	164.7	20.8	1.3	140	92	7.9	..
France	2.26	4	73.7	148.0	15.6	2.2	101	84	26.1	..
French Polynesia	..	..	..	..	..	..	91	61	14.8	..
Gabon	..	50	..	13.8	..	*1.4*	171	10	..	40.0
Gambia, The	..	25	..	53.7	..	1.7	120	16	0.0	65.6
Georgia	5.65	2	*6.0*	48.5	*24.1*	2.3	125	49	3.0	88.9
Germany	*1.29*	11	44.9	140.6	11.6	1.2	120	86	16.0	..
Ghana	*0.90*	14	*10.3*	38.2	*14.9*	0.5	115	19	*4.9*	65.6
Greece	..	13	23.4	138.6	22.8	2.3	110	63	10.3	..
Greenland	..	..	..	..	..	..	106	67	4.4	..
Grenada	2.03	15	..	68.4	*18.7*	..	110	37	..	51.1
Guam	..	..	..	..	..	..	..	69	..	..
Guatemala	*0.52*	19	..	41.7	*10.8*	0.4	107	23	5.0	72.2
Guinea	0.13	8	..	..	..	3.8	72	2	4.9	53.3
Guinea-Bissau	..	9	..	17.1	..	*1.7*	63	3	..	44.4
Guyana	..	18	*21.4*	60.4	..	1.2	71	37	0.2	56.7
Haiti	*0.06*	97	..	29.2	..	..	65	11	..	47.8
Honduras	..	14	..	60.3	15.1	1.3	94	19	2.4	76.7
Hungary	3.66	5	10.5	61.1	22.5	0.8	118	76	13.7	85.6
Iceland	9.48	4	*19.9*	116.1	22.9	*0.1*	111	98	16.9	..
India	0.12	29	76.1	75.5	*10.8*	2.4	74	18	8.6	77.8
Indonesia	*0.29*	48	47.5	43.5	*11.4*	0.8	129	17	7.0	84.4
Iran, Islamic Rep.	..	15	27.4	..	..	*2.2*	88	39	..	73.3
Iraq	*0.13*	29	..	0.4	..	4.3	95	11	..	52.2
Ireland	5.78	6	57.2	165.7	22.8	0.5	105	80	21.3	..
Isle of Man	*45.27*	..	..	..	..	..	..	..	..	..
Israel	3.11	13	65.6	85.1	22.9	5.2	121	71	16.0	..

  Economy | States and markets | Global links | Back

World Development Indicators 2016   **115**

5 States and markets

	Business entry density per 1,000 people ages 15–64 2014	Time required to start a business days June 2015	Stock market capitalization % of GDP 2014	Domestic credit provided by financial sector % of GDP 2014	Tax revenue collected by central government % of GDP 2013	Military expenditures % of GDP 2014	Mobile cellular subscriptions[a] per 100 people 2014	Individuals using the Internet[a] % of population 2014	High-technology exports % of manufactured exports 2014	Overall statistical capacity (0, low, to 100, high) 2015
Italy	2.32	6	..	173.0	23.6	1.4	154	62	7.2	..
Jamaica	1.00	3	21.1	52.4	26.6	0.9	107	41	0.6	77.8
Japan	0.15	10	95.1	373.8	10.9	1.0	120	91	16.7	..
Jordan	0.99	12	71.3	106.2	15.3	3.5	148	44	1.6	74.4
Kazakhstan	1.71	5	10.5	36.6	..	1.1	172	55	37.2	90.0
Kenya	1.80	26	40.5	44.6	15.9	1.3	74	43	3.8	54.4
Kiribati	..	31	..	..	..	..	17	12	0.7	34.4
Korea, Dem. People's Rep.	..	..	..	..	..	..	11	0	..	..
Korea, Rep.	2.30	4	86.0	162.4	14.4	2.6	116	84	26.9	..
Kosovo	4.27	11	..	26.7	..	..	..	..	..	40.0
Kuwait	..	31	..	60.7	..	3.3	218	79	0.1	..
Kyrgyz Republic	1.08	10	2.5	15.9	18.1	3.4	134	28	5.3	82.2
Lao PDR	..	73	..	..	14.8	0.2	67	14	..	71.1
Latvia	10.61	6	4.0	76.8	14.0	1.0	117	76	15.0	..
Lebanon	..	15	24.4	194.9	14.9	4.6	88	75	2.1	65.6
Lesotho	1.55	29	..	0.7	..	2.2	85	11	0.0	65.6
Liberia	..	5	..	37.8	..	0.8	73	5	..	51.1
Libya	..	35	..	−42.0	..	8.0	161	18	..	22.2
Liechtenstein	1.17	..	..	..	..	..	109	95	..	..
Lithuania	4.19	4	9.2	13.2	13.6	2.7	147	72	10.1	..
Luxembourg	6.10	19	97.4	194.5	25.7	0.5	149	95	5.7	..
Macedonia, FYR	3.70	1	5.7	54.6	16.4	1.2	106	68	3.1	83.3
Madagascar	0.70	13	..	16.8	10.1	0.7	41	4	0.6	58.9
Malawi	..	38	17.8	21.5	..	1.2	33	6	2.5	75.6
Malaysia	2.37	4	135.8	140.5	15.6	1.5	149	68	43.9	74.4
Maldives	..	9	..	70.7	13.7	..	189	49	..	55.6
Mali	..	9	..	23.1	15.8	1.4	149	7	1.2	65.6
Malta	17.26	28	44.1	151.5	28.1	0.6	127	73	34.4	..
Marshall Islands	..	17	..	..	..	..	29	17	..	37.8
Mauritania	..	8	..	31.9	..	2.9	94	11	..	66.7
Mauritius	5.14	6	69.3	115.5	18.7	0.3	132	41	0.0	93.3
Mexico	0.94	6	37.1	50.2	..	0.7	82	44	16.0	92.2
Micronesia, Fed. Sts.	..	16	..	..	..	..	30	30	..	35.6
Moldova	..	4	..	38.9	18.6	0.3	108	47	4.8	95.6
Monaco	..	..	..	..	..	..	88	92	..	..
Mongolia	6.31	6	10.5	67.2	15.3	0.9	105	27	19.5	74.4
Montenegro	6.85	10	92.6	..	..	1.7	163	61	..	72.2
Morocco	1.54	10	47.9	112.4	23.9	3.7	132	57	5.3	81.1
Mozambique	..	19	..	34.7	20.4	1.0	70	6	5.6	72.2
Myanmar	..	13	..	28.3	..	3.7	54	2	..	55.6
Namibia	0.85	66	14.8	54.6	23.1	4.2	114	15	2.7	47.8
Nepal	0.69	17	22.1	71.5	15.3	1.5	82	15	0.2	72.2
Netherlands	5.34	4	89.5	230.5	20.0	1.1	116	93	19.9	..
New Caledonia	..	..	..	..	..	..	94	70	13.1	..
New Zealand	16.63	1	37.2	..	27.2	1.2	112	86	9.1	..
Nicaragua	..	13	..	47.2	15.1	0.7	115	18	0.4	70.0
Niger	..	15	..	12.3	..	1.0	44	2	57.1	71.1

 Front   User guide    World view   People   Environment

	Business entry density per 1,000 people ages 15–64 2014	Time required to start a business days June 2015	Stock market capitalization % of GDP 2014	Domestic credit provided by financial sector % of GDP 2014	Tax revenue collected by central government % of GDP 2013	Military expenditures % of GDP 2014	Mobile cellular subscriptions[a] per 100 people 2014	Individuals using the Internet[a] % of population 2014	High-technology exports % of manufactured exports 2014	Overall statistical capacity (0, low, to 100, high) 2015
Nigeria	0.76	31	11.2	21.8	1.6	0.4	78	43	2.1	71.1
Northern Mariana Islands	..	..	..	..	..	..	..	..	..	..
Norway	7.72	4	43.9	..	25.2	1.4	116	96	20.7	..
Oman	1.02	7	46.2	41.2	2.6	11.8	158	70	4.3	..
Pakistan	0.04	19	..	47.5	11.2	3.4	73	14	1.4	75.6
Palau	..	28	..	..	..	..	91	..	20.2	42.2
Panama	14.10	6	29.8	83.7	..	..	158	45	0.2	78.9
Papua New Guinea	..	53	18.6	51.0	..	0.6	45	9	3.5	45.6
Paraguay	..	35	..	40.8	12.8	1.5	106	43	6.1	72.2
Peru	2.44	26	38.9	24.8	16.5	1.4	104	40	3.8	93.3
Philippines	0.27	29	91.9	55.8	12.9	1.2	111	40	49.0	82.2
Poland	..	30	31.0	71.0	15.5	1.9	149	67	8.7	85.6
Portugal	4.62	3	25.1	173.3	22.1	1.8	112	65	4.4	..
Puerto Rico	..	6	..	..	..	..	87	79	..	..
Qatar	1.70	9	88.5	80.4	..	..	146	91	0.0	..
Romania	4.07	8	11.2	38.0	17.4	1.3	106	54	6.4	82.2
Russian Federation	4.20	11	20.7	52.4	14.3	4.5	155	71	11.5	..
Rwanda	1.49	6	..	..	13.4	1.1	64	11	11.9	73.3
Samoa	1.04	9	..	77.4	0.0	..	56	21	1.7	53.3
San Marino	..	17	..	..	..	..	119	..	..	..
São Tomé and Príncipe	3.04	5	..	26.2	13.9	..	65	24	0.8	65.6
Saudi Arabia	..	19	64.1	1.8	..	10.7	180	64	0.7	..
Senegal	0.30	6	..	34.1	19.2	1.5	99	18	3.6	75.6
Serbia	1.62	12	..	52.8	19.7	2.2	122	54	..	90.0
Seychelles	..	32	..	33.1	28.4	1.1	162	54	..	65.6
Sierra Leone	0.32	10	..	14.8	..	0.8	77	2	0.0	63.3
Singapore	9.51	3	244.5	126.3	13.8	3.2	147	82	47.2	..
Sint Maarten	..	..	..	..	..	..	..	..	..	..
Slovak Republic	3.10	12	4.9	65.7	13.2	1.0	117	80	10.2	86.7
Slovenia	4.44	6	15.2	68.7	17.6	1.0	112	72	5.8	..
Solomon Islands	..	9	..	22.2	..	..	66	9	0.0	48.9
Somalia	..	..	..	..	..	0.0	51	2	..	20.0
South Africa	6.54	46	266.7	185.6	25.5	1.1	149	49	5.9	81.1
South Sudan	0.33	14	..	..	..	8.2	25	16	..	34.4
Spain	2.97	14	71.9	210.6	13.9	0.9	108	76	7.0	..
Sri Lanka	0.51	10	30.0	43.0	10.4	2.3	103	26	0.9	73.3
St. Kitts and Nevis	..	19	..	81.1	20.2	..	119	65	..	56.7
St. Lucia	0.56	11	..	108.2	22.9	..	103	51	5.2	61.1
St. Martin	..	..	..	..	..	..	..	..	..	..
St. Vincent & the Grenadines	1.37	10	..	57.9	..	..	105	56	0.1	55.6
Sudan	..	36	..	20.9	..	..	72	25	..	51.1
Suriname	1.36	84	..	38.9	19.5	..	171	40	20.7	62.2
Swaziland	..	30	..	16.5	..	1.8	72	27	..	58.9
Sweden	6.87	7	..	157.5	26.3	1.2	128	93	13.9	..
Switzerland	2.53	10	213.3	176.0	9.5	0.7	137	87	26.4	..
Syrian Arab Republic	..	13	..	..	..	..	64	28	..	47.8
Tajikistan	0.26	11	..	19.5	..	1.1	95	17	..	81.1

	Business entry density per 1,000 people ages 15–64 2014	Time required to start a business days June 2015	Stock market capitalization % of GDP 2014	Domestic credit provided by financial sector % of GDP 2014	Tax revenue collected by central government % of GDP 2013	Military expenditures % of GDP 2014	Mobile cellular subscriptions[a] per 100 people 2014	Individuals using the Internet[a] % of population 2014	High-technology exports % of manufactured exports 2014	Overall statistical capacity (0, low, to 100, high) 2015
Tanzania	..	26	..	20.2	*11.7*	1.0	63	5	2.7	75.6
Thailand	0.90	28	106.3	168.6	17.3	1.4	144	35	20.4	85.6
Timor-Leste	4.63	9	..	–1.1	..	2.1	119	1	*9.8*	62.2
Togo	0.26	10	..	39.7	18.8	..	65	6	*0.2*	65.6
Tonga	*1.91*	16	..	29.5	..	..	64	40	2.4	47.8
Trinidad and Tobago	..	12	..	29.1	..	0.8	147	65	..	56.7
Tunisia	*1.52*	11	19.2	84.6	*21.1*	1.9	128	46	*4.9*	76.7
Turkey	1.13	8	27.5	88.1	21.4	2.2	95	51	1.9	82.2
Turkmenistan	..	..	..	..	..	..	136	12	..	33.3
Turks and Caicos Islands	..	..	..	..	..	..	..	..	*1.9*	..
Tuvalu	..	..	..	..	..	..	38	*37*	..	37.8
Uganda	*1.17*	27	*31.4*	16.8	*11.0*	1.2	52	18	2.4	72.2
Ukraine	*0.92*	7	*11.8*	109.9	*18.3*	3.1	144	43	6.5	91.1
United Arab Emirates	*1.38*	8	50.5	83.0	0.4	5.7	178	90	..	..
United Kingdom	*12.90*	5	106.5	168.8	25.4	2.0	124	92	20.6	..
United States	..	6	151.2	253.5	10.5	3.5	110	87	18.2	..
Uruguay	*2.49*	7	..	35.5	*18.8*	1.6	161	61	7.9	88.9
Uzbekistan	*0.64*	7	..	..	..	..	78	44	..	51.1
Vanuatu	..	35	..	72.1	*16.0*	..	60	19	..	45.6
Venezuela, RB	..	144	..	*61.9*	..	*1.4*	99	57	*1.1*	82.2
Vietnam	..	20	24.7	113.8	..	2.3	147	48	26.9	82.2
Virgin Islands (U.S.)	..	..	..	..	..	..	..	50	..	..
West Bank and Gaza	..	44	25.0	9.8	4.8	..	72	54	..	80.0
Yemen, Rep.	..	40	..	*33.9*	..	4.6	68	23	1.2	55.6
Zambia	1.33	8	..	25.9	*16.0*	1.6	67	17	1.7	60.0
Zimbabwe	..	90	..	..	..	2.6	81	20	1.7	62.2
World	**4.01 u**	**20 u**	**94.3 w**	**173.6 w**	***14.0 w***	**2.3 w**	**97 w**	**41 w**	**18.4 w**	**.. u**
East Asia & Pacific	8.28	23	91.8	205.6	*11.7*	1.8	103	47	27.4	72.0[c,d]
Europe & Central Asia	4.63	10	64.3	142.6	18.8	1.8	126	69	15.5	77.1[c,d]
Latin America & Caribbean	1.98	29	36.2	75.8	..	1.3	115	50	10.9	77.3[c,d]
Middle East & North Africa	4.20	19	51.4	50.8	..	6.5	110	38	..	64.4[c,d]
North America	1.28	4	148.0	253.5	10.6	3.3	107	87	17.6	..
South Asia	0.23	16	70.3	70.1	*10.7*	2.4	75	17	8.1	71.1[c,d]
Sub-Saharan Africa	2.28	27	..	61.4	*13.5*	1.0	71	19	4.0	59.9[c,d]
Low income	0.55	27	..	23.4	..	1.5	57	6	*5.3*	59.8[d]
Lower middle income	1.69	20	65.1	61.3	*11.0*	1.8	88	23	11.5	70.4[d]
Upper middle income	2.89	24	55.7	132.8	*13.5*	1.9	101	48	20.6	71.5[d]
High income	6.41	15	111.2	202.2	14.6	2.5	126	81	18.5	..

a. Data are from the International Telecommunication Union's (ITU) World Telecommunication/ICT Indicators database. Please cite ITU for third party use of these data. b. Differs from the official value published by the government of China (1.3 percent; see National Bureau of Statistics of China, www.stats.gov.cn). c. Excludes high-income countries. d. Excludes countries with a population below 1 million.

 Front | User guide | World view | People | Environment

Entrepreneurial activity

The rate new businesses are added to an economy is a measure of its dynamism and entrepreneurial activity. Data on business entry density are from the World Bank's 2015 Entrepreneurship Database, which includes indicators for more than 150 countries for 2004–14. Survey data are used to analyze firm creation, its relationship to economic growth and poverty reduction, and the impact of regulatory and institutional reforms. Data on total registered businesses were collected from national registrars of companies. For cross-country comparability, only limited liability corporations that operate in the formal sector are included. For additional information on sources, methodology, calculation of entrepreneurship rates, and data limitations see www.doingbusiness.org/data/exploretopics/entrepreneurship.

Data on time required to start a business are from the Doing Business database, whose indicators measure business regulation, gauge regulatory outcomes, and measure the extent of legal protection of property, the flexibility of employment regulation, and the tax burden on businesses. The fundamental premise is that economic activity requires good rules and regulations that are efficient, accessible, and easy to implement. Some indicators give a higher score for more regulation, such as stricter disclosure requirements in related-party transactions, and others give a higher score for simplified regulations, such as a one-stop shop for completing business startup formalities. There are 11 sets of indicators covering starting a business, registering property, dealing with construction permits, getting electricity, enforcing contracts, getting credit, protecting investors, paying taxes, trading across borders, resolving insolvency, and employing workers. The indicators are available at www.doingbusiness.org.

Doing Business data are collected with a standardized survey that uses a simple business case to ensure comparability across economies and over time—with assumptions about the legal form of the business, its size, its location, and nature of its operation. Surveys in 189 countries are administered through more than 10,700 local experts, including lawyers, business consultants, accountants, freight forwarders, government officials, and other professionals who routinely administer or advise on legal and regulatory requirements.

Over the past two years Doing Business has introduced important improvements in 8 of the 10 sets of Doing Business indicators to provide a new conceptual framework in which the emphasis on efficiency of regulation is complemented by increased emphasis on quality of regulation. Moreover, Doing Business has changed the basis for the ease of doing business ranking, from the percentile rank to the distance to frontier score. The distance to frontier score benchmarks economies with respect to a measure of regulatory best practice—showing the gap between each economy's performance and the best performance on each indicator. This measure captures more information than the simple rankings previously used as the basis because it shows not only how economies are ordered on their performance on the indicators, but also how far apart they are. The Doing Business methodology has limitations that should be considered when interpreting the data. First, the data collected refer to businesses in the economy's largest business city and may not represent regulations in other locations of the economy. To address this limitation, subnational indicators are being collected for selected economies, and coverage has been extended to the second largest business city in economies with a population of more than 100 million. Subnational indicators point to substantial differences in the speed of reform and the ease of doing business across cities in the same economy. Second, the data often focus on a specific business form—generally a limited liability company of a specified size—and may not represent regulation for other types of businesses such as sole proprietorships. Third, transactions described in a standardized business case refer to a specific set of issues and may not represent all the issues a business encounters. Fourth, the time measures involve an element of judgment by the expert respondents. When sources indicate different estimates, the Doing Business time indicators represent the median values of several responses given under the assumptions of the standardized case. Fifth, the methodology assumes that a business has full information on what is required and does not waste time in completing procedures. In constructing the indicators, it is assumed that entrepreneurs know about all regulations and comply with them. In practice, entrepreneurs may not be aware of all required procedures or may avoid legally required procedures altogether.

Financial systems

The development of an economy's financial markets is closely related to its overall development. Well functioning financial systems provide good and easily accessible information. That lowers transaction costs, which in turn improves resource allocation and boosts economic growth (Beck and Levine 2001). At low levels of economic development commercial banks tend to dominate the financial system, while at higher levels domestic stock markets become more active and efficient.

Open economies with sound macroeconomic policies, good legal systems, and shareholder protection attract capital and thus have larger financial markets (Claessens, Klingebiel, and Schmukler 2002). The table includes market capitalization as a share of GDP as a measure of stock market size. Market size can be measured in other ways that may produce a different ranking of countries. Recent research on stock market development shows that modern communications technology and increased financial integration have resulted in more cross-border capital flows, a stronger presence of financial firms around the world, and the migration of trading activities to international exchanges. Many firms in emerging markets now cross-list on international exchanges, which provides them with lower cost capital and more liquidity-traded shares. However, this also means that exchanges in emerging markets may not have enough financial activity to sustain them. Comparability across countries may be limited by conceptual and statistical weaknesses, such as inaccurate reporting and differences in accounting standards.

Domestic credit provided by the financial sector as a share of GDP measures banking sector depth and financial sector development in terms of size. Data are taken from the financial corporation survey of the International Monetary Fund's (IMF) *International Financial Statistics* or, when unavailable, from its depository corporation survey. The financial corporation survey includes monetary authorities (the central bank), deposit money banks, and other banking institutions, such as finance companies, development banks, and savings and loan institutions. In a few countries governments may hold international reserves as deposits in the banking system rather than in the central bank. Claims on the central government are a net item (claims on the central government minus central government deposits) and thus may be negative, resulting in a negative value for domestic credit provided by the financial sector.

Tax revenues

Taxes are the main source of revenue for most governments. Tax revenue as a share of GDP provides a quick overview of the fiscal obligations and incentives facing the private sector across countries. The table shows only central government data, which may significantly understate the total tax burden, particularly in countries where provincial and municipal governments are large or have considerable tax authority. Data are based on the IMF's Government Finance Statistics Manual 2014.

Low ratios of tax revenue to GDP may reflect weak administration and large-scale tax avoidance or evasion. Low ratios may also reflect a sizable parallel economy with unrecorded and undisclosed incomes. Tax revenue ratios tend to rise with income, with higher income countries relying on taxes to finance a much broader range of social services and social security than lower income countries are able to.

Military expenditures

Although national defense is an important function of government, high expenditures for defense or civil conflicts burden the economy and may impede growth. Military expenditures as a share of GDP are a rough indicator of the portion of national resources used for military activities. As an "input" measure, military expenditures are not directly related to the "output" of military activities, capabilities, or security. Comparisons across countries should take into account many factors, including historical and cultural traditions, the length of borders that need defending, the quality of relations with neighbors, and the role of the armed forces in the body politic.

Data are from the Stockholm International Peace Research Institute (SIPRI), whose primary source of military expenditure data is official data provided by national governments. These data are derived from budget documents, defense white papers, and other public documents from official government agencies, including government responses to questionnaires sent by SIPRI, the United Nations Office for Disarmament Affairs, or the Organization for Security and Co-operation in Europe. Secondary sources include international statistics, such as those of the North Atlantic Treaty Organization (NATO) and the IMF's *Government Finance Statistics Yearbook*. Other secondary sources include country reports of the Economist Intelligence Unit, country reports by IMF staff, and specialist journals and newspapers.

In the many cases where SIPRI cannot make independent estimates, it uses country-provided data. Because of differences in definitions and the difficulty of verifying the accuracy and completeness of data, data are not always comparable across countries. However, SIPRI puts a high priority on ensuring that the data series for each country is comparable over time. More information on SIPRI's military expenditure project can be found at www.sipri.org/research/armaments/milex.

Infrastructure

The quality of an economy's infrastructure, including information and communications technology, is an important element in investment decisions and economic development.

The International Telecommunication Union (ITU) estimates that there were 7 billion mobile subscriptions globally in 2015. No technology has ever spread faster around the world. Mobile communications have a particularly important impact in rural areas. The mobility, ease of use, flexible deployment, and relatively low and declining rollout costs of wireless technologies enable them to reach rural populations with low levels of income and literacy. The next billion mobile subscribers will consist mainly of the rural poor.

Operating companies have traditionally been the main source of telecommunications data, so information on subscriptions has been widely available for most countries. This gives a general idea of access, but a more precise measure is the penetration rate—the share of households with access to telecommunications. During the past few years more information on information and communication technology use has become available from household and business surveys. Also important are data on actual use of telecommunications services. The quality of data varies among reporting countries as a result of differences in regulations covering data provision and availability.

High-technology exports

The method for determining high-technology exports was developed by the Organisation for Economic Co-operation and Development in collaboration with Eurostat. It takes a "product approach" (rather than a "sectoral approach") based on research and development intensity (expenditure divided by total sales) for groups of products from Germany, Italy, Japan, the Netherlands, Sweden, and the United States. Because industrial sectors specializing in a few high-technology products may also produce low-technology products, the product approach is more appropriate for international trade. The method takes only research and development intensity into account, but other characteristics of high technology are also important, such as knowhow, scientific personnel, and technology embodied in patents. Considering these characteristics would yield a different list (see Hatzichronoglou 1997).

Statistical capacity

Statistical capacity is a country's ability to collect, analyze, and disseminate high-quality data about its population and economy.

When statistical capacity improves and policy makers use accurate statistics to inform their decisions, this results in better development policy design and outcomes. The Statistical Capacity Indicator is an essential tool for monitoring and tracking the statistical capacity of low- and middle-income countries and helps national statistics offices worldwide identify gaps in their capabilities to collect, produce, and use data.

Definitions

• **Business entry density** is the number of newly registered limited liability corporations per 1,000 people ages 15–64. • **Time required to start a business** is the number of calendar days to complete the procedures for legally operating a business using the fastest procedure, independent of cost. • **Stock market capitalization** is the share price times the number of shares outstanding (including their several classes) for listed domestic companies. Investment funds, unit trusts, and companies whose only business goal is to hold shares of other listed companies are excluded. • **Domestic credit provided by financial sector** is all credit to various sectors on a gross basis, except to the central government, which is net. The financial sector includes monetary authorities, deposit money banks, and other banking institutions for which data are available. • **Tax revenue collected by central government** is compulsory transfers to the central government for public purposes. Certain compulsory transfers such as fines, penalties, and most social security contributions are excluded. Refunds and corrections of erroneously collected tax revenue are treated as negative revenue. The analytic framework of the IMF's *Government Finance Statistics Manual 2001* (GFSM 2001) is based on accrual accounting and balance sheets. For countries still reporting government finance data on a cash basis, the IMF adjusts reported data to the GFSM 2001 accrual framework. These countries are footnoted in the table. • **Military expenditures** are SIPRI data derived from NATO's former definition (in use until 2002), which includes all current and capital expenditures on the armed forces, including peacekeeping forces; defense ministries and other government agencies engaged in defense projects; paramilitary forces, if judged to be trained and equipped for military operations; and military space activities. Such expenditures include military and civil personnel, including retirement pensions and social services for military personnel; operation and maintenance; procurement; military research and development; and military aid (in the military expenditures of the donor country). Excluded are civil defense and current expenditures for previous military activities, such as for veterans benefits, demobilization, and weapons conversion and destruction. This definition cannot be applied for all countries, however, since that would require more detailed information than is available about military budgets and off-budget military expenditures (for example, whether military budgets cover civil defense, reserves and auxiliary forces, police and paramilitary forces, and military pensions). • **Mobile cellular subscriptions** are the number of subscriptions to a public mobile telephone service that provides access to the public switched telephone network using cellular technology. Postpaid subscriptions and active prepaid accounts (that is, accounts that have been used during the last three months) are included. The indicator applies to all mobile cellular subscriptions that offer voice communications and excludes subscriptions for data cards or USB modems, subscriptions to public mobile data services, private-trunked mobile radio, telepoint, radio paging, and telemetry services. • **Individuals using the Internet** are the percentage of individuals who have used the Internet (from any location) in the last 12 months. Internet can be used via a computer, mobile phone, personal digital assistant, games machine, digital television, or similar device. • **High-technology exports** are products with high research and development intensity, such as in aerospace, computers, pharmaceuticals, scientific instruments, and electrical machinery. • **Overall statistical capacity** is the composite score assessing the capacity of a country's statistical system. It is based on a diagnostic framework that assesses methodology, data sources, and periodicity and timeliness. Countries are scored against 25 criteria in these areas, using publicly available information and country input. The overall statistical capacity score is then calculated as simple average of all three area scores on a scale of 0–100.

Data sources

Data on business entry density are from the World Bank's Entrepreneurship Database (www.doingbusiness.org/data/exploretopics /entrepreneurship). Data on time required to start a business are from the World Bank's Doing Business project (www.doingbusiness .org). Data on market capitalization are from the World Federation of Exchanges. Data on domestic credit are from the IMF's *International Financial Statistics*. Data on central government tax revenue are from the IMF's *Government Finance Statistics*. Data on military expenditures are from SIPRI's Military Expenditure Database (www.sipri.org/research/armaments/milex/milex_database/milex _database). Data on mobile cellular phone subscriptions and individuals using the Internet are from the ITU's World Telecommunication/ICT Indicators database. Data on high-technology exports are from the United Nations Statistics Division's Commodity Trade (Comtrade) database. Data on Statistical Capacity Indicator are from the World Bank's Bulletin Board on Statistical Capacity (http://bbsc .worldbank.org).

References

Beck, T., and R. Levine. 2001. "Stock Markets, Banks, and Growth: Correlation or Causality?" Policy Research Working Paper 2670. World Bank, Washington, DC.

Claessens, S., D. Klingebiel, and S. L. Schmukler. 2002. "Explaining the Migration of Stocks from Exchanges in Emerging Economies to International Centers." Policy Research Working Paper 2816, World Bank, Washington, DC.

Hatzichronoglou, T. 1997. "Revision of the High-Technology Sector and Product Classification." STI Working Paper 1997/2. Organisation for Economic Co-operation and Development, Directorate for Science, Technology, and Industry, Paris.

5 States and markets

To access the World Development Indicators online tables, use the URL http://wdi.worldbank.org/table/ and the table number (for example, http://wdi.worldbank.org/table/5.1). To view a specific indicator online, use the URL http://data.worldbank.org/indicator/ and the indicator code (for example, http://data.worldbank.org /indicator/IE.PPI.TELE.CD).

5.1 Private sector in the economy

Telecommunications investment	IE.PPI.TELE.CD
Energy investment	IE.PPI.ENGY.CD
Transport investment	IE.PPI.TRAN.CD
Water and sanitation investment	IE.PPI.WATR.CD
Domestic credit to private sector	FS.AST.PRVT.GD.ZS
Businesses registered, New	IC.BUS.NREG
Businesses registered, Entry density	IC.BUS.NDNS.ZS

5.2 Business environment: enterprise surveys

Time dealing with government regulations	IC.GOV.DURS.ZS
Average number of times meeting with tax officials	IC.TAX.METG
Time required to obtain operating license	IC.FRM.DURS
Bribery incidence	IC.FRM.BRIB.ZS
Losses due to theft, robbery, vandalism, and arson	IC.FRM.CRIM.ZS
Firms competing against unregistered firms	IC.FRM.CMPU.ZS
Firms with female top manager	IC.FRM.FEMM.ZS
Firms using banks to finance working capital	IC.FRM.BKWC.ZS
Value lost due to electrical outages	IC.FRM.OUTG.ZS
Internationally recognized quality certification ownership	IC.FRM.ISOC.ZS
Average time to clear exports through customs	IC.CUS.DURS.EX
Firms offering formal training	IC.FRM.TRNG.ZS

5.3 Business environment: Doing Business indicators

Number of procedures to start a business	IC.REG.PROC
Time required to start a business	IC.REG.DURS
Cost to start a business	IC.REG.COST.PC.ZS
Number of procedures to register property	IC.PRP.PROC
Time required to register property	IC.PRP.DURS
Number of procedures to build a warehouse	IC.WRH.PROC
Time required to build a warehouse	IC.WRH.DURS
Time required to get electricity	IC.ELC.TIME
Time required to enforce a contract	IC.LGL.DURS
Business disclosure index	IC.BUS.DISC.XQ
Time required to resolve insolvency	IC.ISV.DURS

5.4 Stock markets

Market capitalization, $	CM.MKT.LCAP.CD
Market capitalization, % of GDP	CM.MKT.LCAP.GD.ZS
Value of shares traded	CM.MKT.TRAD.GD.ZS
Turnover ratio	CM.MKT.TRNR
Listed domestic companies	CM.MKT.LDOM.NO
S&P/Global Equity Indices	CM.MKT.INDX.ZG

5.5 Financial access, stability, and efficiency

Strength of legal rights index	IC.LGL.CRED.XQ
Depth of credit information index	IC.CRD.INFO.XQ
Depositors with commercial banks	FB.CBK.DPTR.P3
Borrowers from commercial banks	FB.CBK.BRWR.P3
Commercial bank branches	FB.CBK.BRCH.P5
Automated teller machines	FB.ATM.TOTL.P5
Bank capital to assets ratio	FB.BNK.CAPA.ZS
Ratio of bank nonperforming loans to total gross loans	FB.AST.NPER.ZS
Domestic credit to private sector by banks	FD.AST.PRVT.GD.ZS
Interest rate spread	FR.INR.LNDP
Risk premium on lending	FR.INR.RISK

5.6 Tax policies

Tax revenue collected by central government	GC.TAX.TOTL.GD.ZS
Number of tax payments by businesses	IC.TAX.PAYM
Time for businesses to prepare, file and pay taxes	IC.TAX.DURS
Business profit tax	IC.TAX.PRFT.CP.ZS
Business labor tax and contributions	IC.TAX.LABR.CP.ZS
Other business taxes	IC.TAX.OTHR.CP.ZS
Total business tax rate	IC.TAX.TOTL.CP.ZS

5.7 Military expenditures and arms transfers

Military expenditure, % of GDP	MS.MIL.XPND.GD.ZS
Military expenditure, % of central government expenditure	MS.MIL.XPND.ZS
Arm forces personnel	MS.MIL.TOTL.P1
Arm forces personnel, % of total labor force	MS.MIL.TOTL.TF.ZS
Arms transfers, Exports	MS.MIL.XPRT.KD
Arms transfers, Imports	MS.MIL.MPRT.KD

5.8 Fragile situations

International Development Association Resource Allocation Index	IQ.CPA.IRAI.XQ
Peacekeeping troops, police, and military observers	VC.PKP.TOTL.UN
Battle related deaths	VC.BTL.DETH
Intentional homicides	VC.IHR.PSRC.P5
Military expenditures	MS.MIL.XPND.GD.ZS
Losses due to theft, robbery, vandalism, and arson	IC.FRM.CRIM.ZS
Firms formally registered when operations started	IC.FRM.FREG.ZS
Children in employment ♂	SL.TLF.0714.ZS
Refugees, By country of origin	SM.POP.REFG.OR
Refugees, By country of asylum	SM.POP.REFG

Internally displaced persons	VC.IDP.TOTL.HE
Access to an improved water source	SH.H2O.SAFE.ZS
Access to improved sanitation facilities	SH.STA.ACSN
Maternal mortality ratio, National estimate	SH.STA.MMRT.NE
Maternal mortality ratio, Modeled estimate	SH.STA.MMRT
Under-five mortality rate ♂	SH.DYN.MORT
Depth of food deficit	SN.ITK.DFCT
Primary gross enrollment ratio ♂	SE.PRM.ENRR

5.9 Public policies and institutions

International Development Association Resource Allocation Index	IQ.CPA.IRAI.XQ
Macroeconomic management	IQ.CPA.MACR.XQ
Fiscal policy	IQ.CPA.FISP.XQ
Debt policy	IQ.CPA.DEBT.XQ
Economic management, Average	IQ.CPA.ECON.XQ
Trade	IQ.CPA.TRAD.XQ
Financial sector	IQ.CPA.FINS.XQ
Business regulatory environment	IQ.CPA.BREG.XQ
Structural policies, Average	IQ.CPA.STRC.XQ
Gender equality	IQ.CPA.GNDR.XQ
Equity of public resource use	IQ.CPA.PRES.XQ
Building human resources	IQ.CPA.HRES.XQ
Social protection and labor	IQ.CPA.PROT.XQ
Policies and institutions for environmental sustainability	IQ.CPA.ENVR.XQ
Policies for social inclusion and equity, Average	IQ.CPA.SOCI.XQ
Property rights and rule-based governance	IQ.CPA.PROP.XQ
Quality of budgetary and financial management	IQ.CPA.FINQ.XQ
Efficiency of revenue mobilization	IQ.CPA.REVN.XQ
Quality of public administration	IQ.CPA.PADM.XQ
Transparency, accountability, and corruption in the public sector	IQ.CPA.TRAN.XQ
Public sector management and institutions, Average	IQ.CPA.PUBS.XQ

5.10 Transport services

Rail lines	IS.RRS.TOTL.KM
Railway passengers carried	IS.RRS.PASG.KM
Railway goods hauled	IS.RRS.GOOD.MT.K6
Port container traffic	IS.SHP.GOOD.TU
Registered air carrier departures worldwide	IS.AIR.DPRT
Air passengers carried	IS.AIR.PSGR
Air freight	IS.AIR.GOOD.MT.K1

5.11 Power and communications

Electric power consumption per capita	EG.USE.ELEC.KH.PC
Electric power transmission and distribution losses	EG.ELC.LOSS.ZS
Fixed telephone subscriptions	IT.MLT.MAIN.P2
Mobile cellular subscriptions	IT.CEL.SETS.P2

Fixed telephone international voice traffic	..[a]
Mobile cellular network international voice traffic	..[a]
Population covered by mobile cellular network	..[a]
Fixed telephone sub-basket	..[a]
Mobile cellular sub-basket	..[a]
Telecommunications revenue	..[a]
Mobile cellular and fixed-line subscribers per employee	..[a]

5.12 The information age

Households with television	..[a]
Households with a computer	..[a]
Individuals using the Internet	..[a]
Fixed broadband Internet subscriptions	IT.NET.BBND.P2
International Internet bandwidth	..[a]
Fixed broadband sub-basket	..[a]
Secure Internet servers	IT.NET.SECR.P6
Information and communications technology goods, Exports	TX.VAL.ICTG.ZS.UN
Information and communications technology goods, Imports	TM.VAL.ICTG.ZS.UN
Information and communications technology services, Exports	BX.GSR.CCIS.ZS

5.13 Science and technology

Research and development (R&D), Researchers	SP.POP.SCIE.RD.P6
Research and development (R&D), Technicians	SP.POP.TECH.RD.P6
Scientific and technical journal articles	IP.JRN.ARTC.SC
Expenditures for R&D	GB.XPD.RSDV.GD.ZS
High-technology exports, $	TX.VAL.TECH.CD
High-technology exports, % of manufactured exports	TX.VAL.TECH.MF.ZS
Charges for the use of intellectual property, Receipts	BX.GSR.ROYL.CD
Charges for the use of intellectual property, Payments	BM.GSR.ROYL.CD
Patent applications filed, Residents	IP.PAT.RESD
Patent applications filed, Nonresidents	IP.PAT.NRES
Trademark applications filed, Total	IP.TMK.TOTL

5.14 Statistical capacity

Overall level of statistical capacity	IQ.SCI.OVRL
Methodology assessment	IQ.SCI.MTHD
Source data assessment	IQ.SCI.SRCE
Periodicity and timeliness assessment	IQ.SCI.PRDC

♂ Data disaggregated by sex are available in the World Development Indicators database.
a. Available online only as part of the table, not as an individual indicator.

GLOBAL LINKS

The world economy is bound together by trade in goods and services, financial flows, and movements of people. As national economies develop, their links expand and grow more complex. The indicators in *Global links* measure the size and direction of these flows and document the effects of policy interventions, such as tariffs, trade facilitation, and aid flows, on the development of the world economy.

The accommodative monetary policy implemented by the major central banks in 2014 through unchanged interest rates lowered risk premiums, improved liquidity in financial markets, and supported economic growth. However, global markets remain surrounded by uncertainties related to geopolitical tension in some regions.

International lending to low- and middle-income economies fell 18 percent in 2014, driven by a sharp 60 percent contraction in short-term debt, reflecting fresh turbulence and uncertainty in the global economy. Just over half of long-term debt inflows went to nonguaranteed private sector borrowers, compared with 62 percent in 2013. Bond issuance by public and private entities remained an important source of external financing, totaling $242 billion in 2014. There was also an important shift in borrower composition: bond issuance by public sector borrowers rose 32 percent to $146 billion, equivalent to 60 percent of total bond issuance in 2014 (compared with 46 percent in 2013). A principal driver was the purchase of domestically issued bonds by nonresidents.

Global inflows of foreign direct investment (FDI) declined 20 percent in 2014, due mainly to a 30 percent decrease into high-income economies. FDI inflows to these economies amounted to $899 billion, only 36 percent of the levels prior to the financial crisis. FDI inflows into low- and middle-income countries proved more resilient and were about 4 percent higher than 2013 levels, accounting for more than 40 percent of global FDI. Investors continue to be attracted by improved business and regulatory environments, growth prospects, and buoyant and expanding domestic markets. Although many economies receive FDI, flows remain highly concentrated: Brazil, China, and India account for more than half.

Global portfolio equity flows rebounded substantially, with an overall annual increase of 41 percent at the end of 2014. Equity flows to high-income economies increased 42 percent, and equity flows to middle-income economies increased 27 percent. Investors sought emerging markets perceived as offering high returns, leading to some diversification in the destination of portfolio equity flows, but in general portfolio equity flows remained highly concentrated in only a handful of middle-income countries. China recorded a 58 percent increase in net portfolio equity flows, to $52 billion; India recorded a 40 percent decline, to $12 billion; and Brazil's net inflows remained unchanged, at $12 billion.

In 2014 inflows of international personal remittances totaled $528 billion, a 6 percent increase over 2013. Personal remittances are calculated in balance of payments statistics as the sum of personal transfers (payments between resident and nonresident individuals) and compensation of employees (the income of short-term nonresident workers and of residents employed by nonresident entities). Some 72 percent ($378 billion) of personal remittances were received by low- and middle-income economies. High-income economies received $150 billion, mostly as compensation of employees; the three top receivers, with about 37 percent, were Belgium, France, and Germany.

Over the past decade flows of foreign direct investment (FDI) to low- and middle-income economies have increased substantially. It has long been recognized that FDI flows can carry the benefits of knowledge and technology transfer to domestic firms and the labor force, productivity spillover, enhanced competition, and improved access for exports abroad. Moreover, they are the preferred source of capital for financing a current account deficit because FDI is non-debt-creating. Global inflows of FDI declined 20 percent in 2014, to $1.6 trillion, due mainly to a 30 percent decrease into high-income economies. Low- and middle-income economies continued to prove more resilient, with FDI inflows decreasing only 1.4 percent.

Foreign direct investment

Foreign direct investment
net inflows, 2014 (% of GDP)

- 6.0 or more
- 4.0–5.9
- 2.0–3.9
- 1.0–1.9
- Less than 1.0
- No data

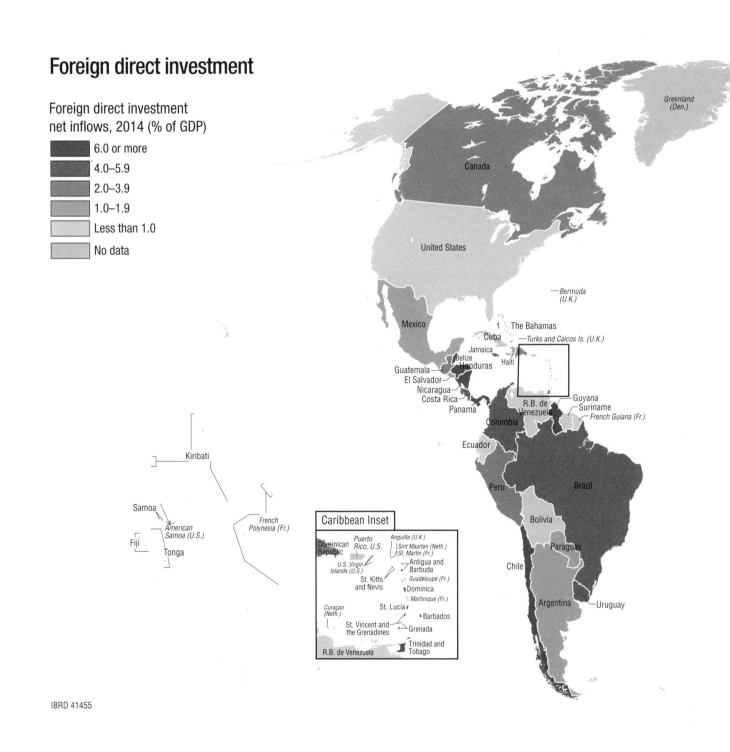

IBRD 41455

A large share of the Republic of Congo's GDP—39 percent in 2014— is from FDI inflows.

China was the top overall recipient of FDI in 2014, with $289 billion.

FDI inflows in the United States dropped 54 percent in 2014.

Brazil is the top receiver of foreign direct investment in Latin America and the Caribbean, with $97 billion.

6 Global links

	Merchandise trade	Net barter terms of trade index	Inbound tourism expenditure	Net official development assistance	Net migration	Personal remittances, received	Foreign direct investment	Portfolio equity	Total external debt stock	Total debt service
							Net inflow	Net inflow		% of exports of goods, services, and primary income
	% of GDP	2000 = 100	% of exports	% of GNI	thousands	$ millions	$ millions	$ millions	$ millions	
	2014	**2014**	**2014**	**2014**	**2010–15**	**2014**	**2014**	**2014**	**2014**	**2014**
Afghanistan	41.4	138.5	4.9	23.3	473	268	49	..	2,555	1.8
Albania	58.0	89.8	49.5	2.1	−92	1,142	1,149	34	8,000	8.6
Algeria	56.8	264.5	0.5	0.1	−143	304	1,505	..	5,453	0.4
American Samoa	..	137.3	..	..	..	..	..	..	..	..
Andorra	..	..	..	..	..	..	..	..	..	..
Angola	..	239.8	2.6	..	102	0	1,922	..	28,450	11.9
Antigua and Barbuda	45.5	57.0	..	0.2	0	21	167	..	..	..
Argentina	25.5	170.3	6.1	0.0	30	502	6,055	−688	..	..
Armenia	50.8	112.7	29.9	2.2	−10	2,079	404	1	8,551	31.7
Aruba	..	133.5	70.8	..	1	7	248	..	..	..
Australia	32.9	165.1	11.6	..	1,023	2,332	46,333	10,887	..	..
Austria	82.4	87.7	9.0	..	147	3,315	8,202	1,206	..	..
Azerbaijan	50.0	184.2	8.3	0.3	−16	1,846	4,430	10	11,693	5.2
Bahamas, The	48.4	81.0	66.1	..	10	..	266	..	..	..
Bahrain	101.6	125.4	7.9	..	30	..	958	−7,689	..	..
Bangladesh	42.0	59.3	0.5	1.3	−2,226	14,983	2,497	358	34,925	5.2
Barbados	49.9	113.6	..	..	2	87	275	..	..	..
Belarus	101.4	116.9	2.8	0.2	121	1,231	1,862	5	40,014	12.1
Belgium	173.8	95.4	3.4	..	270	11,453	−20,097	3,232	..	..
Belize	93.8	100.3	35.1	..	8	80	141	..	1,288	8.4
Benin	46.9	115.0	..	6.3	−10	217	377	..	1,984	..
Bermuda	..	112.6	..	..	..	1,290	−17	−57	..	..
Bhutan	69.7	122.7	19.0	7.1	10	14	8	..	1,840	12.2
Bolivia	68.8	202.5	5.5	2.1	−62	1,184	73	..	8,781	7.3
Bosnia and Herzegovina	91.2	98.2	12.4	3.4	−3	2,086	497	..	10,591	11.8
Botswana	98.3	84.5	..	0.6	20	48	393	0	2,384	0.6
Brazil	19.2	130.2	2.8	0.0	16	2,645	96,895	11,773	556,871	21.6
Brunei Darussalam	82.5	200.7	..	..	2	..	568	..	..	..
Bulgaria	113.0	107.8	12.4	..	−50	1,684	1,971	−77	48,742	15.2
Burkina Faso	49.6	114.4	..	9.0	−125	121	342	66	2,544	2.7
Burundi	28.9	137.8	..	16.2	40	51	..	..	690	..
Cabo Verde	45.4	101.3	53.1	12.9	−11	191	132	..	1,537	4.9
Cambodia	144.8	68.6	28.6	5.1	−150	377	1,730	..	6,811	1.4
Cameroon	36.9	156.4	..	2.7	−60	251	501	..	5,289	..
Canada	53.2	125.4	3.1	..	1,176	1,184	57,168	23,127	..	..
Cayman Islands	..	61.6	..	..	..	..	18,553	..	..	..
Central African Republic	20.0	73.7	..	35.3	10	..	3	..	657	..
Chad	56.7	196.6	..	2.9	100	..	761	..	2,857	..
Channel Islands	..	..	..	..	4	..	..	..	..	..
Chile	57.3	135.5	3.6	0.1	201	136	22,002	2,321	..	..
China	41.5	84.0	2.3	0.0	−1,800	29,911	289,097	51,916	959,510	1.9
Hong Kong SAR, China	386.6	64.6	7.4	..	150	372	115,980	17,648	..	..
Macao SAR, China	22.8	86.7	93.7	..	35	50	2,550	..	..	..
Colombia	31.5	145.9	7.7	0.3	−145	4,166	16,151	3,833	102,345	19.5
Comoros	48.1	94.2	..	11.9	−10	121	14	..	145	0.7
Congo, Dem. Rep.	40.8	122.6	0.0	8.3	−96	22	−344	−14	5,508	3.3
Congo, Rep.	102.0	215.0	..	0.9	−60	..	5,502	..	3,901	..

 Front | User guide | World view |  People | Environment

	Merchandise trade	Net barter terms of trade index	Inbound tourism expenditure	Net official development assistance	Net migration	Personal remittances, received	Foreign direct investment	Portfolio equity	Total external debt stock	Total debt service
							Net inflow	Net inflow		% of exports of goods, services, and primary income
	% of GDP	2000 = 100	% of exports	% of GNI	thousands	$ millions	$ millions	$ millions	$ millions	
	2014	2014	2014	2014	2010–15	2014	2014	2014	2014	2014
Costa Rica	57.4	62.8	18.5	0.1	20	594	2,578	..	20,974	21.1
Côte d'Ivoire	69.0	158.8	..	2.8	50	378	462	..	10,857	11.6
Croatia	64.2	99.3	37.9	..	−20	2,149	3,937	−21	..	..
Cuba	..	112.0	..	..	−80	..	..	..	..	..
Curaçao	..	98.9	..	..	6	143	69	..	..	..
Cyprus	36.8	92.2	..	..	35	260	861	1,178	..	..
Czech Republic	159.0	103.4	4.4	..	30	1,893	4,871	270	..	..
Denmark	61.4	99.0	3.8	..	97	1,377	−677	11,167	..	..
Djibouti	69.8	84.1	..	..	−16	36	153	..	957	6.1
Dominica	46.5	97.4	..	3.1	..	24	41	..	291	10.5
Dominican Republic	42.4	67.4	33.2	0.3	−153	4,810	2,385	..	26,708	18.5
Ecuador	53.0	181.7	5.1	0.2	−38	2,472	773	1	26,333	13.8
Egypt, Arab Rep.	31.4	149.6	16.9	1.2	−216	19,570	4,783	485	39,624	12.7
El Salvador	62.7	81.2	19.8	0.4	−240	4,235˙	475	..	14,536	19.0
Equatorial Guinea	123.0	219.3	..	0.0	20	..	1,933	..	..	..
Eritrea	..	83.5	..	..	−160	..	47	..	908	..
Estonia	129.6	94.2	10.0	..	−12	544	1,571	−58	..	..
Ethiopia	42.1	136.9	..	6.5	−60	646	1,200	..	16,585	..
Faroe Islands	..	98.4	..	..	..	161	..	..	..	..
Fiji	102.0	106.7	..	2.1	−29	209	279	..	864	..
Finland	55.5	88.7	3.5	..	107	974	14,812	3,966	..	..
France	44.5	89.1	7.8	..	332	25,195	7,957	15,287	..	..
French Polynesia	..	80.7	..	..	−1	669	129	..	..	..
Gabon	65.6	214.2	..	0.7	5	..	973	..	4,326	..
Gambia, The	56.2	103.4	..	12.1	−13	191	28	..	500	..
Georgia	69.3	130.6	28.0	3.4	−296	1,986	1,647	210	13,912	23.2
Germany	70.4	96.7	3.2	..	1,250	17,629	8,390	3,764	..	..
Ghana	71.9	178.6	6.7	3.1	−50	2,008	3,363	..	17,612	5.1
Greece	42.3	86.9	25.4	..	−136	735	1,683	11,267	..	..
Greenland	..	80.1	..	..	..	..	..	..	..	..
Grenada	41.3	87.5	..	4.6	−4	31	40	..	651	10.4
Guam	..	100.6	..	..	0	..	..	..	..	..
Guatemala	49.5	100.2	11.3	0.5	−120	5,837	1,205	..	18,761	14.3
Guinea	51.8	96.2	..	9.1	−10	95	566	..	1,407	..
Guinea-Bissau	38.1	81.0	..	10.6	−10	47	21	..	271	..
Guyana	95.1	107.0	5.9	5.2	−27	330	238	..	2,379	4.7
Haiti	51.8	88.3	34.9	12.4	−150	1,977	99	..	1,937	1.4
Honduras	98.7	50.8	9.7	3.3	−80	3,370	1,294	..	7,331	10.6
Hungary	155.9	99.8	6.0	..	30	4,656	12,400	−341	..	..
Iceland	61.2	86.3	15.0	..	0	206	746	−61	..	..
India	38.3	134.9	4.3	0.1	−2,598	70,389	33,871	12,369	463,230	18.6
Indonesia	39.9	121.5	5.8	0.0	−700	8,551	26,349	3,259	293,397	23.1
Iran, Islamic Rep.	32.9	183.0	..	..	−300	..	2,105	..	5,495	0.5
Iraq	64.3	209.1	..	0.6	549	271	4,782	..	..	..
Ireland	75.2	89.4	3.9	..	−140	719	86,766	230,003	..	..
Isle of Man	..	..	..	..	..	..	..	..	..	..
Israel	47.0	101.4	6.5	..	19	859	6,738	3,600	..	..

6 Global links

	Merchandise trade	Net barter terms of trade index	Inbound tourism expenditure	Net official development assistance	Net migration	Personal remittances, received	Foreign direct investment	Portfolio equity	Total external debt stock	Total debt service
							Net inflow	Net inflow		% of exports of goods, services, and primary income
	% of GDP	2000 = 100	% of exports	% of GNI	thousands	$ millions	$ millions	$ millions	$ millions	
	2014	**2014**	**2014**	**2014**	**2010–15**	**2014**	**2014**	**2014**	**2014**	**2014**
Italy	46.7	100.3	7.2	..	528	9,982	13,727	26,676	..	..
Jamaica	52.5	84.8	51.8	0.7	−97	2,269	595	140	14,046	32.7
Japan	32.7	58.4	2.4	..	350	3,733	9,070	32,997	..	..
Jordan	86.8	71.1	35.7	7.6	230	3,737	1,760	−31	24,256	8.5
Kazakhstan	54.8	215.6	1.8	0.0	160	229	7,598	−135	157,595	35.6
Kenya	40.2	88.1	16.5	4.4	−50	1,441	944	954	16,179	11.0
Kiribati	60.2	94.1	16.9	25.7	−2	16	8	..	..	..
Korea, Dem. People's Rep.	67.0	..	..	0	..	134	..	..	..	..
Korea, Rep.	77.9	52.7	3.2	..	300	6,481	9,899	6,753	..	..
Kosovo	..	..	..	7.7	..	1,192	200	..	2,242	8.8
Kuwait	83.0	211.9	0.6	..	518	4	486	586	..	..
Kyrgyz Republic	99.7	105.4	16.8	8.7	−114	2,243	211	6	7,257	14.2
Lao PDR	49.6	105.8	..	4.1	−118	60	721	..	10,724	..
Latvia	103.1	104.1	6.7	..	−73	1,774	878	58	..	..
Lebanon	56.2	99.7	36.8	1.8	1,250	7,404	2,954	496	30,608	16.4
Lesotho	143.6	74.8	2.0	4.0	−20	380	47	0	876	3.1
Liberia	80.9	127.8	10.6	44.3	−20	495	363	..	633	1.9
Libya	97.2	221.8	..	0.5	−502	..	50	..	..	..
Liechtenstein	..	..	..	..	..	..	..	..	..	..
Lithuania	139.9	94.4	3.5	..	−170	2,113	351	16	..	..
Luxembourg	70.8	74.1	4.4	..	49	1,784	7,087	385,524	..	..
Macedonia, FYR	107.8	90.7	5.5	1.9	−5	367	61	−4	7,241	17.5
Madagascar	50.8	84.3	..	5.7	−5	432	351	..	2,853	..
Malawi	102.1	99.9	2.2	22.8	−30	38	716	0	1,637	4.0
Malaysia	131.0	96.2	9.0	0.0	450	1,573	10,609	..	210,820	4.9
Maldives	75.7	91.2	79.5	0.9	0	3	363	−1	1,026	2.3
Mali	50.5	138.9	..	10.9	−302	923	199	..	3,416	..
Malta	..	126.5	9.9	..	6	196	−13	−139	..	..
Marshall Islands	131.2	107.7	..	24.2	..	26	9	..	..	..
Mauritania	91.1	140.5	1.9	5.4	−20	..	502	..	3,522	9.9
Mauritius	69.0	75.8	27.3	0.4	0	1	418	801	11,288	26.9
Mexico	62.5	97.2	4.0	0.1	−524	24,462	24,154	4,833	432,602	12.2
Micronesia, Fed. Sts.	78.9	75.2	..	33.9	−8	22	1	..	..	..
Moldova	96.2	70.7	10.7	5.9	−10	2,084	350	10	6,463	14.6
Monaco	..	..	..	..	..	..	..	..	..	..
Mongolia	91.6	172.2	3.4	2.8	−15	255	384	−1	20,826	21.2
Montenegro	61.2	..	52.1	2.2	−2	431	497	16	2,454	12.6
Morocco	63.2	125.2	..	2.1	−311	6,962	3,582	..	42,772	15.1
Mozambique	84.5	94.6	4.8	13.4	−25	155	4,999	..	7,793	3.7
Myanmar	42.4	115.3	12.1	2.2	−474	3,103	1,398	..	6,351	0.5
Namibia	92.6	123.0	9.1	1.8	−1	10	493	15	..	..
Nepal	42.7	77.3	21.2	4.4	−372	5,770	6	..	4,010	8.2
Netherlands	143.3	92.1	2.0	..	110	1,540	48,225	4,732	..	..
New Caledonia	..	182.1	..	..	6	479	2,288	..	..	..
New Zealand	42.1	138.9	..	..	7	462	4,454	2,247	..	..
Nicaragua	102.3	87.7	8.9	3.7	−135	1,140	884	..	10,216	14.8
Niger	45.9	157.8	..	11.6	−28	157	769	..	2,585	..

 Front | User guide | World view | People | Environment

	Merchandise trade	Net barter terms of trade index	Inbound tourism expenditure	Net official development assistance	Net migration	Personal remittances, received	Foreign direct investment	Portfolio equity	Total external debt stock	Total debt service
							Net inflow	Net inflow		% of exports of goods, services, and primary income
	% of GDP	2000 = 100	% of exports	% of GNI	thousands	$ millions	$ millions	$ millions	$ millions	
	2014	2014	2014	2014	2010–15	2014	2014	2014	2014	2014
Nigeria	27.6	210.7	0.7	0.5	−300	20,829	4,656	1,037	26,858	0.8
Northern Mariana Islands	..	81.5	..	..	..	..	3	..	..	..
Norway	46.6	157.1	3.4	..	236	761	10,586	−414	..	..
Oman	102.2	239.1	3.5	..	1,211	39	739	910	..	..
Pakistan	29.7	58.8	3.2	1.4	−1,082	17,066	1,778	772	62,184	19.1
Palau	74.2	88.1	..	9.7	..	2	40	..	..	..
Panama	74.4	79.7	21.0	−0.4	28	760	5,214	..	19,343	4.6
Papua New Guinea	57.1	189.0	0.0	3.5	0	10	−30	−6	20,920	13.0
Paraguay	70.7	102.8	2.3	0.2	−87	507	523	..	14,092	19.5
Peru	40.3	205.9	8.5	0.2	−240	2,639	7,885	−79	66,469	10.9
Philippines	45.5	65.2	8.0	0.2	−700	28,403	6,202	1,196	77,659	7.2
Poland	80.1	98.6	4.8	..	−74	7,409	17,275	3,290	..	..
Portugal	61.8	94.0	18.9	..	−140	424	12,410	2,087	..	..
Puerto Rico	..	..	..	..	−104	..	..	..	..	..
Qatar	79.2	213.9	7.5	..	364	499	1,040	2,482	..	..
Romania	74.1	107.4	2.7	..	−437	3,381	3,864	535	111,290	28.9
Russian Federation	43.3	182.0	3.5	..	1,118	7,777	22,891	−12,922	..	..
Rwanda	40.5	181.0	24.5	13.3	−75	128	292	1	2,022	4.5
Samoa	57.7	83.9	65.1	12.0	−13	141	23	..	450	7.9
San Marino	..	..	..	..	..	..	..	..	..	..
São Tomé and Príncipe	55.4	133.8	64.5	11.5	−6	27	27	..	212	13.7
Saudi Arabia	68.6	205.4	2.6	..	850	269	8,012	..	..	..
Senegal	60.4	108.8	..	7.2	−100	1,644	343	..	5,655	..
Serbia	80.8	103.3	7.0	0.9	−100	3,696	2,000	−22	33,103	41.4
Seychelles	118.3	88.1	35.0	0.7	−2	15	108	−21	..	..
Sierra Leone	69.8	56.3	2.4	20.9	−21	62	690	..	1,238	2.3
Singapore	252.1	77.5	3.3	..	398	..	67,523	−1,290	..	..
Sint Maarten	..	..	..	..	..	62	48	..	..	..
Slovak Republic	168.3	93.9	2.8	..	1	2,395	85	18	..	..
Slovenia	141.9	95.5	7.8	..	4	757	1,030	123	..	..
Solomon Islands	82.8	104.0	11.3	18.1	−12	16	21	..	187	2.8
Somalia	..	111.7	..	21.1	−400	..	106	..	2,920	..
South Africa	60.8	135.1	9.6	0.3	600	913	5,741	2,551	144,006	8.6
South Sudan	..	..	..	16.6	865	..	−700	..	..	..
Spain	49.5	88.9	14.5	..	−593	3,119	34,233	27,940	..	..
Sri Lanka	39.0	105.9	19.6	0.7	−485	7,036	944	184	43,609	14.7
St. Kitts and Nevis	37.1	68.0	..	..	..	52	120	..	..	..
St. Lucia	53.5	96.2	..	1.3	0	30	75	..	528	..
St. Martin	..	..	..	..	..	..	..	..	..	..
St. Vincent & the Grenadines	56.2	93.9	..	1.3	−5	33	139	..	339	..
Sudan	18.4a	..	16.4a	1.2	−800	507a	1,251	2a	21,759a	4.4a
Suriname	79.8	122.1	4.4	0.2	−5	9	−210	..	..	..
Swaziland	79.2	107.0	0.8	2.0	−6	24	27	..	438	1.3
Sweden	57.3	91.6	5.0	..	273	4,442	−2,535	2,008	..	..
Switzerland	83.7	102.3	4.7	..	382	2,349	22,741	3,753	..	..
Syrian Arab Republic	..	139.9	..	..	−4,030	1,623	..	..	4,597	..
Tajikistan	60.4	91.4	12.8	3.9	−117	3,975	261	1	4,047	13.2

	Merchandise trade	Net barter terms of trade index	Inbound tourism expenditure	Net official development assistance	Net migration	Personal remittances, received	Foreign direct investment	Portfolio equity	Total external debt stock	Total debt service
	% of GDP	2000 = 100	% of exports	% of GNI	thousands	$ millions	Net inflow $ millions	Net inflow $ millions	$ millions	% of exports of goods, services, and primary income
	2014	2014	2014	2014	2010–15	2014	2014	2014	2014	2014
Tanzania	35.4	135.7	23.4	5.6	−200	389	2,045	4	14,436	2.9
Thailand	112.5	95.2	15.0	0.1	100	5,655	3,719	−5,824	135,799	5.2
Timor-Leste	67.7	..	39.1	7.6	−50	44	34	..	..	..
Togo	91.8	111.1	..	5.1	−10	343	292	..	995	..
Tonga	50.6	85.4	..	18.2	−8	114	56	..	196	..
Trinidad and Tobago	69.5	145.4	..	..	−5	131	2,423	..	..	..
Tunisia	85.5	115.6	14.1	2.0	−33	2,347	1,005	72	26,405	8.7
Turkey	50.1	91.8	17.0	0.4	2,000	1,128	12,765	2,559	408,203	25.0
Turkmenistan	58.0	223.5	..	0.1	−25	..	3,164	..	441	..
Turks and Caicos Islands	..	71.4	..	..	..	..	..	..	..	..
Tuvalu	32.5	..	..	63.3	..	4	..	..	..	..
Uganda	30.2	114.6	17.1	6.2	−150	887	1,147	5	5,135	2.1
Ukraine	82.3	91.3	3.5	1.1	195	7,354	847	−391	130,686	25.2
United Arab Emirates	155.7	180.3	..	..	405	..	10,066	..	..	..
United Kingdom	39.8	100.9	7.4	..	900	4,923	45,457	49,402	..	..
United States	23.2	95.9	9.4	..	5,008	6,908	131,829	155,077	..	..
Uruguay	35.9	128.5	13.6	0.2	−30	122	2,805	..	..	..
Uzbekistan	43.4	171.3	..	0.5	−195	..	751	..	13,389	..
Vanuatu	45.8	95.4	71.5	12.1	1	28	13	..	181	1.8
Venezuela, RB	..	..	..	..	−69	121	..	..	..	..
Vietnam	161.0	129.8	4.5	2.4	−200	..	9,200	252	71,890	4.2
Virgin Islands (U.S.)	..	..	..	..	−4	..	..	..	..	..
West Bank and Gaza	..	77.4	23.6	17.6	−44	2,182	127	53	..	..
Yemen, Rep.	..	159.2	11.0	..	−50	3,351	−738	..	7,710	3.3
Zambia	71.1	172.2	5.8	3.9	−34	58	1,508	6	7,373	3.7
Zimbabwe	51.2	108.4	..	5.8	−220	..	545	..	10,570	..
World	**48.9 w**	..	**6.0[b] w**	**0.2[c] w**	**0 s**	**527,849 s**	**1,561,365 s**	**1,116,140 s**	**.. s**	**.. w**
East Asia & Pacific	54.8	..	5.2	0.0	−1,457	93,101	611,633	120,035	1,816,587[d]	3.8[d]
Europe & Central Asia	63.6	..	6.0	0.0	5,547	160,947	410,388	775,908	1,025,915[d]	23.7[d]
Latin America & Caribbean	37.0	..	6.2	0.2	−2,082	64,987	214,679	22,134	1,346,821[d]	15.5[d]
Middle East & North Africa	71.0	..	5.9	..	−213	49,653	50,093	826	187,878[d]	5.5[d]
North America	25.9	..	8.2	0.0	6,184	9,382	188,980	178,147	..	..
South Asia	37.9	..	5.0	0.6	−6,281	115,529	39,517	13,683	613,379[d]	17.6[d]
Sub-Saharan Africa	45.8	..	6.8	2.8	−1,689	34,249	46,074	5,408	402,811[d]	7.4[d]
Low income	50.8	..	15.0	8.8	−1,166	13,914	16,846	62	167,105[d]	6.1[d]
Lower middle income	44.7	..	5.8	0.9	−16,002	248,353	119,050	20,760	1,527,246[d]	14.5[d]
Upper middle income	46.0	..	5.5	0.1	719	115,541	525,894	73,416	3,699,039[d]	7.5[d]
High income	50.4	..	6.2	0.0	16,458	150,040	899,575	1,021,902	..	..

a. Includes South Sudan. b. Calculated using the World Bank's weighted aggregation methodology (see *Sources and methods*) and thus may differ from data reported by the World Tourism Organization. c. Based on the World Bank classification of economies and thus may differ from data reported by the Organisation for Economic Co-operation and Development. d. Covers only Debtor Reporting System countries.

Starting with *World Development Indicators 2013,* the World Bank changed its presentation of balance of payments data to conform to the International Monetary Fund's (IMF) Balance of Payments Manual, 6th edition (BPM6). The historical data series based on BPM5 ends with data for 2005. Balance of payments data from 2005 forward have been presented in accord with the BPM6 methodology, which can be accessed at www.imf.org/external/np/sta /bop/bop.htm.

Trade in goods

Data on merchandise trade are from customs reports of goods moving into or out of an economy or from reports of financial transactions related to merchandise trade recorded in the balance of payments. Because of differences in timing and definitions, trade flow estimates from customs reports and balance of payments may differ. Several international agencies process trade data, each correcting unreported or misreported data, leading to other differences. The most detailed source of data on international trade in goods is the United Nations Statistics Division's Commodity Trade Statistics (Comtrade) database. The IMF and the World Trade Organization also collect customs-based data on trade in goods.

The "terms of trade" index measures the relative prices of a country's exports and imports. The most common way to calculate terms of trade is the net barter (or commodity) terms of trade index, or the ratio of the export price index to the import price index. When a country's net barter terms of trade index increases, its exports have become more expensive or its imports cheaper.

Tourism

Tourism is defined as the activity of people traveling to and staying in places outside their usual environment for no more than one year for leisure, business, and other purposes not related to an activity remunerated from within the place visited. Data on inbound and outbound tourists refer to the number of arrivals and departures, not to the number of unique individuals. Thus a person who makes several trips to a country during a given period is counted each time as a new arrival. Data on inbound tourism show the arrivals of nonresident tourists (overnight visitors) at national borders. When data on international tourists are unavailable or incomplete, the table shows the arrivals of international visitors, which include tourists, same-day visitors, cruise passengers, and crew members. The aggregates are calculated using the World Bank's weighted aggregation methodology (see *Sources and methods*) and differ from the World Tourism Organization's aggregates.

For tourism expenditure, the World Tourism Organization uses balance of payments data from the IMF supplemented by data from individual countries. These data, shown in the table, include travel and passenger transport items as defined by the BPM6. When the IMF does not report data on passenger transport items, expenditure data for travel items are shown.

Official development assistance

Data on official development assistance received refer to aid to eligible countries from members of the Organisation of Economic Co-operation and Development's (OECD) Development Assistance Committee (DAC), multilateral organizations, and non-DAC donors. Data do not reflect aid given by recipient countries to other low- and middle-income countries or distinguish among types of aid (program, project, or food aid; emergency assistance; or postconflict peacekeeping assistance), which may have different effects on the economy.

Ratios of aid to gross national income (GNI), gross capital formation, imports, and government spending measure a country's dependency on aid. Care must be taken in drawing policy conclusions. For foreign policy reasons some countries have traditionally received large amounts of aid. Thus aid dependency ratios may reveal as much about a donor's interests as about a recipient's needs. Increases in aid dependency ratios can reflect events affecting both the numerator (aid) and the denominator (GNI).

Data are based on information from donors and may not be consistent with information recorded by recipients in the balance of payments, which often excludes all or some technical assistance—particularly payments to expatriates made directly by the donor. Similarly, grant commodity aid may not always be recorded in trade data or in the balance of payments. DAC statistics exclude aid for military and antiterrorism purposes. The aggregates refer to World Bank classifications of economies and therefore may differ from those reported by the OECD.

Migration and personal remittances

The movement of people, most often through migration, is a significant part of global integration. Migrants contribute to the economies of both their host country and their country of origin. Yet reliable statistics on migration are difficult to collect and are often incomplete, making international comparisons a challenge.

Since data on emigrant stock is difficult for countries to collect, the United Nations Population Division provides data on net migration, taking into account the past migration history of a country or area, the migration policy of a country, and the influx of refugees in recent periods to derive estimates of net migration. The data to calculate these estimates come from various sources, including border statistics, administrative records, surveys, and censuses. When there are insufficient data, net migration is derived through the difference between the growth rate of a country's population over a certain period and the rate of natural increase of that population (itself being the difference between the birth rate and the death rate).

Migrants often send funds back to their home countries, which are recorded as personal transfers in the balance of payments. Personal transfers thus include all current transfers between resident and nonresident individuals, independent of the source of income of the sender (irrespective of whether the sender receives income from labor, entrepreneurial or property income, social benefits, or any other types of transfers or disposes of assets) and the relationship between the households (irrespective of whether they are related or unrelated individuals).

Compensation of employees refers to the income of border, seasonal, and other short-term workers who are employed in an economy where they are not resident and of residents employed by nonresident entities. Compensation of employees has three main components: wages and salaries in cash, wages and salaries in kind, and employers' social contributions. Personal remittances are the sum of personal transfers and compensation of employees.

Equity flows

Equity flows comprise foreign direct investment (FDI) and portfolio equity. The internationally accepted definition of FDI (from BPM6) includes the following components: equity investment, including investment associated with equity that gives rise to control or influence; investment in indirectly influenced or controlled enterprises; investment in fellow enterprises; debt (except selected debt); and reverse investment. The Framework for Direct Investment Relationships provides criteria for determining whether cross-border ownership results in a direct investment relationship, based on control and influence.

Direct investments may take the form of greenfield investment, where the investor starts a new venture in a foreign country by constructing new operational facilities; joint venture, where the investor enters into a partnership agreement with a company abroad to establish a new enterprise; or merger and acquisition, where the investor acquires an existing enterprise abroad. The IMF suggests that investments should account for at least 10 percent of voting stock to be counted as FDI. In practice many countries set a higher threshold. Many countries fail to report reinvested earnings, and the definition of long-term loans differs among countries.

Portfolio equity investment is defined as cross-border transactions and positions involving equity securities, other than those included in direct investment or reserve assets. Equity securities are equity instruments that are negotiable and designed to be traded, usually on organized exchanges or "over the counter." The negotiability of securities facilitates trading, allowing securities to be held by different parties during their lives. Negotiability allows investors to diversify their portfolios and to withdraw their investment readily. Included in portfolio investment are investment fund shares or units (that is, those issued by investment funds) that are evidenced by securities and that are not reserve assets or direct investment. Although they are negotiable instruments, exchange-traded financial derivatives are not included in portfolio investment because they are in their own category.

External debt

External indebtedness affects a country's creditworthiness and investor perceptions. Data on external debt are gathered through the World Bank's Debtor Reporting System (DRS). Indebtedness is calculated using loan-by-loan reports submitted by countries on long-term public and publicly guaranteed borrowing and using information on short-term debt collected by the countries, from creditors through the reporting systems of the Bank for International Settlements, or based on national data from the World Bank's *Quarterly External Debt Statistics*. These data are supplemented by information from major multilateral banks and official lending agencies in major creditor countries. Currently, 120 low- and middle-income countries report to the DRS. Debt data are reported in the currency of repayment and compiled and published in U.S. dollars. End-of-period exchange rates are used for the compilation of stock figures (amount of debt outstanding), and projected debt service and annual average exchange rates are used for the flows. Exchange rates are taken from the IMF's *International Financial Statistics*. Debt repayable in multiple currencies, goods, or services and debt with a provision for maintenance of the value of the currency of repayment are shown at book value.

While data related to public and publicly guaranteed debt are reported to the DRS on a loan-by-loan basis, data on long-term private nonguaranteed debt are reported annually in aggregate by the country or estimated by World Bank staff for countries. Private nonguaranteed debt is estimated based on national data from the World Bank's *Quarterly External Debt Statistics*.

Total debt service as a share of exports of goods, services, and primary income provides a measure of a country's ability to service its debt out of export earnings.

Definitions

• **Merchandise trade** includes all trade in goods and excludes trade in services. • **Net barter terms of trade index** is the percentage ratio of the export unit value indexes to the import unit value indexes, measured relative to the base year 2000. • **Inbound tourism expenditure** is expenditures by international inbound visitors, including payments to national carriers for international transport and any other prepayment made for goods or services received in the destination country. They may include receipts from same-day visitors, except when these are important enough to justify separate classification. Data include travel and passenger transport items as defined by BPM6. When passenger transport items are not reported, expenditure data for travel items are shown. Exports refer to all transactions between residents of a country and the rest of the world involving a change of ownership from residents to non-residents of general merchandise, goods sent for processing and repairs, nonmonetary gold, and services. • **Net official development assistance** is flows (net of repayment of principal) that meet the DAC definition of official development assistance and are made to countries and territories on the DAC list of aid recipients, divided by World Bank estimates of GNI. • **Net migration** is the net total of migrants (immigrants less emigrants, including both citizens and noncitizens) during the period. Data are five-year estimates. • **Personal remittances, received,** are the sum of personal transfers (current transfers in cash or in kind made or received by resident households to or from nonresident households) and compensation of employees (remuneration for the labor input to the production process contributed by an individual in an employer-employee relationship with the enterprise). • **Foreign direct investment** is cross-border investment associated with a resident in one economy having control or a significant degree of influence on the management of an enterprise that is resident in another economy. • **Portfolio equity** is net inflows from equity securities other than those recorded as direct investment or reserve assets, including shares, stocks, depository receipts, and direct purchases of shares in local stock markets by foreign investors • **Total external debt stock** is debt owed to nonresident creditors and repayable in foreign currency, goods, or services by public and private entities in the country. It is the sum of long-term external debt, short-term debt, and use of IMF credit. • **Total debt service** is the sum of principal repayments and interest actually paid in foreign currency, goods, or services on long-term debt; interest paid on short-term debt; and repayments (repurchases and charges) to the IMF. Exports of goods and services and primary income are the total value of exports of goods and services, receipts of compensation of nonresident workers, and primary investment income from abroad.

Data sources

Data on merchandise trade are from the World Trade Organization. Data on trade indexes are from the United Nations Conference on Trade and Development's (UNCTAD) annual *Handbook of Statistics*. Data on tourism expenditure are from the World Tourism Organization's *Yearbook of Tourism Statistics* and World Tourism Organization (2016) and updated from its electronic files. Data on net official development assistance are compiled by the OECD (http://stats .oecd.org). Data on net migration are from United Nations Population Division (2015). Data on personal remittances are from the IMF's *Balance of Payments Statistics Yearbook* supplemented by World Bank staff estimates. Data on FDI are World Bank staff estimates based on IMF balance of payments statistics and UNCTAD data (http://unctadstat.unctad.org/ReportFolders/reportFolders.aspx). Data on portfolio equity are from the IMF's *Balance of Payments Statistics Yearbook*. Data on external debt are mainly from reports to the World Bank through its DRS from member countries that have received International Bank for Reconstruction and Development loans or International Development Assistance credits, with additional information from the files of the World Bank, the IMF, the African Development Bank and African Development Fund, the Asian Development Bank and Asian Development Fund, and the Inter-American Development Bank. Summary tables of the external debt of low- and middle-income countries are published annually in the World Bank's *International Debt Statistics* and International Debt Statistics database.

References

IMF (International Monetary Fund). Various issues. *International Financial Statistics.* Washington, DC.

———. Various years. *Balance of Payments Statistics Yearbook. Parts 1 and 2.* Washington, DC.

UNCTAD (United Nations Conference on Trade and Development). Various years. *Handbook of Statistics.* New York and Geneva.

United Nations Population Division. 2015. *World Population Prospects: The 2015 Revision.* New York: United Nations, Department of Economic and Social Affairs.

World Bank. Various years. *International Debt Statistics.* Washington, DC.

World Tourism Organization. 2016. *Compendium of Tourism Statistics 2016.* Madrid.

———. Various years. *Yearbook of Tourism Statistics. Vols. 1 and 2.* Madrid.

6 Global links

To access the World Development Indicators online tables, use the URL http://wdi.worldbank.org/table/ and the table number (for example, http://wdi.worldbank.org/table/6.1). To view a specific indicator online, use the URL http://data.worldbank.org/indicator/ and the indicator code (for example, http://data.worldbank.org /indicator/TX.QTY.MRCH.XD.WD).

6.1 Growth of merchandise trade

Export volume	TX.QTY.MRCH.XD.WD
Import volume	TM.QTY.MRCH.XD.WD
Export value	TX.VAL.MRCH.XD.WD
Import value	TM.VAL.MRCH.XD.WD
Net barter terms of trade index	TT.PRI.MRCH.XD.WD

6.2 Direction and growth of merchandise trade

This table provides estimates of the flow of trade in goods between groups of economies.	..a

6.3 High-income economy trade with low- and middle-income economies

This table illustrates the importance of low- and middle-income economies in the global trading system.	..a

6.4 Direction of trade of low- and middle-income economies

Exports to low- and middle-income economies within region	TX.VAL.MRCH.WR.ZS
Exports to low- and middle-income economies outside region	TX.VAL.MRCH.OR.ZS
Exports to high-income economies	TX.VAL.MRCH.HI.ZS
Imports from low- and middle-income economies within region	TM.VAL.MRCH.WR.ZS
Imports from low- and middle-income economies outside region	TM.VAL.MRCH.OR.ZS
Imports from high-income economies	TM.VAL.MRCH.HI.ZS

6.5 Primary commodity prices

This table provides historical commodity price data.	..a

6.6 Tariff barriers

All products, Binding coverage	TM.TAX.MRCH.BC.ZS
Simple mean bound rate	TM.TAX.MRCH.BR.ZS
Simple mean tariff	TM.TAX.MRCH.SM.AR.ZS
Weighted mean tariff	TM.TAX.MRCH.WM.AR.ZS
Share of tariff lines with international peaks	TM.TAX.MRCH.IP.ZS
Share of tariff lines with specific rates	TM.TAX.MRCH.SR.ZS
Primary products, Simple mean tariff	TM.TAX.TCOM.SM.AR.ZS
Primary products, Weighted mean tariff	TM.TAX.TCOM.WM.AR.ZS
Manufactured products, Simple mean tariff	TM.TAX.MANF.SM.AR.ZS
Manufactured products, Weighted mean tariff	TM.TAX.MANF.WM.AR.ZS

6.7 Trade facilitation

Logistics performance index	LP.LPI.OVRL.XQ
Burden of customs procedures	IQ.WEF.CUST.XQ
Lead time to export	LP.EXP.DURS.MD
Lead time to import	LP.IMP.DURS.MD
Documents to export	IC.EXP.DOCS
Documents to import	IC.IMP.DOCS
Liner shipping connectivity index	IS.SHP.GCNW.XQ
Quality of port infrastructure	IQ.WEF.PORT.XQ

6.8 External debt

Total external debt, $	DT.DOD.DECT.CD
Total external debt, % of GNI	DT.DOD.DECT.GN.ZS
Long-term debt, Public and publicly guaranteed	DT.DOD.DPPG.CD
Long-term debt, Private nonguaranteed	DT.DOD.DPNG.CD
Short-term debt, $	DT.DOD.DSTC.CD
Short-term debt, % of total debt	DT.DOD.DSTC.ZS
Short-term debt, % of total reserves	DT.DOD.DSTC.IR.ZS
Total debt service	DT.TDS.DECT.EX.ZS
Present value of debt, % of GNI	DT.DOD.PVLX.GN.ZS
Present value of debt, % of exports of goods, services and primary income	DT.DOD.PVLX.EX.ZS

6.9 Global private financial flows

Foreign direct investment net inflows, $	BX.KLT.DINV.CD.WD
Foreign direct investment net inflows, % of GDP	BX.KLT.DINV.WD.GD.ZS
Portfolio equity	BX.PEF.TOTL.CD.WD
Bonds	DT.NFL.BOND.CD
Commercial banks and other lendings	DT.NFL.PCBO.CD

6.10 Net official financial flows

Net financial flows from bilateral sources	DT.NFL.BLAT.CD
Net financial flows from multilateral sources	DT.NFL.MLAT.CD
World Bank, IDA	DT.NFL.MIDA.CD
World Bank, IBRD	DT.NFL.MIBR.CD
IMF, Concessional	DT.NFL.IMFC.CD
IMF, Nonconcessional	DT.NFL.IMFN.CD
Regional development banks, Concessional	DT.NFL.RDBC.CD
Regional development banks, Nonconcessional	DT.NFL.RDBN.CD
Regional development banks, Other institutions	DT.NFL.MOTH.CD

 Front | User guide | World view | People | Environment

6.11 Aid dependency

Net official development assistance (ODA)	DT.ODA.ODAT.CD
Net ODA per capita	DT.ODA.ODAT.PC.ZS
Grants, excluding technical cooperation	BX.GRT.EXTA.CD.WD
Technical cooperation grants	BX.GRT.TECH.CD.WD
Net ODA, % of GNI	DT.ODA.ODAT.GN.ZS
Net ODA, % of gross capital formation	DT.ODA.ODAT.GI.ZS
Net ODA, % of imports of goods and services and income	DT.ODA.ODAT.MP.ZS
Net ODA, % of central government expenditure	DT.ODA.ODAT.XP.ZS

6.12 Distribution of net aid by Development Assistance Committee members

Net bilateral aid flows from DAC donors	DC.DAC.TOTL.CD
United States	DC.DAC.USAL.CD
EU institutions	DC.DAC.CECL.CD
Germany	DC.DAC.DEUL.CD
France	DC.DAC.FRAL.CD
United Kingdom	DC.DAC.GBRL.CD
Japan	DC.DAC.JPNL.CD
Netherlands	DC.DAC.NLDL.CD
Australia	DC.DAC.AUSL.CD
Norway	DC.DAC.NORL.CD

Sweden	DC.DAC.SWEL.CD
Other DAC donors	..[a,b]

6.13 Movement of people

Net migration	SM.POP.NETM
International migrant stock	SM.POP.TOTL
Emigration rate of tertiary educated to OECD countries	SM.EMI.TERT.ZS
Refugees by country of origin	SM.POP.REFG.OR
Refugees by country of asylum	SM.POP.REFG
Personal remittances, Received	BX.TRF.PWKR.CD.DT
Personal remittances, Paid	BM.TRF.PWKR.CD.DT

6.14 Travel and tourism

International inbound tourists	ST.INT.ARVL
International outbound tourists	ST.INT.DPRT
Inbound tourism expenditure, $	ST.INT.RCPT.CD
Inbound tourism expenditure, % of exports	ST.INT.RCPT.XP.ZS
Outbound tourism expenditure, $	ST.INT.XPND.CD
Outbound tourism expenditure, % of imports	ST.INT.XPND.MP.ZS

a. Available online only as part of the table, not as an individual indicator.
b. Derived from data elsewhere in the World Development Indicators database.

Front | User guide | World view | People | Environment

Sources and methods

As a major user of development data, the World Bank recognizes the importance of data documentation to inform users of the methods and conventions used by primary data collectors—usually national statistical agencies, central banks, and customs services—and by international organizations, which compile the statistics that appear in the World Development Indicators database.

This section describes some of the statistical practices and procedures used in preparing *World Development Indicators.* It covers data consistency, reliability, comparability, reporting standards of key indicators, and the methods employed for calculating regional and income group aggregates and for calculating growth rates. It also describes the *World Bank Atlas* method for deriving the conversion factor used to estimate gross national income (GNI) and GNI per capita in U.S. dollars. Other statistical procedures and calculations are described in the *About the data* sections following each table. Additional documentation and metadata are available in the World Development Indicators database at http://databank.worldbank.org/wdi and from a dashboard of the statistical capacity of countries at http://datatopics.worldbank.org/statisticalcapacity.

Data availability, reliability, and comparability

Many factors affect data availability, reliability, and comparability. Statistical systems in many of the poorest countries are limited; statistical methods, coverage, practices, and definitions differ widely; and cross-country and intertemporal comparisons involve complex technical and conceptual problems that cannot be resolved unequivocally. Data relevant at the national level may not be suitable for standardized international use due to methodological concerns or the lack of clear documentation. Delays in reporting data and the use of old surveys as the basis for current estimates may further compromise the quality of data reported. Data coverage may not be complete because of special circumstances affecting the collection and reporting of data, such as problems stemming from conflicts.

Considerable effort has been made to standardize the data, but full comparability cannot be assured, so care must be taken in interpreting the indicators. Although drawn from sources thought to be the most authoritative, data should be understood only as indicating trends and characterizing major differences among economies rather than as offering precise quantitative measures of those differences.

Discrepancies in data presented in different editions of *World Development Indicators* reflect updates by countries as well as revisions to historical series and changes in methodology. Therefore readers are advised not to compare data series between printed editions of *World Development Indicators* or between different World Bank publications. Consistent time series data for 1960–2014 are available at http://databank.worldbank.org/wdi.

Sources and methods

	Currency	National accounts						Balance of payments and trade			Government finance	IMF data dissemination standard
		Base year	Reference year	System of National Accounts	SNA price valuation	Alternative conversion factor	PPP survey year	Balance of Payments Manual in use	External debt	System of trade	Accounting concept	
Afghanistan	Afghan afghani	2002/03		1993	B			6	A	G	C	G
Albania	Albanian lek	[a]	1996	1993	B		Rolling	6	A	S	C	G
Algeria	Algerian dinar	1980		1968	B		2011	6	A	S	B	G
American Samoa	U.S. dollar			1968			2011[b]					
Andorra	Euro	2000		1968	B							
Angola	Angolan kwanza	2002		1993	P	1991–96	2011	6	A		B	G
Antigua and Barbuda	East Caribbean dollar	2006		1968	B		2011	6		G	B	G
Argentina	Argentine peso	2004		2008	B	1971–84		6		S	C	S
Armenia	Armenian dram	[a]	1996	1993	B	1990–95	2011	6	A	G	C	S
Aruba	Aruban florin	2000		1993	B		2011	6		G		
Australia	Australian dollar	[a] 2013/14		2008	B		2011	6		G	C	S
Austria	Euro	[a]	2010	2008	B		Rolling	6		S	C	S
Azerbaijan	New Azeri manat	2000		1993	B	1992–95	2011	6	A	G	C	G
Bahamas, The	Bahamian dollar	2006		1993	B		2011	6		G	C	G
Bahrain	Bahraini dinar	2010		2008	P		2011	6		G	B	G
Bangladesh	Bangladeshi taka	2005/06		1993	B		2011	6	P	G	C	G
Barbados	Barbados dollar	1974		1993	P		2011	6		G	B	G
Belarus	Belarusian rubel	[a]	2000	1993	B	1990–95	2011	6	A	G	C	S
Belgium	Euro	[a]	2010	2008	B		Rolling	6		S	C	S
Belize	Belize dollar	2000		1993	B		2011	6	A	G	B	G
Benin	CFA franc	2007		1968	B	1992	2011	6	A	G	B	G
Bermuda	Bermuda dollar	2006		1993	B		2011	6		G		
Bhutan	Bhutanese ngultrum	2000		1993	B		2011	6	A	G	C	G
Bolivia	Bolivian Boliviano	1990		1968	B	1960–85	2011	6	A	G	C	G
Bosnia and Herzegovina	Bosnia and Herzegovina convertible mark	[a]	2010	1993	B		Rolling	6	A	S	C	G
Botswana	Botswana pula	2006		1993	B		2011	6	E	G	B	G
Brazil	Brazilian real	1995	2000	1993	B		2011	6	A	S	C	S
Brunei Darussalam	Brunei dollar	2000		1993	P		2011	6		S		G
Bulgaria	Bulgarian lev	[a]	2010	1993	B	1978–89, 1991–92	Rolling	6	A	S	C	S
Burkina Faso	CFA franc	1999		1993	B	1992–93	2011	6	A	G	B	G
Burundi	Burundi franc	2005		1993	B		2011	6	A	G	B	G
Cabo Verde	Cabo Verde escudo	2007		1993	P		2011	6	A	S	C	G
Cambodia	Cambodian riel	2000		1993	B		2011	6	A	G	B	G
Cameroon	CFA franc	2000		1993	B		2011	6	A	S	B	G
Canada	Canadian dollar	[a]	2010	2008	B		2011	6		G	C	S
Cayman Islands	Cayman Islands dollar	2007		1993			2011					
Central African Republic	CFA franc	2000		1968	B		2011	6	A	S	B	G
Chad	CFA franc	2005		1993	B		2011	6	E			G
Channel Islands	Pound sterling	2003	2007	1968	B							
Chile	Chilean peso	2008		1993	B		2011	6		G	C	S
China	Chinese yuan	2000		1993	P	1978–93	2011	6	P	G	C	S
Hong Kong SAR, China	Hong Kong dollar	[a]	2013	2008	B		2011	6		G	C	S
Macao SAR, China	Macao pataca	2012		1993	B		2011	6		G	C	G
Colombia	Colombian peso	2005		1993	B	1992–94	2011	6	A	S	C	S
Comoros	Comorian franc	1990		1968	P		2011	6	A			G
Congo, Dem. Rep.	Congolese franc	2005		1968	B	1999–2001	2011	6	P	S	B	G
Congo, Rep.	CFA franc	1990		1968	P	1993	2011	6	A	S	B	G
Costa Rica	Costa Rican colon	1991		1993	B		2011	6	A	G	C	S
Côte d'Ivoire	CFA franc	2009		1968	P		2011	6	A	S	B	G
Croatia	Croatian kuna	[a]	2010	1993	B		Rolling	6		S	C	S
Cuba	Cuban peso	1997	2005	1993	B		2011					
Curaçao	Netherlands Antillean guilder			1993			2011					
Cyprus	Euro	[a]	2005	1993	B		Rolling	6		G	C	S

 Front User guide World view People Environment

	Latest population census	Latest demographic, education, or health household survey	Source of most recent income and expenditure data	Vital registration complete	Latest agricultural census	Latest industrial data	Latest trade data	Latest water withdrawal data
Afghanistan	1979	DHS, 2015	IHS, 2011				2014	2000
Albania	2011	DHS, 2008/09	LSMS, 2012	Yes	2012	2012	2014	2006
Algeria	2008	MICS, 2012/13	IHS, 1995			2010	2014	2012
American Samoa	2010			Yes	2008			
Andorra	2011c			Yes			2014	
Angola	2014	DHS, 2015	IHS, 2008/09					2005
Antigua and Barbuda	2011			Yes	2007		2014	2012
Argentina	2010	MICS, 2011/12	IHS, 2013	Yes	2008	2002	2014	2011
Armenia	2011	DHS, 2015	IHS, 2013	Yes	2014		2014	2012
Aruba	2010			Yes			2014	
Australia	2011		ES/BS, 2010	Yes	2011	2012	2014	2013
Austria	2011c		IHS, 2012	Yes	2010	2012	2014	2002
Azerbaijan	2009	DHS, 2006	LSMS, 2013	Yes	2015	2012	2014	2012
Bahamas, The	2010						2014	
Bahrain	2010c			Yes		2010	2014	2003
Bangladesh	2011	DHS, 2014; HIV/MCH SPA, 2014	IHS, 2010		2008	2011	2011	2008
Barbados	2010	MICS, 2012		Yes			2014	2005
Belarus	2009	MICS, 2012	IHS, 2013	Yes		2011	2014	2013
Belgium	2011d		IHS, 2012	Yes	2010	2012	2014	2009
Belize	2010	MICS, 2015/16	LFS, 1999		2011		2014	2000
Benin	2013	MICS, 2014	CWIQ, 2011/12				2014	2001
Bermuda	2010			Yes			2014	
Bhutan	2005	MICS, 2010	IHS, 2012		2009e		2012	2008
Bolivia	2012	DHS, 2008	IHS, 2013		2013	2001	2014	2009
Bosnia and Herzegovina	2013	MICS, 2011/12	LSMS, 2007	Yes		2011	2014	2012
Botswana	2011	MICS, 2000	ES/BS, 2009/10		2015	2012	2014	2000
Brazil	2010	WHS, 2003	IHS, 2013		2006	2012	2014	2010
Brunei Darussalam	2011			Yes			2014	1994
Bulgaria	2011	LSMS, 2007	ES/BS, 2012	Yes	2010	2012	2014	2009
Burkina Faso	2006	LSMS, 2014; MIS, 2014	CWIQ, 2009		2006–10		2014	2005
Burundi	2008	MIS, 2012	CWIQ, 2006			2010	2014	2000
Cabo Verde	2010	DHS, 2005	CWIQ, 2007	Yes	2014/15		2014	2001
Cambodia	2008	DHS, 2014	IHS, 2012		2013	2000	2013	2006
Cameroon	2005	MICS, 2014	PS, 2007		2013e	2002	2014	2000
Canada	2011		LFS, 2010	Yes	2011	2012	2014	2009
Cayman Islands	2010			Yes			2013	
Central African Republic	2003	MICS, 2010	PS, 2008				2014	2005
Chad	2009	DHS, 2014/15	PS, 2011				1995	2005
Channel Islands	2009/11f			Yesg				
Chile	2012		IHS, 2013	Yes	2007		2014	2006
China	2010	NSS, 2013	IHS, 2014		2007	2007	2014	2005
Hong Kong SAR, China	2011			Yes		2012	2014	
Macao SAR, China	2011			Yes		2012	2014	
Colombia	2006	DHS, 2015	IHS, 2014		2014/15	2012	2014	2008
Comoros	2003	DHS, 2012	IHS, 2004				2013	1999
Congo, Dem. Rep.	1984	DHS, 2013/14	1-2-3, 2012/13					2005
Congo, Rep.	2007	MICS 2014/15	CWIQ/PS, 2011		2014/15	2009	2014	2002
Costa Rica	2011	MICS, 2011	IHS, 2015	Yes	2014	2012	2013	2013
Côte d'Ivoire	2014	DHS, 2011/12	IHS, 2015		2014/15		2014	2005
Croatia	2011	WHS, 2003	IHS, 2012	Yes	2010e		2014	2010
Cuba	2012	MICS, 2014		Yes			2006	2013
Curaçao	2011			Yes				
Cyprus	2011			Yes	2010	2012	2014	2009

Sources and methods

	Currency	National accounts						Balance of payments and trade			Government finance	IMF data dissemination standard
		Base year	Reference year	System of National Accounts	SNA price valuation	Alternative conversion factor	PPP survey year	Balance of Payments Manual in use	External debt	System of trade	Accounting concept	
Czech Republic	Czech koruna	[a]	2010	2008	B		Rolling	6		S	C	S
Denmark	Danish krone	[a]	2010	2008	B		Rolling	6		G	C	S
Djibouti	Djibouti franc	1990		1968	B		2011	6	A			G
Dominica	East Caribbean dollar	2006		1993	B		2011	6	A	S	B	G
Dominican Republic	Dominican peso	2007		1993	B		2011	6	A	G	C	G
Ecuador	U.S. dollar	2007		2008	B		2011	6	A	S	B	S
Egypt, Arab Rep.	Egyptian pound	2011/12		1993	B		2011	6	A	G	C	S
El Salvador	U.S. dollar	1990		1968	B		2011	6	A	G	C	S
Equatorial Guinea	CFA franc	2006		1968	B	1965–84	2011				B	
Eritrea	Eritrean nakfa	2000		1968	B			6	E			
Estonia	Euro	[a]	2010	2008	B	1987–95	Rolling	6		G	C	S
Ethiopia	Ethiopian birr	2010/11		1993	B		2011	6	A	G	B	G
Faroe Islands	Danish krone			1993	B			6				
Fiji	Fijian dollar	2005		1993	B		2011	6	A	G	B	G
Finland	Euro	[a]	2010	2008	B		Rolling	6		S	C	S
France	Euro	[a]	2010	2008	B		Rolling	6		S	C	S+
French Polynesia	CFP franc	1990		1993			2011[b]	6		S		
Gabon	CFA franc	2001		1993	B	1993	2011	6	E			G
Gambia, The	Gambian dalasi	2004		1993	P		2011	6	A	G	C	G
Georgia	Georgian lari	[a]	1996	1993	B	1990–95	2011	6	A	G	C	S
Germany	Euro	[a]	2010	2008	B		Rolling	6		S	C	S+
Ghana	New Ghanaian cedi	2006		1993	B	1973–87	2011	6	A	G	B	G
Greece	Euro	[a]	2010	2008	B		Rolling	6		S	C	S
Greenland	Danish krone	1990		1993						G		
Grenada	East Caribbean dollar	2006		1968	B		2011	6	A		B	G
Guam	U.S. dollar			1993			2011[b]					
Guatemala	Guatemalan quetzal	2001		1993	B		2011	6	A	G	B	G
Guinea	Guinean franc	2003		1993	B		2011	6	A		B	G
Guinea-Bissau	CFA franc	2005		1993	B		2011	6	E			G
Guyana	Guyana dollar	2006		1993	B			6	A	S		G
Haiti	Haitian gourde	1986/87		1968	B	1991	2011	6	A			G
Honduras	Honduran lempira	2000		1993	B	1988–89	2011	6	A	S	C	G
Hungary	Hungarian forint	[a]	2010	2008	B		Rolling	6		S	C	S
Iceland	Iceland krona	[a]	2010	2008	B		Rolling	6		S	C	S
India	Indian rupee	2011/12		2008	B		2011	6	A	G	C	S
Indonesia	Indonesian rupiah	2010		1993	B		2011	6	A	G	C	S
Iran, Islamic Rep.	Iranian rial	2004/05		1993	B	1980–2002	2011	6	A	S	C	G
Iraq	Iraqi dinar	2007		1968	P	1997, 2004	2011	6			B	G
Ireland	Euro	[a]	2010	2008	B		Rolling	6		G	C	S
Isle of Man	Pound sterling	2003		1968								
Israel	Israeli new shekel	[a]	2010	2008	P		2011	6		S	C	S
Italy	Euro	[a]	2010	2008	B		Rolling	6		G	C	S+
Jamaica	Jamaican dollar	2007		1993	B		2011	6	A	S	C	S
Japan	Japanese yen	[a]	2010	1993	B		2011	6		G	C	S
Jordan	Jordanian dinar	1994		1968	B		2011	6	A	S	B	S
Kazakhstan	Kazakh tenge	[a]	2005	1993	B	1987–95	2011	6	A	G	C	S
Kenya	Kenyan shilling	2009		2008	B		2011	6	A	G	B	G
Kiribati	Australian dollar	2006		1993	B		2011[b]	6		S	C	G
Korea, Dem. People's Rep.	Democratic People's Republic of Korean won			1968				6				
Korea, Rep.	Korean won	2010		2008	B		2011	6		G	C	S
Kosovo	Euro	2008		1993	B			6	A			G
Kuwait	Kuwaiti dinar	2010		1993	B		2011	6		S	C	G
Kyrgyz Republic	Kyrgyz som	[a]	1995	1993	B	1990–95	2011	6	A	G	B	S
Lao PDR	Lao kip	2002		1993	B		2011	6	A		B	
Latvia	Euro	[a]	2010	2008	B	1987–95	Rolling	6		S	C	S
Lebanon	Lebanese pound	1997		1993	B		2011	6	A	S	B	G

 Front | User guide | World view | People | Environment

	Latest population census	Latest demographic, education, or health household survey	Source of most recent income and expenditure data	Vital registration complete	Latest agricultural census	Latest industrial data	Latest trade data	Latest water withdrawal data
Czech Republic	2011[d]	WHS, 2003	IHS, 2012	Yes	2010	2012	2014	2012
Denmark	2011[c]		ITR, 2012	Yes	2010	2012	2014	2012
Djibouti	2009	MICS, 2006	PS, 2012		2015[e]		2009	2000
Dominica	2011			Yes	2015		2012	2010
Dominican Republic	2010	MICS, 2014	IHS, 2013				2014	2010
Ecuador	2010	RHS, 2004	IHS, 2014			2008	2014	2005
Egypt, Arab Rep.	2006	HIS, 2015	ES/BS, 2010/11	Yes	2009/10	2010	2014	2000
El Salvador	2007	MICS, 2014	IHS, 2014	Yes	2007/08		2014	2005
Equatorial Guinea	2002	DHS, 2011	PS, 2006		2015			2000
Eritrea	1984	DHS, 2002	PS, 1993			2012	2003	2004
Estonia	2012[d]	WHS, 2003	IHS, 2012	Yes	2010	2012	2014	2012
Ethiopia	2007	HIV/MCH SPA, 2014	ES/BS, 2010/11			2009	2014	2002
Faroe Islands	2011			Yes			2009	
Fiji	2007		ES/BS, 2008/09	Yes	2009	2011	2014	2000
Finland	2010[c]		IHS, 2012	Yes	2010	2012	2014	2006
France	2006[h]		ES/BS, 2012	Yes	2010	2012	2014	2010
French Polynesia	2007			Yes			2014	
Gabon	2013	DHS, 2012	CWIQ/IHS, 2005				2009	2005
Gambia, The	2013	DHS, 2013	IHS, 2010		2011/12	2004	2014	2000
Georgia	2014	MICS, 2005; RHS, 2005	IHS, 2013	Yes		2012	2014	2008
Germany	2011		IHS, 2011	Yes	2010	2012	2014	2010
Ghana	2010	DHS, 2014	LSMS, 2012			2003	2013	2000
Greece	2011		IHS, 2012	Yes	2009	2012	2014	2007
Greenland	2010[c]			Yes			2014	
Grenada	2011	RHS, 1985		Yes	2012		2009	2014
Guam	2010			Yes	2007			
Guatemala	2002	DHS, 2014/15	LSMS, 2011	Yes	2013		2014	2006
Guinea	2014	DHS, 2012	CWIQ, 2012				2014	2001
Guinea-Bissau	2009	MICS, 2014	CWIQ, 2010				2005	2000
Guyana	2012	MICS, 2014	IHS, 1998				2014	2010
Haiti	2003	HIV/MCH SPA, 2013	IHS, 2012		2008/09		1997	2009
Honduras	2013	DHS, 2011/12	IHS, 2014				2014	2003
Hungary	2011	WHS, 2003	IHS, 2012	Yes	2010	2012	2014	2012
Iceland	2011[d]		IHS, 2012	Yes	2010	2005	2014	2005
India	2011	DHS, 2005/06	IHS, 2011/12		2010/11	2011	2014	2010
Indonesia	2010	DHS, 2012	IHS, 2014		2013	2011	2014	2000
Iran, Islamic Rep.	2011	IrMIDHS, 2010	ES/BS, 2005	Yes	2014	2011	2011	2004
Iraq	1997	LSMS, 2012	IHS, 2012		2011/12	2011	2013	2000
Ireland	2011		IHS, 2012	Yes	2010	2011	2014	2009
Isle of Man	2011			Yes				
Israel	2009[d]		ES/BS, 2010	Yes		2011	2014	2004
Italy	2012[d]		IS, 2012	Yes	2010	2012	2014	2008
Jamaica	2011	MICS, 2011	LSMS, 2004		2007		2014	2007
Japan	2010		IHS, 2008	Yes	2010	2012	2014	2009
Jordan	2004	DHS, 2012	ES/BS, 2010		2007	2012	2014	2005
Kazakhstan	2009	MICS, 2015	ES/BS, 2013	Yes	2006/07		2014	2010
Kenya	2009	DHS, 2014	IHS, 2005/06			2012	2013	2010
Kiribati	2010	KDHS, 2009					2013	
Korea, Dem. People's Rep.	2008	MICS, 2009						2005
Korea, Rep.	2010		ES/BS, 1998	Yes	2010	2012	2014	2005
Kosovo	2011	MICS, 2013/14	IHS, 2011		2014			
Kuwait	2011	FHS, 1996		Yes		2012	2014	2002
Kyrgyz Republic	2009	MICS, 2014	ES/BS, 2014	Yes		2010	2013	2006
Lao PDR	2005	MICS/DHS, 2011/12	ES/BS, 2012		2010/11			2005
Latvia	2011[d]	WHS, 2003	IHS, 2012	Yes	2010	2012	2014	2002
Lebanon	1943	FHS, 2004		Yes	2010	2007	2014	2005

Sources and methods

	Currency	Base year	Reference year	System of National Accounts	SNA price valuation	Alternative conversion factor	PPP survey year	Balance of Payments Manual in use	External debt	System of trade	Accounting concept	IMF data dissemination standard
Lesotho	Lesotho loti	2004		1993	B		2011	6	A	G	B	G
Liberia	U.S. dollar	2000		1968	P		2011	6	A		C	G
Libya	Libyan dinar	2003		1993	B	1986		6		G		G
Liechtenstein	Swiss franc	1990		1993	B							
Lithuania	Euro	a	2010	2008	B	1990–95	Rolling	6		S	C	S
Luxembourg	Euro	a	2010	2008	B		Rolling	6		S	C	S
Macedonia, FYR	Macedonian denar	2005		1993	B		Rolling	6	A	S	C	S
Madagascar	Malagasy ariary	1984		1968	B		2011	6	A	G	C	G
Malawi	Malawi kwacha	2009		1993	B		2011	6	A	G	B	G
Malaysia	Malaysian ringgit	2010		1993	P		2011	6	E	G	B	G
Maldives	Maldivian rufiyaa	2003		1993	B		2011	6	A	G	C	G
Mali	CFA franc	1987		1968	B		2011	6	A	G	B	G
Malta	Euro	a	2005	1993	B		Rolling	6		G	C	S
Marshall Islands	U.S. dollar	2003/04		1968	B		2011b				B	G
Mauritania	Mauritanian ouguiya	2004		1993	B		2011	6	A	G		G
Mauritius	Mauritian rupee	2006		1993	B		2011	6	A	G	C	S
Mexico	Mexican peso	2008		2008	B		2011	6	A	G	C	S
Micronesia, Fed. Sts.	U.S. dollar	2003/04		1993	B		2011b	6		G	B	G
Moldova	Moldovan leu	a	1996	1993	B	1990–95	2011	6	A	G	C	S
Monaco	Euro	1990		1993								
Mongolia	Mongolian tugrik	2010		1993	B		2011	6	A	G	C	G
Montenegro	Euro	2000		1993	B		Rolling	6	A	S		G
Morocco	Moroccan dirham	2007		1993	B		2011	6	A	S	C	S
Mozambique	New Mozambican metical	2009		1993	B	1992–95	2011	6	A	G	B	G
Myanmar	Myanmar kyat	2005/06		1968	P		2011	6	E	G	C	G
Namibia	Namibian dollar	2010		1993	B		2011	6		G	B	G
Nepal	Nepalese rupee	2000/01		1993	B		2011	6	A	S	B	G
Netherlands	Euro	a	2010	2008	B		Rolling	6		S	C	S+
New Caledonia	CFP franc	1990		1993			2011b	6		G		
New Zealand	New Zealand dollar	a	2010	2008	B		2011	6		G	C	
Nicaragua	Nicaraguan gold cordoba	2006		1993	B	1965–95	2011	6	A	G	B	G
Niger	CFA franc	2006		1993	P	1993	2011	6	A	G	B	G
Nigeria	Nigerian naira	2010		2008	B	1971–98	2011	6	A	G	B	G
Northern Mariana Islands	U.S. dollar			1968			2011b					
Norway	Norwegian krone	a	2010	2008	B		Rolling	6		G	C	S
Oman	Rial Omani	2010		1993	P		2011	6		G	B	G
Pakistan	Pakistani rupee	2005/06		1993	B		2011	6	A	G	B	G
Palau	U.S. dollar	2004/05		1993	B		2011b				B	G
Panama	Panamanian balboa	2007		1993	B		2011	6	A	S	C	G
Papua New Guinea	Papua New Guinea kina	1998		1993	B	1989	2011b	6	A	G	B	G
Paraguay	Paraguayan guarani	1994		1993	B		2011	6	A	G	C	G
Peru	Peruvian new sol	2007		1993	B	1985–90	2011	6	A	S	C	S
Philippines	Philippine peso	2000		1993	P		2011	6	A	G	B	S
Poland	Polish zloty	a	2005	2008	B		Rolling	6		S	C	S
Portugal	Euro	a	2010	2008	B		Rolling	6		S	C	S+
Puerto Rico	U.S. dollar	1953/54		1968	P					G		
Qatar	Qatari riyal	2013		1993	P		2011	6		G	B	G
Romania	New Romanian leu	2005		1993	B	1987–89, 1992	Rolling	6	A	S	C	S
Russian Federation	Russian ruble	2000		1993	B	1987–95	2011	6		G	C	S
Rwanda	Rwandan franc	2011		2008	P	1994	2011	6	A	G	B	G
Samoa	Samoan tala	2008/09		1993	B		2011b	6	A	G	B	G
San Marino	Euro	1990		1993	B						C	G
São Tomé and Príncipe	São Tomé and Principe dobra	2001		1993	P		2011	6	A	S	B	G
Saudi Arabia	Saudi Arabian riyal	2010		1993	P		2011	6		G		G
Senegal	CFA franc	1999		1993	B		2011	6	A	G	B	G

Front | User guide | World view | People | Environment

	Latest population census	Latest demographic, education, or health household survey	Source of most recent income and expenditure data	Vital registration complete	Latest agricultural census	Latest industrial data	Latest trade data	Latest water withdrawal data
Lesotho	2006	DHS, 2014	ES/BS, 2010		2010		2012	2000
Liberia	2008	DHS, 2013	CWIQ, 2007					2000
Libya	2006	FHS, 2007			2014/15		2010	2000
Liechtenstein	2010^d			Yes				
Lithuania	2011^d		ES/BS, 2012	Yes	2010	2012	2014	2007
Luxembourg	2011			Yes	2010	2011	2014	2012
Macedonia, FYR	2002	MICS, 2011	ES/BS, 2010	Yes	2007	2010	2014	2007
Madagascar	1993	MIS, 2013	PS, 2010			2006	2014	2000
Malawi	2008	DHS, 2015/16	IHS, 2010/11		2006/07	2010	2014	2005
Malaysia	2010	WHS, 2003	IS, 2014	Yes	2015	2012	2014	2005
Maldives	2014	DHS, 2009	IHS, 2009/10	Yes			2014	2008
Mali	2009	MICS, 2015; MIS, 2015	IHS, 2009/10				2012	2006
Malta	2011			Yes	2010	2010	2014	2002
Marshall Islands	2011	RMIDHS, 2007	IHS, 1999					
Mauritania	2013	MICS, 2015	IHS, 2008				2014	2005
Mauritius	2011	WHS, 2003	IHS, 2012	Yes	2014	2012	2014	2003
Mexico	2010	MICS, 2015	IHS, 2014	Yes	2007	2010	2014	2011
Micronesia, Fed. Sts.	2010		IHS, 2000				2013	
Moldova	2014	MICS, 2012	ES/BS, 2013	Yes	2011	2012	2014	2007
Monaco	2008^c			Yes				2009
Mongolia	2010	MICS, 2013/14	LSMS, 2014	Yes	2011	2011	2014	2009
Montenegro	2011	MICS, 2013	ES/BS, 2013	Yes	2010		2014	2010
Morocco	2014	EPSF, 2010/11	ES/BS, 2007			2012	2014	2010
Mozambique	2007	AIS, 2014	ES/BS, 2008/09		2009/10		2014	2001
Myanmar	2014	DHS, 2015/16			2010		2010	2000
Namibia	2011	DHS, 2013	ES/BS, 2009/10		2014/15	2012	2014	2002
Nepal	2011	MCH SPA, 2015	LSMS, 2010/11		2011/12	2011	2014	2006
Netherlands	2011^d		IHS, 2012	Yes	2010	2012	2014	2010
New Caledonia	2009			Yes			2014	
New Zealand	2013			Yes	2012	2010	2014	2010
Nicaragua	2005	RHS, 2006/07	LSMS, 2014		2011		2014	2011
Niger	2012	DHS, 2012	CWIQ/PS, 2011		2004–08	2002	2014	2005
Nigeria	2006	MIS, 2015	IHS, 2009/10		2013		2014	2005
Northern Mariana Islands	2010				2007			
Norway	2011^c		IS, 2012	Yes	2010	2012	2014	2006
Oman	2010	MICS, 2014			2012/13	2012	2014	2003
Pakistan	1998	DHS, 2012/13	IHS, 2010/11		2010	2006	2014	2008
Palau	2010			Yes			2014	
Panama	2010	MICS, 2013	IHS, 2013		2011	2001	2014	2010
Papua New Guinea	2011	LSMS, 1996	IHS, 2009/10			2001	2012	2005
Paraguay	2012	RHS, 2008	IHS, 2014		2008	2010	2014	2012
Peru	2007	Continuous DHS, 2014	IHS, 2014		2012	2011	2014	2008
Philippines	2010	DHS, 2013	ES/BS, 2012	Yes	2012	2010	2014	2009
Poland	2011^d		ES/BS, 2012	Yes	2010	2011	2014	2012
Portugal	2011			Yes	2009	2011	2014	2007
Puerto Rico	2010	RHS, 1995/96		Yes	2012	2006		2005
Qatar	2010	MICS, 2012		Yes		2010	2014	2005
Romania	2011	RHS-Ro, 2004	ES/BS, 2012	Yes	2010	2012	2014	2009
Russian Federation	2010	WHS, 2003	IHS, 2013	Yes	2006	2012	2014	2001
Rwanda	2012	DHS, 2014/15	IHS, 2010/11		2013		2014	2000
Samoa	2011	DHS, 2009			2009		2014	
San Marino	2010			Yes				
São Tomé and Príncipe	2012	MICS, 2014	PS, 2010		2011/12		2014	1993
Saudi Arabia	2010	Demographic survey, 2007			2010	2006	2013	2006
Senegal	2013	Continuous DHS, 2015; HIV/MCH SPA, 2015	PS, 2011/12		2014	2012	2014	2002

Sources and methods

	Currency	National accounts						Balance of payments and trade			Government finance	IMF data dissemination standard
		Base year	Reference year	System of National Accounts	SNA price valuation	Alternative conversion factor	PPP survey year	Balance of Payments Manual in use	External debt	System of trade	Accounting concept	
Serbia	New Serbian dinar	[a]	2010	1993	B		Rolling	6	A	G	C	G
Seychelles	Seychelles rupee	2006		1993	B		2011	6			C	S
Sierra Leone	Sierra Leonean leone	2006		1993	B		2011	6	A		C	G
Singapore	Singapore dollar	2010		2008	B		2011	6		G	C	S
Sint Maarten	Netherlands Antillean guilder			1993			2011					
Slovak Republic	Euro	[a]	2010	2008	B		Rolling	6		S	C	S
Slovenia	Euro	[a]	2010	2008	B		Rolling	6		S	C	S
Solomon Islands	Solomon Islands dollar	2004		1993	B		2011[b]	6	E	S	B	G
Somalia	Somali shilling	1985		1968	B	1977–90			E			
South Africa	South African rand	2010		2008	B		2011	6	P	G	C	S
South Sudan	South Sudanese pound	2009		1993								
Spain	Euro	[a]	2010	2008	B		Rolling	6		S	C	S+
Sri Lanka	Sri Lankan rupee	2010		1993	P		2011	6	A	G	B	S
St. Kitts and Nevis	East Caribbean dollar	2006		1993	B		2011	6		S	B	G
St. Lucia	East Caribbean dollar	2006		1968	B		2011	6	A		B	G
St. Martin	Euro			1993								
St. Vincent and the Grenadines	East Caribbean dollar	2006		1993	B		2011	6	A	S	C	G
Sudan	Sudanese pound	1981/82[i]	1996	1968	B		2011	6	P	G	B	G
Suriname	Suriname dollar	2007		1993	B		2011	6		G	B	G
Swaziland	Swaziland lilangeni	2011		1993	B		2011	6	A		B	G
Sweden	Swedish krona	[a]	2010	2008	B		Rolling	6		S	C	S+
Switzerland	Swiss franc	[a]	2010	2008	B		Rolling	6		S	C	S
Syrian Arab Republic	Syrian pound	2000		1968	B	1970–2010	2011	6	E	S	B	G
Tajikistan	Tajik somoni	[a]	2000	1993	B	1990–95	2011	6	A		C	G
Tanzania	Tanzanian shilling	2007		2008	B		2011	6	A	G	B	G
Thailand	Thai baht	2002		1993	P		2011	6	A	S	C	S
Timor-Leste	U.S. dollar	2010		2008	B			6			C	G
Togo	CFA franc	2000		1968	P		2011	6	A	S	B	G
Tonga	Tongan pa'anga	2010/11		1993	B		2011[b]	6	A	G		G
Trinidad and Tobago	Trinidad and Tobago dollar	2000		1993	B		2011	6		S	C	G
Tunisia	Tunisian dinar	2010		1993	B		2011	6	A	G	C	S
Turkey	New Turkish lira	1998		1993	B		Rolling	6	A	S	C	S
Turkmenistan	New Turkmen manat	2005		1993	B	1987–95, 1997–2007		6	E			
Turks and Caicos Islands	U.S. dollar			1993			2011			G		
Tuvalu	Australian dollar	2005		1968	B		2011[b]	6				G
Uganda	Ugandan shilling	2009/10		2008	B		2011	6	A	G	B	G
Ukraine	Ukrainian hryvnia	[a]	2003	1993	B	1987–95	2011	6	A	G	C	S
United Arab Emirates	U.A.E. dirham	2007		1993	P		2011	6		S	C	G
United Kingdom	Pound sterling	[a]	2010	2008	B		Rolling	6		G	C	S
United States	U.S. dollar	[a]	2010	2008	B		2011	6		G	C	S+
Uruguay	Uruguayan peso	2005		1993	B		2011	6		S	C	S
Uzbekistan	Uzbek sum	[a]	1997	1993	B	1990–95		6	A	G	C	
Vanuatu	Vanuatu vatu	2006		1993	B		2011[b]	6	E	G	B	G
Venezuela, RB	Venezuelan bolivar fuerte	1997		1993	B		2011	6		G	C	G
Vietnam	Vietnamese dong	2010		1993	P	1991	2011	6	A	G		G
Virgin Islands (U.S.)	U.S. dollar	1982		1968						G		
West Bank and Gaza	Israeli new shekel	2004		1968	B		2011	6			C	S
Yemen, Rep.	Yemeni rial	2007		1993	P	1990–96	2011	6	E	S	C	G
Zambia	New Zambian kwacha	2010		2008	B	1990–92	2011	6	A	G	B	G
Zimbabwe	U.S. dollar	2009		1993	B	1991, 1998	2011	6	A	G	B	G

	Latest population census	Latest demographic, education, or health household survey	Source of most recent income and expenditure data	Vital registration complete	Latest agricultural census	Latest industrial data	Latest trade data	Latest water withdrawal data
Serbia	2011	MICS, 2014	IHS, 2011	Yes	2012	2012	2014	2009
Seychelles	2010		BS, 2006/07	Yes	2011		2008	2005
Sierra Leone	2004	DHS, 2013; MIS, 2013	IHS, 2011				2014	2005
Singapore	2010c	NHS, 2010		Yes		2012	2014	1975
Sint Maarten	2011			Yes				
Slovak Republic	2011	WHS, 2003	IS, 2013	Yes	2010	2011	2014	2007
Slovenia	2011c	WHS, 2003	ES/BS, 2012	Yes	2010	2012	2014	2012
Solomon Islands	2009	SIDHS, 2006/07	IHS, 2005/06				2014	
Somalia	1987	MICS, 2006						2003
South Africa	2011	DHS, 2003; WHS, 2003	ES/BS, 2010/11		2007	2010	2014	2000
South Sudan	2008	MICS, 2010	ES/BS, 2009					2011
Spain	2011d		IHS, 2012	Yes	2009	2011	2014	2010
Sri Lanka	2012	DHS, 2006/07	ES/BS, 2012/13	Yes	2013	2011	2014	2005
St. Kitts and Nevis	2011			Yes			2011	2012
St. Lucia	2010	MICS, 2012	IHS, 1995	Yes	2007		2014	2007
St. Martin								
St. Vincent and the Grenadines	2011			Yes			2012	2013
Sudan	2008	MICS, 2014	ES/BS, 2009		2015	2001	2012	2011
Suriname	2012	MICS, 2010	ES/BS, 1999	Yes	2008/09	2003	2014	2006
Swaziland	2007	MICS, 2014	ES/BS, 2009/10				2007	2000
Sweden	2011c		IS, 2012	Yes	2010	2012	2014	2010
Switzerland	2010d		ES/BS, 2012	Yes	2010	2012	2014	2012
Syrian Arab Republic	2004	MICS, 2006	ES/BS, 2007			2005	2010	2005
Tajikistan	2010	DHS, 2012	LSMS, 2014		2013		2000	2006
Tanzania	2012	DHS, 2015/16	ES/BS, 2011/12		2007/08	2010	2014	2002
Thailand	2010	MICS, 2012/13	IHS, 2013		2013	2011	2014	2007
Timor-Leste	2010	DHS, 2009/10	LSMS, 2007				2013	2004
Togo	2010	DHS, 2013/14	CWIQ, 2011		2011–14		2013	2002
Tonga	2006	Tonga DHS, 2012	IHS, 2009		2014		2014	
Trinidad and Tobago	2011	MICS, 2011	IHS, 1992	Yes		2006	2010	2011
Tunisia	2014	MICS, 2011/12	IHS, 2012			2010	2013	2011
Turkey	2011d	Turkey DHS, 2008	ES/BS, 2012	Yes	2014	2009	2014	2003
Turkmenistan	2012	MICS, 2015/16	LSMS, 1998				2000	2004
Turks and Caicos Islands	2012			Yes			2012	
Tuvalu	2012	Tuvalu DHS, 2007					2008	
Uganda	2014	MIS, 2014/15	IHS, 2012/13		2008/09	2000	2014	2008
Ukraine	2001	MICS, 2012	ES/BS, 2013	Yes		2012	2014	2010
United Arab Emirates	2010	WHS, 2003			2012		2014	2005
United Kingdom	2011		IS, 2012	Yes	2010	2012	2014	2011
United States	2010		LFS, 2013	Yes	2012	2008	2014	2005
Uruguay	2011	MICS, 2012/13	IHS, 2014	Yes	2011	2010	2014	2000
Uzbekistan	1989	MICS, 2006	ES/BS, 2011	Yes				2005
Vanuatu	2009	MICS, 2007/08	IHS, 2010		2007		2011	
Venezuela, RB	2011	MICS, 2000	IHS, 2013	Yes	2008		2013	2007
Vietnam	2009	MICS, 2013/14	IHS, 2014	Yes	2011	2012	2014	2005
Virgin Islands (U.S.)	2010			Yes	2012			
West Bank and Gaza	2007	MICS, 2014	IHS, 2011		2010	2010	2014	2005
Yemen, Rep.	2004	DHS, 2013	ES/BS, 2005			2009	2014	2005
Zambia	2010	DHS, 2013/14	IHS, 2010				2014	2002
Zimbabwe	2012	DHS, 2015	IHS, 2011/12				2014	2002

Note: For explanation of the abbreviations used in the table, see notes following the table.

a. Original chained constant price data are rescaled. b. Household consumption only. c. Population data compiled from administrative registers. d. Population data compiled from administrative registers in combination with other sources of data, such as a sample surveys. e. Natural resources census, livestock census, livestock and aquaculture census, or sample agricultural census. f. Latest population census: Guernsey, 2009; Jersey, 2011. g. Vital registration for Guernsey and Jersey. h. Rolling census based on continuous sample survey. i. Reporting period switch from fiscal year to calendar year from 1996. Pre-1996 data converted to calendar year.

• **Base year** is the base or pricing period used for constant price calculations in the country's national accounts. Price indexes derived from national accounts aggregates, such as the implicit deflator for gross domestic product (GDP), express the price level relative to base year prices. • **Reference year** is the year in which the local currency constant price series of a country is valued. The reference year is usually the same as the base year used to report the constant price series. However, when the constant price data are chain linked, the base year is changed annually, so the data are rescaled to a specific reference year to provide a consistent time series. When the country has not rescaled following a change in base year, World Bank staff rescale the data to maintain a longer historical series. To allow for cross-country comparison and data aggregation, constant price data reported in *World Development Indicators* are rescaled to a common reference year (2005) and currency (U.S. dollars). • **System of National Accounts** identifies whether a country uses the 1968, 1993, or 2008 System of National Accounts (SNA). The 2008 SNA is an update of the 1993 SNA and retains its basic theoretical framework. • **SNA price valuation** shows whether value added in the national accounts is reported at basic prices (B) or producer prices (P). Producer prices include taxes paid by producers and thus tend to overstate the actual value added in production. However, value added can be higher at basic prices than at producer prices in countries with high agricultural subsidies. • **Alternative conversion factor** identifies the countries and years for which a World Bank–estimated conversion factor has been used in place of the official exchange rate (line rf in the International Monetary Fund's [IMF] *International Financial Statistics*). See *Sources and methods* for further discussion of alternative conversion factors. • **Purchasing power parity (PPP) survey year** is the latest available survey year for the International Comparison Program's estimates of PPPs. • **Balance of Payments Manual in use** refers to the classification system used to compile and report data on balance of payments. 6 refers to the 6th edition of the IMF's *Balance of Payments Manual* (2009). • **External debt** shows debt reporting status for 2014 data. *A* indicates that data are as reported, *P* that data are based on reported or collected information but include an element of staff estimation, and *E* that data are World Bank staff estimates. • **System of trade** refers to the United Nations general trade system (G) or special trade system (S). Under the general trade system goods entering directly for domestic consumption and goods entered into customs storage are recorded as imports at arrival. Under the special trade system goods are recorded as imports when declared for

domestic consumption whether at time of entry or on withdrawal from customs storage. Exports under the general system comprise outward-moving goods: (a) national goods wholly or partly produced in the country; (b) foreign goods, neither transformed nor declared for domestic consumption in the country, that move outward from customs storage; and (c) nationalized goods that have been declared for domestic consumption and move outward without being transformed. Under the special system of trade, exports are categories a and c. In some compilations categories b and c are classified as re-exports. Direct transit trade—goods entering or leaving for transport only—is excluded from both import and export statistics. • **Government finance accounting concept** is the accounting basis for reporting central government financial data. For most countries government finance data have been consolidated (C) into one set of accounts capturing all central government fiscal activities. Budgetary central government accounts (B) exclude some central government units. • **IMF data dissemination standard** shows the countries that subscribe to the IMF's Special Data Dissemination Standard (SDDS) or General Data Dissemination System (GDDS). S refers to countries that subscribe to the SDDS and have posted data on the Dissemination Standards Bulletin Board at http://dsbb.imf.org. S+ countries must observe additional coverage, periodicity, and timeliness requirements. G refers to countries that subscribe to the GDDS. The SDDS was established for member countries that have or might seek access to international capital markets to guide them in providing their economic and financial data to the public. The GDDS helps countries disseminate comprehensive, timely, accessible, and reliable economic, financial, and sociodemographic statistics. IMF member countries elect to participate in either the SDDS or the GDDS. Both standards enhance the availability of timely and comprehensive data and therefore contribute to the pursuit of sound macroeconomic policies. The SDDS is also expected to improve the functioning of financial markets. • **Latest population census** shows the most recent year in which a census was conducted and in which at least preliminary results have been released. The preliminary results from the very recent censuses could be reflected in timely revisions if basic data are available, such as population by age and sex, as well as the detailed definition of counting, coverage, and completeness. Countries that hold register-based censuses produce similar census tables every 5 or 10 years. A rare case, France conducts a rolling census every year; the 1999 general population census was the last to cover the entire population simultaneously. • **Latest demographic, education, or health household survey**

indicates the household surveys used to compile the demographic, education, and health data in section 2. AIS is AIDS Indicator Survey, DHS is Demographic and Health Survey, EPSF is National Survey on Population and Family Health, FHS is Family Health Survey, HIS is Health Issues Survey, HIV/MCH SPA is HIV/Maternal and Child Health Service Provision Assessment Survey, IrMIDHS is Iran's Multiple Indicator Demographic and Health Survey, KDHS is Kiribati Demographic and Health Survey, LSMS is Living Standards Measurement Study, MCH SPA is Maternal and Child Health Service Provision Assessment Survey, MICS is Multiple Indicator Cluster Survey, MIS is Malaria Indicator Survey, NHS is National Health Survey, NSS is National Sample Survey on Population Changes, RHS is Reproductive Health Survey, RHS-Ro is Romania Reproductive Health Survey, RMIDHS is Republic of the Marshall Islands Demographic and Health Survey, SIDHS is Solomon Islands Demographic and Health Survey, Tonga DHS is Tonga Demographic and Health Survey, Turkey DHS is Turkey Demographic and Health Survey, Tuvalu DHS is Tuvalu Demographic and Health Survey, and WHS is World Health Survey. Detailed information on AIS, DHS, HIS, HIV/MCH SPA, MCH SPA, and MIS is available at www.dhsprogram.com; detailed information on MICS is available at www.childinfo.org; detailed information on RHS is available at www.cdc.gov/reproductivehealth; and detailed information on WHS is available at www.who.int/healthinfo/survey/en. • **Source of most recent income and expenditure data** shows household surveys that collect income and expenditure data. Names and detailed information on household surveys can be found on the website of the International Household Survey Network (www.surveynetwork.org). Core Welfare Indicator Questionnaire Surveys (CWIQ), developed by the World Bank, measure changes in key social indicators for different population groups—specifically indicators of access, utilization, and satisfaction with core social and economic services. Expenditure survey/budget surveys (ES/BS) collect detailed information on household consumption as well as on general demographic, social, and economic characteristics. Integrated household surveys (IHS) collect detailed information on a wide variety of topics, including health, education, economic activities, housing, and utilities. Income surveys (IS) collect information on the income and wealth of households as well as various social and economic characteristics. Income tax registers (ITR) provide information on a population's income and allowance, such as gross income, taxable income, and taxes by socioeconomic group. Labor force surveys (LFS) collect information on employment, unemployment, hours of work, income, and wages. Living Standards

Measurement Study Surveys (LSMS), developed by the World Bank, provide a comprehensive picture of household welfare and the factors that affect it; they typically incorporate data collection at the individual, household, and community levels. Priority surveys (PS) are a light monitoring survey, designed by the World Bank, that collect data from a large number of households cost-effectively and quickly. 1-2-3 (1-2-3) surveys are implemented in three phases and collect sociodemographic and employment data, data on the informal sector, and information on living conditions and household consumption. • **Vital registration complete** identifies countries that report at least 90 percent complete registries of vital (birth and death) statistics to the United Nations Statistics Division and are reported in its *Population and Vital Statistics Reports*. Countries with complete vital statistics registries may have more accurate and more timely demographic indicators than other countries. • **Latest agricultural census** shows the most recent year in which an agricultural census was conducted or planned to be conducted, as reported to the Food and Agriculture Organization of the United Nations. • **Latest industrial data** show the most recent year for which manufacturing value added data at the three-digit level of the International Standard Industrial Classification (revision 2 or 3) are available in the United Nations Industrial Development Organization database. • **Latest trade data** show the most recent year for which structure of merchandise trade data from the United Nations Statistics Division's Commodity Trade (Comtrade) database are available. • **Latest water withdrawal data** show the most recent year for which data on freshwater withdrawals have been compiled from a variety of sources.

Exceptional reporting periods

In most economies the fiscal year is concurrent with the calendar year. Exceptions are shown in the table at right. The ending date reported here is for the fiscal year of the central government. Fiscal years for other levels of government and reporting years for statistical surveys may differ.

The **reporting period for national accounts data** is designated as either calendar year basis (CY) or fiscal year basis (FY). Most economies report their national accounts and balance of payments data using calendar years, but some use fiscal years. In *World Development Indicators* fiscal year data are assigned to the calendar year that contains the larger share of the fiscal year. If a country's fiscal year ends before June 30, data are shown in the first year of the fiscal period; if the fiscal year ends on or after June 30, data are shown in the second year of the period. Balance of payments data are reported in *World Development Indicators* by calendar year.

Revisions to national accounts data

National accounts data are revised by national statistical offices when methodologies change or data sources improve. National accounts data in *World Development Indicators* are also revised when data sources change. The following notes, while not comprehensive, provide information on revisions from previous data. • **Andorra.** The base year has changed to 2000. Price valuation is in basic prices. • **Barbados.** Price valuation is in producer prices. Barbados reports using SNA1993. • **Benin.** Based on official government statistics, the new base year is 2007. Price valuation is in basic prices. • **Brazil.** Based on official government statistics, the new reference year is 2000. • **Cuba.** Based on official government statistics, the new reference year is 2005. • **Dominican Republic.** Based on data

Economies with exceptional reporting periods

Economy	Fiscal year end	Reporting period for national accounts data
Afghanistan	Mar. 20	FY
Australia	Jun. 30	FY
Bangladesh	Jun. 30	FY
Botswana	Mar. 31	CY
Canada	Mar. 31	CY
Egypt, Arab Rep.	Jun. 30	FY
Ethiopia	Jul. 7	FY
Gambia, The	Jun. 30	CY
Haiti	Sep. 30	FY
India	Mar. 31	FY
Indonesia	Mar. 31	CY
Iran, Islamic Rep.	Mar. 20	FY
Japan	Mar. 31	CY
Kenya	Jun. 30	CY
Kuwait	Jun. 30	CY
Lesotho	Mar. 31	CY
Malawi	Mar. 31	CY
Marshall Islands	Sep. 30	FY
Micronesia, Fed. Sts.	Sep. 30	FY
Myanmar	Mar. 31	FY
Namibia	Mar. 31	CY
Nepal	Jul. 14	FY
New Zealand	Mar. 31	CY
Pakistan	Jun. 30	FY
Palau	Sep. 30	FY
Puerto Rico	Jun. 30	FY
Samoa	Jun. 30	FY
Sierra Leone	Jun. 30	CY
Singapore	Mar. 31	CY
South Africa	Mar. 31	CY
Swaziland	Mar. 31	CY
Sweden	Jun. 30	CY
Thailand	Sep. 30	CY
Tonga	Jun. 30	FY
Uganda	Jun. 30	FY
United States	Sep. 30	CY
Zimbabwe	Jun. 30	CY

from the Central Bank of Dominican Republic, the new base year is 2007. • **Egypt, Arab Republic.** The Egyptian Ministry of Planning rebased national accounts to 2011/12. • **Hong Kong SAR, China.** Based on data from the Hong Kong Census and Statistics Office, the new reference year is 2013. • **Gabon.** Price valuation is in basic prices. • **Indonesia.** Statistics Indonesia revised national accounts based on SNA2008. The new base year is 2010. Price valuation is in basic prices. • **Iran, Islamic Republic.** Based on data from the Central Bank of Iran, the new base year is 2004/05. • **Iraq.** Based on official government statistics, the new base year is 2007. • **Kuwait.** Price valuation is in basic prices. • **Latvia.** Based on data from Eurostat, the new reference year is 2010. • **Libya.** Official statistics for Libya are not available; data are based on World Bank estimates. The new base year is 2003. • **Lithuania.** Based on data from Eurostat, the new reference year is 2010. • **Macedonia, FYR.** Based on revisions by the Macedonia State Statistics Office, the new base year is 2005. • **Malaysia.** Based on data from the Malaysian Department of Statistics and Bank Negara Malaysia, the new base year is 2010. • **Mauritania.** Based on official statistics from the Mauritania Ministry of Economic Affairs and Development, the new base year is 2004. • **Mongolia.** Based on data revised by the National Statistics Office of Mongolia, the new base year is 2010. • **Morocco.** Based on data from the Moroccan Haut Commissariat au Plan, the new base year is 2007. • **Qatar.** Based on data from the Qatar Ministry of Development Planning and Statistics and the Qatar Central Bank, the new base year is 2013. • **Romania.** Based on data from Eurostat, the Romanian National Institute of Statistics, the National Bank of Romania, and World Bank estimates, the new base year is 2005. • **São Tomé and Príncipe.** The base year has changed to 2001. • **Saudi Arabia.** Based on data from the Saudi Central Department of Statistics and Information under the authority of the Ministry of Economy and Planning, the new base year is 2010. • **Seychelles.** Price valuation is in basic prices. • **Sri Lanka.** The Sri Lankan government has changed its methodology and revised the production side of national accounts from 2010 to 2014. The new base year is 2010. • **Swaziland.** Based on data from the Central Statistics Office of Swaziland and the IMF, the new base year is 2011. • **Thailand.** Based on data from the Bank of Thailand and the National Economics and Social Development Board, the new base year is 2002. • **Tunisia.** Based on data from Tunisia's Ministry of Development and International Cooperation, Central Bank, and National Institute of Statistics, the new reference year is 2010. • **Uganda.** Price valuation is in basic prices.

Sources and methods

Aggregation rules

Aggregates based on the World Bank's regional and income classifications of economies appear at the end of the tables, including most of those available online. The 214 economies included in these classifications are shown on the flaps on the front and back covers of the book. Aggregates also contain data for Taiwan, China. Beginning with this edition, regional aggregates include data for economies at all income levels, unless otherwise noted.

Because of missing data, aggregates for groups of economies should be treated as approximations of unknown totals or average values. The aggregation rules are intended to yield estimates for a consistent set of economies from one period to the next and for all indicators. Small differences between sums of sub-group aggregates and overall totals and averages may occur because of the approximations used. In addition, compilation errors and data reporting practices may cause discrepancies in theoretically identical aggregates such as world exports and world imports.

Five methods of aggregation are used in *World Development Indicators*:

- For group and world totals denoted in the tables by a *t*, missing data are imputed based on the relationship of the sum of available data to the total in the year of the previous estimate. The imputation process works forward and backward from 2005. Missing values in 2005 are imputed using one of several proxy variables for which complete data are available in that year. The imputed value is calculated so that it (or its proxy) bears the same relationship to the total of available data. Imputed values are usually not calculated if missing data account for more than a third of the total in the benchmark year. The variables used as proxies are GNI in U.S. dollars; total population; exports and imports of goods and services in U.S. dollars; and value added in agriculture, industry, manufacturing, and services in U.S. dollars.

- Aggregates marked by an *s* are sums of available data. Missing values are not imputed. Sums are not computed if more than a third of the observations in the series or a proxy for the series are missing in a given year.

- Aggregates of ratios are denoted by a *w* when calculated as weighted averages of the ratios (using the value of the denominator or, in some cases, another indicator as a weight) and denoted by a *u* when calculated as unweighted averages. The aggregate ratios are based on available data. Missing values are assumed to have the same average value as the available data. No aggregate is calculated if missing data account for more than a third of the value of weights in the benchmark year. In a few cases the aggregate ratio may be computed as the ratio of group totals after imputing values for missing data according to the above rules for computing totals.

- Aggregate growth rates are denoted by a *w* when calculated as a weighted average of growth rates. In a few cases growth rates may be computed from time series of group totals. Growth rates are not calculated if more than half the observations in a period are missing. For further discussion of methods of computing growth rates see below.

- Aggregates denoted by an *m* are medians of the values shown in the table. No value is shown if more than half the observations for countries with a population of more than 1 million are missing.

Exceptions to the rules may occur. Depending on the judgment of World Bank analysts, the aggregates may be based on as little as 50 percent of the available data. In other cases, where missing or excluded values are judged to be small or irrelevant, aggregates are based only on the data shown in the tables.

Growth rates

Growth rates are calculated as annual averages and represented as percentages. Except where noted, growth rates of values are in real terms computed from constant price series. Three principal methods are used to calculate growth rates: least squares, exponential endpoint, and geometric endpoint. Rates of change from one period to the next are calculated as proportional changes from the earlier period.

Least squares growth rate. Least squares growth rates are used wherever there is a sufficiently long time series to permit a reliable calculation. No growth rate is calculated if more than half the observations in a period are missing. The least squares growth rate, r, is estimated by fitting a linear regression trend line to the logarithmic annual values of the variable in the relevant period. The regression equation takes the form

$$\ln X_t = a + bt$$

which is the logarithmic transformation of the compound growth equation,

$$X_t = X_o (1 + r)^t.$$

In this equation X is the variable, t is time, and $a = \ln X_o$ and $b = \ln (1 + r)$ are parameters to be estimated. If $b*$ is the least squares estimate of b, then the average annual growth rate, r, is obtained as $[\exp(b*) - 1]$ and is multiplied by 100 for expression as a percentage. The calculated growth rate is an average rate that is representative of the available observations over the entire period. It does not necessarily match the actual growth rate between any two periods.

Exponential growth rate. The growth rate between two points in time for certain demographic indicators, notably labor force and population, is calculated from the equation

$$r = \ln(p_n/p_0)/n$$

where p_n and p_0 are the last and first observations in the period, n is the number of years in the period, and ln is the natural logarithm operator. This growth rate is based on a model of continuous, exponential growth between two points in time. It does not take into account the intermediate values of the series. Nor does it correspond to the annual rate of change measured at a one-year interval, which is given by $(p_n - p_{n-1})/p_{n-1}$.

Geometric growth rate. The geometric growth rate is applicable to compound growth over discrete periods, such as the payment and reinvestment of interest or dividends. Although continuous growth, as modeled by the exponential growth rate, may be more realistic, most economic phenomena are measured only at intervals, in which case the compound growth model is appropriate. The average growth rate over n periods is calculated as

$$r = \exp[\ln(p_n/p_0)/n] - 1.$$

World Bank Atlas method

In calculating GNI and GNI per capita in U.S. dollars for certain operational and analytical purposes, the World Bank uses the *Atlas* conversion factor instead of simple exchange rates. The purpose of the *Atlas* conversion factor is to reduce the impact of exchange rate fluctuations in the cross-country comparison of national incomes.

The *Atlas* conversion factor for any year is the average of a country's exchange rate (or alternative conversion factor) for that year and its exchange rates for the two preceding years, adjusted for the difference between the rate of inflation in the country and the rate of international inflation.

The objective of the adjustment is to reduce any changes to the exchange rate caused by inflation.

A country's inflation rate between year t and year $t-n$ (r_{t-n}) is measured by the change in its GDP deflator (p_t):

$$r_{t-n} = \frac{p_t}{p_{t-n}}$$

International inflation between year t and year $t-n$ ($r_{t-n}^{SDR\$}$) is measured using the change in a deflator based on the International Monetary Fund's unit of account, special drawing rights (or SDRs). Known as the "SDR deflator," it is a weighted average of the GDP deflators (in SDR terms) of Japan, the United Kingdom, the United States, and the euro area, converted to U.S. dollar terms; weights are the amount of each currency in one SDR unit.

$$r_{t-n}^{SDR\$} = \frac{p_t^{SDR\$}}{p_{t-n}^{SDR\$}}$$

Sources and methods

The *Atlas* conversion factor (local currency to the U.S. dollar) for year t (e_t^{atlas}) is given by:

$$e_t^{atlas} = \frac{1}{3}\left[e_t + e_{t-1}\left(\frac{r_{t-1}}{r_{t-1}^{SDR\$}}\right) + e_{t-2}\left(\frac{r_{t-2}}{r_{t-2}^{SDR\$}}\right)\right]$$

where e_t is the average annual exchange rate (local currency to the U.S. dollar) for year t.

GNI in U.S. dollars (*Atlas* method) for year t ($Y_t^{atlas\$}$) is calculated by applying the *Atlas* conversion factor to a country's GNI in current prices (local currency) (Y_t) as follows:

$$Y_t^{atlas\$} = Y_t / e_t^{atlas}$$

The resulting *Atlas* GNI in U.S. dollars can then be divided by a country's midyear population to yield its GNI per capita (*Atlas* method).

Alternative conversion factors

The World Bank systematically assesses the appropriateness of official exchange rates as conversion factors. An alternative conversion factor is used when the official exchange rate is deemed to be unreliable or unrepresentative of the rate effectively applied to domestic transactions of foreign currencies and traded products. This applies to only a small number of countries. Alternative conversion factors are used in the *Atlas* methodology and elsewhere in *World Development Indicators* as single-year conversion factors.

Credits

1. World view

Section 1 was prepared by a team led by Neil Fantom and Umar Serajuddin. The overviews of each of the Sustainable Development Goals were prepared by many World Bank staff. Contributors included Husein Abdul-Hamid, Paola Agostini, Oya Pinar Ardic Alper, Luis Benveniste, Carter Brandon, Randall Brummett, Raffaello Cervigni, Tamirat Yacob Chulta, Stephane Raphael Dahan, Simon Davies, Chandan Deuskar, Adam Stone Diehl, Leslie K. Elder, Patrick Hoang-Vu Eozenou, Mahyar Eshragh-Tabary, Juan Feng, Eduardo Ferreira, Saulo Teodoro Ferreira, Vivien Foster, Habiba Gitay, Roger Gorham, Mary C. Hallward-Driemeier, Ellen Hamilton, Lucia Hanmer, Lewis Hawke, Timothy Grant Herzog, Barbro Hexeberg, Masako Hiraga, Maddalena Honorati, Aira Maria Htenas, Atsushi Iimi, Sarah Iqbal, Arvind Jain, Miguel Jorge, Bala Bhaskar Naidu Kalimili, Haruna Kashiwase, Buyant Erdene Khaltarkhuu, Tariq Khokhar, Silvia Lubenova Kirova, Glenn-Marie Lange, Victoria Louise Lemieux, Hiroko Maeda, Eliana Carolina Rubiano Matulevich, Carole Megevand, Nicholas Menzies, Samuel Lantei Mills, Esther G. Naikal, Ulf Gerrit Narloch, Fernanda Ruiz Nunez, Ana Florina Pirlea, Malvina Pollock, Elizabeth Purdie, Leila Rafei, Evis Rucaj, Christopher Sall, Umar Serajuddin, Meera Shekar, Rebecca Soares, Rubena Sukaj, Emi Suzuki, Steven Jay Silverstein, Siv Elin Tokle, Robert Townsend, Nancy L. Vandycke, Dereje Ketema Wolde, Mizuki Yamanaka, Junhe Yang, and Nobuo Yoshida. Tables were produced by Parul Agarwal, Mahyar Eshragh-Tabary, Juan Feng, Masako Hiraga, Bala Bhaskar Naidu Kalimili, Haruna Kashiwase, Buyant Erdene Khaltarkhuu, Hiroko Maeda, Evis Rucaj, Rubena Sukaj, Emi Suzuki, and Dereje Ketema Wolde. Signe Zeikate of the World Bank's Economic Policy and Debt Department provided the estimates of debt relief for the Heavily Indebted Poor Countries Debt Relief Initiative and Multilateral Debt Relief Initiative. The map was produced by Juan Feng and William Prince. Editorial help was provided by Tariq Khokhar and Elizabeth Purdie.

2. People

Section 2 was prepared by Juan Feng, Masako Hiraga, Haruna Kashiwase, Hiroko Maeda, Elizabeth Purdie, Umar Serajuddin, Emi Suzuki, and Dereje Ketema Wolde in partnership with the World Bank's various Global Practices and Cross-Cutting Solutions Areas—Education, Gender, Health, Jobs, Poverty, and Social Protection and Labor. Emi Suzuki prepared the demographic estimates and projections. The indicators on shared prosperity were prepared by the Global Poverty Working Group, a team of poverty experts from the Poverty Global Practice, the Development Research Group, and the Development Data Group. Poverty estimates at national poverty lines were compiled by the Global Poverty Working Group. Shaohua Chen and Prem Sangraula of the World Bank's Development Research Group and the Global Poverty Working Group prepared the poverty estimates at international poverty lines. Lorenzo Guarcello, Furio Rosati, and Cristina Valdivia of the Understanding Children's Work project prepared the data on children at work. Other contributions were provided by Sarah Iqbal, Eliana Carolina Rubiano Matulevich, and Alena Sakhonchik (gender) and Samuel Mills (health); Alan Wittrup of the International Labour Organization (labor force); Priscilla Idele, Colleen Murray, and Tyler Porth (health), Julia Krasevec (malnutrition), and Rolf Luyendijk and Andrew Trevett (water and sanitation) of the United Nations Children's Fund; Chiao-Ling Chien, Friedrich Huebler, Weixin Lu, Adriano Miele, and Said Ould A. Voffal of the United Nations Educational, Scientific and Cultural Organization Institute for Statistics (education and literacy); Patrick Gerland, Danan Gu, and François Pelletier of the United Nations Population Division (population); Callum Brindley and Chandika Indikadahena (health expenditure), Monika Bloessner, Elaine Borghi, Mercedes de Onis, and Leanne Riley (malnutrition), Teena Kunjumen (health workers), Jessica Ho (hospital beds), Rifat Hossain (water and sanitation), Luz Maria de Regil and Gretchen Stevens (anemia), Hazim Timimi (tuberculosis), Wahyu Mahanani and Colin Mathers (cause of death), Ryan Williams (malaria), Lori Marie Newman (syphilis), and Kacem Iaych (road safety), all of the World Health Organization; Juliana Daher and Mary Mahy of the Joint United Nations Programme on HIV/AIDS (HIV/AIDS); John Meara, Joshua Ng, and Mark Shrime of the Lancet

Credits

Commission on Global Surgery (surgery); and Leonor Guariguata of the International Diabetes Federation (diabetes). The map was produced by Hiroko Maeda, William Prince, and Dereje Ketema Wolde.

3. Environment

Section 3 was prepared by Mahyar Eshragh-Tabary in partnership with the World Bank's Environment and Natural Resources Global Practices and Energy and Extractives Global Practices. Mahyar Eshragh-Tabary wrote the introduction with editorial help from Elizabeth Purdie. Christopher Sall wrote the about the data sections on air pollution. Esther G. Naikal, Urvashi Narain, and Christopher Sall prepared the data and metadata on population-weighted exposure to ambient $PM_{2.5}$ pollution and natural resources rents. Gabriela Elizondo Azuela, Sudeshna Ghosh Banerjee, Jiemei Liu, and Elisa Portale prepared the data and metadata on access to electricity, access to nonsolid fuel, energy intensity, renewable energy, and renewable electricity. Emi Suzuki wrote the about the data sections on urban population growth, access to an improved water source, and access to improved sanitation facilities. Neil Fantom, Bala Bhaskar Naidu Kalimili, and William Prince provided instrumental comments, suggestions, and support at all stages of production. Several other staff members from the World Bank made valuable contributions: Gabriela Elizondo Azuela, Marianne Fay, Vivien Foster, Rowena M. Gorospe, Glenn-Marie Lange, Ulf Gerrit Narloch, and Jonathan Edwards Sinton. Contributors from other institutions included Michael Brauer, Aaron Cohen, Mohammad H. Forouzanfar, and Peter Speyer from the Institute for Health Metrics and Evaluation; Pierre Boileau and Maureen Cropper from the University of Maryland; Sharon Burghgraeve, Dan Dorner, and Jean-Yves Garnier of the International Energy Agency; Armin Wagner of German International Cooperation; and Craig Hilton-Taylor and Caroline Pollock of the International Union for Conservation of Nature. The team is grateful to the Center for International Earth Science Information Network, the Emissions Database for Global Atmospheric Research and Joint Research Centre, the Food and Agriculture Organization, the Global Burden of Disease of the Institute for Health Metrics and Evaluation, the International Energy Agency, the International Union for Conservation of Nature, the Office of Foreign Disaster Assistance of the U.S. Agency for International Development, the Socioeconomic Data and Applications Center of the U.S. National Aeronautics and Space Administration, the United Nations Environment Programme and World Conservation Monitoring Centre, and the U.S. Department of Energy's Carbon Dioxide Information Analysis Center for access to their online databases. The World Bank's Environment and Natural Resources Global Practices and Energy and Extractives Global Practices devoted generous staff resources. The map was produced by Mahyar Eshragh-Tabary and William Prince.

4. Economy

Section 4 was prepared by Bala Bhaskar Naidu Kalimili in close collaboration with the Environment and Natural Resources Global Practice and Economic Data Team of the World Bank's Development Data Group. Bala Bhaskar Naidu Kalimili wrote the introduction, with inputs from Liu Cui and invaluable comments and editorial help from Neil Fantom and Elizabeth Purdie. The national accounts data for low- and middle-income economies were gathered by the World Bank's regional staff through the annual Fall Survey. Maja Bresslauer, Liu Cui, Saulo Teodoro Ferreira, Bala Bhaskar Naidu Kalimili, Alagiriswamy Venkatesan, and Tamirat Yacob Chulta updated, estimated, and validated the databases for national accounts. Esther G. Naikal and Christopher Sall prepared the data on adjusted savings and adjusted income. The team is grateful to Eurostat, the International Monetary Fund, the Organisation for Economic Co-operation and Development, the United Nations Industrial Development Organization, and the World Trade Organization for access to their databases. The map was produced by Bala Bhaskar Naidu Kalimili and William Prince.

5. States and markets

Section 5 was prepared by Buyant Erdene Khaltarkhuu and Junhe Yang in partnership with the World Bank Group's Finance and Markets, Macroeconomics and

 Front | User guide | World view | People | Environment

Fiscal Management, Transport and Information and Communication Technologies Global Practices and its Public–Private Partnerships and Fragility, Conflict, and Violence Cross-Cutting Solution Areas; the International Finance Corporation; and external partners. Buyant Erdene Khaltarkhuu wrote the introduction with substantial input from William Prince and Elizabeth Purdie. Tatiana Chekanova (World Federation of Exchanges) provided the data and metadata on stock markets. Other contributors include Fernanda Ruiz Nunez and Zichao Wei (investment in infrastructure projects with private participation); Leora Klapper and Frederic Meunier (business registration); Jorge Luis Rodriguez Meza, Valeria Perotti, and Joshua Wimpey (Enterprise Surveys); Frederic Meunier and Rita Ramalho (Doing Business); Michael Orzano (Standard & Poor's global stock market indexes); James Hackett of the International Institute for Strategic Studies (military personnel); Sam Perlo-Freeman of the Stockholm International Peace Research Institute (military expenditures); Therese Petterson (battle-related deaths); Clare Spurrell (internally displaced persons); Enrico Bisogno and Michael Jandl of United Nations Office on Drugs and Crime (homicide); Ananthanarayan Sainarayan and Antonin Combes of the International Civil Aviation Organization, and Andreas Dietrich Kopp (transport); Vincent Valentine of the United Nations Conference on Trade and Development (ports); Azita Amjadi (high-technology exports); Renato Perez of the International Monetary Fund (financial soundness indicators); Vanessa Grey, Esperanza Magpantay, Susan Teltscher, and Ivan Vallejo Vall of the International Telecommunication Union (information communication and technology); Torbjörn Fredriksson, Scarlett Fondeur Gil, and Diana Korka of the United Nations Conference on Trade and Development (information and communication technology goods trade); Martin Schaaper and Rohan Pathirage of the United Nations Educational, Scientific and Cultural Organization Institute for Statistics (research and development, researchers, and technicians); Carsten Fink and Mosahid Khan of the World Intellectual Property Organization (patents and trademarks); and Barbro Hexeberg and Mizuki Yamanaka (statistical capacity). The map was produced by Buyant Erdene Khaltarkhuu and William Prince.

6. Global links

Section 6 was prepared by the Financial Data Team of the Development Data Group, led by Evis Rucaj under the management of Neil Fantom, and comprising Parul Agarwal, Peter Bourke, Cynthia Nyanchama Nyakeri, Sun Hwa Song, and Rubena Sukaj, and in partnership with the World Bank's Development Research Group (trade), Development Prospects Group (commodity prices and remittances), International Trade Department (trade facilitation), and external partners. Other contributors include Azita Amjadi (trade and tariffs), Frédéric Docquier (emigration rates), Flavine Creppy and Yumiko Mochizuki of the United Nations Conference on Trade and Development, and Mondher Mimouni of the International Trade Centre (trade); Cristina Savescu (commodity prices); Jeff Reynolds and Joseph Siegel of DHL (freight costs); Yasmin Ahmad, Elena Bernaldo, Aimée Nichols, and Ann Zimmerman of the Organisation for Economic Co-operation and Development (aid); Tarek Abou Chabake of the Office of the UN High Commissioner for Refugees (refugees); and Teresa Ciller and Leandry Moreno of the World Tourism Organization (tourism). Ramgopal Erabelly, Shelley Fu, and William Prince provided technical assistance. The map was produced by Rubena Sukaj and William Prince.

Other parts of the book

Bruno Bonansea of the World Bank's Map Design Unit coordinated preparation of the maps on the inside covers and within each section. William Prince prepared *User guide* and the lists of online tables and indicators for each section and wrote *Sources and methods* with input from Neil Fantom. Azita Amjadi and Jomo Tariku prepared *Partners*.

Database management

William Prince coordinated management of the World Development Indicators database, with assistance from Mathieu Djayeola, Shelley Fu, and Junhe Yang in the Sustainable Development and Data Quality Team.

Credits

Operation of the database management system was made possible by Ramgopal Erabelly and Karthik Krishnamoorthy working with the Data and Information Systems Team under the leadership of Soong Sup Lee.

Design, production, and editing

Azita Amjadi coordinated all stages of production with Communications Development Incorporated, which provided overall design direction, editing, and layout, led by Bruce Ross-Larson and Christopher Trott. Elaine Wilson created the cover and graphics and typeset the book. Peter Grundy, of Peter Grundy Art & Design, and Diane Broadley, of Broadley Design, designed the report.

Administrative assistance, office technology, and systems development support

Elysee Kiti provided administrative assistance. Jean-Pierre Djomalieu, Gytis Kanchas, and Nacer Megherbi provided information technology support. Ugendran Machakkalai, Atsushi Shimo, and Malarvizhi Veerappan provided software support on the DataBank application.

Publishing and dissemination

The World Bank's Publishing and Knowledge Division, under the direction of Carlos Rossel, provided assistance throughout the production process. Denise Bergeron, Jewel Monique McFadden, Stephen McGroarty, Nora Ridolfi, and Janice Tuten coordinated printing, marketing, and distribution.

World Development Indicators mobile applications

Software preparation and testing were managed by Shelley Fu with assistance from Prashant Chaudhari, Neil Fantom, Mohammed Omar Hadi, Soong Sup Lee, Parastoo Oloumi, William Prince, Jomo Tariku, and Malarvizhi Veerappan. Systems development was undertaken in the Data and Information Systems Team led by Soong Sup Lee. William Prince and Junhe Yang provided data quality assurance.

Online access

Coordination of the presentation of the World Development Indicators online, through the Open Data website, the DataBank application, the table browser application, and the Application Programming Interface, was provided by Neil Fantom and Soong Sup Lee. Development and maintenance of the website were managed by a team led by Azita Amjadi and comprising George Gongadze, Timothy Herzog, Jeffrey McCoy, Parastoo Oloumi, Leila Rafei, and Jomo Tariku. Systems development was managed by a team led by Soong Sup Lee, with project management provided by Malarvizhi Veerappan. Design, programming, and testing were carried out by Prasanth Alluri, Ying Chi, Rajesh Danda, Shelley Fu, Mohammed Omar Hadi, Siddhesh Kaushik, Karthik Krishnamoorthy, Ugendran Machakkalai, Nacer Megherbi, Parastoo Oloumi, Atsushi Shimo, and Jomo Tariku. William Prince and Junhe Yang coordinated production and provided data quality assurance. Multilingual translations of online content were provided by a team in the General Services Department.

Client feedback

The team is grateful to the many people who have taken the time to provide feedback and suggestions, which have helped improve this year's edition. Please contact us at data@worldbank.org.

 Front | ? User guide | World view | People | Environment

ECO-AUDIT
Environmental Benefits Statement

The World Bank Group is committed to reducing its environmental footprint. In support of this commitment, the Publishing and Knowledge Division leverages electronic publishing options and print-on-demand technology, which is located in regional hubs worldwide. Together, these initiatives enable print runs to be lowered and shipping distances decreased, resulting in reduced paper consumption, chemical use, greenhouse gas emissions, and waste.

The Publishing and Knowledge Division follows the recommended standards for paper use set by the Green Press Initiative. The majority of our books are printed on Forest Stewardship Council (FSC)–certified paper, with nearly all containin   e recycled fiber in our book paper is   tally chlorine-free (TCF), processed   ntal chlorine-free (EECF) processes.

More informat   hilosophy can be found at http://wv   ity.

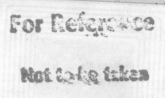